THE STORY OF JESUS

ALL FOUR GOSPELS IN ONE

D. B. RYEN

Second Edition

The Story of Jesus

All Four Gospels in One

Study Bible

D. B. Ryen

Second Edition, Version 2.12

All instances of biblical text are original works derived from various Greek and English sources. Although many sections of *THE STORY OF JESUS* are similar to existing English translations of the Bible, every effort was made to create original text and avoid copyright infringement. Please forgive any instances that are overly similar to other Bible translations; there are only so many ways to translate the same verse from Greek. Refer to Appendix G for major references used.

Contact us at: email@dbryen.com

Visit our website: www.dbryen.com

ISBN-13: 9781096406501

Palestine
Circa 30 AD
0 5 10 15 20 25 km
Sidon
Mt Hermon
Damascus
Caesarea Philippi
PHOENICIA
SYRIA
Tyre
LAKE HULEH
Chorazin
SEA OF GALILEE
Capernaum
Bethsaida
MEDITERRANEAN SEA
GALILEE
Gennesaret
Tiberias
Yarmuk River
Canatha
Mt Carmel
Cana
Sepphoris
Nazareth
Abila
Nain
Gadara
Caesarea
Pella
DECAPOLIS
Scythopolis
Samaria
Gerasa
Salim
Mt Ebal
SAMARIA
Shechem
Mt Gerizim
Jordan River
Jabbok River
Ephraim
Joppa
Philadelphia
PEREA
JUDEA
Jericho
Emmaus
Mt of Olives
Bethany (beyond the Jordan)
Jerusalem
Bethany
Bethlehem
Tekoa
Gaza
Hebron
IDUMEA
Arnon River
Beersheba
DEAD SEA
Masada

Who has believed our message? And who has been shown the arm of the Lord*?*

He grew up before him like a sapling and like a root from dry land. He didn't have a form or honor that we'd look at him, nor an appearance that we'd want him.

He was hated and betrayed by men, a man of sadness, familiar with sickness. He was hated enough to hide one's face from him. And we didn't think much of him.

But he certainly carried our sickness and bore our pain, while we figured he was struck, beaten, and oppressed by God.

He was stabbed for our rebellion and broken for our guilt. The discipline for our good fell on him and we're healed by his bruises.

Like sheep, we've all wandered and each has turned his own way, but the Lord *made all our depravity meet him.*

He was oppressed and mistreated, but he didn't open his mouth. Like a lamb led to slaughter and like a sheep silent before shearers, he still didn't open his mouth.

He was taken by restraint and judgment. And who would've thought that he was cut off from the living land for my people's rebellion, his own generation, whose disease it was?

His grave was set among the wicked, but he was wealthy in death because he had done nothing violent, nor was deception in his mouth.

But the Lord *was happy to crush him, to make him diseased. If he could make himself their guilt, then he'd see his seed, he'd lengthen his days, and the* Lord*'s pleasure would flourish in his hand.*

Because of his soul's trouble, he'll see it and be satisfied. By his knowledge, the righteous one, my servant, will justify many by carrying their guilt.

So I'll give him a part with the great, and he'll divide the plunder with the strong because of this: he poured himself out to death and was counted with the lawless, but he carried the sin of many and interceded for the lawless.

– Isaiah 53

TABLE OF CONTENTS

APPENDICES

INTRODUCTION

Disclaimer

Religious education isn't new. Scholars have been studying, interpreting, and teaching theology based on sacred writings for millennia. But the Scriptures are for everyone, not just the learned. In the same way, religion and faith are for everyone, regardless of education, scholarship, race, gender, or social status. The original Gospel writers weren't scholars themselves, at least not originally. They were a tax collector, a missionary's companion, a physician, and a fisherman; it's unknown whether they had any formal religious education. But it didn't matter – they penned the most popular biography in history.

Such is this account.

THE STORY OF JESUS attempts to put the events of Jesus' life into chronological order. It draws primarily from the four books of the Bible that record his life, that is, the Gospels of Matthew, Mark, Luke, and John. These sources have been combined into one complete seamless narrative as accurately as possible. When details vary between the four Gospels, round parentheses ( ) denote differences in wording from one Gospel writer to the next. And when details are not stated at all, but rather implied, square brackets [ ] contain the extra text.

Efforts have been made to thoroughly research historical facts and language translations, but always from the perspective of an interested follower, not a certified biblical scholar, historian, or linguist. As such, there may be details that are less than accurate despite the best of intentions. For example, the order of events in this account may not be in the precise order they occurred in history, as established by teams of scholars with far greater expertise.

Similarly, it's always difficult to translate the Bible literally while still being readable. The translation used in *THE STORY OF JESUS* is original text, based on various contemporary English translations and the original Greek, Aramaic, and Hebrew versions of the Bible. This applies both to the main text of Jesus' life story and the sidebars of the various scriptural references. *THE STORY OF JESUS* attempts to be as faithful as possible to the original languages it was written in, even at the expense of being readable. Hopefully any discrepancies in fact or translation will be graciously overlooked, because this book's purpose isn't to be a historical textbook but the retelling of a story, one that has changed many lives.

THE STORY OF JESUS is divided up into 38 chapters, which are further subdivided into sections. The start of each section includes a brief description of what it's about and a list of biblical references for where the text came from. *THE STORY OF JESUS* also includes extra information to help explain the context and translation of Jesus' story. Footnotes that correspond to a particular topic are marked accordingly with an alphabetic marker within the text ([a]). Larger text boxes may have no specific reference to the text, but generally help to explain the world in which Jesus walked during the first century.

Everyone should study the Scriptures for themselves. That's how this account started. *THE STORY OF JESUS* is quite simply the full story of Jesus' time on earth.

PREFACE

First Century Judea

Israel's history all started with one man: Abram. The Bible records that God told him to leave his home, promising to give him his own land and make him into a great nation.[a] This promised land was Canaan, a fertile green belt bordered by the Mediterranean Sea to the west and the Jordan River to the east. After arriving there, Abram was renamed Abraham and had a son by his previously-barren wife, Sarah. His son, Isaac, fathered twins. The younger twin, Jacob, deceptively received the blessing and inheritance of the firstborn. Jacob was renamed Israel and had twelve sons, who, with their descendants, would become the twelve tribes of Israel. Jacob was forced to relocate away from Canaan to Egypt due to a seven-year famine. In Egypt, Jacob's family of seventy grew into a nation, and over time Israel's population became so large that the Egyptian Pharaoh feared revolt and subsequently oppressed them as slaves. Then, four hundred years after arriving in Egypt, Moses[b]

A. *The LORD told Abram, "Go from your country, your relatives, and your father's house, to the land I'll show you. I'll make you a great nation. I'll bless you and make your name great, and then you'll be a blessing. I'll bless those who bless you and curse those who curse you. And all the families on earth will be blessed through you." – Genesis 12:2-3*

B. *The LORD said to Moses, "Go to Pharaoh and tell him, 'The LORD says, "Let my people go, so they can serve me."'" – Exodus 8:1*

led the entire nation back to the land promised to them by God.

Under Joshua, Moses' successor, the people of Israel drove out the residents of Canaan and were established as a kingdom of their own right. Successive judges ruled Israel after their settlement in Canaan, frequently rescuing them from neighboring nations, until Saul was established as Israel's first king. However, a shepherd-turned-warrior named David was the one to truly lead Israel, becoming Israel's second king after Saul's death.

During the reign of David[c] and his son Solomon, Israel reached the peak of its power, becoming the richest nation in the Middle East at the time, according to the Bible. But it didn't last long. Crumbling morality, heavy taxation, and labor conscription led to Israel's division. Around 950 BC, under David's grandson Rehoboam, the nation split into the southern kingdom of Judah, which maintained the Davidic dynasty, and the northern kingdom of Israel, which adopted a new king, Jeroboam. Various kings rose and fell in Israel and Judah as they warred with each other and with their neighbors. Then around 720 BC, the Assyrians conquered Israel, taking much of its population into exile. Judah was also conquered, this time in two campaigns by the Babylonians in 597 and 587 BC, who captured Jerusalem[d] and similarly exiled many of the survivors. The Persians later conquered Babylon, taking over their massive empire, but they allowed groups of Jewish exiles to return to their homeland. In 333 BC, Alexander the Great conquered Persia, gaining control of Israel and the rest of the Middle East and establishing Greek culture and language throughout. After his death, Alexander's generals divided his empire between themselves, but subsequent revolts re-established an independent Jewish nation in 164 BC under the Hasmonean dynasty. However, Jerusalem was again captured, with Judea becoming a province of the Roman Empire in 63 BC. Herod the Great ruled the Jews as a client-king under Rome and was the current ruler at the time of Jesus' birth in 4 BC.

Throughout Israel's tumultuous history, various prophets (messengers from God) encouraged the Jews and warned them to repent and return to God[e] and follow the laws given to them during their exodus from Egypt to Canaan. The prophets frequently stressed that Israel's

---

C. *He raised David up to be their king, and he witnessed about him, saying, "I've found David, Jesse's son, to be a man after my heart, who'll do all I want." – Acts 13:22*

D. *How lonely sits the city that was full of people! She who was great among the nations has become a widow! – Lamentations 1:1*

rebellion away from God had led to their downfall, and that turning back to him would lead to freedom and blessing. However, any religious reformation soon reverted back to immorality and subsequent oppression.

Despite the dire circumstances of Israel's national identity, Jews lived in constant expectation of the Messiah,[f] which means "anointed one" in Hebrew. The Greek equivalent, *christos*, is where the term "Christ" comes from. The Jews understood the Messiah to be a powerful king who would defeat their enemies and bring prosperity and peace. Although many messiahs temporarily delivered Israel throughout its history, none fulfilled all the requirements, as detailed by various prophets' contributions to Scripture.

So this was the situation in Judea during the first century: Israel was living under Roman rule; revolts were common, but were swiftly and brutally subdued; religious reform had expanded Moses' Law into thousands of rules and rituals about cleanliness; and the Jews were waiting for their Messiah, a mighty king who would sit on David's throne and establish an empire.

It was into this world that Jesus was born.

E. *"Repent and turn from all of your rebelling, so that sin won't trip you up. Throw away all the rebelling you've done and make a new heart and a new spirit for yourselves. O Israel's house, why will you die? I'm not happy with anyone's death," says the Lord God. "So repent and live!" – Ezekiel 18:30-32*

F. *Look at my servant, whom I hold. He's my chosen, who pleases my soul. I've put my Spirit on him and he'll bring justice out to the nations. He won't get discouraged or crushed until he sets up justice on earth. – Isaiah 42:1,4a*

The Bible

Although it can vary in content and translation, the **Bible** is the primary text of multiple world religions, most notably Christianity and Judaism. In its most common form, the Bible is divided into two major sections, each containing multiple smaller books:

1. The Old Testament follows the history of Israel as a nation through its formation, settlement, exile, and restoration. It also includes books of songs, poetry, prophecy, and law.
2. The New Testament starts with four different accounts – written by Matthew, Mark, Lukeand John – that detail the life of a teacher named Jesus, who claimed to be God's Son. It goes on to describe the beginning of the church, including letters addressed to various churches of the day.

This sacred text, particularly the Old Testament, is also simply called the **Scripture**.

Originally written in Hebrew, Aramaic, and Greek, the Bible has become the most widely reproduced book in the world. And despite having multiple authors and being written over centuries, the Bible claims to be the inspired words of God.

The first five books of the Bible, in the Old Testament, are collectively referred to as **Moses' Law**. It's also called the Pentateuch, the Torah, the "Book of the Law," or simply "The Law." This ancient Scripture records the development of Israel as a nation, as well as the laws God gave them for fulfilling their destiny as his people.

1. Genesis records the early history of the world and the establishment of Abraham's descendants as the nation of God. It follows Israel's first four generations, from Abraham to the twelve patriarchs of Israel, ending with their settlement in Egypt. It also includes accounts of creation, the first sin, the worldwide flood with Noah's ark, and Babel's tower to heaven.
2. Exodus records Israel's flight from slavery under Pharaoh in Egypt. It also details God's covenant with them as a nation.
3. Leviticus lays out instructions on holiness.
4. Numbers records 40 years of wandering in the desert and how Israel's territory should be divided once they got there.
5. Deuteronomy records final commands to serve God as Israel prepared to enter their promised land.

These books served as the foundation for Jewish government, law, religion, and culture. Additionally, Moses' Law dictated what was clean and unclean. God called Israel to be **holy** (set apart) for himself, and, as such, Israel's rules about external purity were outward signs of that inward holiness. Specific uncleanliness was described in Moses' Law.

- Eating or handling certain animals, such as ravens, vultures, eagles, owls, hares, pigs, camels, mice, bats, lizards, shellfish, and all insects except locusts. Other animals were implied based on general characteristics, such as alligators, cats, dogs, horses, squid, snakes, and turtles.
- People with certain physical conditions, such as menstrual periods, leprosy, open sores, post-childbirth, and having any discharge from the body.
- Touching the dead bodies of both people and animals. Even the tent that a dead body was found in was considered unclean.

Purification rituals were detailed for all unclean conditions, which typically involved a period of social isolation, sprinkling of water or blood, immersion in water, and/or offering sacrifices to become clean again. These regulations about **cleanliness** were the cornerstone of Israel's religious rituals.

CHAPTER 1

Foreword to the Gospel

1.1 LUKE'S PURPOSE

Mark 1:1
Luke 1:1-4

The beginning of the good news of Jesus Christ, God's Son.

Greatest Theophilus,[a] even though many have set their hand to put together an account of the things done among us, as they were given to us by those who were eyewitnesses from the beginning and servants of the word, I thought it would be good for me also to write it out chronologically, after carefully investigating everything from the beginning, so that you might know for sure about the word you've been taught.

1.2 JOHN'S PROLOGUE: THE "WORD"

John 1:1-18

A. Luke addressed his version of Jesus' life, as well as his history of the early church (the book of Acts), to "**greatest Theophilus**." *Kratistos* is the Greek word that translates to "strongest," "greatest," or "most excellent." It was used as a title of respect when addressing someone important. Theophilus, on the other hand, translates to "God lover." Although this term could be applied to the church as a whole, it was likely the name of a specific person, possibly the one who commissioned the writing.

In the beginning was the word and the word was with God. The word was God. He was with God in the beginning. All things came to be through him, and apart from him nothing came to be that has come to be. In him was life, and that life was the light of men. The light is shining in the darkness and the darkness can't grasp it.

There was a man named John who was sent from God. He came as a witness to testify about the light, for all to believe through him. He wasn't the light, but a witness to the light. The true light coming into the world illuminates every man. He was in the world and the world was made through him, but the world didn't know him. He came to his own, but his own didn't accept him. But whoever accepted him, he gave the right to become God's children, to those who believed in his name, who weren't born of blood or of the body's will or of man's will, but born of God.

The word became a body and lived with us. We saw his glory, glory like the only one born of the Father, full of grace and truth. John testifies[b] about him. He cried out, "This is the one I spoke about: 'The one who comes after me is greater than I am, because he existed before I did.'"

Out of his abundance, we've all received grace for grace. The Law was given through Moses, but grace and truth came through Jesus

B. Occasionally, Greek authors used the present tense of a verb to emphasize an action in the midst of a story told in the past tense. This literary feature occurs in the New Testament, which was originally written in Greek. However, English doesn't employ this method of emphasis, so a direct translation can seem awkward. In other Bible translations, the present tense Greek is often translated into past tense English and marked with an asterisk to note the emphasis. However, a more literal translation keeps those few words in the present tense, as it's rendered here. In this first occurrence, the original Gospel writer emphasized John's testifying by writing "**testifies**," contrary to the tense of the rest of the passage.

The Word

Logos is the Greek word for "speech" or "**word**," but John uses this term to refer specifically to God's word personified as Jesus. No other Gospel writer uses *logos* like this. However, since Heraclitus first used the term around 500 BC, ancient Greek philosophers used *logos* to mean wisdom in general, particularly pertaining to divine order and reasoning.

Many Bible translations capitalize "word" when referring to Jesus. Similarly, pronouns ("he" or "his") referring to God or Jesus are typically capitalized throughout Scripture. However, there was no concept of capitalization in the original languages of the Bible. Over time, church tradition has capitalized any titles or pronouns referring to God, but this practice isn't directly biblical. So to keep with a more literal translation of the original Scriptures, pronouns referring to Jesus or God are not capitalized here. Nor is "word" capitalized, despite being a reference to Jesus' divinity. However, "Father" and "Son" are capitalized when they're clear references to God.

Christ. No one has ever seen God, but the only God who was born, who's at the Father's chest, has made him known.

1.3 JESUS' GENEALOGY

Matthew 1:1-17
Luke 3:23b-38

The record of the genealogy of Jesus the Christ, the son of David and the son of Abraham:

Abraham fathered Isaac, Isaac fathered Jacob, and Jacob fathered Judah and his brothers.
Judah fathered Perez and Zerah by Tamar, Perez fathered Hezron, and Hezron fathered Ram.
Ram fathered Amminadab, Amminadab fathered Nahshon, and Nahshon fathered Salmon.
Salmon fathered Boaz by Rahab, Boaz fathered Obed by Ruth, and Obed fathered Jesse.
Jesse fathered David the king.
David fathered Solomon by her of Uriah.
Solomon fathered Rehoboam, Rehoboam fathered Abijah, and Abijah fathered Asa.
Asa fathered Jehoshaphat, Jehoshaphat fathered Joram, and Joram fathered Uzziah.
Uzziah fathered Jotham, Jotham fathered Ahaz, and Ahaz fathered Hezekiah.
Hezekiah fathered Manasseh, Manasseh fathered Amon, and Amon fathered Josiah.

Jesus' Different Genealogies

Both Matthew and Luke record Jesus' genealogy. Matthew's starts with Abraham, the patriarch of all Israel, and lists descendants forward to Jesus' father Joseph. Luke, on the other hand, begins with Jesus and records backward all the way to Adam, the first man. One explanation for Jesus' **two different genealogies** is that Matthew records only the heirs to David's throne, while Luke records the complete lineage. Ancient genealogies weren't necessarily exhaustive lists – ancestors were sometimes only included for a specific reason.

Another possibility is that Matthew records Joseph's line (Jesus' legal father), while Luke records Mary's (Jesus' biological mother). Reading closely in Luke's account (page 19), the text states Jesus was "**considered**" (Greek *nomizo*) to be Joseph's son, thereby making Joseph the son of Eli through marriage. Therefore, Jesus was possibly a descendant of David by both parents, fulfilling the prophet Jeremiah's words long before.

The LORD says, "David will never lack a man to sit on the throne of Israel's house."
– Jeremiah 7:14

Women in Jesus' Genealogy

Besides his mother Mary, four women are mentioned in Matthew's account of Jesus' genealogy. The first, **Tamar**, was originally Judah's daughter-in-law, being married to his two oldest sons. Genesis 38 records that after their deaths, with Tamar widowed twice, she was engaged to Judah's next son, but the marriage never occurred. So after disguising herself as a prostitute, Tamar slept with Judah. Upon becoming pregnant, Judah condemned his daughter-in-law to be burned for her sin, not knowing she was pregnant by him. But after confronting him with proof, she was allowed to live and subsequently gave birth to twin boys, Perez and Zerah.

Rahab was a prostitute in the city of Jericho during Israel's conquest of Canaan. She hid two Israelite spies and helped them escape the city by sending their pursuers in a different direction. For her service to Israel, Rahab's whole household was spared when Jericho was conquered, and she lived among Israel from then on. Her story is recorded in the book of Joshua.

Ruth is one of only two women to have a book of the Bible named after her. After her husband died, Ruth committed herself to her mother-in-law, Naomi, and they travelled back to Naomi's homeland, Israel, even though Ruth herself was from Moab. Although widows in ancient Israel had nobody to provide for them, Ruth found favor with a man named Boaz, Naomi's relative. Boaz was so impressed with Ruth's character that he married her and took her and Naomi into his household.

Finally, Bathsheba was originally the wife of Uriah, a warrior in King David's army. However, while Uriah was away on campaign, David saw her bathing on a rooftop, sent for her, and slept with her. Upon finding out she was pregnant, David commanded Uriah to be abandoned in battle, leading to his death. David then took Bathsheba as his wife, but was soon confronted about his sin. Although he quickly repented, their child became sick and died. However, Bathsheba later bore him four other children, one of which, Solomon, went on to rule Israel after David (see 2 Samuel 11). Her name isn't explicitly stated in Jesus' genealogy, but it's certainly implied as "**her of Uriah**."

In such a patriarchal world, it's not insignificant that women were mentioned at all in a genealogy.

Josiah fathered Jeconiah and his brothers during the exile to Babylon.

After the exile to Babylon, Jeconiah fathered Shealtiel, and Shealtiel fathered Zerubbabel.

Zerubbabel fathered Abihud, Abihud fathered Eliakim, and Eliakim fathered Azor.

Azor fathered Zadok, Zadok fathered Achim, and Achim fathered Eliud.

Eliud fathered Eleazar, Eleazar fathered Matthan, and Matthan fathered Jacob.

Jacob fathered Joseph, the husband of Mary, by whom Jesus was born, who is called the Christ.

So all the generations from Abraham to David are 14 generations; from David to the exile in Babylon, 14 generations; and from the exile in Babylon to the Christ, 14 generations.

Jesus was considered to be from[c] Joseph, from Eli, from Matthat, from Levi, from Melchi, from Jannai, from Joseph, from Mattathias, from Amos, from Nahum, from Hesli, from Naggi, from Maath, from Mattathias, from Semein, from Josech, from Joda, from Joanan, from Rhesa, from Zerubbabel, from Shealtiel, from Neri, from Melchi, from Addi, from Cosam, from Elmadam, from Er, from Joshua, from Eliezer, from Jorim, from Matthat, from Levi, from Simeon, from Judah, from Joseph, from Jonam, from Eliakim, from Melea, from Menna, from Mattatha, from Nathan, from David, from Jesse, from Obed, from Boaz, from Salmon, from Nahshon, from Amminadab, from Admin, from Ram, from Hezron, from Perez, from Judah, from Jacob, from Isaac, from Abraham, from Terah, from Nahor, from Serug, from Reu, from Peleg, from Heber, from Shelah, from Cainan, from Arphaxad, from Shem, from Noah, from Lamech, from Methuselah, from Enoch, from Jared, from Mahalaleel, from Cainan, from Enosh, from Seth, from Adam, from God.

C. *Ho* is a very common Greek article that can mean various things. *Ho* can be translated to many words in English, including (but not limited to) "the," "this," and "which." In the case of a genealogy, it means "son of" or simply "**from**."

Joseph

Joseph is the name of many men in the Bible who lived long before Jesus' father Joseph. The most notable of them was the eleventh of Jacob's twelve sons. Joseph was favored by Jacob more than any of his brothers, being the only son of Jacob's favorite wife, Rachel. His name means "may God add," referring to Rachel's desire for more children after his birth. Upon receiving a colorful coat from his father and relating a dream of his lordship over his brothers, Joseph's ten brothers sold him in a fit of envy to slave traders travelling to Egypt.

Throughout years of slavery, promotion, jail, dream interpretation, and famine, Joseph eventually worked his way up to becoming the second most powerful man in Egypt, all the while maintaining his integrity and deferring praise to God. He ended up saving his entire extended family from famine, and brought them down to live with him in Egypt. It was in Egypt that the family of Israel developed into a nation, became enslaved, and was finally delivered from slavery. Joseph was also the father of Ephraim and Manasseh, two future half-tribes of Israel.

The City of Jerusalem

The Jewish capital of **Jerusalem** was (and still is) a prominent city in the Middle East, but it has a tumultuous history of repeated conquest, glory, rebellion, war, destruction, and restoration. Unlike other ancient capitals that were well-positioned around natural resources and trade routes, Jerusalem was located far inland, between the Mediterranean Sea and the Dead Sea, away from major trade routes and waterways. It also lacked an adequate water supply, until an underground spring was diverted within its walls. The city sat on the southern spur of a plateau in the Judean mountains. Two steep valleys flanked Jerusalem east and west, while another shallow one ran through it. The Hinnom Valley, also called the Gehenna Valley, lay south and west of Jerusalem's walls, wrapping around the base of the city's highest point, Mount Zion, where Herod's palace was built; the Kidron Valley was east of the city, separating the Mount of Olives from Jerusalem's temple mount, also called Mount Moriah; and through the middle of the city, the shallow Tyropoeon Valley ran southward to join with the Kidron and Hinnom outside the walls. But despite its apparent geographic impracticality, Jerusalem's hostile location made it a strong fortress, easily defended against attack. However, Jerusalem's walls and gates have been built, destroyed, rebuilt, and expanded so many times that little of what stood in the first century remains to this day.

The name Jerusalem has various proposed meanings: the first half of the word can mean "foundation," "cornerstone," "house," or "instruction," while the second half can mean "peace," "safety" or refer to Shalim, the Canaanite god of the setting sun. Similarly, Jerusalem has various pseudonyms. The city is first mentioned in the Bible as Salem (1), which was ruled by a Canaanite priest named Melchizedek during the time of Abraham. Hundreds of years later, Jerusalem is again mentioned in the Bible during Joshua's campaign to conquer Canaan. The city was then inhabited by the Jebusites, and was therefore called Jebus (2). Although Israel attacked and invaded the city, they couldn't drive the Jebusites out until the reign of King David. Despite the city's strong defense atop steep slopes, David's army conquered the city around 1003 BC through a secret underground water tunnel. David then expanded the city walls and made Jerusalem his capital. Jerusalem helped to unite Israel because it sat, ideally, near the border of Judah (southern kingdom) and Benjamin (northern kingdom). Thus Jerusalem was also known as the City of David (3). Finally, David's son Solomon built the first Temple in Jerusalem on the second-highest point in the city, Mount Moriah, which may be the same location as where Abraham tied up and nearly sacrificed his son Isaac in an act of faith centuries earlier. However, the Temple mount (and Jerusalem itself) was thereafter called Zion (4), after Mount Zion, the highest point within the city, located across the Tyropoeon Valley just west of Mount Moriah.

After construction of the Jewish Temple, Jerusalem became the center of religion and culture for Israel. It was during Solomon's reign that Jerusalem reached the pinnacle of its splendor, with envoys from all over the world visiting to admire and pay tribute to Israel. However, civil strife and widespread immorality soon led to its downfall. Twenty years after the northern kingdom of Israel fell to Assyria, Jerusalem (the capital of the southern kingdom of Judah) miraculously survived a siege in 701 BC by the Assyrians after a plague supposedly decimated their army. However, Babylon succeeded where Assyria could not, capturing Jerusalem in 597 and again in 587 BC, and taking exiles back east on both occasions. Seventy years later, Jewish exiles were allowed to return to their homeland under the Persians to rebuild the Temple, which was completed in 516 BC, but paled in comparison to the original Temple. Judah existed as a vassal state in the Persian Empire, and as a territory in the Greek Empire after Alexander the Great conquered Persia. But Jerusalem revolted against the Greeks in 167 BC and established an independent Hebrew nation. However, the city was recaptured in 37 BC, this time by Herod the Great, who ruled Judea and the surrounding nations as a client-king under Rome. During Herod's rule, Jerusalem's Temple and walls were renovated and expanded. The Jews again rebelled in 66 AD, leading to a Roman-Jewish war and the subsequent destruction of Jerusalem in 70 AD under the Roman commander Titus.

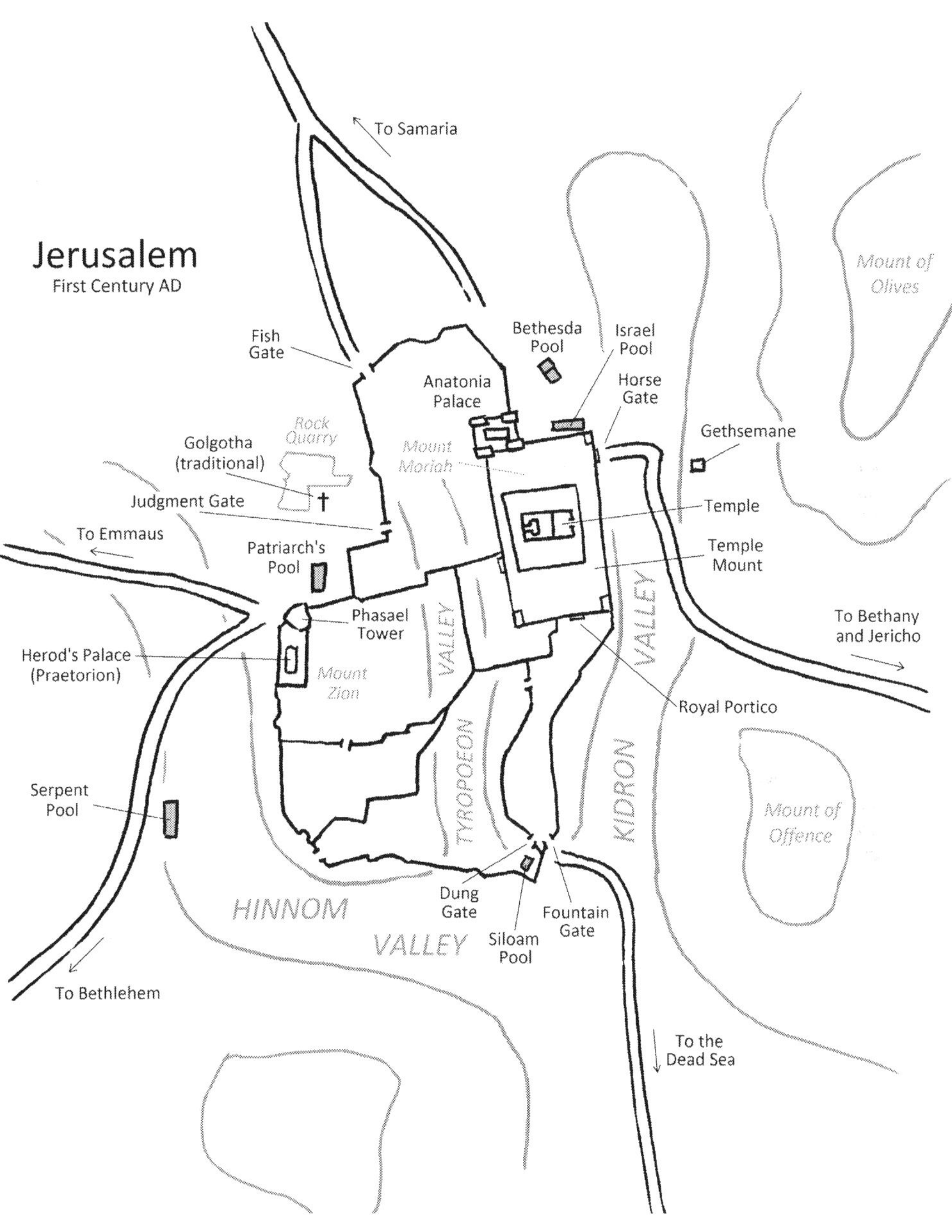
Jerusalem
First Century AD
To Samaria
Mount of Olives
Fish Gate
Bethesda Pool
Israel Pool
Anatonia Palace
Horse Gate
Rock Quarry
Golgotha (traditional)
Mount Moriah
Gethsemane
Judgment Gate
Temple
To Emmaus
Patriarch's Pool
Temple Mount
Phasael Tower
To Bethany and Jericho
Herod's Palace (Praetorion)
Mount Zion
VALLEY
VALLEY
Royal Portico
TYROPOEON
KIDRON
Serpent Pool
Mount of Offence
HINNOM
VALLEY
Dung Gate
Fountain Gate
Siloam Pool
To Bethlehem
To the Dead Sea

Priesthood

A **priest** is a mediator between God and man. More specifically, Jewish priests were the official ministers of Israel and descendants of Moses' brother Aaron, from the tribe of Levi. Aaron was ordained as Israel's first High Priest as they journeyed from Egypt to Canaan, and his family subsequently became the official priestly line. The Greek term *archiereus* ("first priest") referred to the current or past priest who governed all the other priests as the religious head of Israel. This position is often translated "High Priest" or "Chief Priest."

A priest was to be set apart for service in all things, from appearance (no physical defects) to family life (wife must be a virgin from Israel). The High Priest's purification process involved a week-long ceremony of bathing, dressing in specially-made priestly clothes, and being anointed with oil. A priest's duties included burning incense, tending to ceremonial lamps, ensuring offerings were properly prepared, teaching the Law, and judging court cases. But most importantly, the High Priest would enter the innermost room of the Temple, the Holy of Holies, once each year and offer sacrifices for himself and the people.

The role of priests diminished somewhat over time as they were overshadowed by other religious groups, such as scribes and Pharisees. As well, the role of High Priest was no longer hereditary under Roman rule, but could be appointed or deposed as the current ruler desired.

[Aaron and his sons] will be anointed for an everlasting priesthood throughout their generations.

– Exodus 40:15

CHAPTER 2

The Birth of John

2.1 JOHN'S BIRTH FORETOLD TO ZACHARIAS

Luke 1:5-25

During the days of Herod, king of Judea, there was a priest named Zacharias,[a] who belonged to the division of Abijah.[b] He had a wife from Aaron's daughters,[c] whose name was Elizabeth. They were both righteous in God's sight, walking blamelessly in all the Lord's commandments and regulations. However, they had no children, because Elizabeth was barren and they were both well along in days.

It happened that while he was acting as priest before God in the order of his division, he was chosen by lot, according to the priestly custom, to enter the Lord's Temple and burn incense. Meanwhile, the

A. The name **Zacharias**, which means "God has remembered," is the Greek version of Zechariah. Over 30 men in the Bible had the same name.

B. When David was king of Israel, he divided the priesthood into 24 divisions, of which **Abijah** was the eighth. Each division was responsible for the daily administration of the temple for a week at a time.

C. Aaron was Moses' older brother and was ordained as the first High Priest of Israel. His male descendants carried on in this role throughout subsequent generations. Female descendants, however, did not serve as priests, but to be one of **Aaron's daughters** denoted priestly descent.

whole assembly of people prayed outside at the hour of incense.[d] An angel from the Lord appeared to him, standing to the right of the incense altar. Zacharias was alarmed when he saw it and fear seized him. But the angel told him, "Don't be afraid, Zacharias. Your request has been heard. Your wife Elizabeth will give birth to a son and you'll name him John. You'll have joy and happiness, and many will celebrate his birth, because he'll be great in the Lord's sight. He won't drink wine or liquor,[e] and he'll be filled with the Holy Spirit from within his mother's womb. He'll turn many of Israel's sons back to the Lord their God. And it's he who will go before him in the spirit and the power of Elijah[f] to turn the hearts of fathers back to their children and the disobedient to a righteous attitude, and to prepare a people equipped for the Lord."

"How will I know this?" Zacharias asked the angel. "I'm an old man and my wife is well along in days."

"I am Gabriel, who stands in God's presence," the angel answered. "I've been sent to speak to you and bring you this good news. Look, you'll be silent and unable to speak until the day this happens, because you didn't believe my words, which will be completed in their time."

The people were waiting for Zacharias, wondering about his delay in the Temple. But when he came out, he couldn't speak to them, so they realized that he'd seen a vision in the Temple. And although he kept signing to them, he stayed mute.

After the days of his service were done, he returned home. And after those days, his wife Elizabeth became pregnant, but she hid herself for five months, saying, "This is how the Lord has dealt with me in the days when he looked at me to remove my disgrace[g] from among men."[h]

D. Incense was burned continuously on a golden altar in the Temple. The supply was refreshed by a priest first thing in the morning and again after the evening sacrifices. Therefore, the **hour of Incense** could either be at dawn or twilight.

E. Anyone who **abstained from alcohol** was called a Nazirite, from the Hebrew word *nazir* ("separated"). Also included in the Nazirite vow was never cutting one's hair or touching a corpse. The Old Testament records that the hero Sampson and the prophet Samuel were both Nazirites.

F. *Look, I'm going to send Elijah the prophet to you before the great and fearful day of the LORD comes. He'll turn fathers' hearts to their children and children's hearts to their fathers, so that I won't come and strike the land with a curse. – Malachi 4:5-6*

G. Ancient cultures valued children immensely as a means to continue one's legacy and a sign of God's blessing. Barrenness was therefore **disgraceful**, and even considered a curse by God.

H. *He makes the barren live in the house like the joyful mother of children. Praise the LORD! – Psalm 113:9*

2.2 JESUS' BIRTH FORETOLD TO MARY

Luke 1:26-38

In the sixth month, Gabriel the angel was sent from God to a city in Galilee called Nazareth,[i] to a virgin engaged to a man from David's house named Joseph. The virgin's name was Mary. Coming in, he said, "Rejoice,[j] favored one! May the Lord be with you!"

She was troubled at these words and kept wondering what kind of a greeting this was. Then the angel told her, "Don't be afraid, Mary, because you've found God's favor! Look, you'll conceive in your womb and bear a son, and you'll name him Jesus. He'll be great and will be called the Son of the Highest.[k] The Lord God will give him the throne of David his father. He'll reign over Jacob's house forever and his kingdom will have no end."

Mary asked the angel, "How can this happen, since I haven't known[l] a man?"

The angel answered, "The Holy Spirit will come upon you and the power of the Highest will overshadow you, which is why the Holy One born will be called God's Son. Look, even your relative Elizabeth has conceived a son in her old age too, and the one who was called barren is now in her sixth month, because nothing will be impossible with God."

Then Mary said, "Look, the Lord's slave. May it happen to me just as you've said."

Then the angel left her.

I. **Nazareth** was a town in the Roman province of Galilee, somewhat secluded from the rest of the land. It sat in a high valley, surrounded by hills and apart from major highways. However, Nazareth was just a few miles south of Sepphoris, a prominent Roman city in Galilee. The extensive building projects in Sepphoris in the early first century would likely have attracted skilled workers from the surrounding area. However, despite its proximity to Sepphoris, Nazareth may have had a reputation for being unimportant in Israel, as well as for immorality. It was not a place where the Messiah would have been expected to come from.

J. In addition to meaning "**rejoice**," "be glad," or "be well," the Greek word *chairo* could also be used as a salutation, meaning "hail" or "greetings." It was particularly used at the beginning of written letters and was the standard greeting to Caesar ("Hail, Caesar!").

K. In terms of the physical position of an object, "**highest**" could refer to being elevated above everything else. However, in reference to God, it referred to his being exalted above all.

L. The Greek verb *ginosko* means "**know**" or "understand." It was also a euphemism for intercourse.

The Holy Spirit

Holy Spirit comes from the Greek *hagios* ("holy," "saintly") and *pneuma* ("breath," "wind," "spirit") and was understood to be the Spirit of God. It has also been translated "Holy Ghost," from the Old English word for "spirit" (*gast*). "Holy Spirit" only occurs three times in the Old Testament, although the Hebrew word for "spirit" (*ruwach*) occurs many times alone or with other descriptors in reference to God. The New Testament, however, uses "Holy Spirit" 98 times, hinting at the Christian theology of the Trinitarian nature of God.

Christianity holds that God has three distinct entities making up the same one God: the Father, the Son, and the Holy Spirit. Understandably confusing, and in sharp contrast to Judaism's strict monotheism, this doctrine has been described in a variety of metaphors. The three parts of God are said to be like three pieces of the same pie. Or similar to each person having three distinct parts – a body, a mind, and a spirit – which are separate dimensions of oneself, yet intimately unified as one person. Another understanding is that God the Father produced God the Son and their relationship is the Spirit of God. However it's understood, each entity of the Trinity is completely God. Like a cube exists in three dimensions, so God is three in one. Outside of the Gospels, one of the most explicit references to Trinitarian theology was made by Paul the Apostle: *"The grace of the Lord Jesus Christ and the love of God and the partnership of the Holy Spirit be with you all." (2 Corinthians 13:14)*

Trinitarian theology developed after Jesus' time, but the understanding during the first century was that the Holy Spirit was God's breath or essence, not a separate being.

2.3 MARY VISITS ELIZABETH

Luke 1:39-56

In those days, Mary got up and went to the hills in a hurry, to a city in Judah. Then she entered Zacharias' house and greeted Elizabeth. When Elizabeth heard Mary's greeting, the baby leaped in her womb and Elizabeth was filled with the Holy Spirit. She cried out in a loud voice, "You're blessed[m] among women! And the fruit of your womb is blessed! And why me, that the mother of my Lord would come to me? Because look, when the sound of your greeting entered my ears, the baby in my womb leaped for joy! Blessed is she who believed, because what the Lord has told her will be fulfilled."

Then Mary said,

"My soul amplifies[n] the Lord and my spirit is overjoyed in God my savior!

M. "**Blessed**" comes from the Greek word *makarios*, which can also mean "happy." It represents the wishing of favor or goodness on another, with the hope that God will make it happen. God promised Israel blessings if they obeyed his Law. A father would often bless his children before his death, symbolically passing on God's favor. The opposite of a blessing – a curse – is wishing injury, harm, or misfortune on another.

Look, I'm putting a blessing and a curse before you today: the blessing if you listen to the LORD your God's commands, which I'm commanding you today; and the curse if you don't listen to the LORD your God's commands, but turn from the way I'm commanding you today by following other gods that you don't know. – Deuteronomy 11:26-28

Because he looked at the lowliness of his slave, and look, all generations will call me blessed from now on.
Because the Strong One has done something great for me, and his name is Holy.[o]
His mercy is on generation after generation toward those who fear him.[p]
He has done great things with his arm and he has scattered those proud in the thoughts of their hearts.
He took down rulers from their thrones and lifted up the humble.
He filled the hungry with good things,[q] but sent the rich away empty.
Reminded of his mercy, he helped his servant Israel as he spoke to our fathers, Abraham and his descendants forever."

So Mary stayed with her about three months and then returned home.

2.4 JOHN'S BIRTH

Luke 1:57-80

The time came for Elizabeth to deliver and she gave birth to a son. Her neighbors and relatives heard that the Lord had amplified his mercy toward her and they celebrated with her.

Then it happened that they came to circumcise[r] the child on the eighth day. They were going to call him Zacharias, after his father, but his mother said, "No! He'll be called John."

But they told her, "None of your relatives are called by that name."

N. *Megalyno* is Greek for "make great" or "exalt." It's translated here as **amplifies**. It's used only twice in the gospels.

O. *Let them praise your great and awesome name – it is Holy. – Psalm 99:3*

P. *The LORD's kindness is from forever to forever on those who fear him, and his righteousness is on the children's children of those who keep his covenant and remember and follow his rules. – Psalm 103:17*

Q. *He satisfied the thirsty soul and filled the hungry soul with good things. – Psalm 107:9*

R. Starting with Abraham, Genesis records that God commanded all males to be circumcised as a sign of God's covenant with his people. **Circumcision** is the surgical removal of the foreskin on the penis. It was also practiced in other ancient cultures, such as Egypt and Canaan, as a rite of passage into adulthood, often occurring during puberty. However, Israel traditionally circumcised a newborn male at eight days old, in conjunction with naming him. Over time, the Jews took great pride in circumcision, often degrading foreigners as "the uncircumcised."

You'll circumcise the flesh of your foreskin to be the sign of the covenant between me and you. – Leviticus 17:11

So they signed to his father as to what he wanted to call him. He asked for a tablet and wrote, "His name is John." They were all amazed. Then immediately his mouth and his tongue were opened and he began to speak, praising God. Fear came on all those living around them, and all this talk was discussed throughout all the hill country of Judea. All who heard it kept it in mind, saying, "What will this child be?" because the hand of the Lord was with him too.

His father Zacharias was filled with the Holy Spirit, and prophesied, saying,

"Blessed be the Lord God of Israel, because he has visited us and has made his people redeemed!
He has raised up a horn[s] of salvation for us in the house of David his servant, as he spoke by the mouth of his holy prophets ages ago:
'For salvation from our enemies and from the hand of all who hate us;[t]
To show our fathers mercy and remember his holy covenant, the promise he swore to our father Abraham;[u]
To let us serve him without fear, in holiness and righteousness before him all our days, being rescued from our enemies' hands.'
And you, child, will be called the prophet of the Highest, because you'll go on ahead of the Lord to prepare his ways,[v]
To give his people knowledge of salvation through the forgiveness of their sins,
Because of the tender mercy of our God, which the sunrise from the heights will visit us with,
To shine on those who sit in darkness and the shadow of death,[w]

S. Animal **horns** served multiple purposes in Israel. As musical instruments (*shofar*), they called the nation together for festivals or battles. Horns were also oil containers, which could be used to anoint a new king. And since an animal's horns were its weapons, they became a symbol of strength and courage.

The LORD is my cliff, my fortress, my savior, my God, my rock, and my shelter. He's my shield, the horn of my salvation, and my high place. – Psalm 18:2

T. *He saved them from the hand of those who hated them and redeemed them from the enemy's hand. – Psalm 106:10*

U. Genesis records that **God's covenant with Abraham** was to give him land, bless him, and bless others through him. The covenant was confirmed with his name being changed from Abram and all of his male descendants being circumcised as a sign of the covenant throughout subsequent generations.

V. *"Look, I'm going to send my messenger to clear the way ahead of me. Then the Lord you seek will suddenly come to his Temple. Look, the messenger of the covenant, the one you enjoy – he's coming!" says the LORD of armies. – Malachi 3:1*

To guide our feet into the way of peace."

So the child kept growing and getting strong in his spirit, and he lived in the deserts until the day of his presentation to Israel.

W. *The people walking in darkness will see an intense light, and the light will shine on those living in a dark land. – Isaiah 9:2*

CHAPTER 3

The Birth of Jesus

3.1 JOSEPH'S DREAM

Matthew 1:18-25

The birth of Jesus the Christ was like this: when his mother Mary was engaged to Joseph, she was found to be pregnant by the Holy Spirit before they had come together.[a] Her fiancé, Joseph, being a righteous man and not wanting to disgrace her, planned to send her away secretly. But when he thought about this, look, an angel from the Lord appeared to him in a dream, saying, "Joseph, son of David, don't be afraid to take Mary as your wife, because this pregnancy is from the Holy Spirit. She'll give birth to a son and you'll call his name Jesus, because he'll save his people from their sins."

This all happened to fulfill what the Lord said through the prophet: "Look, the virgin will be pregnant and will give birth to a son, and they'll call his name *Immanuel*," which translates to "God with us."

A. By law, the penalty for **sex outside marriage** (also called having an affair, adultery, or fornication) was death.

If a virgin girl is engaged to a man and another man finds her in the city and lies with her, then bring the two of them to the city gate and stone them to death – the girl because she didn't cry out in the city and the man because he humiliated his neighbor's wife. So you'll burn the evil from among you. – Deuteronomy 22:23-24

The Name of Jesus

The name **Jesus** (Greek *Iesous*) is the Greek form of the Hebrew name Joshua, which means "the LORD saves." It was a common name at that time. In the Old Testament, Joshua was the name of Moses' right hand man and successor. He's first mentioned in the Bible as a Hebrew spy in the promised land before Israel entered it. He was only one of two spies that reported back favorably to Israel, but his report was widely disregarded and Israel failed to enter their land. As a result, God banished them into the wilderness for 40 years. During this time, Joshua acted as Moses' assistant, and, after a faithless act by Moses, he led Israel on their second attempt at entering Canaan. This time they were successful and Joshua took the army on a virtually unstoppable military campaign through their new land to eradicate the current residents, the account of which is recorded in the biblical book that bears his name. Therefore, Jesus can be considered a symbolic "second Joshua," who delivered his people into a new promised land.

Generations before Jesus' birth, Isaiah prophesied that the coming messiah would be called **Immanuel**. This symbolic name means "God with us."

The Lord himself will give you a sign: look, a virgin will become pregnant and give birth to a son, and she'll call his name Immanuel.

– Isaiah 7:14

Joseph got up from his sleep and did what the angel of the Lord commanded and took her as his wife, but he didn't know her until she gave birth to a son. He named him Jesus.

3.2 JESUS' BIRTH

Luke 2:1-20

In those days an order went out from Caesar Augustus[b] for a census[c] to be taken of the whole world. This was the first census while Quirinius[d] was governor of Syria. So everyone went to be registered, each to his own city. Joseph went up too, from the city of Nazareth in Galilee to the City of David in Judea, which is called Bethlehem,

B. **Caesar Augustus** (also called Gaius Julius Caesar Augustus) was the first and arguably the greatest Roman emperor, ruling from 27 BC to 14 AD. He expanded his rule throughout the Mediterranean world and established *Pax Romana* ("Roman Peace"), which was two centuries of peace throughout the empire. Like other Roman rulers, he periodically imposed a census to be taken of the entire empire to assess for taxation and military service.

C. During a **census**, everyone had to return to their hometown to declare to the censor their name, age, family, and property (land, slaves, livestock). Single women and orphans were represented by their guardians. A person who deliberately missed the census was subject to severe punishment, including property seizure, imprisonment, and/or death.

D. When **Quirinius** took over the reign of Syria from Herod Archelaus in 6 AD, one of his first tasks was to conduct a census in Syria and Judea. However, Matthew's Gospel states Jesus' birth was during the reign of Herod the Great, who died ten years earlier in 4 BC. Thus there is some discrepancy as to what Quirinius' role was at that time, since he didn't take power until a decade later. Most scholars agree that Jesus was born in late 5 BC or early 4 BC.

Bethelehem

Eight kilometers south of Jerusalem in the fertile hill country of Judah was a city called **Bethlehem**. Its name means "house of bread," but it was also called David's City in the New Testament, since that was where David was born, raised, and anointed king (Jerusalem is also called David's City for other reasons). Bethlehem is first mentioned in Genesis as the burial place of Jacob's wife Rachel after she died following the birth to her second son Benjamin. It's later recorded as where Ruth and Naomi, David's ancestors, returned after their husbands' deaths. Finally, the prophet Micah prophesied the Messiah would be born there, hundreds of years before Jesus' arrival.

As for you, Bethlehem Ephrathah, too small to be among the thousands from Judah, someone will go out from you to be the ruler of Israel. His origins are ancient, from the days of eternity.

– Micah 5:2

because he was from David's house and family. He went to register with Mary, who was engaged to him and was pregnant.

While they were there, the days were fulfilled for her to give birth, and she delivered her firstborn, a son. She wrapped him in cloths and laid him in a manger,[e]) because there wasn't any room for them at the lodge.

That night, in the same area, there were shepherds camping[f] out and guarding their flocks. Suddenly, an angel from the Lord stood in front of them and the Lord's glory shone around them, and they were terribly afraid. But the angel told them, "Don't be afraid! Look, I bring you good news of great joy that will be for all people! A savior has been born today in the City of David. He is Christ the Lord. This is your sign: you'll find a baby wrapped in cloths and lying in a manger."

Suddenly a multitude of heaven's armies appeared with the angel, praising God, saying, "Glory to God in the highest! Peace on earth among men that please him!"

After the angels left them for heaven, the shepherds said to each other, "Let's go to Bethlehem and see what has happened, about these words that the Lord has let us know!"

So they came quickly and found Mary and Joseph, with the baby lying in a manger. When they saw him, they let them know about the

E. A box or trough used to hold food for animals was called a **manger** (*phatne* in Greek. In Judea, they were often made of clay mixed with straw or stones. Mangers could also be carved into a rock wall within a stable.

F. *Agrauleo* is a Greek verb derived from *agros* ("field" or "land") and *aule* ("courtyard"). It refers to a shepherd's practice of sleeping out in the fields, under the open sky. It's translated here as "**camping**."

The Gospel

The term "gospel" comes from the Old English for "**good news**" or "glad tidings." It's the direct translation of the Greek word *euangelion*, which literally means "good message." Although it has come to refer to the story of Jesus' life, its meaning during the first century was much broader. The gospel represented good news for a kingdom or empire in a variety of ways: a new king had been crowned, the king had defeated his enemies, or a new heir to the throne had been born. In any of these occurrences, messengers would be dispatched throughout the kingdom to proclaim the gospel, that is, the good news. It was also common practice for messengers to be dispatched following a battle to relay news of victory to an expectant king and country back home. In keeping with Christian tradition, the Gospel (capital "G") refers to Jesus' story, as recorded in the New Testament books of Matthew, Mark, Luke, and John.

How beautiful on the mountains are the feet of him who brings good news, who announces peace and brings good news of happiness, who announces salvation, saying in Zion, "Your God reigns!"

– Isaiah 52:7

speech they had been told regarding this child. All who heard it wondered about what the shepherds had told them. But Mary treasured all these words, thinking about them in her heart. Then the shepherds returned, glorifying and praising God for all they had seen and heard, just as it had been told to them.

3.3 JESUS PRESENTED AT THE TEMPLE

Luke 2:21-39

When the eight days were fulfilled before his circumcision, he was named Jesus, the name the angel had given him before he was conceived in the womb. And when the days for [Mary's] purification[g] were complete, according to Moses' Law, they brought him up to Jerusalem to present him to the Lord (as it's written in the Law of the Lord, "Every male that opens the womb will be called holy to the Lord"),[h] and to offer a sacrifice according to the Law of the Lord, a pair of turtledoves or two young doves.[i]

G. According to Moses' Law, a mother was considered unclean for 40 days after giving birth to a son. However, if she gave birth to a daughter, she was unclean for 73 days (see Leviticus 12). After the **days of her purification**, she would bring a one-year-old lamb and a dove to the priest as an offering, and then she would be clean again. However, if she couldn't afford a lamb, she could offer two doves instead.

H. *Dedicate every firstborn to me, the first offspring of every womb among Israel's sons, of both man and animals. It belongs to me.... The males belong to the LORD. – Exodus 13:2,12b*

I. The **doves** (*peristera*) mentioned in the Bible were similar to modern-day pigeons. **Turtledoves** (*trygon*), however, were migrants to Palestine, living there from April to

Prophets

A **prophet** is God's mouthpiece and, accordingly, a prophecy is a message relayed from God. Although the Greek term *prophitis* translates to "foreteller," which is where the English term comes from, the equivalent Hebrew word (*nabiy*) translates to "spokesman." The understanding of a prophet in first century Judea wasn't necessarily someone who could predict the future, but someone who simply acted as God's messenger. In fact, the majority of prophecies in the Bible didn't foretell future events but rather instructed, warned, encouraged, or corrected the people they were intended for. Such messages were received by prophets in all sorts of ways (through angels, in dreams, by seeing visions), just as prophets in the Bible came from all walks of life (shepherds, farmers, princes, kings, priests, women), and they could be called to lifelong or temporary service. Yet however they spoke, the Bible states that prophets carried the authority of God himself as they spoke his words, not their own. A prophet speaking apart from God was considered a great sin and was harshly denounced. When a prophet did foretell future events, the Bible records that his words should be used to verify or falsify his status as a prophet. Unfortunately, the role of being a prophet was not particularly pleasant in ancient times – many of the prophets in the Bible faced abuse when their messages were not well-received.

I'll raise up a prophet like [Moses] from among his brothers. I'll put my words in his mouth and he'll tell them all that I command him. – Deuteronomy 18:18

There was a man in Jerusalem named Simeon, who was righteous and devoted. He was looking for Israel to be comforted, and the Holy Spirit was on him. The Holy Spirit had told him that he wouldn't see death before he had seen the Lord's Christ. He came into the Temple in the Spirit and when Jesus' parents brought in the child to do the Law's custom, he took him into his arms and blessed God, saying,

"Master, now you're setting your slave free in peace, just as you've said.
My eyes have seen your salvation, which you've prepared in front of everyone,
A light of revelation to the Gentiles[j] and the glory of your people Israel!"[k]

His father and mother were amazed at what was being said about him. Simeon blessed them and told his mother Mary, "Look, even though a sword will pierce your soul, this one is laid down for the fall

October and filling the air with their soft cooing. Because they were relatively common, doves and turtledoves were often used as food and inexpensive sacrifices.

If she can't find enough for a lamb, she'll take two turtledoves or two young doves, one for a burnt offering and the other for sin. The priest will cover her and she'll be clean. – Leviticus 12:8

J. The Jews called any non-Jews **Gentiles**, from *ethnos*, the Greek word for "nations." Segregation between Jews and Gentiles was extreme under Roman rule, and Jews wouldn't normally eat with or associate with any foreigners.

K. *I'll make you a light to the nations, so my salvation can reach to the end of the earth. – Isaiah 49:6*

and rise of many in Israel, and as a sign to be opposed, so that the thoughts of many hearts will be revealed."

There was also a prophetess, Anna, Phanuel's daughter, from the tribe of Asher.[l] She was well along in days and had lived with her husband seven years after her marriage, and then as a widow until the age of 84. She never left the Temple, serving night and day with fasting and prayer. At that hour, she came up and thanked God, and she spoke about him to all who were looking for Jerusalem's deliverance.

Then, when they had done everything according to the Law of the Lord, they returned to their city, Nazareth in Galilee.

3.4 MAGI VISIT

Matthew 2:1-23
Luke 2:40

After Jesus was born in Bethlehem in Judea, during the days of King Herod, Magi[m] from the East arrived in Jerusalem, saying, "Where's the one born as the king of the Jews? We saw his star in the East and have come to worship him."

When King Herod heard this, he was troubled, along with all of Jerusalem. So gathering together all the High Priests and the scribes from the people, he asked them where the Christ would be born. They told him, "Bethlehem in Judea, because the prophet wrote this:

> 'And you, Bethlehem, land of Judah, aren't at all least among the leaders of Judah.
> A ruler will come out of you, who'll shepherd Israel, my people.'"[n]

So Herod called the Magi secretly and figured out the time the star

L. When Joshua divided the promised land among Israel's tribes, the land of western Galilee was given to the tribe of **Asher**. Despite its rich soil and thick forests, its distance from the rest of Israel made it somewhat isolated. Much of its territory was taken over by the ancient nation of Phoenicia. Asher, the patriarch of the tribe, was Jacob's eighth son, the second of two sons born to Leah's maid-servant Zilpah.

M. The term *magus* referred to someone who divined future events from the stars. The practice was rooted in the teaching of Zoroaster, an ancient sorcerer and astrologist who was considered the founder of the **Magi**. However, their role in ancient times may have also included advising rulers, acting as priests, studying science, and/or practicing sorcery. The Greek word *magus* is where the English "magician" originates.

N. *And as for you, Bethlehem Ephrathah, too small to be among the thousands from Judah, someone will go out from you to be the ruler of Israel for me. His origins are ancient, from the days of eternity... He'll rise up and shepherd in the LORD's strength and in the pride of the LORD's name... And he'll be peace. – Micah 5:2,4-5*

Herod the Great

Herod was the name of various rulers in and around Judea, the first of which was **Herod the Great**. He was appointed king of the Roman province of Judea in 36 BC, ruling until 4 BC, around the time of Jesus' birth. Herod the Great remained loyal to Rome throughout his reign, maintaining favor and peace with generous gifts. He also sought to please the Jews, claiming to be a convert to Judaism himself, and undertook various building projects across Judea, particularly the rebuilding of the Temple in Jerusalem. But despite this, Herod was a harsh, violent ruler. He presumably suffered from depression and paranoia, which prompted him to have three of his sons – and the mother of two of them – killed. During his final days, he made plans for an extravagant funeral. He died after a long bout of agonizing illness.

After Herod's death, his kingdom was divided into three regions, each ruled by one of his sons:

- Herod Archelaus ruled Judea and Samaria briefly, until 6 AD. He was deposed after complaints of his brutality reached Rome.
- Herod Antipas ruled Galilee and Perea until 39 AD. He became infatuated with his half-brother's wife Herodias, and he married her despite both of them being married to others at the time.
- Herod Philip II ruled the northern part of his father's kingdom until 30 AD. He also had many building projects, most notably rebuilding the city of Caesarea Philippi, which he named after himself.

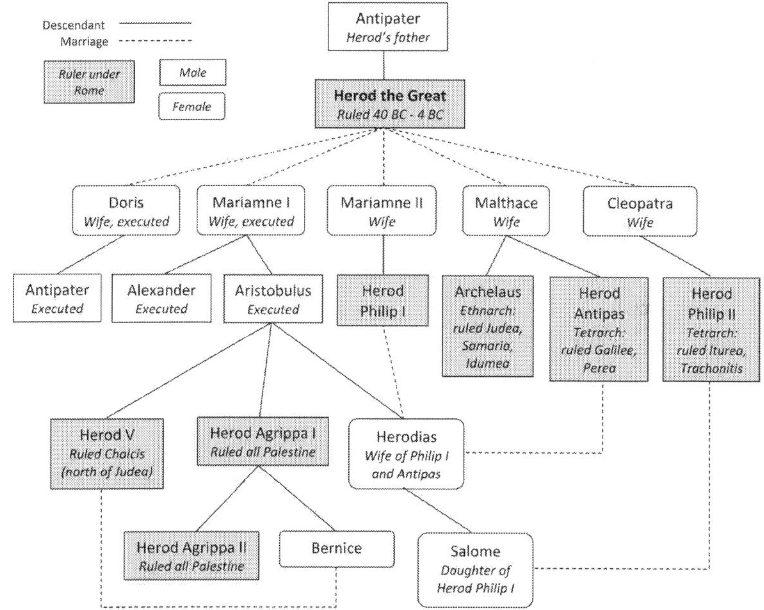

Archelaus was called an *ethnarch* ("ruler of the people"), taking over half of his father's kingdom and ruling over the descendants of Abraham (Jews, Samaritans, Idumeans). Antipas and Philip II were called *tetrarchs* ("ruler of a quarter"), dividing the other half of the kingdom between them.

One of Herod the Great's grandsons also became a ruler. After Herod had his son Aristobulus executed, his grandson – Herod Agrippa – was raised in the imperial court of Rome. By winning the favor of successive emperors, Agrippa was granted his uncles' territories one at a time, beginning in 37 AD, eventually acquiring his grandfather's entire kingdom.

The Gifts of the Magi

As a soft, yellow metal that doesn't tarnish, **gold** was ideal for jewelry and currency in ancient times, as it is today. It was a common gift for royalty, such as when the Queen of Sheba visited Solomon to witness his splendor firsthand. It also decorated the Temple in Jerusalem.

Boswellia trees are exceptionally hardy plants, able to grow in the harsh arid climate of the Middle East and northern Africa. They can survive in mountainous conditions too dry and rocky for most other plants. **Frankincense** is the scented, dried resin of the *Boswellia* tree, harvested by "milking" the trees of their sap. The milky sap is where the Aramaic name for frankincense comes from (*olibanum*, "the result of milking"). Frankincense was used in various anointing oils, incense, perfumes, and religious offerings throughout the Middle East and Northern Africa. Certain sacrifices mandated by Moses' Law were to be made along with pure frankincense.

Similar to frankincense, **myrrh** (from the Aramaic for "bitter") was a fragrant blend of oil and resin from the small, thorny *Commiphora* bush. It was used in incense, perfumes, anointing oils, and as an embalming agent to prepare a corpse for burial. It may also have been used as a primitive anesthetic. Its value in ancient times was so great that it was typically worth its weight in gold.

had appeared to them. Then he sent them to Bethlehem, saying, "Go and ask about the child thoroughly, and report back to me when you find him, so I can come and worship him too."

Then after hearing from the king, they left. The star they had seen in the East led them until it came and stood over where the child was. When they saw the star, they celebrated exceedingly with great happiness. Coming into the house, they saw the child with his mother Mary, and they fell down and worshipped him. They opened their treasuries and brought him gifts of gold, frankincense, and myrrh. Then, having been warned in a dream not to return to Herod, they left for their own country by another road.

Now after they left, look, an angel from the Lord appears to Joseph in a dream. "Get up!" he told him. "Take the child and his mother and escape to Egypt, and stay there until I tell you. Herod's going to look for the child to destroy him."

So he got up, took the child and his mother at night, and left for Egypt. He was there until the death of Herod, to fulfill what the Lord spoke through the prophet: "I called my son out of Egypt."[o]

When Herod saw that he had been tricked by the Magi, he got very angry and ordered all the boys in Bethlehem and its territory to be killed, from two years old and under, according to the time he figured from the Magi. Then what was said through Jeremiah the prophet was

O. *When Israel was a boy, I loved him, and I called my son out of Egypt. – Hosea 11:1*

fulfilled: "A voice was heard in Ramah, weeping and much mourning. Rachel is weeping for her children, but she won't be comforted, because they are no more."[p]

But look, after Herod died, an angel from the Lord appears to Joseph in a dream in Egypt. "Get up," he told him. "Take the child and his mother, and go into the land of Israel, because those who sought the child's life are dead."

So he got up, took the child and his mother, and came to the land of Israel. But when he heard that Archelaus was ruling Judea instead of his father Herod, he was afraid to go there. So after being warned in a dream, he left for the area of Galilee and came to live in a city called Nazareth. This fulfilled what the prophets spoke: "He'll be called a Nazarene."[q]

The child grew up, becoming strong and full of wisdom. And the grace of God was on him.

3.5 PASSOVER IN JERUSALEM

Luke 2:41-52

Now his parents went to Jerusalem every year for the Passover Feast. So when he was twelve years old, they went up, according to the feast's custom. But when they returned, after completing the days, Jesus the boy stayed back in Jerusalem. His parents didn't know of it and went a day's journey, thinking he was in the caravan. But they didn't find him when they looked among their relatives and friends, so they returned to Jerusalem to look for him there. After three days, they found him in the Temple, sitting among the teachers, listening to them

P. When Isaac's son Jacob ran away from home out of fear of his brother, he lived with his uncle Laban for 14 years. During that time, he fell in love with and married Laban's daughter (Jacob's cousin) **Rachel**. She was unable to conceive after her marriage and considered herself dead without children. Although she competed fiercely with her older sister Leah (Jacob's other wife who bore him seven children), Rachel was Jacob's favorite and eventually gave birth to two of his twelve sons. She was buried near Bethlehem after dying following the birth of her second son, Benjamin.

Ramah was the name of various cities in the Bible, but the one most likely referred to here is in the territory of Benjamin, within the northern kingdom of Israel, 8 kilometers north of Jerusalem. It may have been the same town as Ramoth-Gilead, the birthplace of Samuel the prophet.

The LORD says, "A voice is heard in Ramah, mourning and bitter weeping. Rachel is weeping for her children, but she refuses to be comforted for her children, because they are no more." –Jeremiah 31:15

Q. The prophecy of Jesus being a **Nazarene** is not recorded in the Bible. It may have been an oral tradition.

The Passover Feast

Exodus records that God sent ten plagues against the Egyptians because Pharaoh repeatedly didn't allow Moses to lead the nation of Israel out of slavery. First, the Nile River turned to blood (1), then frogs covered the land (2), followed by infestations of lice (3) and flies (4). Disease then struck livestock (5), with boils breaking out on people as well (6). Severe hailstorms (7) led to swarms of locusts that devastated crops (8), followed by three days of darkness (9). The final plague was the death of every firstborn male in Egypt (10). During each plague, only the Egyptians and their property were affected, not Israel. But to prevent the last and most severe plague from striking Israel's sons, Moses instructed the entire nation to sacrifice a lamb and wipe its blood on their doorposts the night before the angel of death was to come. The blood would be a sign for the angel to pass over the house, sparing the firstborn sons of Israel. That night, after finding dead sons in every Egyptian house, Pharaoh finally let Israel go.

Thus the tradition of celebrating the **Passover Feast** began, to commemorate when the angel of death passed over Israel's homes. It was celebrated in the spring, and all of Israel's men were required to gather in Jerusalem to feast and rest for a week. On the first night, a flawless lamb was sacrificed and eaten, and for the rest of the week, all bread had to be flat and unleavened. In fact, any form of yeast or leavening agent was prohibited during the feast, since, in their haste to leave Egypt centuries prior, Israel had no time to include yeast in their bread and wait for it to rise. The Passover was therefore also called the Feast of the Unleavened.

and asking questions, and everyone who heard him was amazed at his understanding and his answers.

When they saw him, they were blown away.[r] Then his mother said, "Son, why have you treated us like this?! Look, your father and I have been in agony searching for you!"

"Why were you looking for me?" he answered. "Didn't you know I'd be at my Father's?"

But they didn't understand the words he said. Then he went down with them and came to Nazareth, and he submitted to them. His mother kept all these words in her heart.

Jesus kept increasing in wisdom and age, and in favor with God and men.

R. All of the Gospel writer except John use the Greek word *ekplesso*. It's derived from *ek* ("away") and *plesso* ("strike"), which literally translates to "strike off," "drive out," or "**blow away**." However, when used figuratively, *ekplesso* describes being dumbfounded and common renderings in English include "astonished" or "amazed." Coincidentally, to be "blown away" in today's language is a colloquial way of referring to profound amazement, so this literal translation is used here.

CHAPTER 4

John's Ministry

4.1 JOHN'S MINISTRY

Matthew 3:1-12
Mark 1:2-8
Luke 3:1-18

In the 15th year of Tiberius Caesar's reign – when Pontius Pilate was governor of Judea, Herod was tetrarch of Galilee, his brother Philip was tetrarch of the region of Ituraea and Trachonitis, and Lysanias was tetrarch of Abilene, in the high priesthood of Annas and Caiaphas[a] – the word of God came to John, Zacharias' son, in the wilderness.

In those days, John the Baptizer came from the wilderness of Judea into the entire area around the Jordan, preaching a baptism of repentance for the forgiveness of sins, saying, "Repent, because the kingdom of heaven[b] is coming!"

This is the one Isaiah the prophet wrote about in his book, saying,

A. Before a worldwide **dating system** was established, ancient authors identified times in history by who was ruling in various parts of the world. In this case, a date of 25-26 AD is most likely.

B. The phrases "God's kingdom" (used by all Gospel writers) and "**the kingdom of heaven**" (used only by Matthew) mean the same thing. Theologically, God's kingdom is anywhere his will is done, regardless of geographic location or political presence. However, Jews in the first century believed God's kingdom was the nation of Israel as a sovereign state.

Repentance

There are two Hebrew words for "**repent**" – *nacham* means "be sorry" or "comfort," while *shuwb* means "turn" or "return." The Greek equivalent (*metanoeo*) is a combination of *meta* ("after," "with") and *noeo* ("understand," "think"), commonly understood to mean "change one's mind." In Jewish theology, repentance was turning one's heart away from immorality and submitting to God's sovereignty. It was paramount to Jewish religion, and was the basis for making animal sacrifices to cover sin.

Nearly every prophet in Israel's history called people to repentance and reconciliation with God. The entire nation repented from worshiping a golden calf during its journey through the desert after Moses' rebuke. King David famously repented after sleeping with Uriah's wife, Bathsheba, as recorded in the remorseful Psalm 51. The Bible even records that the great Babylonian king Nebuchadnezzar repented and worshipped God after a period of insanity and isolation.

If my people, who are called by my name, will humble themselves, pray, seek my face, and turn from their evil paths, then I'll hear from heaven, forgive their sin, and heal their land.
– 2 Chronicles 7:14

"Look, I'm sending my messenger ahead of you, who will make your way ready.
The voice of one shouting in the wilderness: 'Make the Lord's way ready, make his paths straight!
Every valley will be filled, and every mountain and hill will be lowered.
The crooked will become straight and the rough roads smooth.
And everybody will see God's salvation.'"[c]

John had clothes of camel hair and a leather belt around his waist. His food was locusts[d] and wild honey. All of Jerusalem, all of the regions

C. *A voice is calling, "Clear the LORD's road in the wilderness! Make the desert highway smooth for our God. Let every valley be lifted up and every mountain and hill lowered. Let the crag become a plain and the ridges a valley. Then the LORD's glory will be shown and everybody will see it together. The mouth of the LORD has spoken." – Isaiah 40:3-5*

D. When conditions are ideal, grasshoppers of the *Acrididae* family can reproduce so rapidly that they form huge swarms in response to the sudden overcrowding. The masses of grasshoppers in these destructive swarms are called **locusts**, which are the same species, but have a slightly different appearance and behavior from solitary grasshoppers. Swarms are virtually unstoppable. They can travel huge distances and quickly reduce crops to stubble with each insect eating its weight in food every day. Their bodies are 2-3 inches long, with six legs and two pairs of wings. According to Moses' Law, only grasshoppers, locusts, and crickets were edible out of all the winged insects.

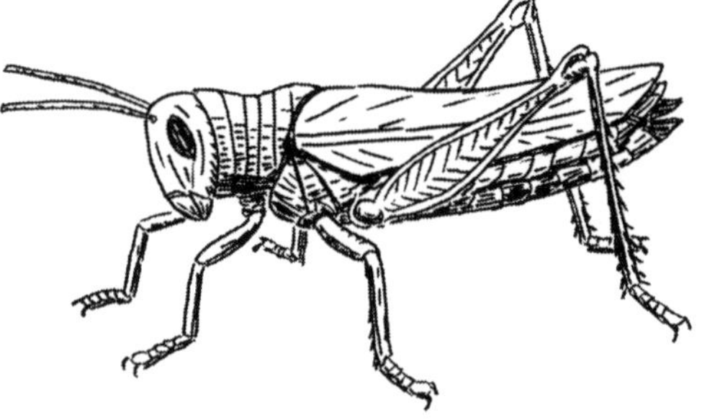

Jordan River

The **Jordan River** winds its way southward from the Sea of Galilee to the Dead Sea, through a rift valley that runs into northern Africa. It descends to one of the lowest elevations on earth, dropping to almost 400 meters below sea level by the time it reaches the Dead Sea. As a large river, the Jordan served as a formidable obstacle in ancient times and the shallow sections where crossing on foot was possible were important military strongholds. The Jordan River was the eastern border of Israel's promised land and Joshua 3 records that the water miraculously parted as Israel crossed it to begin their campaign of conquering the land.

of Judea, and the whole area around the Jordan went out to him, and they were baptized by him in the Jordan River as they confessed their sins. But when he saw many of the Pharisees and Sadducees coming for baptism, he told them, "You spawn of snakes! Who warned you to escape the anger that's coming? Produce fruit according to repentance, and don't tell yourselves, 'We have Abraham as our father,' because I tell you that God can raise up children of Abraham from these stones. In fact, the axe is already lying at the root of the trees, so every tree that doesn't produce good fruit is cut down and thrown into the fire."

"Then what should we do?" the crowds asked him.

"Whoever has two shirts, share with the one who has none," he answered. "And whoever has food, do the same."

Tax collectors also came to be baptized and asked him, "Teacher, what should we do?"

"Charge no more than what you were ordered," he told them.

Soldiers asked him, "And about us, what should we do?"

"Don't extort or cheat anyone," he said, "and be content with your pay."[e]

The people were all expecting, wondering, and debating in their hearts about John, whether he was the Christ. But John told them all, "As for me, I baptize you with water for repentance, but someone's coming after me who's more powerful than I am, and I'm not worthy to even bend down and untie the strap of his sandals. He'll baptize you with the Holy Spirit and fire. His pitchfork is in his hand to clear out his threshing floor and gather the wheat into his barn. But he'll burn the chaff with an unquenchable fire."[f]

In many other speeches he brought the good news to the people.

E. The annual **wage of Roman soldiers** was 225 denarii, some of which was held back as tax for clothing and food. Soldiers would supplement their meager pay with whatever plunder they could get from battle or raids on enemy settlements. They could also take prisoners of war as slaves, which could be sold for profit later on. At the completion of their service (20 years), discharged soldiers received a bonus of 3000 denarii and farmland in frontier regions of the empire.

F. During the harvest, after the wheat had been reaped and bundled, the grain was separated from the stalk at **threshing floors**. These were flat, paved surfaces, typically on elevated ground exposed to wind. The wheat would first be beaten on the ground to separate the grain from the stalk, accomplished either by hand, by tools, or by animals walking on it. Once threshed, a **pitchfork** was used to throw the stalks into the air, where they would be carried away by the wind. The heavier grain, however, would fall straight down and be collected. The remaining wheat stalks and husks – called **chaff** – were typically burned afterwards.

CHAPTER 5

The Beginning of Jesus' Ministry

5.1 JESUS' BAPTISM

Matthew 3:13-17
Mark 1:9-11
Luke 3:21-23a

Jesus arrives at the Jordan from Nazareth in Galilee to be baptized[a] by John, just like all the people were being baptized. But John objected, saying, "I need to be baptized by you, and you come to me?"

"Let it happen now," Jesus answered, "because this is the way for all righteousness to be fulfilled."

So he lets it happen. Then after being baptized, Jesus came straight up out of the water. And as he was praying, look, the sky opened up and he saw the Spirit of God descending in a form shaped like a dove,

A. The Greek word *baptizo* means "submerge" or "wash." It could describe an ordinary process of cleaning or a ceremonial washing during religious purification. *Baptizo* is derived from *bapto* ("dip" or "immerse"). Although the two terms seem the same, their difference in Greek is quite profound. Centuries before Jesus, the Greek poet and physician Nicander used both terms in a recipe for making pickles. Vegetables were first dipped (*bapto*) in boiling water, then baptized (*baptizo*) in a vinegar solution. The first was a temporary process, while the second produced a permanent change. Thus **baptism** in the context of the New Testament was an outward sign of a repentant heart turning to God, representing a change in one's life.

and it came to him. Then look,[b] a voice out of the sky said, "You're my dear Son. I'm happy with you."

Jesus was about thirty years old when he began.

5.2 TEMPTATION IN THE WILDERNESS

Matthew 4:1-11
Mark 1:12-13
Luke 4:1-13

Then right away, the Spirit takes him out into the wilderness. So Jesus, full of the Holy Spirit, returned from the Jordan and was led around the wilderness by the Spirit for forty days and forty nights,[c] being tempted by Satan, the Devil. He ate nothing (fasted) during those days, and when they were done, he was hungry. Then the tempter, the Devil, came to him, saying, "If you're God's Son, tell this stone to become bread."

Jesus answered him, "It's written, 'Man won't live on only bread, but on every word that goes out from God's mouth.'"[d]

Then the Devil takes him into the holy city, Jerusalem, to stand on the pinnacle of the Temple. He tells him, "If you're God's Son, throw yourself down from here, as it's written, 'He'll command his angels around you to guard you,' and, 'They'll lift you up in their hands so you won't hit your foot on a stone.'"[e]

"Again, it's written," Jesus answered him, "'Don't test the Lord your God.'"[f]

B. The Gospel writers often used the word "**look**" (*idou* in Greek) to emphasize or draw the reader's attention to a certain statement. It has traditionally been translated "behold" in the Bible.

C. The number **forty** is mentioned repeatedly in the Bible during periods of transition. Genesis records that it rained forty days and nights when God flooded the earth, while Noah and his family were safely in the ark. Although all life on land was wiped out, Noah carried enough animals with him to repopulate the earth afterwards. Similarly, Israel was led through the desert for forty years before entering their promised land, during which Moses spent two 40 day periods on a mountain with God, receiving instruction on God's Law.

D. *He humbled you and made you hungry, then he fed you with manna, which neither you nor your fathers knew about, so you would understand that man doesn't live on only bread. Man lives on everything that goes out from God's mouth. – Deuteronomy 8:3*

E. *He'll give his angels orders regarding you, to guard you on every road. They'll lift you up in their hands so you don't hit your foot on a rock. – Psalm 91:11-12*

F. *Fear the LORD your God alone. Worship him and swear by his name. Don't go after other gods, any gods from the nations around you, because the LORD your God among you is a jealous God. Or else the LORD your God's anger will burn against you and he'll destroy you from the face of the earth. Don't test the LORD your God, like you tested him at Massah. – Deuteronomy 6:13-16*

Again, the Devil leads him up a very high mountain and shows him all the kingdoms of the world and their glory in a moment of time. Then the Devil told him, "I'll give you all of this power, because it was given to me and I give it to whomever I want. If you bow down and worship me, it'll be all yours."

Jesus answers him, "Go away Satan! It's written, 'Worship the Lord your God and serve only him.'"[f]

Then the Devil leaves him until the next time, having finished every temptation. [Jesus] was with the wild animals, but look, angels came and served him.

5.3 JOHN'S TESTIMONY

John 1:19-34

This is John's testimony when the Jews sent priests and Levites from Jerusalem to ask him, "Who are you?"

He didn't deny them, but confessed, "I'm not the Christ."

"Then what?" they asked him. "Are you Elijah?"[g]

"I'm not," he says.

"Are you the prophet?"

"No," he answered.

Then they asked, "Who are you, so we can give an answer to those who sent us? What do you say about yourself?"

He replied, "I'm the voice of someone shouting in the wilderness: 'Straighten the way of the Lord!'[h] just like Isaiah the prophet said."

G. In the northern kingdom of Israel, a prophet named **Elijah** roamed the land, judging Israel and delivering messages from God during a time of widespread idol worship. The Bible records that he was a hairy man who wore rugged clothes and lived in caves. He didn't get along well with Ahab, Israel's king, and on occasion had to run for his life.

During the peak of his ministry, 1 Kings 18 records that Elijah famously challenged 850 prophets of other gods to a contest: each side would build an altar and offer a sacrifice, and the god that answered with fire was the real one. The idol prophets shouted out for fire, and even cut themselves until they bled profusely, but nothing happened. Then, after Elijah prepared his altar and drenched it with water, fire fell from the sky and burned everything up. This led to the execution of the 850 other prophets and ended over three years of drought and famine.

At the end of his time on earth, Elijah didn't die but was miraculously swept up to heaven in a fiery chariot, leaving his apprentice Elisha to continue his work. Centuries later, another prophet, Malachi, predicted Elijah's eventual return.

H. *A voice is calling, "Clear the LORD's road in the wilderness!" – Isaiah 40:3*

Then the Pharisees, who had sent them, asked, "Then why are you baptizing, if you're not the Christ, Elijah, or the prophet?"

"I baptize with water," John answered, "but someone stands among you who you don't know. He comes after me, and I'm not worthy to untie the strap of his sandal."

All this took place in Bethany across the Jordan,[i] where John was baptizing.

The next day, he sees Jesus coming to him and says, "Look, God's lamb,[j] who takes away the sin of the world! This is who I spoke about when I said, 'A man is coming after me who's actually before me, because he existed before I did.' I didn't recognize him, but I came baptizing in water so that Israel would know him."

John testified saying, "I saw the Spirit descending like a dove out of the sky, and he stayed on him. I didn't recognize him, but the one who sent me to baptize with water told me, 'The one you see the Spirit descending and staying on, this is the one who baptizes with the Holy Spirit.' I saw it myself, and I've testified that this is God's Son."

5.4 FIRST DISCIPLES

John 1:35-51

The next day John was standing with two of his disciples,[k] and again he saw Jesus walking. "Look," he says, "God's lamb!"

The two disciples heard him speak, and they followed Jesus. Jesus turned and saw them following him. "What are you looking for?" he asks them.

I. The town of Bethabara in modern-day Jordan is the traditional site of Bethany east of the Jordan River, as distinguished from the town of Bethany near Jerusalem. The town wasn't on the Jordan itself, but among the streams and springs flowing into it. Modern excavations have shown early chapels built to commemorate Jesus' baptism, but scholars are divided on whether Bethabara is truly the "**Bethany across the Jordan**" mentioned by John.

J. John is the only Gospel writer to use the term "**God's lamb**." It's mentioned twice in John's Gospel, but dozens of times in his apocalyptic book of Revelation, always in reference to Jesus. According to Moses' Law, a flawless lamb was sacrificed annually by each family during the Passover Feast. Lambs were also used for various sin and peace offerings, as prescribed by Moses' Law.

K. A Jewish law teacher was an expert on the Scripture and its interpretation. Each teacher would hand-pick the best students in Jewish schools to become his **disciples**. This word comes from the Greek *mathetes*, which is derived from the word for "learn" (*manthano*). "Student" is a more literal translation, but the traditional "disciple" is used here. Disciples would follow their teacher for years and devote themselves to learning how to live like him, adopting his knowledge and interpretation of Scripture, until they became teachers themselves and chose disciples of their own.

"Rabbi," they said (which translates to "Teacher"),[l] "where are you staying?"

"Come and see," he replies.

So they came and saw where he was staying and stayed with him that day, because it was about the tenth hour.[m] One of the two who heard John and followed was Andrew, Simon Peter's brother. He first finds his brother Simon and tells him, "We've found the Messiah!" which translates to "Christ."

He brought him to Jesus, who looked at him and said, "You're Simon, John's son, but you'll be called Cephas," which translates to "Peter."[n]

The next day Jesus wanted to go to Galilee. He finds Philip and tells him, "Follow me."

Philip was from Bethsaida,[o] which was Andrew and Peter's city. Then Philip finds Nathanael and tells him, "We've found the one that Moses wrote about in the Law, and also the prophets! Jesus from Nazareth, Joseph's son!"

But Nathanael said, "Can anything good come out of Nazareth?"

"Come and see!" Philip tells him.

Jesus saw Nathanael coming to him. "Look," he says, "a true Israelite, who has no deception in him."

"How do you know me?" Nathanael says.

L. **Rabbi** was the Hebrew word for "master," but was used as a title of respect for law teachers.

M. Judea during the first century, an hour was the smallest unit of time, defined as one twelfth of daylight, which changed slightly through the seasons. The first hour began at sunrise, the sixth was noon, and the twelfth hour ended at sunset. Accordingly, the **tenth hour** was in the late afternoon, around four o'clock.

N. Names have meaning in the Bible, and occasionally a person was given a **new name** at a turning point in his life. Abram ("high father") was renamed Abraham ("father of a multitude") when God made a covenant with him. Similarly, Jacob ("hold the heel") was renamed Israel ("contend with God") after wrestling with an angel.

Simon's new name, **Peter** (Greek *Petros*), comes from *petra*, meaning "rock." **Cephas** means the same thing in Aramaic, another common language of the time. *Petra* refers to a massive boulder or rock foundation; this is distinct from *lithos*, which translates to "stone" or "pebble."

O. There is some discrepancy as to whether there were two cities named **Bethsaida** or just one. The best known Bethsaida is a city north of the Sea of Galilee, east of the Jordan River. Herod Philip II (the tetrarch) renamed it Julias, after Julia, the third wife of Caesar Augustus. However, the Gospel writers mention there was another Bethsaida in Galilee, on the west side of the Jordan River, near the fishing town of Capernaum. The name Bethsaida translates to "fishing house," suggesting it was located on the Sea of Galilee, but exactly where is unknown.

"When you were under the fig tree, before Philip called you, I saw you." Jesus answered.

"Rabbi," Nathanael said, "you're God's Son! You're the king of Israel!"

"You believe because I told you that I saw you under the fig tree?" Jesus answered. "You'll see better than that."

Then he tells him, "Truly truly,[p] I tell you, you'll see the skies open up and the angels of God rising and descending on the Son of Man."

5.5 FIRST MIRACLE: WATER TO WINE

John 2:1-12

On the third day, there was a wedding in Cana,[q] in Galilee. Jesus' mother was there, and both Jesus and his disciples were also invited to the wedding. When the wine[r] ran out, Jesus' mother tells him, "They have no wine."

P. "**Truly**" is the most common translation of the Greek word *amen*. It's similar to the Hebrew word *amam*, which means "believe" or "faithful." When used at the beginning of a sentence, it typically means "surely" or "certainly." But when spoken at the end, it could mean "so be it" or "may it be done." A custom of the early church was to say *amen* after another had prayed, which has continued until today.

Furthermore, ancient writers used the repetition of words to emphasize a point. Most notably, Jesus often said "**truly truly**" while teaching, which would translate to "absolutely truly" or "truly indeed." Most times a word is repeated three times in the Bible – indicating the most extreme degree – is in describing God or his Temple ("holy, holy, holy").

Q. It's unknown where in Galilee the town or city of **Cana** was located, since there's no record of it outside of the Bible.

R. **Wine** was a common drink among Jews, frequently consumed during feasts and celebrations. Additionally, Moses' Law prescribed portions of wine to be offered along with other sacrifices. Following the harvest in September, grapes were pressed by foot in large vats (winepresses) amidst much celebration. The juice was then fermented in wineskins to produce the alcohol content.

The Son of Man

In the Old Testament, the phrase "**son of man**" refers to man in general. It comes from being a descendant of Adam, the first man, whose name serves as the Hebrew word for "man" or "mankind." Adam's name is derived from the Hebrew word for ground (*adamah*), so "son of man" is also a reference to men's origin, being formed in the beginning from dirt. Of note, the prophet Daniel described a vision where *"someone like the son of man" (Daniel 7:13)* approached God (the "Ancient of Days") to be given sovereignty over everything forever. In this sense, it was used in reference to the coming Messiah. However, the predominant understanding of "son of man" was likely related to its original meaning, as a reference to a man or mankind in general. Ezekiel recorded being called "son of man" by God numerous times, but Jesus is the only person in the Bible to refer to himself in the third person in this way.

"Woman, what's that to us?" Jesus replies. "My time hasn't come yet."

Then his mother tells the servants, "Do whatever he tells you."

There were six stone water jars set there for Jewish purifications, each containing two or three measures.[s] Jesus tells them, "Fill the jars with water."

So they filled them to the brim. Then he says, "Now draw some out and take it to the table master."[t]

So they took it to him. When the table master tasted the water that had become wine, not knowing where it had come from (but the servants who had drawn the water knew), the table master called the groom. He tells him, "Every man serves the good wine first, and then the worst when they're drunk. But you've kept the good wine until now!"

Jesus did this first miracle in Cana, Galilee, revealing his glory, and his disciples believed in him. After this he went down to Capernaum – he, his mother and brothers, and his disciples – and they stayed there for many days.

5.6 JESUS GREATER THAN JOHN

John 3:22-36

Afterwards, Jesus and his disciples came to the land of Judea. He was staying with them and baptizing. John was baptizing as well, in Aenon, near Salim,[u] because there was lots of water there. They were coming to be baptized because John hadn't been thrown into prison yet.

A discussion about purification came up between John's disciples and a Jew. So they came to John and said, "Rabbi, the one who was with

---

S. One measure of water was about 37 liters (9-10 gallons), so a pot holding **two or three measures** would hold 75-110 liters (20-30 gallons of fluid).

T. At a feast, one of the guests was traditionally chosen to be the **table master**, in charge of arranging the tables and tasting the food and wine beforehand. The Greek word for this role is *architriklinos*, which literally translates to "ruler of three couches." The term came from the arrangement of reclining seats around three sides of a table, allowing servants access to the table on the fourth side. The table master acted as the conductor of a feast, similar to a modern-day master of ceremonies.

U. ***Aenon*** is a Greek word derived from the Hebrew word for "spring" or "fountain." Accordingly, **Salim** was presumably a town with a nearby spring, but the location is largely unknown. It may have been south of Scythopolis (also called Beth-Shean) just west of the Jordan, in Samaria.

you across the Jordan, who you witnessed about, look, he's baptizing and everyone's coming to him."

"A man can't receive anything unless it has been given to him from heaven," John answered. "You're my witnesses, that I said I'm not the Messiah, but that I've been sent ahead of him. The one with the bride is the groom. The groom's friend, who stands and hears him, happily celebrates at the groom's voice. So my joy is complete. He must increase, but I must decrease.

"The one coming from above is over everything, but the one on the ground is from the ground and talks about the ground. The one from heaven is above everything. He testifies about what he has seen and heard, but no one accepts his testimony. Whoever has received his testimony has sealed[V] that God is true. The one God sent speaks God's words, because he gives the Spirit endlessly. The Father loves the Son and has given everything over into his hand. Whoever believes in the Son has eternal life, but whoever disobeys the Son won't see life – God's anger stays on him instead."

5.7 SAMARITAN WOMAN

Matthew 4:12
Mark 1:14a
Luke 3:19-20
John 4:1-42

When John criticized Herod the tetrarch because of Herodias, his brother's wife, Herod added this to all the evil he had done: he locked John in prison. So when the Lord found out that John had been arrested, and that the Pharisees had heard that Jesus was making and baptizing more disciples than John (even though his disciples were baptizing, not Jesus himself) he left Judea and returned to Galilee. But he had to pass through Samaria.

So he comes to a city in Samaria called Sychar, near the land Jacob gave his son Joseph. Jacob's well[W] was there, and Jesus, tired from his

V. Ancient **seals** were carved out of soft stone or ivory and were used to impress a particular pattern or picture in wax. Later, seals were made of metal and worn on the finger (signet rings). A wax seal, unique to the one who sealed it, authenticated and approved a document, similar to a modern-day signature. If applied on the outside of a message, an unbroken seal ensured the message was not read before reaching its destination.

W. In the arid landscape of Judea and Samaria, the most consistent sources of water were **wells**, typically dug deep into solid rock (usually limestone). Most wells were accessed by lowering a container by rope to the water below. Their narrow openings were commonly reinforced

journey, was sitting by the well. Around the sixth hour,[x] a Samaritan woman comes to draw water and Jesus tells her, "Give me a drink."

His disciples had left for the city to buy food, so the Samaritan woman asks him, "How do you, a Jew, ask me for a drink, since I'm a Samaritan woman?" – because Jews don't associate with Samaritans.

But Jesus answered her, "If you only knew God's gift and who it is that says, 'Give me a drink,' you would've asked him instead, and he would've given you living water."

"Lord," she says, "you don't have anything to draw with, and the well's deep, so where would you get living water? Are you greater than Jacob our father, who gave us the well and drank from it himself, with his sons and his cattle?"

"Everyone who drinks this water will thirst again," Jesus answered, "but whoever drinks the water I give him will never thirst. Instead, the water I give will become a well of water springing up to eternal life inside him."[y]

"Lord," the woman says, "give me this water so I won't thirst and have to come here to draw."

But he tells her, "Go, call your husband and come back here."

"I don't have a husband," the woman replied.

"Well said, that you don't have a husband, because you've had five husbands," Jesus says. "And the one you have now is not your husband. You've spoken truthfully."

"Lord," the woman says, "I can see that you're a prophet. Our fathers worshipped on this mountain, but you say that Jerusalem is the place where men should worship."

"Woman, believe me that a time is coming when you won't worship the Father on this mountain or in Jerusalem," Jesus replies. "You worship what you don't know, but we worship what we know, because

with a short stone ledge. However, some larger wells had steps down into them to allow water to be drawn directly from the pool below. Ancient wells were covered when not in use, especially in desert areas, to prevent sediment from drifting in and filling them up. Their locations were widely known throughout the land. They were often close to towns, and because they were so valuable, disputes over possession were common.

X. The **sixth hour** was around noon, in the heat of the day. Water was typically drawn by women and girls early in the morning or later in the evening, when the temperature was cooler. Drawing water in the heat of midday was unusual, suggesting those who did it then were social outcasts of sorts, wanting to avoid the rest of the community.

Y. *Whoever's thirsty can come. And whoever wants it may take the gift of living water. – Revelation 22:17b*

Samaria

Samaria was the name of the capital city of the northern kingdom of Israel. After it fell to the Assyrians in 722 BC, the land was repopulated with various foreign colonists, who intermarried with the remaining Jews. Over time, the fertile land of central Canaan (around the ruins of the capital) also became known as Samaria. During Jesus' lifetime, Jews despised the pagan practices and mixed race of the Samaritans and wouldn't associate with them. Instead of journeying through Samaria, Jews would typically detour east, across the Jordan River, to avoid any contact with their loathsome neighbors. Samaritans were considered unclean, and any cup or dish handled by them was also considered unclean.

Within the land of Samaria, Shechem was the most prominent city. It is now the modern city of Nablus. Shechem was originally the capital of Israel's northern kingdom, located in the hill country of Ephraim between two mountains: the barren Mount Ebal to the north and the forested Mount Gerizim to the south. Shechem held considerable significance in Israel for a number of reasons: Abram built his first altar to God at Shechem; Jacob built an altar there on his return from a 20 year self-imposed exile; and Joseph's bones were buried there after Israel's long journey from Egypt (near **Jacob's well**). Furthermore, Shechem was considered a holy city in Samaria because of a Samaritan temple build nearby on Mount Gerizim, even after the temple's destruction by the Jews in the second century BC. Shechem was later called **Sychar**, meaning "shoulder."

Jews and Samaritans disagreed fiercely regarding the significance of the two mountains on either side of Shechem. Upon entering Canaan, Jewish Scriptures record that Joshua built an altar on Mount Ebal and read Moses' Law to the entire nation of Israel. Emphasis was placed on the blessings of obedience and the curses of disobedience, as reflected in the fertile slopes of **Mount Gerizim** and the barrenness of Mount Ebal. These two mountains became a major source of conflict between Jews and Samaritans throughout their tumultuous history.

Although Jewish Scriptures identify Mount Ebal as the mountain where Joshua built an altar, Samaritan Scriptures record that the event took place on the other mountain. Thus Mount Gerizim has been considered holy to Samaritans ever since. Samaritan Scriptures don't include anything beyond the Torah (Genesis through Deuteronomy), and even this has its differences from the Jewish Torah, so the scriptural basis for which mountain was sacred was hotly debated between Jews and Samaritans. Consequently, David's establishment of Jerusalem as the central place of worship, and the sanctity of Solomon's Temple, wasn't recognized by Samaritans. In defiance of Jewish claims, Samaritans constructed a temple on Mount Gerizim sometime after the Babylonians destroyed the Temple in Jerusalem, likely around 400 BC. Tensions further escalated when the Jews invaded Samaria in 128 BC and destroyed their temple on Mount Gerizim.

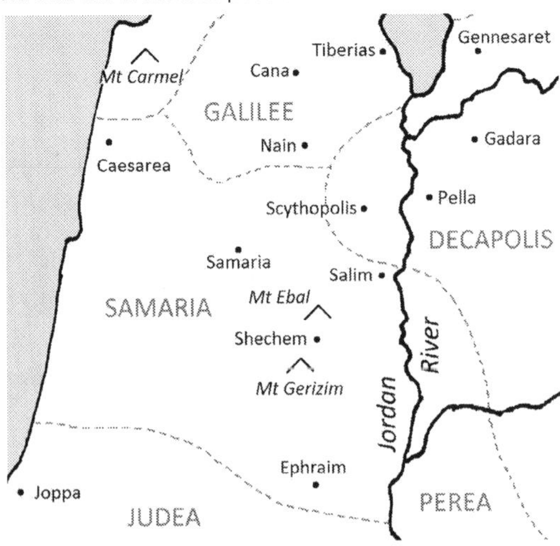

Therefore the issue of where God should formally be worshipped was a bone of contention between Jews and Samaritans, an ancient conflict that spanned centuries.

salvation is from the Jews. But a time's coming – it's now – when the true worshippers will worship the Father in spirit and truth, because the Father looks for them to be his worshippers. God is spirit, and those who worship him must worship in spirit and truth."

Then the woman says, "I know that the Messiah is coming – called the Christ – and when he comes, he'll tell us everything."

Then Jesus says, "I, speaking to you, am."[z]

At this, his disciples arrived and were amazed that he had been talking to a woman, but no one said, "What are you looking for?" or, "Why are you talking to her?"

So the women left her water jar and went into the city. She tells the men, "Come and see a man who has told me all I've done. Isn't this the Christ?"

They went out of the city and came to him. Meanwhile, the disciples urged him, saying, "Rabbi, eat."

But he told them, "I have food to eat that you don't know about."

So the disciples said to one another, "Did somebody bring him something to eat?"

"My food is doing the will of the one who sent me, and finishing his work," Jesus tells them. "Don't you say, 'There are four months then the harvest comes'? But look, I tell you, lift up your eyes and see that the fields are white[a] for harvest. The reaper is already getting paid and is gathering fruit for eternal life so the sower and the reaper can celebrate together. Because the saying that 'one sows and another reaps' is true here. I sent you to reap what you haven't worked for. Others have

Z. In the Old Testament, the most common name of God was designated by four Hebrew letters (יהוה), commonly transliterated into Latin letters as "YHWH." It comes from the Hebrew verb *hayah*, which means "to be." God introduced himself to Moses this way, as recorded in the book of Exodus, *"I Am who I Am.... This is my name forever, and this is my memorial to generations and generations." (Exodus 3:14,15b)* Hebrew originally didn't include any vowels in its written form, so "YHWH" could have been pronounced any number of ways in ancient times, depending on the vowel sounds added. The terms Yahweh and Jehovah were the most common renderings. In English, YHWH is usually translated "LORD" (all capital letters), as it became tradition for Jews to substitute the word *adonai* (Hebrew for "lord") instead of YHWH. However, the original name for God is literally "**I Am**."

El is another common name for God, which is translated as "god," and could refer to the Jewish God or any pagan god. This name is incorporated into the name Israel, which translates to "God strives." Alternately, *Elohim* is the plural form of *El*, which is thought to convey an intensified version of the word, or refer to the three-part nature of God (Father, Son, Holy Spirit), or even describe God together with his angels.

A. Grain (particularly wheat and barley in ancient Palestine) turns from green to light yellow or **white**, indicating it's ripe and ready to be harvested.

worked and you've joined in their work."

Many of the Samaritans from that city believed in him because of the woman's words, who testified, "He told me all I've done."

So when the Samaritans came to Jesus, they asked him to stay with them, and he stayed there two days. Many more believed because of his words, so they told the woman, "We don't believe because of what you said any longer, because we've heard for ourselves and know that this one really is the world's savior!"

CHAPTER 6

Opposition In Galilee

6.1 RETURN TO GALILEE

Matthew 4:17
Mark 1:14b-15
Luke 4:14-15
John 4:43-45

After two days, Jesus left there and returned to Galilee[a] in the power of the Spirit and news about him spread throughout the whole region. He was teaching in their synagogues and was honored by all. From then on, Jesus began to preach God's good news, saying, "The time is fulfilled and God's kingdom is near. Repent and believe in the good news."

Jesus testified that a prophet has no honor in his own fatherland. But when he came to Galilee, the Galileans received him, having seen all the things that he did in Jerusalem at the feast, since they had gone to the feast too.

A. The Roman province of **Galilee** was a fertile region north of Samaria, between the Sea of Galilee to the east and the coastal plains to the west. During Israel's conquest of Canaan under Joshua, the pagan residents of the land that would become Galilee weren't entirely driven out and continued to live there, interspersed among Israel. After Assyria conquered the area, foreign settlers colonized the land, bringing their distant culture and language with them. The intermixing of races produced a distinct dialect and accent, and, like the Samaritans, Galileans were despised and avoided by pure-blooded Jews to the south.

Synagogue

After the fall of Judah, and subsequent destruction of the Temple in Jerusalem in 586 BC, the Jews no longer had a central place of worship. Surrounded by foreigners and pagan religions, the exiles faced extinction of their culture, so the **synagogue** arose as the center of Jewish religion and social life. The term comes from the Greek word for "assembly" or "gathering," and can refer to both the people gathered and the building they gather in. In a synagogue, Jews would regularly study Scripture, worship, and pray as a community, which helped preserve Jewish faith, language, and culture despite isolation from other Jews and separation from the Temple. Unlike the Temple, where only priests could minister, all Jews participated and took turns leading activities. It also served as a local court for deciding legal matters, and an elementary school where Jewish children were taught to read. Synagogues were found throughout the Roman Empire anywhere a community of Jews lived. The buildings themselves had a large seating area, where the congregation sat on the floor or stone benches. At the far end of the room, opposite the doors, a platform held a chest containing Scriptures, which were read at every assembly. Seats on the platform were reserved as places of honor for elders and other synagogue leaders.

6.2 CAPERNAUM CHILD HEALED FROM CANA

John 4:46-54

He came to Cana in Galilee again, where he had changed the water into wine, and there was an official[b] whose son was sick at Capernaum.[c] When he heard that Jesus had come from Judea to Galilee, he went to him and begged him to come and heal his son, because he was about to die. But Jesus told him, "Unless you see affirming signs and miracles, you won't believe."

"Lord," the official says, "come before my boy dies!"

So Jesus tells him, "Go, your son lives."

The man believed the words Jesus told him and left. As he was going, slaves met him saying that his boy was alive. So he asked them what time he had gotten better and they told him, "The fever left him yesterday at the seventh hour."[d]

The father knew that Jesus had told him, "Your son lives," at that

B. The Greek word *basilikos* is used to describe something belonging to a king, whether it be a servant, country, or even clothing. In this case it referred to a person, likely a servant or officer in Herod Antipas' court, translated here as "**official**."

C. One of the most prominent towns in Galilee was **Capernaum**, a large fishing town on the northern shore of the Sea of Galilee. Capernaum's name means "village of Nahum," but it was likely unrelated to the Old Testament prophet of the same name. In fact, Capernaum is not mentioned in the Old Testament at all, suggesting its foundation sometime after the Jews started returning from captivity in 539 BC. Although there was a strong Jewish community in the city, there was also an equally strong Greek and Roman influence. Capernaum had a prominent synagogue in it, which was reportedly built by Roman soldiers stationed there and had an adjacent tax collection office.

D. The **seventh hour** was around one o'clock in the afternoon.

hour, so he and his whole household believed.

This was the second sign that Jesus did when he came from Judea into Galilee.

6.3 REJECTION IN NAZARETH

Luke 4:16-30

He came to Nazareth, where he had been raised, and as usual for him he went into the synagogue on the Sabbath and stood up to read. The scroll of Isaiah[e] the prophet was handed to him. He opened the scroll and found the place where it was written,

> "The Spirit of the Lord is on me, because he has anointed me to bring good news to the poor. He has sent me to declare release to captives and restored vision to the blind, to set the oppressed free and declare the acceptable year of the Lord."[f]

Then he closed the scroll, gave it back to the attendant, and sat down. The eyes of everyone in the synagogue were staring at him, and he said, "This Scripture has been fulfilled in your ears today."

Everyone was testifying about him, wondering about the words of grace that flowed from his mouth. They were saying, "Isn't this Joseph's son?"

He answered them, "You'll certainly quote me this proverb: 'Heal yourself, doctor! Whatever we heard you do in Capernaum, do here in your fatherland as well.' But I tell you that no prophet is welcome in his fatherland. I tell you truly, there were many widows in Israel in Elijah's days, when the sky was closed for three years and six months, and a severe famine came upon the whole land. But Elijah was sent to none of them, only to a widowed woman[g] in Zarephath of Sidon. And there were many lepers in Israel with Elisha the prophet, but none of

E. One of the most famous Old Testament prophets was **Isaiah**, who likely authored much of the large book of history, poetry, and prophecy that bears his name. His book records that he was married to a prophetess, and that their two sons received names based on messages he received from God. He lived after the division of Israel into northern and southern kingdoms, but before the fall of Judea to the Babylonians. His 40 year ministry consisted primarily of delivering messages to various nations of the time. Many prophecies relating to the coming Messiah are found in Isaiah's book.

F. *The Spirit of the Lord God is on me, because the LORD has anointed me to bring good news to the poor. He has sent me to tie up broken hearts, to declare freedom to captives and release to prisoners, to declare the acceptable year of the LORD and the day of vengeance of our God. – Isaiah 61:1-2*

them was cleansed except Naaman,[h] a Syrian!"

Everyone in the synagogue was filled with rage when they heard this. So they got up, drove him out of the city, and led him to the ridge of the mountain that their city was built on to throw him off. But passing right through them, he left.

6.4 TRAVEL TO CAPERNAUM

Matthew 4:13-16
Luke 4:31a

Leaving Nazareth, he came and settled in Capernaum, a city in Galilee by the sea, in the region of Zebulun and Naphtali, to fulfill what was said through Isaiah the prophet:

> "The land of Zebulun and the land of Naphtali by the sea, beyond the Jordan, in Galilee of the Gentiles: people sitting in darkness saw a great light, and a light dawned on those sitting in the land and the shadow of death."[i]

G. During a severe drought, the Old Testament book of 1 Kings records that God told Elijah the prophet to travel away from Israel to Zarephath, a city on the Mediterranean coast. There he stayed with a poor **Phoenician widow** and her son, who were about to die of starvation. Elijah asked her for some of her last food, assuring her that their flour and oil wouldn't run out until the drought was over. She did what he said, and sure enough, their containers never emptied until it finally rained.

H. Years after the Phoenician widow, the Bible records that another foreigner was the beneficiary of a miracle when **Naaman**, a Syrian military commander, came to Elisha (Elijah's successor) to be healed of leprosy. Elisha told him by messenger to go and bathe in the Jordan River seven times. After his initial reluctance, Naaman obeyed and was healed.

I. *There won't be darkness for the one in anguish. In past times, he treated the land of Zebulun and the land of Naphtali lightly, but later, heavily. On the road by the sea, across the Jordan, in Galilee of the Gentiles, people walking in darkness will see an intense light, and the light will shine on those living in a dark land. – Isaiah 9:1-2*

Naphtali and Zebulun

Naphtali (whose name means "my struggle") was Jacob's sixth son, while **Zebulun** (whose name means "gift" or "honor") was his tenth. Both became patriarchs of tribes of Israel that bear their respective names. Their lands were adjacent, west and north of the Sea of Galilee, in northern Israel. The region was mountainous and fertile, but its easy access by land and sea made it subject to frequent attack. Although the area had numerous fortified cities, it was ravaged by the Aramean army and later by the Assyrians, with many exiles taken into captivity.

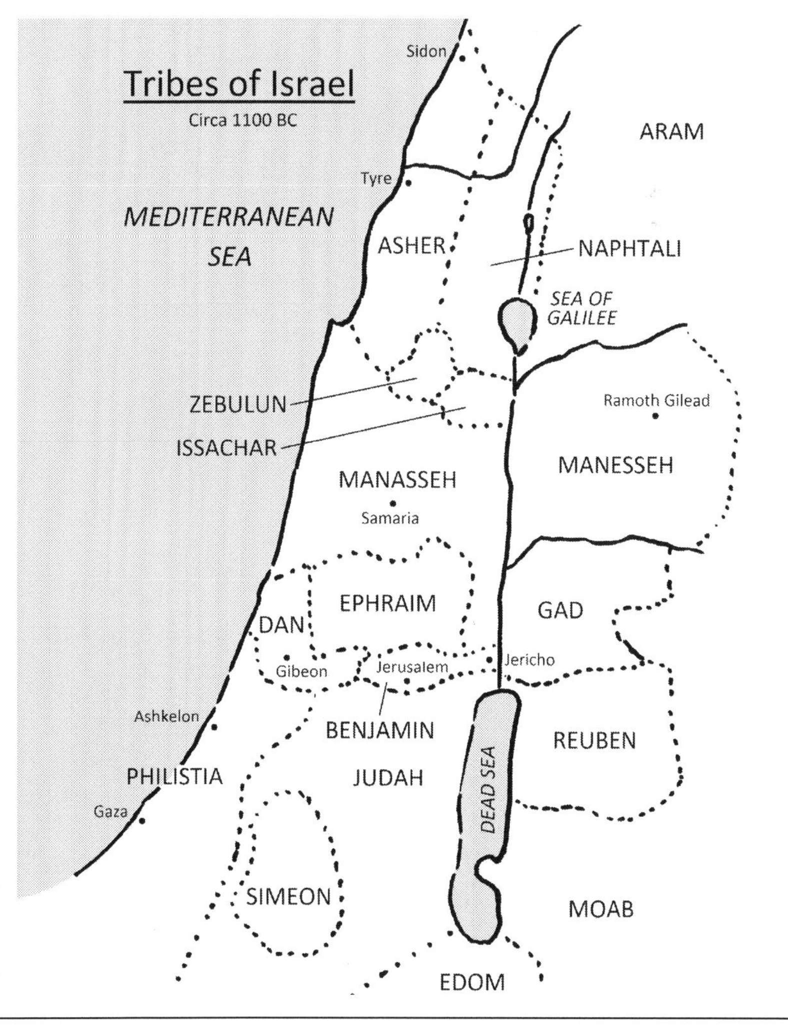

Chapter 7

The Disciples Called

7.1 Four disciples called

Matthew 4:18-22
Mark 1:16-20
Luke 5:1-11

While the crowd pressed in on him and listened to God's word, this happened: he was walking by the Sea of Galilee (the Lake of Gennesaret) and saw two boats standing beside the lake, but the fishermen had come out of them and were washing their nets. Two of the fishermen he saw were brothers: Simon, who was called Peter, and Simon's brother Andrew, who was throwing a net into the sea. Going on from there, he saw another pair of brothers: James and his brother John, who were Zebedee's sons and Simon's partners, in the boat with their father Zebedee, repairing their nets. Then he got into one of the boats (Simon's) and asked him to go out a little from land. Then he sat down and taught the crowds from the boat. When he had finished speaking, he told Simon, "Go out into the depths and lower your nets for a catch."

"Master, we struggled all night and caught nothing," Simon answered. "But at your word, I'll lower the nets."

Fishing

About 100 km north of Jerusalem lies the largest freshwater lake in Israel. The **Sea of Galilee**, also called the Lake of Gennesaret and the Sea of Tiberias, is fed primarily by the Jordan River, but also by underground springs. Its elevation is well below sea level (220 meters), surrounded by steep hills rising into the fertile mountains of the Golan heights. These sharp changes in elevations made for strong winds that could quickly stir up storms on the water. Yet despite the steep slopes and unpredictable weather, cities such as Bethsaida, Tiberias, and Capernaum flourished on its shore.

Fishing around the Sea of Galilee was a thriving industry, with hundreds of boats working the lake daily. The warm waters supported a wide variety of fish, particularly tilapia (pictured below), a 1-2 pound cichlid found throughout lakes in the Middle East and Africa. Although hooks and line were sometimes used, the most common method of fishing in ancient Palestine was with nets. Small casting nets could be handled by one man on shore, while larger dragnets required multiple fishermen in boats. Floats kept one edge of dragnets on the surface, while weighted stones and metal kept the other edge submerged. By drawing a line threaded through the deep edge to close the net, fish could either be hauled into boats or dragged to shore for sorting. After use, nets were cleaned, inspected, and mended for reuse. Most fishing was done at night, when fish came up from the cooler deep waters to feed in the shallows, which was otherwise too warm for large fish during the hot days. Moses' Law stated that fish with fins and scales were considered edible, while catfish, eel, and shellfish were unclean and therefore forbidden as food.

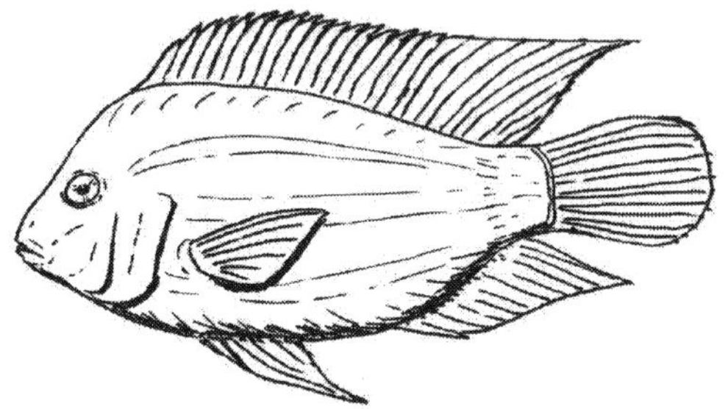

Doing so, they caught such a huge number of fish that their net began to tear. They signaled their partners to come and grab it in the other boat, and they came and filled both boats so much that they began to sink. When Simon Peter saw it, he fell at Jesus' knees, saying, "Go away from me, O Lord, because I'm a sinful man!"

Shock had seized him and all of those with him because of the fish they had caught. Then Jesus told Simon, "Don't be afraid. From now on you'll catch men."

After they brought their boats to land, Jesus tells Simon and Andrew, "Follow me, and I'll make you fishers for men."

Immediately they left their nets and everything else, and they followed him. Then he called James and John, Zebedee's sons, and immediately they left their father Zebedee in the boat with the workers to follow him.

7.2 DEMONIZED MAN HEALED

Mark 1:21-28
Luke 4:31b-37

They go to Capernaum, a city in Galilee. Immediately he went into the synagogue on the Sabbath and began to teach. They were blown away at his teaching, because his words had such authority, unlike the scribes.

A man was there in their synagogue who was possessed by the spirit of an unclean demon. "Get away!" he shouted. "What is it with us and you, Jesus from Nazareth? Have you come to destroy us? I know who you are: the holy one from God!"

But Jesus rebuked it, saying, "Be quiet and come out of him!"

Then the demon (the unclean spirit) threw him down into convulsions in front of them and screamed with a loud voice. But then it came out without harming him. They were all amazed and argued among themselves, saying, "What are these words? New teaching with authority! He even commands the unclean spirits and they obey him."

News about him immediately spread everywhere, to all the regions around Galilee.

Demons

In first century Judea, the Greek word *daimon* (translated "**demon**") referred to a spiritual being, but without the negative connotation that the word carries today. Back then, a demon was a spirit that wasn't necessarily good or bad. However, other names for them in the Bible do suggest their evil nature, such as "unclean spirit" and "evil spirit." Over time Christian tradition adopted the word "demon" to mean fallen angels that rebelled with Satan against God. Jews in the first century understood that demons could possess and control people, causing problems like deafness, blindness, mental disorders, seizures, and the inability to speak. Not all diseases were blamed on demons, since the Gospel writers often differentiated between the same problem as having natural or supernatural causes. However, it's unclear what the criteria were to attribute an affliction to demon possession or simply a medical cause. Exorcism is the act of evicting demons from the people or places they possess, which was practiced throughout the ancient Middle East by Jews and other religious groups.

7.3 PETER'S MOTHER-IN-LAW HEALED

Matthew 8:14-17
Mark 1:29-34
Luke 4:38-41

After they left the synagogue, they went straight to Simon Peter and Andrew's house, along with James and John. Simon's mother-in-law was laying there sick, suffering from a high fever, and immediately they told Jesus about her, asking him to help her. So he came to her. Standing over her, he rebuked the fever, then he took her hand and woke her up, and the fever left. Immediately she got up and served them.

When evening came, after sunset, they brought everyone who was sick or demonized to him and the whole city gathered at the door. Laying his hands on each of them, he healed all the sick from their various diseases and threw out spirits with a word. The many demons that were coming out of them shouted, "You're God's Son!" But he rebuked them and wouldn't let them speak, because they knew who he was – the Christ. This fulfilled what was said through Isaiah the prophet, "He himself took our weakness and carried away our disease."[a]

7.4 TRAVEL AND HEALING THROUGH GALILEE

Matthew 4:23-25
Mark 1:35-39
Luke 4:42-44

Early in the morning, while it was still dark, Jesus got up and went away somewhere remote to pray, but Simon and those with him looked for him and found him. "Everyone's looking for you!" they say.

"Let's go somewhere else," he answers, "to the towns and cities nearby, so I can announce God's kingdom there too, because that's why I came."

The crowds were looking for him too, and they came to keep him from leaving. But Jesus went on throughout all Galilee and Judea, teaching in their synagogues and announcing the good news of the kingdom. He was throwing out demons and healing every disease and every weakness the people had.

News about him spread throughout all Syria and they brought him everyone who was sick – those suffering with various diseases and pains, the demonized, the lunatics, and the paralytics. And he healed them. So huge crowds followed him from Galilee, Decapolis, Jerusalem, Judea, and from across the Jordan.

A. *He certainly carried our sickness and bore our pain, while we figured he was struck, beaten, and oppressed by God. – Isaiah 53:4*

Leprosy

Infection with *Mycobacterium leprae* causes a chronic, disfiguring skin disease called **leprosy**. It's characterized by progressively worsening skin lesions that cause nerve and tissue destruction. The bacteria grow best on cooler areas of the body, so lesions (called granulomas) tend to develop on the limbs and face. Leprosy is spread by prolonged contact with someone infected, and also by nasal droplet (from breathing, sneezing, coughing). Before antibiotics, there was no cure for leprosy, although many remedies were attempted, including bathing in blood, applying snake venom, repeated bee stings, castration, and oil from chaulmoogra trees. Because it was contagious and relatively untreatable, lepers were usually quarantined and segregated from the general population.

The Hebrew word for leprosy (*tsara'ath*) was a nonspecific term for any skin condition, which could also refer to mildew and mould on clothes or houses. Moses' Law included extensive regulations for leprosy on people or their possessions. In general, anyone with an open skin lesion was considered unclean, whether it was true leprosy or something else. Lepers (those with skin lesions) had to live in isolation and shout, "Unclean! Unclean!" when around others. When a skin disorder resolved, the person had to be examined by a priest and be ceremonially cleaned. After bathing, shaving, washing one's clothes, and offering sacrifices, the person could then officially rejoin the community. However, unlike other skin conditions, leprosy rarely self-resolved, so true lepers were typically outcasts for life.

7.5 LEPER HEALED

Matthew 8:2-4
Mark 1:40-45
Luke 5:12-16

Look, while he was in one of the cities, a man covered with leprosy saw him. He comes to Jesus, begging him on his knees and falling on his face, saying, "Lord, if you want to, you can cleanse me."

Jesus was moved, so he reached out his hand and touched him. "I want to," he says. "Be clean."

Immediately the leprosy left him and he was clean. Then he warned him and sent him away. "See that you don't tell anyone," he tells him. "But go and show yourself to the priest and give the offering for your cleansing that Moses commanded, as a witness to them."

But he left and announced it repeatedly and spread the news so much that Jesus couldn't openly enter a city. Instead, he had to stay out in remote areas. They came to him from everywhere, and huge crowds gathered to hear him and be healed of their sickness. However, Jesus would escape to the wilderness to pray.

7.6 PARALYTIC HEALED

Matthew 9:1-8
Mark 2:1-12
Luke 5:17-26

Days later, he got into a boat and crossed back over to his hometown of Capernaum, and when he arrived, it was heard that he was home. One day, he was teaching and speaking the word to them, and there were so many gathered that there wasn't any space, not even near the door. Pharisees and lawyers were sitting there too, having come from Jerusalem and every village of Galilee and Judea. And the Lord's power was there for him to heal.

Four men come carrying a paralyzed man as he lay on a cot. They were trying to bring him in to put him down in front of him, but they couldn't get to him because of the crowd. So they went up to the roof and removed it above him. When they had dug through the roof, they lowered the cot that the paralytic was lying on down through the clay into the midst of them, right in front of Jesus. Seeing their faith, Jesus tells the paralytic, "Cheer up, son! Your sins are forgiven."

Some of the scribes sitting there thought to themselves in their hearts, saying, "Who is this man speaking blasphemies?[b] Who can forgive sins except God alone?"

Houses

Houses in first century Palestine varied widely in size and shape, but the typical family dwelling had one or two storeys and multiple rooms. In the country or un-walled towns, houses were typically only one story (as pictured), whereas houses within walled cities, where space was more limited, typically had two or more storeys. Livestock were kept on the lower floor, while the main living area of the family was above it. Walls were made of brick or stone, then covered with plaster. A flat **roof** was constructed by laying beams across the tops of the walls, which supported branches and straw laid over top. Finally, a layer of clay sealed it from rain. The roof provided extra open space and often had a short ledge around it to prevent people from falling off. An extra room could be built on the roof as a spare bedroom or storage room.

But right away Jesus knew in his spirit what they were thinking to themselves. "Why are you thinking such evil in your hearts?" he says. "What's easier to tell a paralytic, 'Your sins are forgiven,' or 'Get up, pick up your cot, and walk'? But now, so you'll know that the Son of Man has authority on earth to forgive sins –" then he tells the paralytic, "I tell you, get up, pick up your cot, and go home."

So he got up immediately, picked up the cot he had been lying on, and went home praising God in everyone's sight. They were all awe-struck and full of fear. They praised God, who had given such authority to men, saying, "We've never seen anything like this! Today we've seen the extraordinary!"

7.7 MATTHEW CALLED

Matthew 9:9-13
Mark 2:13-17
Luke 5:27-32

Jesus went out by the seashore again, teaching all of the people as they came out to him. As he was passing by, he saw a man sitting in a toll booth, Levi, also called Matthew, Alphaeus' son. "Follow me!" he tells him.

So Levi got up, left everything, and followed him. He threw a big party for him at his house. And look, crowds of tax collectors and other

B. In Judea, speaking contemptuously or irreverently about God, or cursing him, was a terrible sin called **blasphemy** (*nehatsa* in Hebrew, *blasphemeo* in Greek). It translates literally to "injure one's reputation" and is where the English word "blame" originates. Blasphemy violated the third of Moses' Ten Commandments, which directed Israel to keep God's name holy. As punishment, Moses' Law held that a blasphemer must be stoned to death.

Taxation

The Roman Empire levied various **taxes** against its subjects throughout its many provinces. First, a poll or head tax (*tributum capitis*) was a fixed amount that every person had to pay, according the registry of the latest census. Poll taxes fell on Roman subjects, not on Roman citizens, and subsequently provoked numerous revolts. Second, a land tax was charged based on how much land a person owned. Third, tolls were collected when particular highways were travelled. Finally, a temple tax was imposed specifically on Jews, which funded the operation and upkeep of the Temple in Jerusalem.

With all this money to be paid annually, the Roman Empire employed locals in every province to collect its taxes. Unfortunately, with the authority of the Empire and little accountability, **tax collectors** (*telones*) had a reputation for demanding more than what was due and pocketing the difference. And because they were fellow countrymen aligned with the occupying power, tax collectors were viewed as traitors for hire.

sinners were reclining[c] and eating with Jesus and his disciples, because there were many of them following him.

Then it happens that as he was reclining, the Pharisees and the scribes saw that he was eating with sinners and tax collectors, so they grumbled to his disciples, saying, "Why do you and your teacher eat and drink with tax collectors and sinners?"

But overhearing them, Jesus answers, "The healthy don't need a doctor, the sick do. Go and learn what this means: 'I want compassion, not sacrifice,'[d] because I didn't come to call the righteous, but rather sinners, to repentance."

C. The common mealtime practice in ancient Judea was to **recline** on the floor beside a low table. Couches or pillows could be used for such reclining. Utensils and individual dishes weren't used during meals. Instead, food was served in a communal bowl, with bread to dip in and scoop out, all eaten with one's hands. Wine was the drink of choice, for those who could afford it, served in individual cups or goblets.

D. *I enjoy kindness over sacrifice, and the knowledge of God over offerings. – Hosea 6:6*

Scribes, Lawyers, and Pharisees

Scribes and **lawyers** were names for essentially the same occupation: professional experts in Jewish law. These renowned Rabbis continually studied the Torah – the first five books of the Bible – and gave applications for everyday life. Their interpretations and expansions of the Law were handed down verbally through generations of religious teachers before being recorded in the Mishnah around 200 AD. These rules dealt with all aspects of Jewish life, including prayer, agriculture, rest, festivals, marriage, law, courts, Temple rituals, diet, and purity. By the first century, they were as legally binding as the Torah itself. Scribes were responsible for continually studying, revising, and further interpreting Jewish oral tradition. They also meticulously made copies of Scripture and judged court cases.

There are various terms in the New Testament for such positions. The Greek word for "scribe" is *grammateus*, derived from the word for "letter" or "writing." *Didaskalos* means "teacher," a title frequently used for Jesus in the Gospels. Some Bible translations specify *didaskalos* as "teacher of the law" or "doctor of the law" when not referring to Jesus. Finally, *nomikos* comes from the Greek word for "law" (*nomos*) and is therefore translated "lawyer." Unlike modern lawyers, ancient lawyers in Judea didn't represent parties in court cases. They would give their expert opinions on the law in criminal matters, but didn't necessarily act as advocates for the accused.

Scribes and lawyers worked closely with **Pharisees**, a class of Jews firmly committed to Judaism. Insisting that Moses' Law be kept according to the scribes' interpretation, the Pharisees were a religious group that arose during the second century BC when Judea was under strong Greek influence. They enjoyed high social standing for their moral excellence, and were typically called Rabbi in public, the Hebrew word for "master." As a political movement, the Pharisees were the people's party, since most were ordinary Jews who had worked and studied their way into their positions, contrary to the rich ruling class of the Sadducees. The term "Pharisee" comes from the Hebrew word *parash*, meaning "separate." They were so particular about following Jewish purity customs that they wouldn't eat in the homes of non-Pharisees, since they couldn't be sure that the food had been properly prepared. Similarly, they had limited contact with Gentiles (non-Jews). The Pharisee movement became the basis for Rabbinic Judaism, which arose in the first century AD.

Fasting

Voluntarily going without food or water is called **fasting**, often done for the purpose of seeking God's will or favor. Moses fasted for 40 days while receiving God's Law, while King Jehosephat called for all of Judah to fast when a Moabite army marched against them. Similarly, Queen Esther and the exiled Jews fasted when faced with destruction of their nation, in hopes of being delivered by God. Fasting was also done to show repentance, like when the city of Nineveh fasted after hearing the prophet Jonah's message of judgment. Fasting didn't guarantee God's blessing, but it acted as an outward sign of humility and repentance toward God. Fasting also marked periods of mourning, like when Israel mourned the death King Saul and his sons. Although it occurred frequently in Israel's history, fasting was only required in Moses' Law once a year. On Atonement Day, the whole nation fasted, prayed, and made sacrifices to have God cover their sin (the Hebrew word for atonement – *kaphar* – translates to "cover"). This day later became known simply as "The Fast." Sometimes other outwards signs of humility or mourning were practiced along with fasting to publicly emphasize the misery of the person fasting, such as dressing in rough cloth (sackcloth), not bathing, or covering oneself in ashes.

7.8 FEASTING VS. FASTING

Matthew 9:14-17
Mark 2:18-22
Luke 5:33-39

John's disciples and the Pharisees were fasting. They come to him and ask, "Why do we, John's disciples and the Pharisee's disciples, fast and pray so often, but your disciples eat and drink and don't ever fast?"

"Do the groomsmen[e] mourn and fast while the groom is still with them?" Jesus asked. "No! As long as the groom is with them, they can't fast. But the days will come when the groom is taken away from them, and then in that day they'll fast."

Then he told them a parable:[f] "No one tears off a piece of unshrunk cloth from a new coat and sews it on an old coat, because he'll tear the new one and the new patch won't match the old one. The patch will lift off – the new from the old – and a worse tear will occur.

"And no one puts new wine into old wineskins,[g] or else the wine will burst out of the skins and both the wine and the skins will be ruined.

E. "Sons of the wedding chamber" is the literal translation of the New Testament phrase for **groomsmen** (*huios nymphios*).

F. The Greek practice of using illustrations to explain principles was used frequently in the first century. Such an analogy was called a **parable**, from the Greek word *parabole*, which literally means to throw something down beside another. Such a comparison helped to explain the unknown by comparing it with the familiar. A parable typically involved a moral dilemma and its consequences, with its meaning implied rather than explicitly stated.

G. A **wineskin** was a leather bag used to ferment and contain wine. It was typically made of a whole goat skin, lined with tree sap or resin to prevent its contents from seeping out. The

They put new wine into fresh wineskins and both are preserved. But after drinking the old, no one wants the new, because he says, 'The old is better.'"

skin of grapes naturally have yeast growing on them, and, upon pressing the grapes, the yeast digests the natural sugars in the juice to produce alcohol and carbon dioxide gas. New wineskins full of fermenting wine expand as gas accumulates. However, wineskins can only be used to ferment wine once – the gas would burst old wineskins if used to hold fresh grape juice again.

CHAPTER 8

Controversy on the Sabbath

8.1 CRIPPLE HEALED ON THE SABBATH

John 5:1-3a, 5-47

Afterwards, Jesus went up to Jerusalem for a Jewish feast. There's a pool in Jerusalem by the Sheep Gate called *Bethesda* in Hebrew that has five porches where many of the sick, blind, lame, and withered lay. A man was there who had been frail[a] for 38 years. Jesus saw him lying there and knew he had been there a long time. So he asks him, "Do you want to get healthy?"

"Sir," the sick man answered, "I don't have anyone to put me in the pool when the water is stirred up. While I'm going, someone else gets there before me."

Then Jesus tells him, "Get up, pick up your cot, and walk."

Immediately the man got better, and he picked up his cot and walked.

Now that day was the Sabbath and the Jews were telling the man who was healed, "It's the Sabbath, so you're not allowed to carry your

A. *Astheneia* is Greek for "**frailty**," "weakness," or "sickness," from the negative form of the word for "strength" (*sthenos*).

Bethesda

The **Bethesda pool** was a public bath house north of the Temple in Jerusalem. The Hebrew name *Bethesda* translates to "mercy house" or "grace house," and tradition holds that the pool was associated with healing. It was originally formed by building a short dam across a small valley near Jerusalem, thereby creating a reservoir for rain water. From here, a channel cut into the rock brought fresh water from the pool into the city. Eventually, as Jerusalem expanded, Bethesda was incorporated within the city walls and a second pool was added to the south. Its five porches (or porticos) were covered walkways supported by columns. Four of them likely surrounded the two pools in a rectangle, with the fifth dividing them down the middle. Its whereabouts was largely unknown until archeological digs in the 19th century revealed a large pool that matched the biblical description of the Bethesda pool.

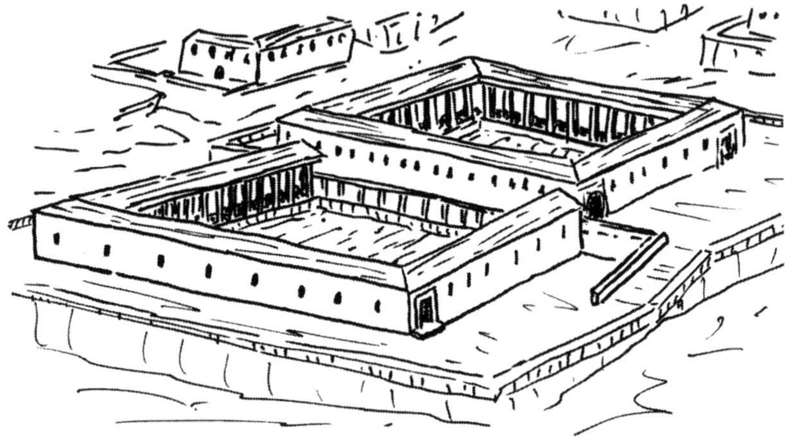

Like many natural springs, legend held that Bethesda had supernatural healing properties. Later copies of John's Gospel include text that sheds light on why it was so popular among the infirm:

> *"... many of the sick, blind, lame, and withered lay [waiting for movement in the waters. Because an angel from Lord would descend at certain times to the pool and stir up the water. Then whoever stepped in the water first after it was stirred up became healthy from whatever disease he was held by.] And so it was for a man..."*
>
> *– John 5:3b-4*

This additional text isn't included in the earliest known copies of John's Gospel, suggesting its incorporation into Scripture later.

cot."

"The one who made me healthy told me to pick up my cot and walk," he answered.

So they asked him, "Which man told you to pick it up and walk?"

But the healed man didn't know who it was, because Jesus had slipped away while a crowd was there. Then afterwards, Jesus finds him in the Temple. "Look, you've gotten better," he said. "Don't sin anymore, so something worse doesn't happen to you."

The man left and told the Jews that it was Jesus who had made him better, so the Jews harassed Jesus because he did it on the Sabbath. But he answered them, "My Father's working now, so I'm working too."

That's why the Jews were looking to kill him so much more: not only was he breaking the Sabbath but he was also calling God his own father, making himself equal with God.

Then Jesus told them, "Truly truly, I tell you that the Son can't do anything by himself, unless it's something he sees the Father doing, because the Son does whatever the Father does, and in the same way too. The Father loves his Son and he shows him everything he's doing. He'll show him even greater actions than this, so that you'll be amazed. Because just as the Father raises the dead and gives them life, the Son also gives life to whoever he wants to. The Father doesn't judge anyone, but he has given all judgment to the Son, so that all will respect the Son just like they respect the Father. Whoever doesn't respect the Son doesn't respect the Father who sent him.[b]

"Truly truly, I tell you that whoever hears my word and believes in the one who sent me has eternal life. He won't come under judgment but has gone from death to life.

"Truly truly, I tell you that a time is coming – and is here now – when the dead will hear the voice of God's Son, and whoever hears it will live. Just like the Father has life within himself, he gave the Son life to have life within himself too. And he gave him authority to make judgments, because he's the Son of Man. Don't be amazed at this, because a time's coming when everyone in their graves will hear his voice and come out – those who did good to a resurrection of life, and those who practiced evil to a resurrection of judgment.

"I can't do anything on my own. I judge as I hear, and my judgment is right, because I don't seek my own desires but the desires of him who sent me.

"If I testify about myself, my testimony isn't true.[c] But there's someone else who testifies about me, and I know that the testimony he testifies about me is true. You sent to John and he testified about the truth. He was the burning, shining lamp, and you were okay with being

---

B. *Whoever denies the Son doesn't have the Father. – 1 John 3:14*

C. Moses' Law stated that a **single testimony** wasn't acceptable as legal evidence on its own. More witnesses were needed.

One witness can't stand up against a man because of a depravity or sin he has committed. But a word will be confirmed by the mouths of two or three witnesses. – Deuteronomy 19:15

The Sabbath

Genesis records that God created the world in six consecutive days, then rested from his work on the seventh. Thus the **Sabbath** (meaning "cease") became a Jewish day of rest and worship every seventh day. Keeping or observing the Sabbath became law for all Israel when Moses delivered the Ten Commandments shortly after they left captivity in Egypt:

> *"Remember the Sabbath day by keeping it holy. You'll work and do all your business in six days, but the seventh day is a Sabbath to the LORD your God. Do not do any work on it, not you, your son or daughter, your slave or maid, your animals, nor any foreigner living in your towns. Because the LORD made the skies, the earth, the sea, and everything in them in six days, but he rested on the seventh day. So the LORD blessed the Sabbath day and made it holy ."*
>
> *– Exodus 20:8-11*

Failing to observe the Sabbath, or even speaking against it, was punishable by death according to Hebrew Law. Jeremiah, a prophet before and during Israel's exile to Babylon, taught that God would bless or destroy Israel for simply keeping or disregarding the Sabbath.

Jewish tradition held various criteria for the definition of work, which was divided into 39 general activities. It included: farming (planting, plowing, reaping, threshing), sorting, food preparation (kneading, baking, killing animals), making clothes (spinning wool, dyeing, weaving more than two threads, sewing more than two stitches, washing), tying and untying, writing and erasing, building and destroying, lighting and extinguishing a fire, and finishing anything. All preparations for the Sabbath were done the day before and all work stopped from sundown on Friday until the appearance of three stars on Saturday night. The only way the Sabbath could be broken was if a human life was in danger, in which case a Jew was not only free from the Sabbath restrictions, but required to act.

The Sabbath was also every seventh year, where any farmed field was to remain fallow until the next year. Furthermore, every seventh Sabbath year (every fiftieth year) was to be a year of jubilee, where everyone was to return to their own land and all debts were to be forgiven.

overjoyed in his light for a while. But so you can be saved, I say this: the testimony I get isn't from man. The testimony I have is better than John, because the actions the Father has given me to do – the actions I do – testify about me, that the Father has sent me. And the Father who sent me has also testified about me. You haven't ever heard his voice or seen his appearance. You don't have his word living in you because you don't believe the one he sent. You search the Scriptures because you think that you have eternal life in them. But they testify about me, and yet you won't come to me to have life.

"I don't get glory from men. But I know you, that you don't have God's love in yourselves. I've come in my Father's name, but you don't accept me. But if someone else comes in his own name, you'll accept him. So how can you believe when you accept glory from one another but don't look for glory from the only God? Don't think that I'll accuse you before the Father – Moses, whom you hope for, is the one who accuses you. If you'd believed Moses, you would believe me, because he wrote about me.[d] But if you don't believe what he wrote, how will you believe my words?"

8.2 PICKING GRAIN ON THE SABBATH

Matthew 12:1-8
Mark 2:23-28
Luke 6:1-5

While Jesus passed through grain fields on the Sabbath, this happened: his disciples got hungry and were picking the grain, rubbing it in their hands,[e] and eating it as they made their way along. When the Pharisees saw it, they asked him, "Look, why are your disciples doing something illegal on the Sabbath?"

But Jesus tells them, "Haven't you read what David did when he was in need, when he and those with him got hungry? While Abiathar was High Priest, he went into the house of God and ate the dedicated bread,[f] which was illegal for anyone to eat except the priests alone. But he ate it and gave it to those who were with him.

"Or haven't you read in the Law that on the Sabbath the priests in the Temple violate the Sabbath but are innocent?[g] I tell you, something

D. *The LORD your God will raise up a prophet like [Moses] for you, from among you and your brothers. You'll listen to him. – Deuteronomy 18:15*

E. Any activities associated with farming were forbidden on the Sabbath, since it violated Moses' Law. This included harvesting ("**picking the grain**") and threshing ("**rubbing it in their hands**"), even for just a few grains.

F. 1 Samuel 21 records that when David was running away from King Saul, he went to Nob, a town in northeastern Israel, and met a priest there named Ahimelech. David lied about his purpose and asked Ahimelech for whatever provisions he had. However, the only food available was the bread set aside specifically for priests. It was called the consecrated bread, the **dedicated bread**, or the bread of the sanctuary, and it consisted of twelve loaves displayed on a gold table. This bread was mandated in Moses' Law to serve as a reminder of God's covenant with Israel. Ahimelech let David have it, provided none of his men had slept with a woman recently. He also gave David the sword of Goliath, a giant he had killed previously, since he had arrived unarmed. In this way, the Law of the Temple was broken, but David was considered guiltless.

The Gospel writer Mark states that **Abiathar** played the role of priest in the story, not Ahimelech (Abiathar's father) as the Old Testament records. There's some discrepancy as to whether a transcription error was made, or if one of the men were called by the other's name. It wasn't uncommon to call a son by his father's name. Conversely, Abiathar was certainly a more renowned figure in Israel's history, appointed High Priest when David was crowned king of Judah, so his presumably erroneous inclusion in the story in the place of his father Ahimelech may be due to his prominence.

G. Numbers records that sacrifices were to be made every day to God: two lambs, grain, oil, and wine. The Sabbath was no exception – the same sacrifices were made as any other day, except that the grain offering was doubled. Priests were responsible for preparing and

greater than the Temple is here. If you'd known what this means, 'I want mercy, not a sacrifice,'[h] you wouldn't have condemned the innocent."

Then Jesus told them, "The Sabbath was made for man, not man for the Sabbath. And the Son of Man is the Lord, even over the Sabbath."

8.3 HAND HEALED ON THE SABBATH

Matthew 12:9-21
Mark 3:1-12
Luke 6:6-11

Leaving there, he went into their synagogue again on another Sabbath and taught. A man was there who had a withered[i] right hand and the scribes and the Pharisees were watching to see if he would heal on the Sabbath, so they could accuse him. They asked Jesus, "Is it legal to heal on the Sabbath?"

But he knew their thoughts. So he tells the man with the withered hand, "Get up into the middle."

So he got up and stood forward. Then he tells them, "I ask you this: is it legal to do good or evil on the Sabbath, to save a life or destroy it? What man among you won't take hold of his sheep and lift it out of a ditch if it falls in on the Sabbath? How much more is a man than a sheep! So yes, it's legal to do good on the Sabbath."

They were silent. Then, after looking at them angrily, upset at their hard hearts, he tells the man, "Stretch out your hand."

When he stretched it out, his hand was restored back to normal, just like his other one. The Pharisees were full of rage and left immediately, and they conspired with the Herodians[j] against him, about how they could destroy him.

---

offering these sacrifices every day, so they weren't at fault for **working on the Sabbath**, despite numerous laws prohibiting it.

H. *I enjoy kindness over sacrifice, and the knowledge of God over offerings. – Hosea 6:6*

I. *Xeros* is a Greek word that translates to "dry," "wasted," or "**withered**." It could also refer to dry land, as a distinction from the sea. However, it's unclear what it means with respect to a limb, whether it described a disease, malformation, or something else.

Those with withered hands or other physical defects were typically ostracized from Jewish society, since physical deformities were thought to be the result of sin. It's unusual that a man with a withered hand would be in allowed the Temple; the situation may have been set up to trap Jesus.

J. Jews who favored Greek customs (Hellenization) and Roman law in Judea, particularly supporting Herod's reign, were called **Herodians**. They were an influential political party

Knowing this, Jesus left for the sea with his disciples. Many crowds followed him from Galilee, and also from Judea, Jerusalem, Idumea,[k] across the Jordan, and the region of Tyre and Sidon. Many people heard of everything he was doing and came to him. He healed them all, but he warned them not to reveal who he was, which fulfilled what was said through Isaiah the prophet:

> "Look at my servant, whom I chose, my dear, who pleases my soul. I'll put my Spirit on him and he'll announce justice to the nations. He won't argue or shout out, nor will anyone hear his voice in the streets. He won't break a crushed reed and he won't put out a smoldering candle until he brings justice to victory.[l] And Gentiles will hope in his name."[m]

He told his disciples that a boat should be ready for him because of the crowds, so they wouldn't crowd him. He had healed so many that whoever was suffering pressed around him just to touch him. And whenever unclean spirits saw him, they would fall before him and shout, "You're God's Son!" But he rebuked them repeatedly to not reveal him.

---

that opposed anyone who threatened Roman rule under Herod. They may have recognized Herod himself as the Messiah. Their political views directly opposed those of the Pharisees, who were opposed to Roman rule. However, little is known about them apart from two brief mentions in the New Testament.

K. South of Judea and the Dead Sea was a region called Edom or **Idumea**. The name means "red," which may refer to the area's red sandstone. Edomites were descendants of Esau, Isaac's firstborn son, who was covered in red hair at birth, another possible source of Edom's name. Esau was a rugged hunter who was scammed out of his birthright as Isaac's heir by his younger twin brother Jacob. He ended up settling the area after reconciling with Jacob, and his descendants by his six wives grew into the nation of Edom.

L. *Look at my servant, whom I hold. He's my chosen, who pleases my soul. I've put my Spirit on him and he'll bring justice out to the nations. He won't cry out or raise his voice or make his voice heard in the streets. He won't break a crushed reed and he won't put out a fading candle. He'll bring justice out honestly. He won't get discouraged or crushed until he sets up justice on earth. – Isaiah 42:1-4a*

M. *At that time, nations will look to Jesse's root, who'll stand as a sign for the people. His rest will be glorious. – Isaiah 11:10*

CHAPTER 9

Teaching on the Mountain

9.1 TWELVE APOSTLES CHOSEN | BLESSINGS AND WOES

Matthew 5:1-12, 10:2-4
Mark 3:13-19
Luke 6:12-26

During this time, Jesus leaves for the mountain to pray and he calls the ones he wanted. He had spent the night praying to God and when the day came, his disciples came to him. He chose twelve of them and named them as his apostles,[a] so that they would be with him and that he could send them out to preach and have authority to throw out demons. These are the names of the twelve he designated as apostles: the first was Simon (whom he also named Peter), and his brother Andrew; James of Zebedee and John, James' brother (he named them *Boanerges*, which means, "sons of thunder"); Philip and Bartholomew; Matthew the tax collector and Thomas; James of Alphaeus and Judas of James[b]

A. The Greek word *apostolos* literally means "someone sent away" and is where the English word "**apostle**" comes from. Although it has come to have a strong religious connotation, the word back in Judea was more generic and referred to a messenger or emissary.

B. Matthew records the tenth disciple as Thaddeus, while Mark records him as **Judas of James**. Luke, on the other hand, shortens his name to Jude of James in the book of Acts, possibly to further distinguish him from Judas Iscariot, the twelfth disciple. Being "of James" usually meant being the son of James, but it could also mean they were brothers. However, despite

(Thaddaeus); Simon, who was called a Zealot;[c] and Judas Iscariot,[d] who became a traitor and betrayed him.

Then Jesus came down with them and stood in a flat area. A large crowd of his disciples was there, as well as a great multitude of people from all of Judea and Jerusalem, and from Tyre and Sidon on the coast, who had come to listen to him and have their diseases healed. Even those who were harassed by unclean spirits were being cured. All of the people were trying to touch him, because power was coming from him and healing everyone.

But when Jesus saw the crowds, he went up the mountain, and his disciples joined him after he had sat down. Then, lifting his eyes toward his disciples, he opened his mouth and taught them.

"Blessed are the poor in spirit, because the kingdom of heaven is theirs. Blessed are those who are hungry now, because they'll be satisfied. Blessed are those who weep now, because they'll laugh. Blessed are those who mourn, because they'll be comforted. Blessed are the meek,[e] because they'll inherit the earth.[f] Blessed are those who hunger and thirst for righteousness, because they'll be satisfied. Blessed are the merciful, because they'll receive mercy. Blessed are the pure in heart, because they'll see God. Blessed are the peacemakers, because they'll be called sons of God. Blessed are those who've been mistreated for righteousness' sake, because the kingdom of heaven is theirs.

---

his many names, little is known about Jude, although some scholars hold that he was one of Jesus' brothers and the writer of the biblical book of the same name.

C. During the Roman occupation of Judea, a group of Jewish rebels sought to expel the Romans from their homeland. Their name – the **Zealots** – reflected their zeal and fierce patriotism for the Jewish nation. Zealots were some of the earliest terrorists on record, regularly murdering Romans and Greeks who were living in Judea. They also targeted other Jews thought to be in league with Rome, such as Sadducees, or those who openly opposed violence against Rome. Zealots had a bleak reputation in Judea for being ruffians. They used violent revolts to undermine Roman rule. In 66 AD, they led a rebellion and succeeded in taking control of Jerusalem, triggering the Roman-Jewish War. However, their success was short-lived: Rome recaptured the city in 70 AD and destroyed the Temple. Shortly thereafter, the Roman army attacked the Zealot stronghold of Masada in 73 AD, prompting the Zealots to commit mass suicide, effectively ending the movement.

D. Iscariot translates to "from Kerioth," referring to a town or region in Judea. Thus **Judas Iscariot** may have been the only non-Galilean disciple.

E. The Greek work *prays* (pronounced "prah-ooce") is a root adjective that is often translated "**meek**" or "humble." However, the usual Greek word for "humble" is *tapeinos*, suggesting that meekness is not the same as humility. *Prays* occurs only three times in the Gospels, while variations of *tapeinos* occur seven. The two terms often occur together.

F. *The humble will inherit the land and delight themselves in abundant prosperity. – Psalm 37:11*

Blessed are you when men hate you, exclude you, insult you, mistreat you, scorn your name as evil, and falsely say all sorts of evil about you because of me, the Son of Man. On that day, leap and celebrate! Be happy, because look, your reward in heaven is huge. Their fathers mistreated the prophets before you the same way.

"But woe[g] you who are rich, because you have your comfort. Woe you who are full now, because you'll be hungry. Woe you who laugh now, because you'll mourn and cry. And woe when all men speak well of you, because their fathers used to treat the false prophets likewise."

9.2 INTERPRETATIONS OF THE LAW

Matthew 5:13-24, 27-48; 6:22-23
Luke 6:27-36; 11:33-36; 16:16-18
Mark 9:49-50; 14:34-35

"You're the salt of the earth. Everyone will be salted with fire. Salt is good, but if salt becomes saltless and bland, how can you flavor it and make it salty again? It's useless for the soil and the manure, not good for anything anymore, except to be thrown out and walked on by men. So have salt in yourselves, and be at peace with one another. Whoever has ears to hear, listen up!

"You're the light of the world. A city set on a hill can't hide. And nobody lights a lamp and puts it in the cellar[h] under a basket. Instead, it

G. **Woe** is pronounced basically the same way in Greek, Hebrew, and English. It's a term of sadness or suffering, an exclamation of grief spoken in the midst of despair.

H. *Krypte* is a Greek word referring to a hidden or secret place. It's where the English "crypt" comes from, but it can also be translated as "basement," "**cellar**," or "vault."

Salt

Common table **salt** is sodium chloride (NaCl), a crystallized solid at room temperature that easily dissolves in water. All life is dependent on salt, which contributes two of the major electrolytes in cells. However, salt can be lethal if levels aren't carefully balanced. In fact, armies used to scatter salt on enemy fields to render the land infertile. Salt was also the most common ancient seasoning, being one of the five basic human tastes. Before refrigeration, it was the primary means of preserving meat for consumption later. Salt production typically occurred at the seaside, particularly at the Dead Sea, by evaporating seawater in saltpans. Throughout human history, salt has always been a valuable commodity. The English word "salary" comes from the Latin word *salarium*, which was money paid to Roman soldiers to purchase salt.

Conversely, Mark uses the Greek word *analos* as the opposite of salty, translating literally to "without salt" or "**saltless**." Matthew and Luke, however, use *moraino*, meaning "**bland**" or "tasteless." *Moraino* could also mean "foolish," as Paul quotes later in the New Testament: *"Professing to be wise, they became foolish (moraino)." (Romans 1:22)*

goes on a lampstand,[i] so it shines on everyone in the house, and those who come in can see the light. Similarly, shine your light before men so they can see the good you do and praise the Father in heaven.

"The eye is the lamp of the body. When your eye is healthy and good, your whole body is full of light as well. But when it's sick and bad, your body will be full of darkness. So watch out that the light inside you isn't darkness. If the light inside you is dark, it'll be dark indeed! But if your whole body is full of light, with no dark part, it'll be completely lit up, like when a lamp illuminates you with its light.

"Don't think that I came to dissolve the Law or the prophets. I didn't come to destroy but to fulfill! The Law and the prophets went until John, and since that time the good news of God's kingdom is being announced and everyone is forcing his way in. I tell you truly that until heaven and earth pass away, not one *iota*[j] from the Law will pass away until everything's done, because it's easier for heaven and earth to pass away than for one stroke[k] of the Law to fail. Whoever voids even one of the smallest of these commandments, and teaches this to men, will be called the smallest in the kingdom of heaven. But whoever does them and teaches them will be called great in the kingdom of heaven.

"I tell you that unless your righteousness exceeds that of the scribes and the Pharisees, you won't enter the kingdom of heaven.

"You've heard that the ancients were told, 'Don't murder,'[k] and that whoever murders will be guilty before the court. But I tell you that anyone who's angry with his brother will be guilty before the court as well; whoever tells his brother '*Raca*'[l] will be guilty before the Sanhedrin;[m] and whoever says, 'You fool!' will be guilty enough for the

---

I. *Lychnia* is derived from the word for lamp or candle (*lychnos*), referring to something that supports or elevates a light. It can be translated "**lampstand**" or "candleholder."

J. The ninth letter of the Greek alphabet, ***iota***, is the smallest of all Greek letters. It's written with a single vertical stroke ("ι"), similar to the English letter "i." Similarly, the Greek word *keraia* refers to a "little horn," serif, or **stroke** of a single letter.

K. Do not murder. – Exodus 20:13

L. ***Raca*** is an Aramaic expression of contempt that means "empty head" or "air head," similar to calling someone an idiot. The term comes from the writings of Jewish scribes, but isn't mentioned elsewhere in the Bible.

M. Every city in Israel had a council of judges called the **Sanhedrin** (Hebrew for "assembly") that heard civil and criminal matters, including violations of Moses' Law. Its 23 members were made up of priests, elders, scribes, Pharisees, Sadducees, and other aristocrats. Although the Sanhedrin had considerable power in Judea, the Romans held ultimate authority and could interfere with its actions at anytime. In Jerusalem, the Great Sanhedrin was Judea's supreme court, which included 71 members. It had authority over the Temple

fires of hell. So if you're offering your gift at the altar[n] and there you remember that your brother has something against you, leave your gift before the altar and go. First make up with your brother, and then come and offer your gift.

"You've heard it said, 'Don't have an affair.'[o] But I tell you that everyone who looks at a woman and lusts[p] for her has already had an affair with her in his heart. If your right eye trips you up, pull it out and throw it away. It's better for you to lose one part of yourself than for your whole body to be thrown into hell. And if your right [hand] trips you up, cut it off and throw it away. It's better for you to lose one part of yourself than for your whole body to go to hell.

"It was said: 'Whoever sends his wife away will give her a divorce.'[q] But I tell you that whoever divorces his wife and marries another (except due to fornication) has an affair[r] and makes her do the same. And whoever marries a woman divorced from a husband has an affair too.

"Again, you've heard that the ancients were told, 'Don't break your promises or promise falsely, but you'll keep your oaths to the Lord.'[s]

---

police, who could arrest people apart from Roman laws, but couldn't legally execute prisoners.

N. Any raised structure used to offer sacrifices to a god was an **altar**. Abraham, Isaac, and Jacob each made or restored altars to God after defining moments in their lives. During Israel's journey through the wilderness, the Tabernacle (God's portable Temple) had two altars: one for burnt offerings, made of wood and bronze, and another for incense, made of wood and gold. Altars were also used to remind future generations of a particular event, like the one erected by Joshua as a monument to the tribes east of the Jordan to symbolize their unity with the rest of Israel. The altar in Jerusalem's Temple was originally built by Solomon, but was rebuilt and rededicated many times throughout Israel's history. However, altars weren't unique to Israel's religion – many ancient cultures used them to offer sacrifices to their gods. In fact, Paul records that Athens had so many altars that one was dedicated to an "unknown god" to make sure no deity was missed.

O. *Do not have an affair. – Exodus 20:14*

P. *Epithymeo* is Greek for "desire," "long," "crave" or "turn toward." However, in the context of desiring something that one cannot legitimately have, it corresponds to "**lust**" or "covet."

Q. *When a man takes and marries a wife, but she doesn't please his eyes because he finds something indecent with her, he can write a divorce certificate, hand it to her, and send her out of his house. – Deuteronomy 24:1*

R. The Greek *moicheuo* and the Hebrew *na'aph* are both traditionally translated "commit adultery," which refers to sex with another's spouse. Here they're translated "**have an affair**." In a broader sense, the Greek *porneia* ("**fornication**") is where the English "pornography" originates and refers to any illicit or immoral sex. In the Bible, this includes affairs, homosexuality, bestiality, and incest. Both terms were used as metaphors for idol worship.

S. *When you make a promise to the LORD your God, don't delay in completing it, because that would be sin and the LORD your God would certainly require it from you. But if you keep*

But I tell you, don't swear at all, either by heaven, because it's God's throne; by the earth, because it's the stool for his feet; or by Jerusalem, because it's the city of the great king. And don't swear by your head, because you can't make one hair white or black. Instead, let your words be 'Yes, yes' or 'No, no.'[t] Anything beyond that is evil.

"You've heard it said, 'An eye for an eye and a tooth for a tooth.'[u] But I tell you, don't resist someone who's evil. Whoever slaps your right cheek, turn your other one to him as well, and if anyone wants to sue you for your shirt, let him have your coat too. Whoever forces you to go one mile,[v] go two with him. Give to anyone who asks something from you, don't turn away from the one who wants to borrow from you, and don't demand what's yours back from someone who takes it.

"You've heard it said, 'Love your neighbor[w] and hate your enemy.' But I tell you, love your enemies, do good to those who hate you,[x] bless those who curse you, lend without expecting anything back, and pray for those who mistreat you,[y] so that you'll be sons of your Father – the Highest – who's in heaven. He makes his sun rise on the evil and the good, he sends rain on the righteous and the unrighteous, and he's kind to the ungrateful and the evil. So treat others how you want them to

---

yourself from promising, it wouldn't be sin. So be careful to do whatever comes out of our lips, because you've freely promised the LORD your God what you've said. – Deuteronomy 23:21-23

T. *Above all, my brothers, don't swear, either by heaven, by earth, or by any other oath. But your "yes" is "yes" and your "no" is "no," so you won't fall under judgment. – James 5:12*

U. *If a man strikes the life of any man, he'll certainly be killed. The one who strikes the life of an animal will make peace – life for life. If a man injures his neighbor, it'll be done to him just as he did – break for break, eye for eye, tooth for tooth. He'll be injured just as he injured a man. The one who strikes an animal will make peace, but the one who strikes a man will die. There's one judgment for you, for the stranger and the native, because I am the LORD your God. – Leviticus 24:17-22*

V. As the ruling power, Roman soldiers could legally force any civilian or their property (horse, mule, oxen, cart, boat) to carry their equipment at any time. This practice was called impressment (*angaria* in Greek). It was often used in the empire-wide postal service, where messengers could seize civilian horses if theirs were worn out. However, such a practice was easily abused and a limit of **one mile** was imposed to reduce hostility between soldiers and civilians.

W. *Do not hate your brother in your heart. You can certainly correct your neighbor, but you won't take on sin because of him. Don't take revenge or hold a grudge against the sons of your people, but you'll love your neighbor like yourself. I am the LORD. – Leviticus 19:17-18*

X. *If your enemy is hungry, feed him. If he's thirsty, give him a drink. And in doing this you'll pile up burning charcoal on his head. Don't be conquered by evil, but conquer evil with good. – Romans 12:20-12*

Y. *They stoned Stephen as he called out and said, "Lord Jesus, receive my spirit!" Then falling on his knees, he cried out with a loud voice, "Lord, don't hold this sin against them!" Saying this, he slept. – Acts 7:59-60*

treat you. What reward will you have if you only love those who love you? Don't tax collectors and sinners love those who love them? What extra are you doing if you only embrace your brothers? Don't the Gentiles do that? What grace[z] is it to be good to those who are good to you? Even sinners do that. And what grace is it if you only lend to those who'll pay you back? Sinners lend to sinners to get the same amount back. So be perfect, just like your heavenly Father is perfect. And be merciful,[z] just like your Father is merciful.

9.3 RELIGIOUS HYPOCRISY

Matthew 6:1-8, 16-18

"Be aware of acting righteously in front of men so they'll notice you, because then you won't have any reward with your Father in heaven. When you give to charity, don't have a trumpet blown before you like the hypocrites[a] do in the synagogues and in the streets so that men will honor them. I tell you truly that they have their reward. But when you give to charity, don't let your left know what your right is doing, so that your giving will be hidden. Then your Father, who sees what's hidden, will reward you.

"When you pray, don't be like the hypocrites, because they love to stand and pray in the synagogues and on the street corners for men to see. I tell you truly, they have their reward. But when you pray, go into your closet,[b] close the door, and pray to your Father who's hidden. And your Father, who sees what's hidden, will reward you.

"And when you pray, don't use repetitions[c] like the Gentiles, who think they'll be heard because of their many words. Don't be like them.

Z. Various theological definitions exist for **grace** and **mercy**. These are two of the simplest: grace (called "favor" in the Old Testament) is giving something good that is undeserved, such as donating to the poor; mercy is not giving something negative that is deserved, like refraining from penalizing a criminal. These definitions correlate with the context of many of their occurrences in the Bible, but not all.

A. Pretending to have certain virtues and morals without actually having them is hypocrisy, a form of deception. A **hypocrite** emphasizes the importance of righteousness and strives for that appearance, but fails to actually practice it. The term *hypokrites* comes from Greek theater, referring to an actor who wore a mask and imitated the speech and behavior of a particular character. It could also be translated "pretender" or "actor".

B. Many houses had inner rooms or **closets** to store goods. They were called *tameion* in Greek, which can also been translated "bedroom" or "secret room."

C. The Greek word *battalogeo* means "stutter" or "stammer," possibly originating from Battus, the king of Cyrene, who was said to have stuttered as a child. It could also refer to speaking in **repetitions** or babbling, related to prayers that were incessantly repeated. Finally,

Your Father knows what you need before you even ask him.

"When you fast, don't be gloomy like the hypocrites. They blemish their faces when they fast so they'll be noticed by men, and I tell you truly, they have their reward. But when you fast, anoint[d] your head and wash your face so your fasting won't be noticed by men, only by your Father in private. And your Father, who sees things in private, will reward you."

9.4 TRUE TREASURE | JUDGMENT

Matthew 6:19-21, 7:1-6
Luke 6:37-42

"Don't gather up treasures on earth, where moth and rust can destroy, and where thieves can dig in and steal. Instead, gather up treasures for yourselves in heaven, where moth[e] and rust can't destroy, and where thieves can't dig in and steal. Because wherever your treasure is, that's where your heart will be too.

"Don't judge, and you won't be judged. Don't condemn, and you won't be condemned. Release, and you'll be released. Give, and it'll be given to you – a beautiful amount will pour onto your chest,[f] pressed

---

battalogeo may imply prayers with unnecessarily long lists of words, to ensure the "right" words were spoken.

D. Ritually smearing with oil, milk, perfume, or water is called **anointing**, which is used by various religions to symbolize a special purpose. The Bible records that oil was used to ceremonially anoint priests and utensils for use in the Temple, which represented a spiritual anointment with God's Holy Spirit. It was also used to crown kings and commission prophets. Olive oil, in particular, was also used medicinally, anointed on the sick or wounded for healing. It could also be rubbed over the body as a means of refreshment, a common practice throughout ancient cultures. Anointing the head and washing the face were possibly part of the daily hygiene routine in first century Judea.

E. All **moths** start out as larvae. When moth eggs are laid on fabric, they hatch into larvae and eat the natural fibers (wool, silk) as they grow, leaving the clothing full of holes. They can also destroy agricultural crops with their vast appetites.

Moths were a symbol of destruction in the Bible. Hosea 5:12 records that God will be *"like a moth"* to his people, slowly and silently punishing them for their disobedience.

F. The Greek word *kolpos* refers to the **chest**. Clothes in that area formed a loose pouch overhanging the belt, which was used to collect and carry numerous smaller items, such as grain.

down, shaken together, and running over. Therefore, you'll be judged how you judge, and it'll be measured back to you how you measure."

He also told them a parable: "Can the blind guide the blind? Won't they both fall into a ditch? A disciples isn't above his teacher, but everyone will be like his teacher after he's completed.[g] Why do you look at the sliver in your brother's eye but don't notice the log in your own eye? Or how can you tell your brother, 'Brother, let me take that sliver out of your eye,' and look, you don't see the log in your own eye? You hypocrite, first take the log out of your own eye and then you'll see clearly to take the sliver out of your brother's eye.

"Don't give something holy to dogs. And don't throw your pearls before pigs, because they'll trample them underfoot, then turn and tear you apart."

9.5 NARROW ROAD | FALSE PROPHETS | OBEDIENCE

Matthew 7:13-29, 8:1
Luke 6:43-44, 46-49

"Go in through the narrow gate. Destruction has a wide gate and a broad road that leads to it, and many go in through it. But life has a small gate and a narrow road that leads to it, and few ever find it.

"Be aware of false prophets. They come to you in sheep's clothing, but on the inside they're ravenous wolves. You'll know them by their fruit. Are grapes gathered from thorns or figs harvested from bushes?[h] No, every good tree produces good fruit, and bad trees produce bad fruit. A good tree can't produce bad fruit and similarly a bad tree can't produce good fruit. Every tree that doesn't produce good fruit is cut down and thrown into the fire. So you'll know them by their fruit, just like each tree is known by its fruit.

"Why do you call me, 'Lord, Lord,' but don't do what I say? Not everyone who calls me that will get into the kingdom of heaven, but only the one who does the will of my Father in heaven. On that day, many will tell me, 'Lord, Lord, didn't we prophesy in your name, throw out demons in your name, and do many miracles in your name?'[i]

G. *Katartizo* is a Greek verb meaning "prepare," "**complete**," or "perfect." Matthew uses this term to describe fishermen mending their nets, and so making them fit for work again. In the sense of a student, it can mean "mature" or "graduated," having completed one's training.

H. *My brothers, can a fig produce olives or a vine produce figs? – James 3:12*

But I'll tell them, 'I never knew you. Leave me, you who act lawlessly.'[j]

"Everyone who comes to me, hears my words, and does them, I'll show you what he's like: he's a wise man building a house, who dug deep and set its foundation on the rock. Then the rain fell and a flood occurred. But even when rivers came and the winds blew, and both slammed against the house, they couldn't shake it. It didn't fall because it had been well built, founded on the rock. But everyone who hears my words and doesn't do them is like a foolish man who built his house on the sand, without any foundation. The rain fell, the rivers came, the winds blew, and they slammed against it. Then immediately the house collapsed, and its ruin was massive."

When Jesus had finished saying this, the crowds were blown away at his teaching, because he was teaching them with authority, not like their scribes. And when he came down from the mountain, many crowds followed him.

I. *Become doers of the word, not only hearers who deceive themselves. – James 1:22*

J. *Leave me, all of you trouble makers, because the LORD has heard the voice of my weeping. – Psalm 6:8*

CHAPTER 10

Authority and Repentance

10.1 CENTURION'S SERVANT HEALED

Matthew 8:5-13
Luke 7:1-10

When Jesus had finished all his speaking for the people to hear, he went to Capernaum. Now a centurion's favorite slave was sick and about to die. So when he heard about Jesus' arrival, he sent some Jewish elders, asking him to come and save his slave's life, saying, "Lord, my servant is lying paralyzed at home, in terrible distress."

When they came to Jesus, they called him urgently, saying, "He deserves your help because he loves our nation. He was the one who built us our synagogue."

"I'll come and heal him," Jesus replies.

So Jesus travelled with them. When he wasn't far from the house, the centurion sent friends to tell him, "Lord, don't trouble yourself. I'm not worthy for you to come under my roof, which is why I wasn't even worthy to come to you myself. But just say the word and my servant will be healed. I'm a man placed under authority too, with soldiers under me. I tell one to go and he goes, and another to come and he comes. And to my slave, 'Do this,' and he does it."

The Roman Centurion

Roman armies were called legions, consisting of about 5000 soldiers and officers, most of whom were Roman citizens. Each legion was divided into cohorts, the basic functional unit of the Roman military. A cohort had 400-600 soldiers further divided into six centuries of 80-100 men each. Each century was commanded by a **centurion**, with the most senior centurion also commanding the cohort. Units of cavalry and light infantry supported the main force of heavy infantry.

Each soldier carried a long spear (*hasta, pilum*) and a large curved rectangular shield (*scutum*) over a meter tall. A short sword (*gladius*) was carried as a secondary weapon. Armor consisted of overlapping strips of metal over the torso (*lorica segmenta*), a helmet with cheek plates (*galea*), and greaves over the shins.

The Romans fought in a phalanx formation, where multiple rows of soldiers moved forward as a single unit, constantly pushing on and crushing the opposing force. Overlapping shields provided protection from enemy weapons, while spears held overhead and thrust downward made short work of the enemies themselves. Roman legions were highly disciplined and trained, and they were considered the most deadly military force of their time.

When Jesus heard this, he was amazed and told the crowd following him, "Truly I tell you, I haven't found such great faith in anyone in Israel! I tell you that many will come from east and west to recline with Abraham, Isaac, and Jacob in the kingdom of heaven. But the sons of the kingdom will be thrown into the darkness outside, where there will be weeping and teeth grinding."

Then Jesus told the centurion, "Go. It'll be done for you just as you've believed."

The servant was healed that very hour, and when the messengers returned to the house, they found him healthy.

10.2 WIDOW'S SON RESURRECTED

Luke 7:11-17

Next he went to a city called Nain.[a] His disciples went with him, as well as a big crowd. As he approached the city gate, someone who had died was being carried out, the only son of his mother, who was also a widow.[b] A considerable crowd from the city was with her too. When the Lord saw her, he was moved for her and told her, "Don't cry."

Then he came up and touched the coffin, and the pallbearers stood still. He said, "Young man, I tell you, get up!"

Then the dead man sat up and began to speak. Jesus gave him back to his mother. Fear gripped them all and they praised God, saying, "A great prophet has risen among us!" and, "God has visited his people!"

News about him spread through all Judea and all the surrounding area.

10.3 JOHN'S QUESTIONS

Matthew 11:2-19
Luke 7:18-35

John's disciples reported all of this to him while he was in prison. When John heard of all Christ's work, he called two of his disciples and sent them to the Lord, saying, "Are you the one coming or should we look for another?"

When the men arrived, they said, "John the Baptizer sent us to ask you, 'Are you the one coming or should we look for another?'"

At that time, he had been healing many diseases, hardships, and evil spirits, and he gave sight to many of the blind. "Go and report to John what you see and hear," he answered them. "The blind get their sight, the lame walk, the lepers are cleaned, the deaf hear,[c] the dead are raised,

A. **Nain** was a Galilean village 14 kilometers south of Nazareth. Although it remains to this day, little is known about its history.

B. In ancient times, the husband was the sole provider of the household, whose death could mean poverty for any family left behind. **Widows**, therefore, had nobody to care for them if they remained unmarried and didn't have an adult son. Thus they were some of the poorest people in Israel. Moses' Law held that widows, orphans, and other poor foreigners could legally gather what was left in fields after the harvesters were finished, since they often had no other means to provide for themselves.

C. *The eyes of the blind will be opened and the ears of the deaf will be cleared. The cripple will jump like a deer and the tongue of the mute will rejoice. – Isaiah 35:5-6*

There are a number of **Messianic Scriptures** in the Old Testament, referring to the Messiah that would deliver Israel from her enemies. Because these Scriptures were likely

and the poor get good news. Whoever isn't tripped up because of me is blessed."

After John's messengers left, he spoke to the crowds about John, "What did you go out into the wilderness to see? A reed shaken by the wind? Well then, what did you go out to see? A man softly dressed?[d] Those who wear fancy clothes and live in luxury are in royal palaces! But what did you go out to see? A prophet? Yes, I tell you, even more than a prophet! This is the one who was written about:

> 'Look, I send my messenger before you, who'll prepare your way ahead of you.'[e]

Truly I tell you, no one is greater than John the Baptizer among all those born by women, but even the smallest in God's kingdom is greater than he is. From the days of John the Baptizer until now, the kingdom of heaven is forced upon and strong men seize it for themselves. All the prophets and the Law prophesied until John, and, if you want to accept it, John is the Elijah[f] who was coming. Whoever has ears to hear, listen up!"

When all the people and the tax collectors heard, they justified God, having been baptized with John's baptism. But the Pharisees and the lawyers rejected God's purpose for themselves, not having been baptized by him.

"What will I compare the men of this generation to? What are they like? They're like children sitting in the market, calling to others, saying, 'We played the flute[g] for you, but you didn't dance. We mourned, but you didn't cry.' John the Baptizer came not eating bread and not drinking wine and you say, 'He has a demon!' Then the Son of

---

well known, it's possible that the Jews would have understood Jesus' quotation of this Scripture about himself to be an assertion that he was the Messiah.

D. *Malakos* is Greek for "soft." In reference to clothing, "**softly dressed**" likely meant wearing luxurious or fancy clothing. However, in reference to a man, it negatively suggested he had a delicate or feminine character, particularly emphasizing his weakness, cowardice, or homosexuality.

E. *"Look, I'm going to send my messenger to clear the way ahead of me. Then the Lord you seek will suddenly come to his Temple. Look, the messenger of the covenant, the one you enjoy – he's coming!" says the LORD of armies. – Malachi 3:1*

F. *Look, I'm going to send Elijah the prophet to you before the great and fearful day of the LORD comes. – Malachi 4:5*

G. Similar to their modern equivalents, early **flutes** were wind instruments that made shrill, high-pitched sounds. They were made of various materials, such as silver, wood, bone, or reeds. Flutes and other wind instruments are mentioned in the Old Testament as far back as Jubal, a descendant of Cain, who was noted as the father of harp and flute players.

Man came eating and drinking and you say, 'Look, a glutton and a drunk! A friend of tax collectors and sinners!' However, wisdom is justified by her actions and all her children."

10.4 WOE TO CHORAZIN AND BETHSAIDA

Matthew 11:20-30
Luke 10:13-15

Then he began to criticize the cities where most of his miracles had been done, because they didn't repent. "Woe, Chorazin![h] Woe, Bethsaida! If the miracles that have happened in you had happened in Tyre and Sidon, they would've repented and sat in sackcloth and ashes long ago. So I tell you, it'll be better for Tyre and Sidon on the judgment day than for you. And Capernaum, will you be lifted up into heaven? No, you'll descend into hell! Because if the miracles that have happened in you had happened in Sodom, it would've remained until today. So I tell you that it'll be better for the land of Sodom on the judgment day than for you."

During that time Jesus said, "Father, I praise you, the Lord of heaven and earth! You've hidden this from the wise and the educated, but you've shown it to babies. Yes, Father, because this way looked good to you.

"My Father has given me everything, and no one knows the Son except the Father. Nor does anyone know the Father except the Son and anyone the Son wants to show.

"Come to me, anyone who's exhausted and weighed down![i] I'll rest you. Take my yoke[j] on yourself and learn from me, because I'm meek

H. Ruins are all that remain of **Chorazin**, a prominent town north of the Sea of Galilee. Its synagogue, in particular, was impressive compared to others in the area.

I. *Throw your burden on the LORD and he'll hold you. He'll never let the righteous be moved. –Psalm 55:22a*

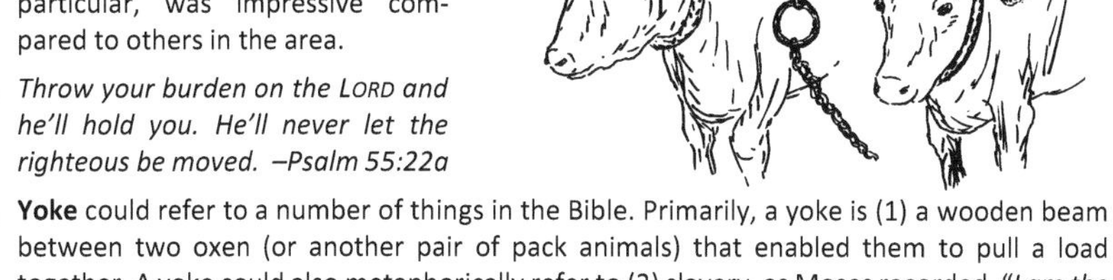

J. **Yoke** could refer to a number of things in the Bible. Primarily, a yoke is (1) a wooden beam between two oxen (or another pair of pack animals) that enabled them to pull a load together. A yoke could also metaphorically refer to (2) slavery, as Moses recorded, *"I am the LORD your God, who brought you out of Egypt's land so you wouldn't be their slaves. I broke the bars of your yoke, making you walk upright." (Leviticus 26:13)* Finally, it was used in Judea to represent (3) a teacher's instruction, so that taking on your teacher's yoke was analogous to adopting his teaching as your own and becoming his disciple.

Tyre and Sidon

North of Israel, on the coast of the Mediterranean Sea, is the Phoenician city of **Tyre**. During the Greek and Roman empires, it was a wealthy and prominent sea port along the coast, with its ships dominating trade and establishing colonies throughout the Mediterranean. Tyre was easily defended: half of the city lay on an island, while the other half was on the mainland, surrounded by mountains and cliffs to the east.

Farther north along the coast was **Sidon**, another prominent port city. It was built on the coastal plains of Canaan, connected to several small islands by bridges. Sidon was repeatedly conquered and destroyed throughout its history, but restored to prominence after each defeat.

Both Tyre and Sidon had reputations for immorality, pride, and idol worship, and consequently they were the target of numerous judgments by Old Testament prophets. The prophet Joel condemned them for plundering the Jews and selling them as slaves after the Babylonians captured Jerusalem. Since they were on the Mediterranean coast, they were heavily influenced by Greek religion and culture. Both cities were compared to the immoral ancient cities of Sodom and Gomorrah.

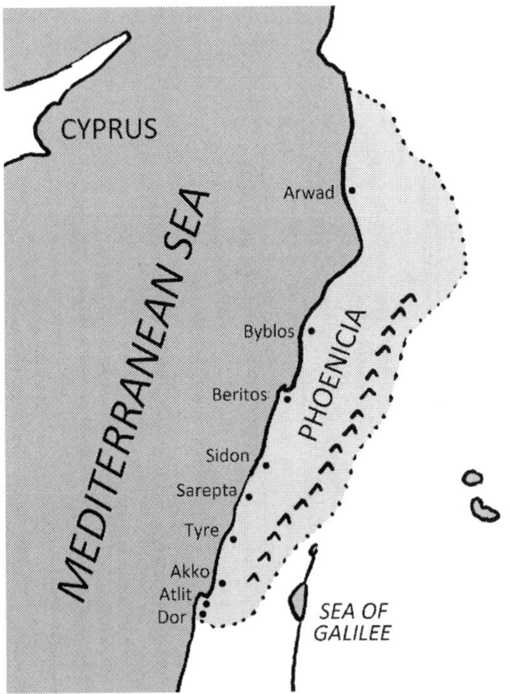

Genesis 19 records that Abraham's nephew Lot settled in the fertile Jordan Valley of southern Canaan near the Dead Sea, away from his uncle so their flocks wouldn't overcrowd each other. There were five cities in that valley – **Sodom**, Gomorrah, Admah, Zeboiim, and Zoar – that were so evil and devoid of good men that, according to the Bible, God determined to destroyed them. But before their destruction, God sent two angels, appearing as men, to rescue Lot and his family. While staying with Lot in Sodom, men from the city stormed the house and demanded the release of Lot's two guests so they could rape them. But just before they broke down the door, the angels miraculously blinded the Sodomites, preventing them from finding the house. The next morning, the angels instructed Lot and his family to escape the city and not look back. Then, shortly after their departure, God rained fiery sulfur (also called brimstone) down on the cities. Unfortunately, Lot's wife didn't heed the angels' advice and was transformed into a salt pillar when she looked back at the destruction, but Lot and his two daughters escaped safely to Zoar. The entire valley was full of smoke the next day and all but one of the cities – Zoar – was completely destroyed. The destruction of Sodom and Gomorrah is referred to in the Bible as an example of God's judgment on immorality.

and humble in my heart. You'll find rest for your souls.[k] My yoke is easy and my burden is light."

10.5 SINFUL WOMAN ANOINTS JESUS' FEET

Luke 7:36-50

One of the Pharisees invited Jesus to eat with him, so he went into the Pharisee's house and reclined. There was a woman in the city who was a sinner, and when she found out he was reclining in the Pharisee's house, she brought perfume in alabaster.[l] Standing behind him at his feet and weeping, she wet his feet with her tears and wiped them with the hair of her head. Then she kissed his feet and anointed them with perfume. When the Pharisee who had invited him saw this, he said to himself, "If this man was a prophet, he'd know who and what this woman is who's touching him, that she's a sinner."

"Simon," Jesus answered him, "I have something to tell you."

"Say it, Teacher," he says.

"A moneylender had two borrowers: one owed 500 denarii[m] and the other owed 50. When neither one could pay him back, he forgave them both. Now which of them will love him more?"

"I suppose the one who had more forgiven," Simon answered.

"You've judged correctly," he replied. Then turning toward the woman, he told Simon, "Do you see this woman? I came into your house and you didn't give me any water for my feet, but she has wet my feet with her tears and wiped them with her hair. You didn't give me a kiss,

K. *The LORD says this: "Stand by the road. See and ask for the ancient paths where the good road is and walk in it. Then you'll find rest for your souls." –Jeremiah 6:16a*

L. The Greek word for "**perfume**" or "ointment" was *myron*, likely referring to the aromatic resin myrrh.

Alabaster is a soft, semi-transparent white stone that was commonly carved into sculptures or ornaments. Alabaster could refer to two similar types of stone: gypsum (calcium sulphate), which was modern alabaster, relatively soft, and easily scratched; and calcite (calcium carbonate), which was ancient alabaster and much harder. Alabaster was highly valued for making small bottles, vases, jars, bowls, lamps, statues, or vials. Because of its translucency, it could also be used as a window if cut thin enough. Alabaster was extensively mined in Egypt and the Jordan Valley. Alabaster jars typically had long necks and were sealed closed. To access the contents, jars had to be broken open, and therefore could not be reused.

M. The most common coin in Roman currency was the **denarius** (denarii plural). It was a small silver coin that circulated from 211 BC until 270 AD. The name translates to "containing ten," meaning it was the same value as ten asses (the *as* or *assarion* was a bronze Roman coin). One denarius was typically paid as the daily wage for unskilled labor.

but she hasn't stopped kissing my feet since I came in. You didn't anoint my head with oil, but she has anointed my feet with perfume. Because of this – that she loved much – I tell you that her sins, which are numerous, have been forgiven. But whoever is forgiven little, loves little."

Then he told her, "Your sins are forgiven."

Those reclining with him said to themselves, "Who is this that even forgives sins?"

"Your faith[n] has saved you," he told the woman. "Go in peace."

N. *Faith is the foundation of what's hoped for and the proof of what's not seen. By this, the elders witnessed. By faith, we understand the worlds were completed by God's word, so what's seen wasn't made out of what's visible.... And without faith, it's impossible to please him, because whoever comes to God must believe that he is and that he becomes the payer of those who search for him. – Hebrews 11:1-3,6*

CHAPTER 11

Disbelief

11.1 WOMEN FOLLOWERS

Luke 8:1-3

After that, he went throughout the cities and villages, proclaiming and preaching God's kingdom. The Twelve were with him, as well as some women who had been healed of evil spirits and sickness: Mary, called Magdalene, who had seventy demons leave her; Joanna, the wife of Chuza, Herod's manager;[a] Susanna; and many others who were supporting them however they could.

11.2 ACCUSATIONS AND BLASPHEMY

Matthew 12:22-37, 43-45
Mark 3:20-30
Luke 6:45; 11:14-15, 17-28; 12:10

Then he comes home and such a crowd gathers again that they couldn't even eat a meal. When his relatives heard about it, they went out to get him, saying, "He's insane."

A. *Epitropos* is a Greek word from *epi* ("on" or "over") and *tropos* ("manner" or "way"). It referred to a **manager** or steward, who was put in charge of managing another's household.

But a demonized man, who was also blind and deaf, was brought to Jesus. He healed him and threw out the demon, so that when the demon left, the deaf man spoke and saw. All the crowds were amazed, saying, "Could this be the son of David?"[b]

But when the scribes and the Pharisees who had come down from Jerusalem heard about it, they said, "This man throws out demons only by the ruler of demons. He's possessed by Beelzebul."[c]

Knowing their thoughts, Jesus called them to himself and spoke in parables: "How can Satan[c] throw out Satan? Every kingdom divided against itself is destroyed and every city or house divided against itself won't stand. If Satan throws out Satan, if he rises up against himself and is divided, how will his kingdom stand? He can't stand – he'll be finished! And if I throw out demons by Beelzebul, the ruler of demons, like you say I do, who do your sons throw them out by? This is why they'll be your judges. But if I throw out demons by the finger and the Spirit of God, then God's kingdom has come to you.

"How can anyone enter the house of the strong and steal his possessions unless he ties the strong one up first? Only then will he rob his house. When someone strong and armed guards his own house, his possessions won't move. But when someone stronger comes and conquers him, he strips away the armor he depended on and divides the plunder. Whoever isn't with me is against me, and whoever doesn't gather with me scatters.

"Truly I tell you, every sin of the sons of men will be forgiven, and also any blasphemies or words they speak against the Son of Man. But

---

B. The Old Testament records that God promised David that he would never lack a person to sit on Israel's throne, and it was expected that the coming Messiah would fulfill this prophecy. Thus the term "**son of David**" became synonymous with the Messiah, who would be a direct descendant of David and come from his hometown, Bethlehem.

A boy will be born to us and a son will be given to us. The government will be upon his shoulder. His name will be called Wonderful, Counselor, Mighty, God, Eternal, Father, Prince of Peace. His dominion and his peace will never stop increasing, on David's throne and over his kingdom, to establish and sustain it with justice and righteousness from now to eternity. The passion of the LORD of armies will do this. – Isaiah 9:6-7

C. The name **Satan** means "obstructer" or "adversary" and is one letter different from the Hebrew word for "hate" or "oppose" (*satam*). In the Bible, Satan is also called the Devil, which comes from the Greek *diabolos* meaning "slanderer," and **Beelzebul**, which means "lord of the flies." In first century Judea, Satan was understood to be the ruler of all demons, in constant opposition to God. He first appears in Genesis as a snake who convinces the first woman, Eve, to eat from a forbidden tree, which leads to human banishment from Eden and various curses on the earth. Satan also appears in the book of Job as an accuser before God. Finally, in the prophetic book of Revelation, he's depicted as a dragon who will ultimately be thrown into a fiery lake to suffer for eternity.

whoever blasphemes or speaks against the Holy Spirit[d] will never be forgiven, not in this age or the next, because he's guilty of an eternal sin." – since they said he had an unclean spirit.

"Either make the tree good and its fruit good, or make the tree bad and its fruit bad, because the tree is known by its fruit. The good man brings good out of the good treasure of his heart, while the evil man brings evil out of evil. You pit of vipers![e] How can you, being evil, say good things? The mouth speaks from whatever fills the heart. I tell you that people will be accountable on the judgment day for every careless word they say, because you'll be justified by your words and you'll also be condemned by your words.

"Now when an unclean spirit leaves a man, it goes through dry places looking for rest, but it doesn't find any. Then it says, 'I'll go back to the house I came from.' When it arrives, it finds it empty, swept, and tidied. Then it goes and takes seven other spirits more wicked than itself and they all go in and live there. In the end, the man is worse off than he was in the beginning. That's how it'll be with this evil generation."

While he was saying this, one of the women in the crowd raised her voice and said, "Blessed is the womb that bore you and the breasts that nursed you."

"On the contrary," he said, "blessed are those who hear God's word and keep it."

D. It's unclear what exactly **blasphemy against the Holy Spirit** is and also what is meant by this concept of unforgiveable sin. Jesus seemed to suggest that it's attributing God's work to Satan. While later in the New Testament, the book of Hebrews says that it's impossible for those who have experienced salvation and the Holy Spirit, and then willfully rejected him, to be saved again. It's a subject of debate among theologians.

E. All snakes from the *Viperidae* family, called vipers or adders, are venomous. Upon biting, their long hinged fangs deliver venom deep into their prey, which paralyzes muscles and destroys tissue on contact. Although the majority of snakes in Judea were not venomous, multiple species of viper were native to the area.

Because snakes are ectothermic (cold-blooded), they need to absorb heat from external sources, such as the sun. But in the winter, when outside temperatures are fatal to snakes, they hibernate in groups until spring. A hibernaculum is the site of dozens of sleeping snakes, typically underground in crevices, caves, or pits. Stepping in such a **pit of vipers** would lead to dozens of lethal viper bites.

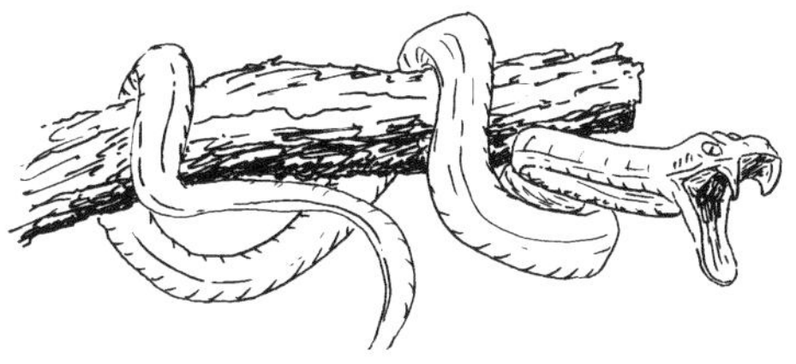

11.3 SIGN REQUESTED

Matthew 12:38-42
Luke 11:16, 29-32

Some of the scribes and the Pharisees were demanding a miracle from heaven to test him, saying, "Teacher, we want to see a sign from you."

But as the crowds were increasing, he answered, "This is an evil and immoral generation. It wants a sign, but no sign will be given except the sign of Jonah the prophet. Just as Jonah became a sign to the Ninevites and was in the belly of the sea monster for three days and three nights, the Son of Man will be in the heart of the earth for three days and three nights for this generation. The men of Nineveh will stand up with this generation at the judgment and condemn it, because they repented at Jonah's preaching, but look, something better than Jonah is here. The Queen of the South will rise up with the men of this generation at the judgment and condemn them, because she came from the ends of the earth to hear the wisdom of Solomon, but look, something better than Solomon is here."

Jonah and the Queen of Sheba

At the peak of Assyria's power, the Bible records that God instructed an Israelite prophet named **Jonah** to travel east to Nineveh, Assyria's massive capital city, to warn them of their impending judgment and destruction for their wickedness. Instead, Jonah ran in the opposite direction, boarding a ship heading west to Tarshish (possibly the city of Tartessus in what is now Spain).

At sea, a fierce storm arose and all the men on board appealed to their gods for salvation, except for Jonah, who was asleep below deck. The crew knew he was running from God and asked him how to stop the storm. Jonah replied, *"Pick me up and throw me into the sea. Then the sea will calm down, because I know this great storm is because of me." (Jonah 1:12)* They reluctantly complied, and once he was overboard, the storm instantly abated. Jonah was subsequently swallowed by a large sea creature and he miraculously lived in its belly for three days before being vomited out onto dry land. Repentant, Jonah journeyed to Nineveh and proclaimed their coming destruction, which was well-received. In fact, the whole city repented and was saved.

However, Jonah's story ends with his embitterment towards God for sparing Israel's enemy from destruction, since Assyria would go on to invade and conquer the northern kingdom of Israel years later as an instrument of God's judgment. Jonah's story is recorded in the biblical book that bears his name.

During Solomon's reign, at the peak of Israel's power and wealth, the **Queen of Sheba**, a kingdom in southwest Arabia, visited him after hearing reports of his wisdom and prosperity. She toured the whole kingdom, heard Solomon's words firsthand, and lavished him with gifts, leaving thoroughly impressed with is wisdom, wealth, and splendor.

11.4 SPIRITUAL FAMILY

Matthew 12:46-50
Mark 3:31-35
Luke 8:19-21

While he was talking to the crowds, look, his mother and brothers arrive, wanting to talk to him. But they couldn't get to him because of the crowd sitting around him, so they sent for him as they stood outside.

"Look," someone tells him, "your mother and brothers are standing outside looking for you, wanting to talk to you."

But he answers the speaker, "Who's my mother and who are my brothers?" Then looking at his disciples sitting around him and stretching out his hand towards them he says, "Look, my mother and brothers! Whoever hears the will of God (my Father in heaven) and does it, he is my brother and sister and mother."

CHAPTER 12

Parables

12.1 PARABLE OF SOILS

Matthew 13:1-23
Mark 4:1-25
Luke 8:4-18

That day, Jesus left the house, sat by the sea, and began to teach again. Travelling there from the cities, so many crowds gathered around him that he got into a boat on the sea and sat down while the all the crowds stood on the shore. He taught them much in parables, saying, "Listen! Look, a sower went out to sow[a] his seed. As he sowed, some fell beside the road, where they were trampled and the birds of the sky came and ate them up. Others fell on the rock, where they didn't have much soil. They sprang up immediately but didn't have depth; after the sun rose, they were scorched and withered away because they didn't have roots or moisture. Others fell among thorns, but the thorns grew

A. Before modern farming machinery, fields were **sown** by hand in ancient Judea. The ground was first broken up with a plow pulled by pack animals, such as oxen or horses. Plowing was labor intensive, but essential to crop growth: turning over the soil aerated it and brought fresh nutrients to the surface, while burying rubble left over from the previous season. Seed was then scattered (sown) over the prepared ground. Harrowing then smoothed out the rough clumps of dirt produced by the plow and buried the seed. Finally, after a season's growth, the mature grain was harvested.

up with them and choked them out, so they didn't produce a crop. Yet others, which fell on good soil, increased as they grew up, producing a crop, some 100, some 60, and some 30."

As he said these things, he would call out, "Whoever has ears, listen up!"

Later, when he was alone, his twelve disciples and those with him asked what this parable meant. They also asked, "Why do you talk to them in parables?"

"You've been allowed to know the mysteries of the kingdom of heaven," Jesus answered, "but they haven't been allowed. Those outside get everything in parables, because more will be given to the one who has, so he'll have plenty. But for the one who doesn't have, even what he has will be taken away. So I talk to them in parables because while seeing, they don't see, and while hearing, they don't hear or understand. Isaiah's prophecy is fulfilled in them, which says,

> 'You'll keep hearing, but you won't understand. You'll keep seeing, but you won't know. Because the heart of this people has become dense; they barely hear with their ears and they've closed their eyes. Otherwise they'd see with their eyes, hear with their ears, and understand with their heart and return, and I'd heal them.'[b]

"But your eyes are blessed because they see, and your ears because they hear. I tell you truly that many prophets and righteous men wanted to see what you see, but didn't get to see, and to hear what you hear, but didn't get to hear.

"Don't you understand this parable?" he asks them. "How then will you understand any of the parables? Therefore hear the parable of the sower: the sower sows the seed of God's word. The ones beside the road where the seed is sown are those who hear the word of the kingdom, but they don't understand it. Satan[c] comes immediately and takes away the word sown in their hearts so they won't believe and be saved. Similarly, the ones in the rocky places where the seed was sown

B. *Go and tell this people, "Keep listening, but don't understand. Keep looking, but don't know. Make these people's hearts fat, their ears dense, and their eyes blind. Or else they might see with their eyes, hear with their ears and understand with their hearts, and then return and be healed." – Isaiah 6:9-10*

C. In Jesus' parable of the sower, Mark records that **Satan** takes away the seed sown by the road; Luke records it as the Devil, while Matthew simply says that Evil does it. These are all referring to the same spiritual being.

are those who hear the word and immediately receive it with joy. They believe for a while, but they're temporary, without any root in themselves. When trouble or persecution or temptation comes because of the word, they immediately fall away too. The ones among the thorns where the seed was sown are those who've heard the word, but as they go on their way, the worries of the world, the deception of wealth, the desire for other things, and the pleasures of life enter in and choke the word, and it doesn't bring fruit to maturity. But the ones in the good soil where the seed was sown are those who hear the word in honest and good hearts. They accept it, understand it, and hold onto it. They will certainly bear fruit with perseverance, some 100, some 60, and some 30."

And he told them, "Is a lamp brought out to be put under a basket or a jar, or under a bed? Instead, it's put on a lampstand so that those who come in can see the light. Because there's nothing hidden that won't become known, nor is there a secret that won't come to light. Therefore, see that you listen, because whoever has, more will be given to him. And whoever doesn't have, even what he thinks he has will be removed from him. So if anyone has ears to hear, listen up!"

12.2 PARABLES OF SEEDS AND YEAST

Matthew 13:24-35
Mark 4:26-34
Luke 13:18-21

Then he said, "God's kingdom is like this: a man throws seed upon the ground; he goes to bed at night and gets up by day, and the seed sprouts and grows, but he doesn't know how. The soil produces crops by itself – first the grass, then the grain, then the ripe kernel within the grain. But when the crop allows it, he immediately sends out the sickle,[d] because the harvest has arrived."

He presented another parable to them, saying, "The kingdom of heaven is like a man who sowed good seed in his field, but while his men were sleeping, his enemy came and sowed weeds[e] among the

D. Crops in first century Judea were harvested by hand using a **sickle**. Various shapes and sizes have been employed throughout history to slice through stalks of grain. Most were made of metal (typically iron), with either a smooth or serrated curved blade on the inner edge.

E. The **weeds** mentioned in the Bible are represented by the Greek word *zizanion*, often translated "tares." The plant itself is a species of ryegrass or darnel (genus *Lolium*) that closely resembles wheat, but produces black seed instead of the yellow grain of wheat. Although ryegrass is good for livestock, it's considered a weed, because it produces a toxic grain unfit for human consumption.

wheat, then left. When the wheat sprouted and produced grain, the weeds appeared too. Then the landlord's slaves came and told him, 'Sir, didn't you sow good seed in your field? So where did the weeds come from?' 'An enemy has done this!' he replied. Then the slaves ask, 'Do you want us to go and gather them up?' 'No,' he says, 'because while you're gathering up the weeds, you might uproot the wheat with them. Let them both grow up together until the harvest. At the harvest I'll tell the reapers to gather up the weeds first and tie them in bundles to burn, and then gather the wheat into my barn.'"

He presented yet another parable, saying, "What is God's kingdom like? What parable can we illustrate it with and what can I compare it to? The kingdom of heaven is like a mustard seed[f] that a man took and threw in his field. Even though it's smaller than all the seeds that are sown into the soil, it's bigger than any vegetable and becomes a tree with huge branches when it's fully grown. Then the birds of the air come and stay in its branches and in its shade."[g]

And he told them another parable, "What can I compare God's kingdom to? It's like yeast that a woman took and hid in three measures of flour[h] until it had all risen."

Jesus told all this to the crowds in parables, and he spoke the word in many parables just like these, according to their ability to hear. In

---

F. One of the smallest seeds of ancient agriculture was from the mustard plant, measuring about 2 mm in diameter. The plants have long, weedy stems with broad leaves and yellow flowers. They were sown and harvested annually, but over many seasons a single plant could grow over three meters (ten feet) tall. **Mustard seeds** were used as a condiment, as they are today, by grinding them and combining the powder with water or vinegar. The mustard plant of first century Judea was likely black mustard (*Brassica nigra*), which grew wild in the fields and along the roads of Palestine.

G. *The Lord God says this: "I'll take the treetop of a high cedar and set it down; I'll pluck off the top of a tender shoot and plant it on a high and lofty mountain. On a mountain in the heights of Israel I'll plant it and it'll produce branches, bear fruit, and become a majestic cedar. All the birds of every wing will nest in the shadow of its branches." – Ezekiel 17:22-23*

The tree you saw that grew big and strong – whose height reached the sky and was visible to the whole world, and whose leaves were beautiful and fruit plentiful, which was food for everyone; the field animals lived under it and the birds of the sky lived in its branches – this is you, O king. You've grown big and strong, and your greatness has become great, reaching the sky, and your sovereignty to the end of the earth. – Daniel 4:20-22

H. There's some discrepancy around exactly how much **three measures of flour** was. The Greek word *saton* and Hebrew word *seah* both translate to "measure" or "peck" and are thought to be about 6-7 liters. Three measures, therefore, was about 20 liters, likely the maximum amount of flour a woman could bake with at one time. Such a huge quantity of bread would produce dozens of loaves and feed over 100 people. The amount occurs only one other time in the Bible: in Genesis 18, when Abraham was visited by three angels, he told his wife Sarah to prepare three measures of flour for them, far more than they could eat alone.

fact, he didn't speak to them without a parable, fulfilling what was spoken through the prophet: "I'll open my mouth in parables. I'll say things hidden since the foundation of the world."[i]

But he explained everything privately to his disciples.

12.3 PARABLE OF SEEDS EXPLAINED | MORE PARABLES OF THE KINGDOM

Matthew 13:36-53

Then he left the crowds and went into the house. His disciples came and said, "Explain the parable about the weeds of the field to us."

So he told them, "The one who sows the good seed is the Son of Man and the field is the world. The good seeds are the sons of the kingdom, while the weeds are the sons of evil. The enemy who sowed them is the Devil, the harvest is the end of time, and the reapers are angels. Just like weeds that are gathered up and burned with fire, so it'll be at the end of time. The Son of Man will send out his angels and they'll gather every snare out of his kingdom, with those who practice anarchy,[j] and will throw them into the fiery furnace, where there will be weeping and teeth grinding.[k] Then the righteous will shine like the sun[l] in their Father's kingdom. Whoever has ears, listen up!

"The kingdom of heaven is like a treasure hidden in a field that a man found and hid again. And because of his happiness over it, he goes and sells all he has and buys the field.

"Again, the kingdom of heaven is like a merchant looking for fine pearls.[m] Upon finding an exceptionally valuable pearl, he went and sold all he had and bought it.

I. *My people, listen to my instruction. Stretch out your ears to the words from my mouth. I'll open my mouth in a parable and I'll pour out ancient riddles that we've heard and known, which our fathers told us. We won't hide them from their children, but we'll tell the coming generation about the LORD's praises, his strength, and the wonders he has done. – Psalm 78:1-4*

J. **Anarchy** is the absence of governmental rule or law. The Greek word, *anomia*, represented this concept, which could also be translated "lawlessness."

K. In Judea during the first century, **teeth grinding** or gnashing was as an expression of extreme anguish or despair, particularly referring to the agony of hell.

L. *Those with understanding will shine like the sky, and those who bring many to righteousness like the stars forever and ever. – Daniel 12:3*

M. When an irritant gets inside the shell of certain mollusks, a pearl sac is created to seal it off. Concentric layers of calcium carbonate (the same material the shell is made of) are deposited, gradually producing a smooth-surfaced **pearl**. Oysters, clams, and mussels all

"And again, the kingdom of heaven is like a net thrown into the sea, gathering up every kind of fish. When it was full, they pulled it up onto the beach and sat down to gather the good ones into containers, but the bad ones they threw away. So it'll be at the end of time: angels will come and separate the wicked from among the righteous and they'll throw them into the fiery furnace, where there will be weeping and teeth grinding. Have you understood this?"

"Yes," they say.

"Therefore," he told them, "every scribe who has become a disciple of the kingdom of heaven is like a home owner who brings new and old things out of his treasury."

When Jesus had finished these parables, he went away from there.

react this way in response to parasites that embed themselves inside the shell. Contrary to popular belief, grains of sand almost never produce such a reaction if stuck in the shell. Natural pearls are very rare, occurring in less than one percent of capable mollusks, which consequently made them very valuable as ornaments and jewels in ancient times. Pearl divers harvested oysters by hand from the ocean floor and river bottoms around the Persian Gulf, Red Sea, and Indian Ocean, and each one was checked individually for pearls. From there, merchants sold them at extraordinary prices around the world. Pearls are rarely mentioned in the Bible, but most notably appear in Revelation, where John records a vision in which he saw a new Jerusalem – the future city of God – with twelve gates each made of a single massive pearl.

Chapter 13

Across the Sea and Back Again

13.1 Storm Calmed

Matthew 8:18, 23-27
Mark 4:35-41
Luke 8:22-25

One day, when evening came, Jesus saw the crowd around him. So he tells his disciples, "Let's go over to the other side of the lake."

He got into a boat and his disciples followed him. Launching out and leaving the crowd, they take him along as he was, and other boats were with him. He fell asleep as they sailed.

But look, a huge windstorm arises, shaking the sea. The wind and the waves crashed over top of the boat so much that it was filling up. But even though they were in danger, Jesus was in the stern, asleep on a cushion. So they come to him, wake him up, and tell him, "Master, Master, we're dying! Teacher, don't you care? Save us, Lord!"[a]

So he got up and rebuked the wind. He told the surging sea, "Silent! Be still!"

A. *They cried to the Lord in their trouble and he took them out of their distress. He made the storm calm and the waves were silenced. – Psalm 107:28-29*

Then the wind died down and a great calm occurred. "You small-faiths!"[b] he tells them. "Why are you so afraid? Where's your faith? Do you still have none?"

Then they became terribly frightened and asked one another, "What kind of a man is this? He even commands the wind and the sea, and they obey him!"

13.2 LEGION THROWN OUT

Matthew 8:28-34
Mark 5:1-20
Luke 8:26-39

They sailed and came to the other side of the sea, into the Gerasenes' country, which is opposite Galilee. When he got out of the boat onto land, immediately a demonized man[c] from the city with an unclean spirit met him as he was coming out of the tombs. He hadn't worn any clothing for a long time, and he didn't live in a house but among the tombs.[d] He was so violent that no one could pass by that way. No one was able to bind him anymore, even with a chain; he had often been bound with shackles[e] and chains and kept under guard, but he tore the chains apart and broke the shackles in pieces. Then he had been driven by the demon into the desert, and no one was strong enough to restrain him. Day and night, he continually screamed among the tombs and in the mountains, and he cut himself with stones.

Seeing Jesus from a distance, he ran up and fell down before him, because he had commanded him, "Come out of the man, you unclean spirit!"

Crying out in a loud voice, he says, "What is it with you and me, Jesus, Son of the Highest God? Have you come here to torture me before the time? I beg you by God, don't torture me!"

B. The Greek noun *oligopistos* is from *pistos* ("faith") and *oligo*, meaning "some," "few," or "scant," emphasizing the smallness of the amount. It has been traditionally translated as "men of little faith," but occurs here as "**small-faiths**."

C. Both Mark and Luke record Jesus meeting one **demonized man** in the Gerasene's country (within Decapolis) while Matthew records that he met two.

D. Ancient Palestinian **tombs** were shallow graves covered with rocks or a large stone slab, or they were caves carved into solid rock. Besides the obvious aversion to living next to graves, tombs were typically located some distance away from towns because of Moses' Law, which stated that anyone who touched a corpse or a grave was unclean for a week.

E. The Greek word *pede*, derived from the word for "feet," refers to any type of bondage on the feet, translated here as "**shackles**." This passage is the only time this term is used in the Bible.

Decapolis

The eastern frontier of the Roman Empire in Palestine included a region called **Decapolis**, or "Ten Cities," most of which were east of the Jordan River. They included:

1. Gerasa (now Jarash)
2. Scythopolis (now Beit-She'an)
3. Hippos
4. Gadara (now Umm Quais)
5. Pella
6. Philadelphia (now Amman)
7. Capitolias (now Beit Ras)
8. Canatha (now Qanawat)
9. Abila (now Quwaylibah)
10. Damascus

The region had a strong Roman culture and emperor worship was routinely practiced. Each city was governed independently under Rome and even minted their own coins.

The area around the cities of Gadara and Gerasa was likely the Biblical location of the **Gerasenes' country** (according to Mark and Luke) or Gadarenes' country (according to Matthew). The terrain had high ridges and steep slopes that descended into the sea, and the surrounding hills could easily have accommodated large herds of livestock.

Then Jesus asked him, "What's your name?"

"My name is Legion,[f] because there are many of us," he replies. And they begged him not to send them out of the country into the depths.[g]

Now a large herd of pigs was feeding there on the mountain some distance away from them. The demons begged him, saying, "If you throw us out, send us into the pigs so we can enter them."

So Jesus gave them permission, saying, "Go!"

Coming out of the man, the unclean spirits entered the pigs[h] and the whole herd of about two thousand rushed down the cliffs into the sea and drowned.

When their herdsmen saw it, they ran away and reported everything in the city and in the country, including everything about him who had been demonized. Then look, the whole city and country came out to meet Jesus and see what had happened. They come to Jesus and see the man who had been demonized by a legion of demons sitting down, clothed and sane. They became very frightened. Those who had seen it described how the demonized man had been made better, and about the pigs. Then all the people of the Gerasenes' country and the surrounding area begged him to leave their region.

As he was getting into the boat, the man who had been demonized begged to go with him, but he didn't let him. Instead, he tells him, "Go home to your people and tell them what God has done for you, how he had mercy on you."

So he went away and proclaimed in Decapolis everything that Jesus had done for him, and everyone was amazed. Then Jesus got into the boat and returned.

13.3 JAIRUS' DAUGHTER AND BLEEDING WOMAN HEALED

Matthew 9:18-26
Mark 5:21-43
Luke 8:40-56

F. A Roman **legion** had up to 5000 soldiers in it.

G. *Abyssos* is Greek for "bottomless" or "**depths**," and is where we get the English word "abyss." According to Strong's Concordance, it refers to an immeasurable depth in the middle of the earth where the dead are sent and demons live.

H. According to Moses' Law, all **pigs** and swine were considered unclean and were therefore forbidden as food. Wild boars lived throughout Palestine, which were dangerous if confronted, and were considered pests because they ruined vineyards by devouring grapes and trampling vines. Domestic pigs were raised in Palestine, but never by Orthodox Jews.

After Jesus crossed back over to the other side in the boat, many crowds gathered around and welcomed him, because they had all been waiting for him. So he stayed by the seashore. While he was talking to them, there was a man named Jairus, who was a synagogue leader with an only daughter about twelve years old that was dying. Upon seeing him, he comes up, falls at his feet, and begs him repeatedly, "My daughter is about to die![i] Come and lay your hands on her so she'll be saved and live!"

So Jesus got up and followed him, along with his disciples. Many crowds were following and pressing up against him too. A woman was there who had been bleeding for twelve years, but she couldn't be healed by anyone. She had suffered much under many doctors, having spent all she had, but nothing had helped. In fact, she had just gotten worse. So after hearing about Jesus, she came up behind him in the crowd and touched the edge of his coat, saying to herself, "If I can just touch his clothes, I'll be saved."

I. Before modern medicine, severe bacterial infection was arguably the most common cause of death from sudden illness in children. The infection likely would have started in the lungs, abdomen, brain, or an open wound. The child's condition would have progressively worsened over the course of just a few days, with high fevers and decreasing responsiveness. Bacteria would eventually spread through the bloodstream to infect the rest of the body. A septic **child on her death bed** would have been deathly pale, severely dehydrated, and largely unconscious as the infection caused her various organ systems to shut down. Sadly, this was all too common before the use of vaccinations and antibiotics; prior to the 1800s up to a third of children died before adulthood.

Bleeding and Unclean

According to Moses' Law, any bloody discharge rendered a woman unclean and therefore excluded her from contact with other Jews. Anyone who touched her would also become unclean. Various medical conditions can cause abnormal bleeding in women, such as endometriosis and polycystic ovarian syndrome. Most of these start in the teenage years after the onset of a woman's monthly period. They also typically cause chronic abdominal pain. Additionally, long term bleeding leads to fatigue from iron-deficiency anemia. Therefore, a woman who had been **bleeding for twelve years** was likely in her mid-20s, unmarried and socially isolated, living with chronic pain and low energy, and likely hadn't been significantly touched by anyone since childhood.

If a woman has bloody discharge apart from menstruation, or if she has discharge beyond menstruation, she's unclean for the whole time of her impure discharge, as if she were menstruating. Any bed she lies on during the whole time of her discharge will be like her bed during menstruation, and everything that she sits on will be unclean, like her impurity during menstruation. Similarly, whoever touches them will be unclean. He'll wash his clothes and bathe in water, and he'll be unclean until that evening. When she's cleaned from her discharge, she'll count off seven days and afterwards she'll be clean.... This is the law for someone with a discharge... whether male or female, or a man who lies with an unclean woman.

– Leviticus 15:25-28, 32-33

Immediately her flow of blood dried up and she felt that she had been healed from the suffering in her body. Jesus felt power going out from him, so he turned around in the crowd and asked, "Who touched my clothes?"

While they were all denying it, Peter said to him, "Master, how can you say, 'Who touched me?' when you see the crowds pressing in on you?"

But Jesus said, "Someone touched me, because I felt power go out from me."

He looked around to see the woman who had done this. And when the woman, aware of what had happened to her, saw that she couldn't hide, she was terrified and fell down trembling before him. She told him the whole truth and declared before all the people the reason why she had touched him and how she had been healed immediately. Then he told her, "Courage, daughter. Your faith has saved you. Go in peace and be healed of your suffering."

While he was still speaking, someone comes from the synagogue leader's house, saying, "Your daughter has died. Don't trouble the Teacher anymore."

But overhearing what was being said, Jesus tells him, "Don't be afraid. Just believe and she'll be saved."

Jesus comes to the house of the synagogue leader and he sees the flute-players and the crowd in a commotion, with people weeping and lamenting out loud.[J] Going in, he tells them, "Why the fuss and the weeping? Stop it and get out. The child hasn't died – she's asleep."

They laughed at him, knowing that she had died. But sending them all out, he takes the child's father and mother, along with Peter, James, and John (James' brother), but he didn't let anyone else go in with him. Then he goes in to where the child was. Taking the child by the hand, he tells her, "*Talitha kum!*" which translates to, "Little girl, I tell you, get up!"

Her spirit returned immediately, and the girl got up and walked,

---

J. In ancient Israel, vivid expressions of grief were encouraged during periods of mourning. As soon as a loved one died, the family began wailing and weeping loudly. Neighbors would soon join in, and professional mourners or flute players further contributed to the lament if the family could afford to hire them. Periods of mourning recorded in the Bible were lengthy: Egypt mourned Jacob's death for 70 days, while Israel mourned Aaron's and Moses' deaths for 30 days each. The Greek verb *kopto* means "cut" or "strike," but it's also used as a word for **lamenting**.

Languages in Palestine

After ages of settling, invasion, exile, and resettling, numerous **languages** and dialects were known in Judea during the first century. The original Jewish language was Hebrew, but after Israel's fall to Assyria and Judah's fall to Babylon, Aramaic began to dominate, especially in the northern lands of Samaria and Galilee. This Aramaic became a western dialect called Syriac, which included various Hebrew and Persian words. However, because much of the Old Testament was written in Hebrew, many Jews still spoke a version of it, especially in rural Judea. Then around the second century BC, Alexander the Great's Hellenization of the Mediterranean brought Greek language and culture to Judea, which quickly became the international language of trade. The earliest available copies of the New Testament were written in Greek and even quotations from the Hebrew Old Testament were translated into Greek. Some Hebrew or Aramaic words were used in the New Testament, but often with a translation included in the text. This heavy Greek influence effectively displaced Latin (Rome's language) in Judea, although some terms related to Roman rule persisted, such as monetary amounts. Thus most literate Jews likely knew Aramaic, Hebrew, and marketplace Greek.

Therefore, the Gospels, which were originally written in Greek, include various Aramaic and Hebrew terms. Sometimes there's a translation within the text itself, as there is in Mark's account (*"**Talitha kum**!" which translates to, "Little girl, I tell you, get up!"*)

because she was twelve years old. They were completely amazed. Then he said that she should be given something to eat. He gave them strict instructions that no one should know about this, but the news spread throughout the entire land.

13.4 BLIND AND OTHERS HEALED

Matthew 9:27-34

As Jesus passed through there, two blind men followed him, crying out, "Have mercy on us, son of David!"

After he went into the house, the blind men came up to him. So Jesus asks them, "Do you believe I can do this?"

"Yes, Lord," they reply.

So he touched their eyes, saying, "Then it'll be done for you, according to your faith."

Their eyes opened, but Jesus warned them, "See that no one knows!"

However, they left and spread it around the entire land. As they were going out, a deaf and demonized man was brought to him, and after the demon was thrown out, the deaf man spoke. The crowds were amazed, saying, "Nothing like this has ever appeared in Israel!"

But the Pharisees were saying, "He throws out demons by the ruler of demons."

13.5 HOMETOWN DISBELIEF

Matthew 13:54-58
Mark 6:1-6a

Then Jesus left there. He comes to his fatherland, with his disciples following. When the Sabbath came, he taught in the synagogue and many who heard it were blown away, saying, "Where did this man get this? What's this wisdom given to him and these miracles done by his hands? Isn't he the craftsman's son and a craftsman[k] himself? Isn't he Mary's son and the brother of James, Joses, Judas, and Simon? Aren't his sisters here with us?"

So they were offended by him. Then Jesus said, "A prophet doesn't lack honor, except in his fatherland, among his relatives, and in his own house."

Therefore he didn't do many miracles there, except for laying his hands on a few sick people and healing them. And he wondered at their disbelief.

K. The Greek word *tekton* is where we get the English word "technology." Historically, *tekton* was often translated as "carpenter" in reference to Jesus' or Joseph's occupation, but it can refer to any sort of **craftsman**, including builder, architect, woodworker, or stonemason.

CHAPTER 14

The Twelve Sent Out

14.1 WORKER SHORTAGE

Matthew 9:35-38
Mark 6:6b

Jesus was going through all the cities and villages, teaching in their synagogues and declaring the good news of the kingdom. And he was healing all diseases and all weaknesses.

He was moved when he saw the crowds, because they were troubled and downcast, like sheep without a shepherd.[a] "The harvest is abundant, but workers are scarce," he tells his disciples, "so ask the Lord of the harvest to send workers out into his harvest."

14.2 TWELVE SENT OUT

Matthew 10:1, 5-16, 23-42; 11:1
Mark 6:7-13
Luke 9:1-6; 12:2-9, 49-53; 14:25-33

Jesus calls his twelve disciples together. He gave them power and

A. *May the LORD, the God of the spirits of everybody, set a man over the assembly who will go out and come in before them, who will lead them out and bring them in, so the assembly won't be like sheep without a shepherd. – Numbers 27:16-17*

authority to throw out all evil spirits, and to heal all diseases and all weaknesses. Then Jesus sent them out in pairs to announce God's kingdom.

"Don't go along Gentile roads and don't go into any Samaritan city," he told them. "Instead, go to the lost sheep of Israel's house. Preach as you go, saying, 'The kingdom of heaven is near.' Heal the sick, raise the dead, cleanse lepers, and throw out demons. You've received freely, now give freely. Don't collect gold, silver, or copper for your money belts.[b] Wear sandals but take nothing else for your journey – not a staff, bag, bread, nor money. Don't even have two coats each, because the worker deserves his food. In whatever city or village you enter, ask for whoever is deserving and stay there until you leave town. As you enter the house, give it your greeting.[c] If the house deserves it, your peace will come upon it, but if it doesn't deserve it, your peace will return to you. Whoever doesn't receive you or listen to your words, shake the dust off the soles of your feet[d] as a testimony against them as you leave that house or that city. Truly I tell you, it'll be better for the land of Sodom and Gomorrah on the judgment day than for that city.

"Look, I send you out as sheep among wolves, so be wise like snakes and innocent like doves. Whenever they mistreat you in this city, escape to another. I tell you that you won't finish the cities of Israel before the Son of Man comes.

"A student isn't over his teacher, nor a slave over his master. It's enough for the student that he becomes like his teacher, and the slave his master. If they've called the housemaster Beelzebub,[e] how much more those in his house! Don't be afraid of them, because there's nothing hidden that won't be shown, covered that won't be uncovered, or secret that won't be known. On the contrary, what I tell you in the dark, speak in the light, and what you hear softly in your ear in the

---

B. Special belts with pouches for coins were called **money belts**. They offered better protection against pickpockets than purses.

C. A common Hebrew **greeting** was *Shalom aleichem* ("peace to you"), so by greeting a household, one also blessed it. The Hebrew word for "peace" (*shalom*) could also mean "completeness" or "well-being." It was used as a greeting and a parting word, and is possibly the root of Jerusalem, the Jewish capital city.

D. The act of deliberately **shaking the dust off one's feet** was considered the cutting off of a relationship. When pious Jews left a Gentile city, they would show their separation from them by shaking the dust from their feet.

E. Another name for the Devil is **Beelzebub**, which means "lord of the flies" or "lord of the house."

closet, shout from the roof. My friends, I tell you, don't be afraid of those who kill the body, but afterwards cannot do more nor kill the soul. But I'll show you whom to fear: fear the one who can destroy both soul and body in hell, and who has the power to throw into hell after he has killed. Yes, I tell you, fear him! Aren't two sparrows sold for a nickel?[f] However, not one of them is forgotten by God or will fall to the ground apart from your Father. Even the hairs on your head are all numbered, so don't be afraid – you're worth more than many sparrows.

"Everyone who affirms me before men, I, the Son of Man, will also affirm him before my Father in heaven and before God's angels. But whoever denies me before men, I'll deny him before my Father in heaven and God's angels too.

"I've come to throw fire upon the earth. How I wish it was already lit! But I have a baptism to be baptized with, and I'm so pent up until it's done! Do you think that I came to give the land peace? No! I tell you, division and a sword instead! From now on five in one house will be divided, three against two and two against three. I came to divide a father against his son and a son against his father; a mother against her daughter and a daughter against her mother; a mother-in-law against her daughter-in-law and a daughter-in-law against her mother-in-law.[g] A man's enemies will be those in his own house."

Many crowds were travelling with him. He turned and told them, "If anyone comes to me and doesn't hate[h] his own father, mother, wife, sons, daughters, brothers, and sisters – yes, even his own life – he doesn't deserve me and can't be my disciple. Whoever doesn't carry his own cross and follow after me doesn't deserve me and can't be my

F. Various small birds were called **sparrows** in the Bible. True sparrows, however, are noisy, social birds that gather in large flocks and build nests in the eaves of houses. They were known in Judea as a poor man's sacrifice, since those who couldn't afford sheep or goats could purchase inexpensive sparrows instead.

The *assarion* or *as*, translated here as "**nickel**," was a small Roman coin. It was made of bronze or copper and was originally worth one tenth of a denarius. Later, it was revalued to be even less, worth one sixteenth of a denarius.

Matthew records that Jesus described two sparrows being sold for a nickel, while Luke records five sparrows for a nickel. Mark and John don't record this teaching.

G. *Don't trust a neighbor and don't trust a friend. Guard your lips from the one who lies in your arms. Because a son disrespects his father, a daughter rises against her mother, and a daughter-in-law against her mother-in-law. A man's enemies will be the men in his own house. – Micah 7:5-6*

H. Both Matthew and Luke record that Jesus taught his followers to choose him over their own families. Matthew says followers must not love (*phileo*) their family more than Jesus, while Luke says that followers must **hate** (*miseo*) their family, as it's stated here.

disciple. Whoever finds his life will lose it, and whoever loses his life because of me will find it.

"Who of you, when he wants to build a tower, doesn't sit down and tally the costs first to see if he has enough to finish it? Otherwise, when he has laid the foundation and isn't able to finish, everyone who sees it will laugh at him, saying, 'This man began to build but couldn't finish!' Or what king, when he goes out to meet another king in battle, won't sit down first and consider whether he's strong enough with 10,000 to meet the one coming against him with 20,000? Then, while the other's still far away, he'll send an ambassador and ask for terms of peace. So none of you can be my disciple if you don't give up all your belongings."

"Whoever receives you receives me, and whoever receives me receives the one who sent me. Whoever receives a prophet in the name of a prophet will receive a prophet's reward, and whoever receives a righteous man in the name of a righteous man will receive a righteous man's reward. And whoever gives even a cup of cold water in the name of a disciple to one of these little ones, truly I tell you that he won't lose his reward."

Leaving there, they went from village to village preaching the good news, proclaiming that men should repent, and healing everywhere. They threw out many demons and anointed with oil many who were sick and healed them.

When Jesus had finished instructing his twelve disciples, he left there to teach and preach in their cities.

14.3 JOHN EXECUTED BY HEROD

Matthew 14:1-12
Mark 6:14-29
Luke 9:7-9

King Herod the tetrarch heard the news about Jesus, because his name had become famous and his servants were saying, "John the Baptizer has risen from death! That's why this power is working in him!" But others were saying, "He's Elijah," and others still, "A prophet, like one of the ancient prophets risen." Yet when Herod heard about it, he was dumbfounded. He kept telling his servants, "I had John the Baptizer beheaded, so who's this man I hear so much about? Has he risen?!" So he kept trying to see him.

Now Herod had sent and had John arrested and chained in prison because he had married Herodias, the wife of his brother Philip. John had been telling Herod, "It's not legal for you to have your brother's wife." Herodias held it against him and wanted to have him killed, but she couldn't do so because Herod was afraid of John, knowing he was a righteous and holy man. He was also afraid of the crowd, because they held John as a prophet. So he kept him safe and enjoyed listening to him, but he got confused whenever he heard him.

An opportunity[i] came when Herod threw a party on his birthday for his nobles, commanders, and the leaders of Galilee. When Herodias' daughter came in and danced, she pleased Herod and his guests so much that the king told the girl, "Ask me for whatever you want and I'll give it to you." He even swore an oath to her: "I'll give you whatever you ask for, up to half of my kingdom."

So she went out and asked her mother, "What should I ask for?"

"The head of John the Baptizer," she said.

Having been prompted by her mother, she hurried back to the king immediately, saying, "I want you to give me the head of John the Baptizer on a platter right away."

Although the king was upset, he didn't want to deny her because of his oath and his guests. So the king immediately sent a guard, commanding him to bring back his head. He went and beheaded him in prison, then brought his head back on a platter and gave it to the girl, and the

---

i. *Eukarios* is a Greek term that translates literally to "good time," from the words *eu* ("good") and *kairos* ("time"). However, it's probably best understood as the moment when conditions are ideal for a particular objective. Many Bibles translate it as "opportune time" or "strategic day." Here it's simply "**opportunity**."

Herodias

When Herod the Great had his son Aristobulus killed, it left his granddaughter, **Herodias**, orphaned as a child. Herod the Great engaged her to another son, Herod Philip I (not Philip the tetrarch) for political reasons, and she subsequently gave birth to a daughter named Salome. Herodias later left her husband to marry another of Herod's sons, Herod Antipas (one of the tetrarchs), even though he was also married to someone else at the time (Phasaelis). The affair and subsequent divorces prompted Phasaelis to escape back to her father, Aretas IV, who was king of Nabatea, a neighboring country to the east. In retaliation for his daughter's rejection, Aretas invaded Herod Antipas' land and defeated his forces in 37 AD. Although the Roman Emperor Tiberius ordered an army sent to rescue Herod Antipas, Tiberius died before they arrived and the order was never carried out. Herod Antipas and his wife Herodias were eventually exiled to Gaul (modern day France) in 39 AD after being accused of conspiracy against the new Roman Emperor, Caligula, and all his territory was given to his nephew, Herod Agrippa.

girl gave it to her mother.

When his disciples heard about it, they came and took away his body and laid it in a tomb. Then they went and reported it to Jesus.

CHAPTER 15

The Bread of Jesus

15.1 FIVE THOUSAND FED

Matthew 14:13-23
Mark 6:30-46
Luke 9:10-17
John 6:1-15

After returning, the apostles told Jesus about everything they had done and taught. So many were coming and going that they didn't even have a chance to eat. So they gather together and he tells them, "Come away now by yourselves to the wilderness and rest a while."

Then after he had heard [about John], Jesus took them away by themselves in a boat to the wilderness. They went to a city called Bethsaida across the Sea of Galilee (Sea of Tiberias). But when the crowds saw them going, many anticipated it and ran from all the cities, getting there ahead of them. The people followed on foot because they had seen the miracles he was doing for the sick.

When Jesus arrived, he went up the mountain and sat down with his disciples. Lifting his eyes, Jesus saw the many crowds coming to him. He was moved[a] because they were like sheep without a shepherd, because the Jewish Passover Feast was soon. So he welcomed them and taught them much about God's kingdom, healing those who needed therapy.[b]

That evening, his twelve disciples came to him, saying, "This place is remote and the time is already late. Send the crowds away so they can go into the surrounding countryside and villages to unpack and buy themselves something to eat."

"They don't need to go away," he answered. "You give them something to eat!"

Then he asks Philip, "Where can we buy bread so they can eat?"

He asked this to test him, because he knew what he was going to do. But Philip answers, "Should we go and spend two hundred denarii[c] on bread to give them food? That's not even enough for everyone to have a little!"

"How many loaves do you have?" he says. "Go and look."

When they found out, Andrew (one of his disciples and Simon Peter's brother) tells him, "There's a boy here who has no more than five barley loaves and two fish. But unless we go and buy food for them, what's that for so many people?"

"Bring them here to me," Jesus told his disciples, "and have the people sit in groups of about fifty or a hundred each."

So they did. They had them all sit down, since there was lots of green grass in the area. Then Jesus took the five loaves and two fish. Looking up toward heaven, he gave thanks and blessed it. Then he broke the loaves. He kept giving it to the disciples to put before the seated crowds, and he divided up the two fish among them all as well. And they all ate as much as they wanted.

When they were full, he tells his disciples, "Gather up the leftover pieces so nothing will be lost."

A. *Splagchnizomai* is a Greek word that directly translates to "move one's bowels." However, Jews in the first century referred to the bowels as the seat of emotion and personhood, in the same way English refers to the heart. So unlike the English meaning of having a bowel movement, *splagchnizomai* referred to having a deep emotional feeling in one's gut. More specifically, it referred to feeling compassion or pity, similar to the English expression of being "**moved**" emotionally.

B. *Therapeia* is where the English "**therapy**" comes from. It means the same in Greek as it does in English: medical treatment of disease or disorder. Of all the Gospel writers, only Luke, the physician, uses this term in this context.

C. A denarius was the daily wage of an unskilled laborer, so **two hundred denarii** would have taken about eight months for one man to earn (working six days of the week).

So they gathered them up and filled twelve baskets[d] full of the broken pieces, and fish too, left over by those who had eaten. There were about five thousand men who ate that bread, besides women and children. When the people saw the miracle he had done, they said, "This is truly the prophet who is coming into the world."

Jesus immediately made his disciples get into the boat and go across to Bethsaida and Capernaum while he dispersed the crowds. But seeing that they were about to seize him to make him king, Jesus withdrew from them and left for the mountain again to pray by himself. And when evening came, he was there alone.

15.2 WALKING ON WATER

Matthew 14:24-33
Mark 6:47-52
John 6:16-21

That evening, his disciples went down to the sea and crossed towards Capernaum. After dark, the boat was in the middle of the sea, many stadia from land, but Jesus was alone on land, because he hadn't come to them yet. Then the sea got woken up. A strong, violent wind blew, harassing the boat in the waves. During the fourth watch[e] that night, after they had rowed about 25 to 30 stadia,[f] Jesus saw them struggling at the oars because the wind was against them. So he came to them, walking on the sea and coming close to the boat. He intended to pass by them, but when the disciples saw him walking on the sea, they were all terrified and screamed in fear, crying out, "It's a ghost!"

But immediately Jesus speaks to them, saying, "Courage! It's me!

D. While on a journey, Jews likely carried a **basket** with provisions, especially in Gentile areas where they couldn't expect hospitality or lodging to be available. Ancient baskets came in all shapes and sizes, depending on their intended purpose, such as food storage, brick transportation, or crop harvesting. They also could be small and delicate for ornate treasures, or even large enough to hold a man, like when Paul was lowered from a city wall in one. Baskets were woven from any sort of plant material, such as willow, rush, or palm branches.

E. Roman guards divided the night watch into four shifts of three hours each. The **fourth watch** of the night was 3:00 to 6:00 in the morning, ending at dawn.

F. The Greeks held running races in arenas called ***stadia***, which is where the English "stadium" comes from. The running event itself was also called the *stadion* or *stade* and was a prestigious part of the original Olympic Games. At the trumpet blast to start the race, participants sprinted nude along a dirt track to the finish line where race officials determined the winner. The *stadion* subsequently became a unit of distance measuring 600 feet (185 meters), according to the length of the race track. A distance of **25 to 30 stadia** was about five kilometers (three miles).

Don't be afraid."

Then Peter said, "Lord, if it's really you, tell me to come to you on the water!"

"Come!" he replied.

Then Peter got out of the boat and walked on the water toward Jesus. But seeing the wind, he got scared and began to sink. "Lord!" he cried, "Save me!"[g]

Jesus immediately stretched out his hand and grabbed him. "You small-faith!" he says. "Why did you doubt?"

They wanted to bring him into the boat, and when he got in, the wind stopped and immediately the boat arrived at the land they were going to. Those in the boat were extremely amazed, because they hadn't understood about the bread, since their hearts were calloused. And they worshipped him, saying, "You're definitely God's Son!"[h]

15.3 BREAD OF LIFE

Matthew 14:34-36
Mark 6:53-56
John 6:22-58

When they had crossed over, they came to land at Gennesaret and tied up. They got out of the boat and the men of the area recognized him. They sent runners throughout the whole region and brought him everyone who was sick, carrying them on cots to wherever they heard he was. Whenever he entered villages, cities, or the countryside, they laid the weak in the market and begged that they could just touch the edge of his coat. And whoever touched it was saved.

The next day, the crowd that stood across the sea saw that there was no other boat there and that Jesus hadn't gotten into the boat with his disciples – they had gone away by themselves. However, other boats came from Tiberias, near where they ate the bread after the Lord had given thanks. So when the crowd saw that Jesus and his disciples weren't there, they got into the boats and went to Capernaum looking for Jesus. When they found him across the sea, they asked him, "Rabbi, when did you get here?"

"I tell you, truly truly, you don't look for me because you saw signs,

G. *All who call on the name of the LORD will be saved. –Joel 2:32*

H. *It's God alone who marches over the waves of the sea. –Job 9:8*

Towns on the Sea of Galilee

On the northwest shore of the Sea of Galilee was the Galilean town of **Gennesaret**, also called Kinnereth or Chinnereth. The surrounding land had rich, fertile soil in a plain extending from the sea. Although it was previously a fortified city in the region of Naphtali, remains of Gennesaret haven't survived to this day.

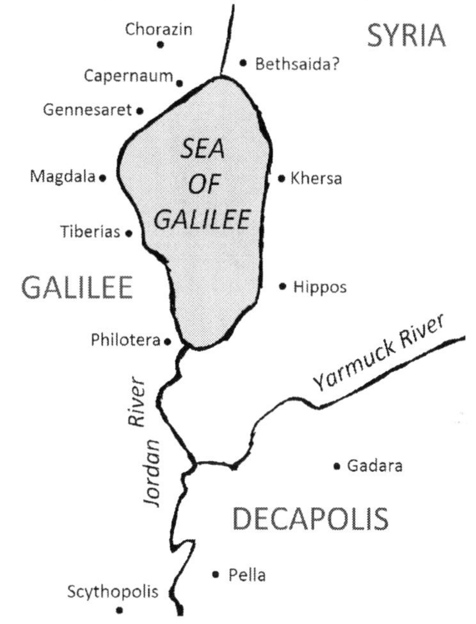

Tiberias, on the other hand, was a wealthy city just south of Gennesaret that still has both ancient ruins and modern inhabitants. Tradition holds that it was originally the Hebrew village of Rakkat, also in the region of Naphtali. Just a few years before Jesus' visit to Tiberias, Herod Antipas founded the city there and named it in honor of the Roman emperor at the time, Tiberius. However, the city was reportedly built on a graveyard, so it was considered unclean by Jews, who refused to enter the city. Because Tiberias was situated on rocky cliffs with a view of the sea and had numerous hot springs in the area, it was a popular lakeside resort for Romans.

The Sea of Galilee was also called the Sea of Gennesaret (by Jews) and the Sea of Tiberias (by Romans).

but because you ate bread and were full," Jesus answered. "However, don't work for food that spoils but for food that lasts into eternal life, which the Son of Man will give to you, because God the Father has put his seal on him."

"What should we do so we can do God's work?" they asked him.

"This is the work of God," Jesus answered, "that you believe in the one he sent."

Then they said, "What will you do as a sign, so we can see and believe in you? What work do you do? Our fathers ate manna[i] in the desert, as it's written, 'He gave them bread from heaven to eat'."[j]

i. As God led Israel out of Egypt, they travelled through barren desert on their way to Canaan. Because there was no food available, Exodus records that God miraculously provided **manna** that covered the ground every morning with the dew. *Manna* is a Hebrew word meaning "What is it?," aptly named after no one in Israel could figure out what it was when it first appeared. Moses recorded that manna was white and seed-like, forming fine flakes like frost on the ground and tasting like honey pastries. Israel ate it every day for 40 years until the day they arrived at their promised land.

"I tell you, truly truly, it's not Moses who gave you bread from heaven," Jesus told them. "It's my Father who gives you the true bread from heaven, because God's bread is what comes down from heaven and gives life to the world."

"Lord, give us this bread forever," they said.

"I am the bread of life," Jesus said. "Whoever comes to me won't hunger and whoever believes in me will never thirst. I've told you that you've seen me, but you don't believe. Everything that the Father gives me will come to me, and the one who comes to me I certainly won't throw away. I've come down from heaven, not to do what I want but what the one who sent me wants. This is what the one who sent me wants: out of everything he has given me, I lose nothing, but raise it up on the last day. And this is what my Father wants, that everyone who sees the Son and believes in him will have eternal life, and that I'll raise him up on the last day."

The Jews were muttering about him, because he said, "I'm the bread that came down from heaven." They were saying, "Isn't this Jesus, Joseph's son, whose father and mother we know? So how can he say, 'I came down from heaven'?"

"Don't mutter among yourselves," Jesus answered. "No one can come to me unless the Father who sent me brings him, and I'll raise him up on the last day. It's written in the prophets, 'They'll be taught by God,'[k] so everyone who has heard and learned from the Father comes to me. However, no one has seen the Father except the one from God – he has seen the Father. I tell you, truly truly, whoever believes has eternal life. I'm the bread of life. Your fathers ate manna in the desert and they died, but this is the bread that comes down from heaven, so you can eat it and not die. I'm the living bread that came down from heaven. If anyone eats this bread, he'll live forever. The bread I'll give for the world's life is my body."

Then the Jews argued with one another, saying, "How can this man give us his body to eat?"

"I tell you, truly truly," Jesus said, "unless you eat the Son of Man's body and drink his blood, you won't have life in yourselves. Whoever

J. *He rained manna on them to eat and gave them food from heaven. Man ate the bread of angels, and he sent them food abundantly. – Psalm 78:24-25*

K. *All of your sons will be taught by the LORD, and your sons' peace will be abundant. You'll be stable in righteousness. You'll be far from oppression, so you won't fear; and from ruin – it won't even come close. – Isaiah 54:13-14*

eats my body and drinks my blood has eternal life, and I'll raise him up on the last day. My body is true food and my blood is true drink. Whoever eats my body and drinks my blood lives in me and I in him. Just like the living Father sent me, and like I live because of the Father, whoever eats me will also live because of me. This is the bread that came down from heaven, but not like the fathers ate and died, because whoever eats this bread will live forever."

15.4 SOME DISCIPLES LEAVE

John 6:59-71

He said this while teaching in the synagogue in Capernaum. When many of his disciples heard it, they said, "That's a harsh word. Who can listen to it?"

Jesus saw that his disciples were muttering about this, so he said, "Does this trip you up? Then what about seeing the Son of Man rising up to where he was before? It's the Spirit that gives life – the body has no benefit. The words I've told you are spirit and life, but some of you don't believe."

Jesus knew who didn't believe and who would betray him from the start, so he was saying, "This is why I've told you that no one can come to me unless the Father lets him."

Because of this, many of his disciples went back and didn't walk with him anymore. But to the Twelve, Jesus asked, "Don't you want to go away too?"

Simon Peter answered, "Lord, who would we go to? You have the words of eternal life. We've believed and have known that you're God's holy one."

"Didn't I choose you – the Twelve – myself?" Jesus replied. "Yet one of you is a devil."

He meant Judas of Simon Iscariot,[l] because he – one of the Twelve – was going to betray him.

L. In a culture without last names, individuals were identified by their father's name. However, instead of explicitly stating that a man was the son of his father (for example, "Judas, son of Simon Iscariot"), the father's name simply became the son's last name ("**Judas of Simon Iscariot**").

CHAPTER 16

The Yeast of the Pharisees

16.1 OUTER VS. INNER CLEANLINESS

Matthew 15:1-20
Mark 7:1-15, 17-23
John 7:1

After this, Jesus walked in Galilee. He didn't want to walk in Judea because the Jews were trying to kill him. However, some Pharisees and scribes come to him from Jerusalem. When they saw some of his disciples eating bread with dirty (unwashed) hands,[a] they gathered around him. Then the Pharisees and the scribes ask, "Why do your disciples eat bread with dirty hands and not walk according to the tradition of the elders?"

Pharisees and all Jews don't eat unless they wash their hands with fists,[b] following the tradition of the elders. Similarly, coming from the

A. Washing hands before eating wasn't commanded in Moses' Law but was included later in the Mishnah, the Pharisees' book of oral traditions and interpretations of the Law. The Greek word *koinos* describes **dirty** hands in this passage. It refers to something common or ordinary, but can also be translated as "defiled" or "polluted." The equivalent term in Latin (*vulgaris*) translates to "common," but, like its Greek counterpart, it acquired a negative connotation over time, becoming "crude" or "unrefined." *Vulgaris* is where the English "vulgar" comes from. Mark uses both *koinos* and *aniptos* (**unwashed**) here, while Matthew only uses *koinos*.

market, they don't eat unless they bathe themselves. And they've been given many other [rules] to follow, such as the washing of cups, pitchers, and brass.[c]

"Why do you break God's command to keep your own tradition?" he answered. "You're experts at it! God said through Moses, 'Honor your father and mother,'[d] and, 'Whoever curses his father or mother should be killed.'[e] But you say that if a man tells his father or mother, 'Whatever I have that would help you is *korban*,'"[f] – which means "given to God" – "you let him do nothing for his father or mother and not honor them, thereby nullifying God's word by the tradition you've been given. You do much like that! Isaiah prophesied perfectly about you hypocrites, as it's written:

> 'These people honor me with their lips, but their heart is far away from me. They worship me uselessly, teaching the rules of men as law.'[g]

Ignoring God's command, you hold onto men's tradition."

Then after Jesus called the crowd to himself again, he said, "Everyone! Listen to me and understand that there's nothing outside a man

---

B. The only place the Greek word *pygme* is mentioned in the Bible is when Mark describes the Jewish tradition of hand washing. It translates to "**fist**" or "clenched hand," possibly referring to the process of washing one hand within the other. However, *pygme* was also a unit of distance in ancient times, measuring from the knuckles to the elbow, suggesting that Jews may have washed all the way up their forearms before meals.

C. *Chalkion* is a Greek word derived from the word for brass (*chalkos*) and refers to anything made of **brass** or bronze. As a gold-colored alloy of copper, zinc, and/or tin, brass was a strong malleable metal that could withstand high heats. The only time *chalkion* is used in the Bible is by Mark in reference to dishes or cooking utensils, but *chalkos* can also refer to coins or musical instruments (gongs, cymbals) in the New Testament. Brass has been used symbolically in the Old Testament to denote strength and permanence.

D. *Honor your father and mother, so your days in the land the LORD your God gives you will be long. – Exodus 20:12*

E. Moses' Law states that if a man **curses his parents**, he must be killed. Furthermore, if a son is consistently stubborn and rebellious, ignoring discipline, Deuteronomy 21:18-21 records that his parents are required to arrest him and bring him to the city elders to be stoned to death, to *"remove the evil among you."*

F. The Hebrew word ***korban*** meant a gift or offering brought to the Temple for dedication to God. It was typically in the form of animals, grain, wine, or incense, but could potentially be anything. Although these gifts were to be made as acts of worship, many prophets condemned Israel for bringing their gifts without a corresponding repentance in their hearts, insisting that their gifts meant nothing without accompanying faith. Apparently, Jews used the *korban* law to circumvent the responsibility of children to support their ailing parents.

G. *Then the Lord said, "This nation approaches me with their words and honors me with their lips, but their hearts are far from me and their reverence for me is just the commands of*

that can make him dirty if it goes into him. Rather, the things that come out of a man are what make him dirty."

Later, after he had left the crowd and gone into the house, his disciples come and say, "Do you know that the Pharisees were offended when they heard those words?"

"Every plant that my heavenly Father hasn't planted will be uprooted," he answered. "Leave them alone. They're blind guides to the blind. And if the blind guides the blind, they'll both fall into a ditch."

Then Peter said, "Explain the parable to us."

"You too?" he replies. "Are you still so senseless? Don't you understand that whatever goes into a man from the outside can't make him dirty because it doesn't go into his heart but into his stomach and out into the toilet?"

So all foods were declared clean.

Then he continued, "Whatever leaves a man comes from the heart, and that makes him dirty. Because out of a man's heart – from the inside – come evil thoughts, fornications, thefts, murders, lusts, envy, wickedness, deception, shamelessness,[h] wicked eyes, blasphemy, arrogance, and foolishness. All of this wickedness comes from the inside and makes a man dirty, but eating without washing his hands doesn't make him dirty."

16.2 PHOENICIAN GIRL HEALED

Matthew 15:21-28
Mark 7:24-30

Jesus got up and returned to the area of Tyre and Sidon. He didn't want anyone to know that he had gone into a house, but he couldn't keep it a secret. Then a Canaanite woman from the area, whose daughter had an unclean spirit, came and immediately fell at his feet. The woman was a Greek of Syrophoenician ancestry. She asked him to throw the demon out of her daughter, crying out, "Have mercy on me, Lord, son of David! My daughter is miserably demonized."

men they've learned. Therefore, look... the wisdom of the wise will disappear, and the understanding of those who understand will be hidden." – Isaiah 29:13-14

H. The Greek word *aselgia* has been called the ugliest word in the New Testament. It translates to "**shamelessness**" or "sensuality" and refers to extreme sexual licentiousness or violence, particularly when someone shocks public decency with blatant sinfulness. *Aselgia* isn't used commonly in the Bible, but appears most frequently in the book of 2 Peter in reference to the behavior of Sodom and Gomorrah before their destruction.

Phoenicia

Along the Mediterranean coast, north of Israel, was the nation of Phoenicia, a sea-faring collection of independent city states. It was a long narrow country stretching from Laodicea to the north to Tyre and Sidon to the south, covering much of modern-day Lebanon. Phoenicians were renowned seamen – the short coastal plain was hemmed in by mountains to the east, so the sea became the basis of the nation's economy and identity. As well, their lush vegetation and vast cedar forests allowed for exceptional shipbuilding and timber export throughout the Middle East. Prolific Phoenician trade routes led to Mediterranean dominance, with colonies established throughout northern Africa and southwestern Europe. The Phoenicians also developed a system of writing that became the basis of various modern alphabets. The name Phoenicia means "purple land," in reference to the purple dyes produced there from shellfish.

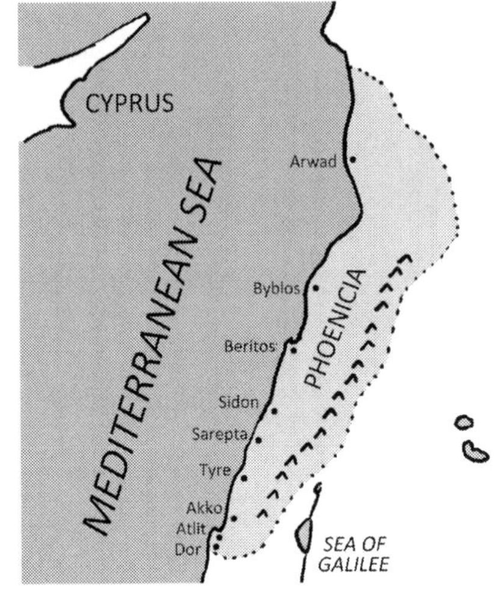

Like much of the ancient Middle East, Phoenicia was conquered by the Persians and then the Greeks. Later, after the Roman Empire conquered the area, Phoenicia became incorporated into the province of Syria. Thus its residents were called **Syrophoenicians** during the first century, distinguished from the Libyan-Phoenicians in North Africa.

But he didn't answer her a word. Finally, his disciples came and begged him, "Send her away. She keeps shouting at us."

So he answered her, "I was sent only to the lost sheep of Israel's house."

But she came and worshipped him,[i] saying, "Lord, help me!"

"Let the children be fed first," he answered. "It isn't right to take the children's bread and throw it to the dogs."

"Yes, Lord," she replies, "but even the dogs eat the children's crumbs that fall from their master's table."

Then Jesus told her, "Woman, your faith is huge. Go! Because of your words, it'll be done just as you wanted. The demon has left your daughter."

Going back home, she found the child lying in bed, the demon

I. *Proskyneo* literally translates to "kiss towards," but is typically rendered "**worship**" or "bow down." The analogous Hebrew term is *shachah*. It described the act of bowing to the ground in an act of profound reverence, possibly accompanied by kissing the hand. Such an act in ancient times would only be done before God, angels, priests, or royalty.

having left her. Her daughter had been healed at that hour.

16.3 HEALING IN DECAPOLIS

Matthew 15:29-31
Mark 7:31-37

Jesus again left the area of Tyre and came through Sidon to the Sea of Galilee, within the area of Decapolis. After going up the mountain, he sat down there. Large crowds came to him, bringing the crippled, injured, blind, mute, and many others. They laid them down at his feet and he healed them all.

Then they bring someone to him who was deaf and had trouble speaking. They beg him to put his hand on him. So Jesus took him by himself away from the crowd, put his fingers into his ears, and after spitting touched his tongue. Then looking up to heaven with a big sigh, he tells him, "*Ephphatha*!"[j] – that is, "Open up!"

Then his ears opened, his tongue's restraint was released, and he spoke clearly. He commanded them not to tell anyone, but the more he commanded them, the more excessively they continued to declare it.

The crowd was completely blown away as they saw the mute speaking, the injured healthy, the crippled walking, and the blind seeing. They glorified the God of Israel. "He has done everything well!" they were saying. "He even makes the deaf hear and the mute speak!"

16.4 FOUR THOUSAND FED

Matthew 15:32-39a
Mark 8:1-9

It was in those days that a large crowd was there again with nothing to eat, so Jesus called his disciples. "I feel for the crowd because they've stayed with me for three days now and don't have anything to eat," he says. "I don't want to send them home hungry or they'll collapse on the way, because some of them have come from far."

But his disciples reply, "Where would we get enough bread here in the wilderness to feed such a crowd?"

"How many loaves do you have?" Jesus asks.

J. *Ephphatha* is a variation of the Aramaic verb *pethach*, meaning "**open**."

"Seven, and some little fish." they replied.

So he tells the crowd to recline on the ground. Then after taking the seven loaves, he gave thanks and broke them, and he gave them to his disciples to put before them. Then he blessed the fish and ordered them to be put before them too. So they served the crowd. They ate and were full, and they picked up seven large baskets full of the broken pieces that were left over. About four thousand men were there, plus women and children. Then he sent them away.

16.5 WARNING AGAINST HYPOCRISY

Matthew 15:39b-16:12
Mark 8:10-21
Luke 12:1b

Jesus got into the boat with his disciples and immediately went to the area of Dalmanutha and Magadan.[k] The Pharisees and the Sadducees came up and argued with him, asking him to show them a sign from heaven to test him. But with a big sigh in his spirit he tells them, "When it's evening, you say, 'Good weather because the sky is red.' And in the morning, 'A storm today because the sky is red and low.'[l] You know how to interpret the appearance of the sky but not the signs of the times? Why does this generation look for a sign? An evil, adulterous[m] generation looks for a sign. Truly I tell you that no sign will be given to this generation except the sign of Jonah."

Leaving them, he got in and went away to the other side. However, the disciples had forgotten to take bread and didn't have more than a loaf with them in the boat. So Jesus told them, "Look out! Watch for the yeast from the Pharisees and the Sadducees, and for the yeast from Herod."

They discussed this among themselves, saying, "It's because we didn't bring bread."

But Jesus knew of it. "You small-faiths," he tells them. "Why are

---

K. The location of ancient **Dalmanutha** is thought to be on the western shore of the Sea of Galilee, near Mount Arbel. Excavations nearby at **Magadan** (presumably another name for Magdala) have revealed an ornate synagogue dating from the first century.

L. Ancient mariner's rhyme: "**Red sky** at night, sailor's delight. Red sky at morning, sailor's warning."

M. An adulteress (Greek noun *moichalis*) was a woman who cheated on her husband. The relationship between God and Israel was frequently compared to a marriage, with Israel repeatedly "playing the harlot" and faithlessly cheating on God. "**Adulterous**" is the adjective describing such a person.

Yeast

Yeast is a type of single-celled fungus. There are many different species, but they all consume oxygen and carbohydrates, while excreting carbon dioxide and various alcohols as waste. In fruit juices, yeast ferments natural sugars to produce alcohol. Once the alcohol gets to a certain concentration, all the yeast dies off in the toxic environment it has created. The liquid is then sterile and fit for consumption. In baking, yeast produces carbon dioxide, which gets trapped in the sticky dough and causes the loaf to rise. Baking the risen loaf sterilizes it with heat and renders the bread fit for consumption. A small amount of yeast will quickly reproduce exponentially to permeate massive amounts of fruit juice or dough, as long as sufficient water and nutrients are present.

Don't you know that a little yeast leavens the whole dough? Clean out the old yeast so you can be new dough, since you're already unleavened. Because Christ, our Passover, has been sacrificed. So let's celebrate the Feast, not with old yeast or the yeast of evil and immorality, but the unleavened bread of purity and truth.

– 1 Corinthians 5:6-8

you discussing with yourselves that you don't have bread? Don't you see or understand yet? Do you have a hard heart? Having eyes, don't you see? And having ears, don't you hear?[n] Don't you remember how many baskets full of pieces you picked up when I broke the five loaves for the five thousand?"

"Twelve," they reply.

"And how many big baskets full of pieces did you pick up after the seven loaves for the four thousand?"

"Seven," they reply.

"Do you still not understand?" he asked. "How do you not understand that I wasn't talking about bread? But watch for the yeast from the Pharisees and the Sadducees, which is hypocrisy."

Then they understood that he didn't say to watch for the yeast of bread, but for the Pharisees' and the Sadducees' teaching.

16.6 BLIND MAN IN BETHSAIDA HEALED

Mark 8:22-26

Then they come to Bethsaida. They bring a blind man to Jesus and beg him to touch him. Taking the blind man by the hand, he brought him out of the village. After spitting on his eyes and laying his hands on him, he asked him, "Do you see anything?"

He gained his sight and said, "I see men, but to me they look like

N. *Now hear this, you foolish heartless people. You have eyes but don't see. You have ears but don't hear. – Jeremiah 5:21*

trees walking around."

Then he laid his hands on his eyes, and he saw everything clearly and was healed. He sent him home, saying, "Don't go into the village."

Caesarea Philippi

At the base of Mount Hermon, northeast of the Sea of Galilee, the city of **Caesarea Philippi** was built on a plateau overlooking a fertile valley. Although the area may have been inhabited earlier, the city itself was founded by the Greeks during the Hellenistic period and was originally called Paneas, after Pan, the Greek god of the wilderness. Despite its location in the midst of arid mountains, a large freshwater spring flowed from a gaping cave in the limestone bedrock, which was one of the four major sources of the Jordan River.

Numerous temples have been built at Caesarea Philippi through the years, and shrines were also erected in caves and niches cut into the rock wall. The city was expanded under Herod the Great in 20 BC, who built a white marble temple dedicated to the Caesars. Then, in 14 AD, Philip II (Philip the tetrarch) changed its name to Caesarea Philippi in honor of Augustus (also called Tiberius), the Caesar at the time, and made it the regional capital. Later, in 61 AD, Agrippa II changed the name again, this time to Neronias in honor of another Roman Emperor, Nero. However, this name lasted only until 68 AD when it reverted to back to Paneas following Nero's suicide. After the fall of Jerusalem in 70 AD, thousands of Jews were executed there as the Roman army passed through. A devastating earthquake in 363 AD may have led to the decline of Caesarea Philippi as a prominent city. Today, only ruins remain and the flow of the mountain spring is a fraction of what it once was. The modern village of Baniyas (Aramaic variation of Paneas) is built on its location.

Jeremiah

Among modern theologians, **Jeremiah** is known as the weeping prophet because of the extreme hardship he suffered throughout his life and ministry, and because of his many tears over Judah's sin. His story is recorded in the biblical book that bears his name, one of the longest in the Bible, and his songs of mourning over the fall of Jerusalem are recorded in a book aptly named Lamentations. Jeremiah was a young Jewish priest from a landowning family who was called by God to proclaim Judah's immorality and imminent destruction by "invaders from the North." His ministry lasted about 40 years, through the reign of multiple Jewish kings, including Josiah, Jehoahaz, Jehoiakim, Jehoichin, and Zedekiah, and ended sometime after Jerusalem's fall. Jeremiah records that God instructed him to refrain from taking a wife and starting a family, and to avoid parties and celebrations. These were to be outward signs of his messages.

Because his preaching was critical of Judah's depravity, Jeremiah was frequently mistreated by the ruling authorities. He was beaten, imprisoned, put in stocks, thrown in a muddy cistern, and attacked by his own brothers. However, once Jerusalem finally fell to the Babylonians in 586 BC, King Nebuchadnezzar ordered his release and proper treatment. Although much of the population was deported to Babylon, Jeremiah was allowed to remain in Jerusalem. However, he was later forced to escape to Egypt after Jerusalem revolted against Babylonian rule.

Like Jesus, Jeremiah often used parables to illustrate his announcements.

CHAPTER 17

Jesus the Christ

17.1 PETER'S FIRST CONFESSION

Matthew 16:13-20
Mark 8:27-30
Luke 9:18-21

Jesus went out with his disciples to the villages in the region of Caesarea Philippi. On the way, he was praying alone and asked his disciples with him, "Who do people say I am? Who's the Son of Man?"

"Some say John the Baptizer, others Elijah," they answered. "Others still that Jeremiah or one of the ancient prophets has risen."

Then he asks them, "Who do you say I am?"

Simon Peter answers, "You're the Christ, the Son of the living God."

"You're blessed, Simon, Jonah's son," Jesus replied, "because flesh and blood didn't show you this. My Father in heaven did. I tell you that you are Peter,[a] and on this rock I'll build my church and the gates of hell won't overpower[b] it. I'll give you the keys to the kingdom of heaven. Whatever you bind on earth will be bound in heaven and whatever you release on earth will be released in heaven."

City Gates

Ancient **city gates** provided a means of controlling access to walled cities. They were typically closed at sunset and reopened at sunrise. Fortified cities could have any number of them. Jerusalem, for example, had dozens of gates throughout its history, each named according to its location, purpose, or history. They could be made of wood, stone, or metal. Gates represented the authority and glory of a city, since possession of the gates meant possession of the city. Because they were often the weakest spots of a city's walls, gateways could have numerous sets of doors, each able to be locked and defended as needed. Armed sentries guarded each gate and constantly watched for impending dangers to the city.

However, city gates were more than just military assets; they were the center of city life. As portals to and from the city, gates were regularly passed through by its citizens and were therefore common sites of public announcements. Ancient prophets frequented them as forums for their messages, and executed criminals were displayed on or around gates as deterrents to future crime. Economically, they were the sites of markets, where citizens met with traders coming from afar to exchange goods. Thus gates also attracted beggars. Local judges presided over trials at gateways. As a covered area, they provided a cool location for public gatherings. Finally, travelers without any place to stay in the city could spend the night in their shelter. Accordingly, any mention of a city gate in ancient manuscripts could refer to a market, court, or public forum, in addition to its obvious role as a military checkpoint and stronghold.

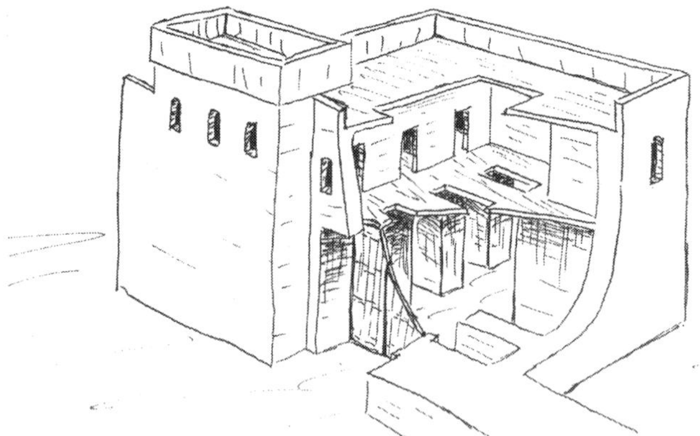

In the Bible, Abraham's nephew Lot was sitting in the gateway of Sodom when angels found him. Sampson famously ripped the gates of Gaza out and carried them away. Boaz went to Bethlehem's gate to settle legal matters regarding his intention to marry Ruth. Eli sat in Shiloh's gate waiting for news of a battle and promptly died when he heard it. David's son Absalom stood in Jerusalem's gate and decided court cases, supplanting his father. The heads of Ahab's 70 sons were piled at Jezreel's gate as a public reminder of judgment on Ahab's corruption. Jeremiah stood in Jerusalem's gates and proclaimed God's messages to Israel, and was subsequently put into stocks there for his inflammatory words. Mordecai, a Jewish community leader, was sitting at the king's gate when he overheard plans to assassinate the king. Daniel also sat at his king's gate as administrator over his kingdom. Ezra gathered all of the returned exiles at Jerusalem's Water Gate to hear Moses' Law recited. Ezekiel commanded that city gates were to remain closed on the Sabbath to discourage work. Finally, near the end of the Bible, John's vision of a restored Jerusalem saw each its twelve gates made of a single giant pearl.

Gates represented the power and glory of a city. Whoever controlled the gates – both in military and everyday matters – controlled the entire city. So when Jesus told Peter, *"the gates of hell won't overpower [my church],"* it was equivalent to saying that Peter and the church would overcome the power of hell and prevail against it.

Then he commanded the disciples not to tell anyone that he was the Christ.

17.2 JESUS PREDICTS HIS DEATH, FIRST TIME

Matthew 16:21-28
Mark 8:31-9:1
Luke 9:22-27

From then on, Jesus taught and showed his disciples that he, the Son of Man, had to go to Jerusalem; suffer much; be rejected by the elders, the High Priests, and the scribes; be killed; and be raised up on the third day. He said it openly. However, Peter took him aside and criticized him, saying, "Mercy, Lord! This will never happen to you!"

But turning around and seeing his disciples, he criticized Peter, saying, "Get behind me, Satan! You're a snare, because you're not thinking about the things of God, but of man."

Then he called the crowd with his disciples and told them, "If anyone wants to follow me, he must reject himself, pick up his cross every day, and follow me. Whoever wants to save his life will lose it, and whoever loses his life for the sake of me and the good news, he's the one who will save it. Because how does a man benefit if he gains the whole world but gives up his life? What can a man give in exchange for his life? Whoever is ashamed of me and my words in this adulterous, sinful generation, the Son of Man will be ashamed of him too. Because the Son of Man is going to come with his holy angels in his Father's glory and pay every man back for his actions.[c]

"I tell you truly," Jesus told them, "that some are standing here who won't taste death until they see the Son of Man coming into his kingdom – God's kingdom!"

17.3 MEETING WITH MOSES AND ELIJAH

Matthew 17:1-13

A. **Peter** is derived from the Greek word *petra*, meaning "rock."

B. *Katischyo* is a Greek term translated here as "**overpower.**" It's a combination of *kata* ("according to" or "against") and *ischyo* ("strong" or "powerful"). *Katischyo* can also be translated "overcome" or "prevail." It's mentioned three times in the New Testament.

C. *God spoke once, and twice I heard this: power is God's and mercy is yours, Lord, because you repay a man for his actions. – Psalm 62:11-12*

Mark 9:2-13
Luke 9:28-36

Six days later,[d] Jesus takes Peter, James, and his brother John and brings them up a high mountain by themselves to pray. While he was praying, he was transformed in front of them: his face changed and shone like the sun, and his clothes became radiant, flashing like lightning, and as white as light, like no launderer[e] can whiten. And look, two men – Moses and Elijah – appeared to them, talking with Jesus. They appeared in glory and spoke about the departure he was about to fulfill in Jerusalem.

Peter and those with him had fallen asleep, but when they woke up, they saw his glory and the two men standing with him. As they were leaving, Peter tells Jesus, "Lord! Rabbi! It's good for us to be here! If you want, I'll make three tents[f] – one for you, one for Moses, and one for Elijah."

He didn't know what to answer, nor did he even realize what he was saying, because they were terrified. But while he was still speaking, a bright cloud[g] formed and covered them. And look, a voice from the cloud said, "This is my dear Son, my chosen, whom I'm happy with.[h] Listen to him!"

D. Both Matthew and Mark record that Jesus went up the mountain **six days later**, while Luke records eight. One explanation for this discrepancy is that six days elapsed in between the two events, while eight days includes the two days of the events themselves in addition to the days in between.

E. Fulling is the process of removing impurities, such as oil and dirt, from wool. First, freshly-cut wool was pounded and stretched to remove any solid material. Then it was washed, often in tubs of human urine (the ammonia helped clean and whiten the material). Finally, the wool was thickened by matting the fibers together in a process called felting. A final wash in water removed any foul smell. The entire process made wool thick and clean. Thus a fuller was essentially an ancient **launderer** or clothes washer. The Greek word, *gnapheus*, only occurs in the Bible in this passage. To describe clothes as beyond any fuller's ability to whiten was to call them supernaturally clean, like nothing seen before.

F. *Skene* is the Greek word for **tent**. It refers to any temporary shelter that is easily broken down and transported elsewhere. The most notable tent in the Bible was the Tabernacle. While Israel was travelling through the wilderness, after leaving Egypt, they built a massive tent that housed the divine presence of God. The Tabernacle was built according to specific guidelines that were given to Moses. It had different partitions inside, with the innermost shrine (Holy of Holies) containing the ark of the covenant. Access was strictly regulated. The Tabernacle was replaced generations later when Solomon finished building the Temple in Jerusalem.

G. The presence of God is associated with **clouds** various times in the Bible. Most notably, God appeared to Israel during their escape from Egypt as a column of clouds during the day and a column of fire during the night.

Clouds and darkness surround him. Righteousness and justice are the foundations of his throne. – Psalm 97:2

H. *Look at my servant, whom I hold. He's my chosen, who pleases my soul. – Isaiah 42:1a*

When the disciples heard it, they fell on their faces and were terrified. But Jesus came and touched them, saying, "Stand up. Don't be afraid."

Then suddenly, they lifted their eyes and looked around, but they didn't see anyone except Jesus alone. As they were coming down the mountain, Jesus commanded them, "Don't tell anyone about what you've seen until the Son of Man has risen from death."

They held onto his words, discussing with one another what rising from death was.

Then his disciples asked him, "Why do the scribes say that Elijah has to come first?"[i]

"Elijah does come first and restore everything," he answered. "But how is it written that the Son of Man will suffer much and be scorned? I tell you that Elijah has already come, but they didn't recognize him. They did whatever they wanted with him, just as it's written about him. And so the Son of Man will suffer by them too."

Then the disciples understood that he had spoken to them about John the Baptizer. Afterwards, they kept silent in those days and didn't tell anyone about anything they'd seen.

I. *Remember the Law of my servant Moses, the rules and judgments I commanded him in Horeb for all Israel. And look, I'm going to send Elijah the prophet to you before the great and fearful day of the LORD comes. He'll turn fathers' hearts to their children and children's hearts to their fathers, so that I won't come and strike the land with a curse. – Malachi 4:4-6*

CHAPTER 18

About Greatness

18.1 MOONSTRUCK BOY HEALED

Matthew 17:14-20
Mark 9:14-29
Luke 9:37-43a

The next day, when they came down the mountain to the disciples, they saw crowds around them and scribes arguing with them. When the whole crowd saw him, they were shocked and immediately ran up to welcome him. "What are you discussing with them?" he asked.

A man from the crowd shouted and came up to Jesus. Kneeling down, he answered, "Teacher, I beg you to look at my son, because he's my one and only. Lord, have mercy on him! I brought him to you because he's moonstruck[a] and very sick, possessed with a spirit that makes him speechless. Whenever it seizes him, he suddenly screams and it throws him into convulsions, then he foams and grinds his teeth

A. Matthew is the only Gospel writer to use the Greek verb *seleniazomai*, which translates literally to "**moonstruck.**" Today, it's the Greek word for seizure, but in ancient times it referred to being affected by the moon in some way. *Lunaticus* is the Latin equivalent, which is where the English "lunatic" comes from. The meaning of *seleniazomai* in this context is unclear, but it may be related to seizure-like activity. The Greeks may have believed that seizures and epilepsy were related to the moon's cycle.

and withers away. Only with exertion does it leave him, crushing him as it goes. I told your disciples to throw it out, but they couldn't!"

"O faithless, contrary generation," he answers. "How long will I be with you? How long will I put up with you? Bring your son to me!"

But as they were bringing him, he saw [Jesus] and immediately the spirit threw him into convulsions. Falling to the ground, he rolled around and foamed.

"How long has this been happening to him?" he asked his father.

"Since childhood," he said. "It has often thrown him into both fire and water to kill him. But if you can do anything, be moved and help!"

Jesus replied, "'If you can?' Everything is possible to him who believes."

Immediately the boy's father cried out, "I do believe! Help my unbelief!"

When Jesus saw that a crowd was running together, he rebuked the unclean spirit, saying, "You deaf and mute spirit, I command you to come out of him and don't enter him again."

After crying out and causing many convulsions, it came out and he became so much like a corpse that many said he was dead. But Jesus took his hand and raised him up. Jesus gave him back to his father and he was healed from then on. Then they were all blown away at God's greatness.

When he came into the house, his disciples asked him privately, "Why couldn't we throw it out?"

"Because of the smallness of your faith," he answers. "I tell you truly that if you have faith like a mustard seed,[b] you can say to this mountain, 'Move from here to there,' and it'll move. Nothing will be impossible for you. But this kind can't come out by anything but prayer."

18.2 JESUS PREDICTS HIS DEATH, SECOND TIME

Matthew 17:22-23
Mark 9:30-32
Luke 9:43b-45

From there they left and went through Galilee. They gathered there, but Jesus didn't want anyone to know. While everyone was

B. **Mustard seeds** are about 2 mm in diameter.

amazed at everything he was doing, he taught his disciples and told them, "Let these words be set in your ears: the Son of Man will be betrayed into men's hands and they'll kill him. Then when he has been killed, he'll rise three days later."

However, they didn't understand these words because it was hidden from them. They were very upset but afraid to ask him about it.

18.3 PAYING THE TWO DRACHMAS

Matthew 17:24-27

When they came to Capernaum, those who collected the two drachmas[c] came to Peter and asked, "Doesn't your teacher pay the two drachmas?"

"Yes," he replies.

But when he came into the house, Jesus spoke to him first, saying, "What do you think, Simon? Who do the kings of the earth collect tolls and taxes from, their sons or strangers?"

"From strangers," Peter replied.

"So the sons are free," Jesus told him. "However, so we don't cause them to trip, go to the sea and throw in a hook. Take the first fish that comes up and when you open its mouth, you'll find a shekel.[d] Take it and give it to them for you and for me."

18.4 GREATNESS IN THE KINGDOM

Matthew 18:1-10
Mark 9:33-43, 45, 47-48
Luke 9:46-50; 17:1-3a

On the road, as they came to Capernaum, an argument started among them about who was the greatest. When they got to the house, Jesus, knowing the thoughts in their hearts, asked them, "What were you discussing on the way?"

But they were silent. Then the disciples approached Jesus and asked

C. Every male over 20 years old was required to pay an annual tax of **two drachmas** for the upkeep of the Temple. The drachma was a Greek coin whose name means "grasp" or "fistful." Each city had its own drachma currency, so its value and exchange rate were based on the economy of the city. However, one drachma in first century Palestine was approximately the daily wage of a skilled worker or soldier.

D. One **shekel** was worth four drachmas, enough for the annual temple tax of two men. The shekel was also called the *tetradrachm* (literally "four-drachma") or *stater* in Greek.

him, "Who's the greatest in the kingdom of heaven?"

Sitting down, he called the Twelve. He tells them, "If anyone wants to be the first, he must be the last of all and the servant of all."

Taking a child, he stood him among them by his side and took him in his arms. "Truly I tell you," he said, "unless you turn and become like children, you won't enter the kingdom of heaven. So whoever humbles himself like this child is the greatest in the kingdom of heaven. Whoever receives one child like this in my name receives me. And whoever receives me doesn't just receive me but also him who sent me. The smallest of you all is the greatest."

Then John said, "Master, Teacher, we saw someone throwing demons out in your name and we tried to stop him because he wasn't following us."

But Jesus said, "Don't stop him, because there isn't anyone who will do a miracle in my name and be able to curse me soon afterward.[e] Whoever isn't against us is for us. And whoever gives you a cup of cold water to drink because of the Christ's name, truly I tell you, he won't lose his reward."

He told his disciples, "It's not impossible that snares come, but woe to the one they come through! Whoever causes one of these little ones who believes in me to trip, it'd be better for him to have a donkey's millstone[f] hung around his neck and be thrown and drowned in the depths of the sea. Be aware!

E. *No one speaking by God's Spirit says, "Jesus is cursed." And no one can say, "Jesus is Lord," except by the Holy Spirit. – 1 Corinthians 12:3*

F. Millstones were large stone wheels with a hole drilled through the middle to facilitate an axle. It was pulled on a slab to grind grain or press olives. Sometimes millstones were so large and heavy that only pack animals could operate them. Thus a **donkey's millstone** (*onikos mylos*) was one of the largest functional rocks in ancient societies.

"Woe to the world because of snares![g] It's unavoidable that snares come, but woe to the man they come through!

"If your hand causes you to trip,[h] cut it off, because it's better to enter life crippled than go to hell, the endless fire, with both your hands. If your foot causes you to trip, cut it off, because it's better to enter life lame than be thrown into hell with both your feet. If your eye causes you to trip, pull it out, because it's better for you to enter God's kingdom with one eye than be thrown into hell, where their worm doesn't die and their fire isn't put out.[i]

"Make sure you don't scorn one of these little ones, because I tell you that their angels in heaven continually see my Father's face in heaven."

18.5 FORGIVENESS

Matthew 18:15-35
Luke 17:3b-4

"If your brother sins, go and correct him between you and him alone. If he listens to you and repents, forgive him – you've won your brother. But if he doesn't listen, take one or two more with you, so that by the mouth of two or three witnesses every word will be confirmed.[j] If he refuses to listen to them, tell the church.[k] And if he refuses to even listen to the church, let him be like a Gentile and a tax collector to you. I tell you truly that whatever you bind on earth will be bound in heaven and whatever you release on earth will be released in heaven.

"Again I tell you, if two of you agree about anything you ask for on

G. The Greek word *skandalon* is a stick or stone that causes someone to trip, often translated as "stumbling block" in the Bible. It can also refer to the trigger of a snare, or to the **snare** itself. But when describing a person, *skandalon* is someone who causes another to sin or err in some way. It's where the English "scandal" originates.

H. *Skandalizo* is the verb form of *skandalon*, that is, the act of **tripping** or stumbling. It can also been translated "fall away."

I. *Then they'll go and look at the corpses of the men who have rebelled against me. Their worm won't die and their fire won't be extinguished, and they'll be revolting to everybody. – Isaiah 66:24*

J. *One witness can't stand up against a man because of a depravity or sin he has committed. But a word will be confirmed by the mouths of two or three witnesses. – Deuteronomy 19:15*

K. Although it occurs numerous times in the rest of the New Testament, "**church**" only occurs in the Gospels twice, both recorded by Matthew. It comes from the Greek *ekklesia*, which refers to an assembly of people in a public place. Over time, "church" has come to signify the worldwide collection of Christian believers or any Christian assembly, but in the first century it would be more accurately translated as simply "assembly" or "congregation," without any religious connotation.

earth, it'll be done for you by my Father in heaven, because where two or three have gathered together in my name, I'm there among them."

Then Peter came and asked him, "Lord, how often should I forgive my brother when he sins against me? Up to seven times?"

"I don't tell you up to seven times," Jesus replies, "but up to seventy times seven.[l] If he sins against you seven times per day but returns to you seven times, saying, 'I repent,' forgive him. Because of this, the kingdom of heaven is compared to a king who wanted to settle accounts with his slaves. When he started settling, one who owed him 10,000 talents[m] was brought to him. But because he couldn't repay it, his lord

L. Lamech, a descendant of Cain, announced a poem of revenge after killing a man: *"If Cain is avenged sevenfold, then Lamech seventy-sevenfold." (Genesis 4:24)* Jesus' use of the number "**seventy times seven**" may also be translated as "seventy-seven," possibly referencing Lamech's words. In the Bible, seven was the number of completeness.

Slavery

By some estimates, up to a third of the Roman Empire's vast population was enslaved, especially in Italy itself. The Roman economy depended on them: **slaves** were the labor force for the massive industries of farming and mining. More domestic roles included butchering, cooking, cleaning, and clothes-making. Educated slaves were even more valuable, working as accountants, doctors, or tutors. A slave's room, board, and overall quality of life weren't as good as free members of the *familia*, but were likely comparable to that of less affluent Romans.

Slaves had fewer rights than citizens, but over time they received increasing legal protection with the ability to file complaints of abuse or mistreatment against their masters. Slave revolts were common, but were swiftly put down by the Roman military. Additionally, professional slave hunters tracked runaway slaves and returned them for a reward. If caught, runaway slaves could be legally beaten, executed, or branded with the Greek letter *phi* ("ϕ") for *fugitivus*.

Most slaves were acquired in war when Roman armies brought captives back from campaigns. Enemy soldiers were far more valuable to enslave than imprison or execute. Other people were enslaved as children when their parents sold them to pay debts. Conversely, freeing a slave was called *manimissio*, meaning "send from the hand," and was typically a public event. Slaves could be freed after performing a particularly good act or lengthy service, while others purchased their freedom from their masters. Any child of a freed slave (*libertus*) would be a full citizen, while children of slaves were born into slavery, even if their parents later attained freedom.

Slavery is mentioned frequently in the Old Testament. Israel was allowed to purchase foreign slaves or enslave captives of war, and Israelites could sell themselves or their children into slavery to pay debts. Abraham had slaves in his household, as did his descendants, and even four of Jacob's twelve sons were born to his wives' female servants (Dan and Naphtali to Bilhah; Gad and Asher to Zilpah). Furthermore, Joseph, one of the twelve sons of Jacob, was sold to slave traders by his brothers. Moses' Law stated that slaves shouldn't be mistreated, especially Hebrew slaves, and if a slave was injured by his master, he was to be freed. Furthermore, Hebrew slaves were to be released after six years of service. Later in the Bible, Paul the Apostle didn't denounce slavery, but encouraged slaves to seek their freedom. He also instructed masters to treat their slaves well, and said that slaves should obey their masters.

commanded him to be sold, along with his wife and children and everything he had, to pay the debt. The slave fell down and bowed before him, saying, 'Have patience with me and I'll pay everything back to you!' The slave's lord was moved and released him, forgiving the debt. But the slave went out and found another slave who owed him 100 denarii.[n] He seized him and choked him, saying, 'Pay back what you owe.' So the other slave fell down and begged him, saying, 'Have patience with me and I'll pay you back!' But he was resolved and went and threw him in prison until he had paid back what was owed. When other slaves saw what had happened, they were very upset and went to tell their lord everything. Summoning him, the lord tells him, 'You wicked slave. I forgave your whole debt because you begged me. Shouldn't you also have had mercy on the other slave like I had mercy on you?' Enraged, his lord handed him over to the torturers until he could repay all he owed. My heavenly Father will do the same to you too if each of you doesn't forgive your brother in your heart."

M. The talent is an ancient unit of mass that varied in quantity throughout history. However, the common talent mentioned in the New Testament was about 59 kilograms (130 pounds). It was the largest unit of silver in the ancient Middle East and was divided into 60 mina, which were further subdivided into 60 shekels each. One silver talent was worth more than 15 years' wages to a common laborer, so **10,000 talents** was an enormous amount of money, beyond the capacity of any worker to earn in his lifetime. In the Bible, this term (*talanton*) is only used by Matthew, a prior tax collector. "Talent" could also refer to the balance scales themselves.

N. One denarius was typically paid as the daily wage for unskilled labor, so **100 denarii** was equal to 25 shekels, since a shekel was worth four denarii.

CHAPTER 19

To Jerusalem

19.1 FOLLOWING JESUS

Matthew 8:19-22
Luke 9:57-62

As they were going along the road, a scribe told him, "Teacher, I'll follow you wherever you go!"

Jesus replies, "Foxes have holes and birds of the air have nests, but the Son of Man has nowhere to lay his head."

Then he told another disciple, "Follow me."

"Lord," he replied, "let me go and bury my father first."

"Let the dead bury their own dead," Jesus replies. "As for you, go and announce God's kingdom."

Another also said, "I'll follow you, Lord, but first let me take leave[a] back home."

But Jesus replied, "No one who puts his hand to the plow and looks back[b] is fit for God's kingdom."

A. The Greek verb *apotasso* translates to "separate from," "**take leave**," or "bid farewell." It was a formal act that likely included arranging one's affairs before leaving.

19.2 DISCUSSION WITH JESUS' BROTHERS

Luke 9:51-56
John 7:2-10

Now the Jewish Feast of Booths was soon, so his brothers told him, "Leave here and go into Judea so your disciples can see the work you're doing too, because no one does anything in secret when he wants to be public. If you're doing this, show yourself to the world."

Not even his brothers believed in him.

"My time hasn't come yet," Jesus tells them, "but your time is always here. The world can't hate you, but it hates me because I testify about it, that its work is evil. Go up to the feast yourselves. I won't go to this feast, because my time hasn't fully come yet."

He told them this and stayed in Galilee. But when the days were approaching for his ascension,[c] he was determined to go to Jerusalem. So when his brothers had gone up to the feast, he went up too, but secretly not openly. He sent messengers ahead of himself and they entered every Samaritan village to prepare for him. However, they didn't receive him because he was continuing on to Jerusalem. When his disciples James and John saw it, they said, "Lord, do you want us to command fire to come down from heaven and destroy them?"

But he turned and rebuked them, and they went on to another village.

B. In ancient agriculture, the best way to **plow in a straight line** was to fix one's eyes on a distant point and continually walk towards it. Diverting one's eyes from the target led to walking a convoluted path.
   Let your eyes look ahead and your eyelids be straight forward. – Proverbs 4:25

C. The only time the word *analempsis* occurs in the Bible is when Luke foreshadows Jesus' **ascension** into heaven. The word literally means "be received up."

The Feast of Booths

On the 15th day of the seventh month (in mid-October), Jews celebrated the **Feast of Booths** after the crops had been harvested. It's also called the Feast of Ingathering, the Feast of Tabernacles, or *Sukkot* (in Hebrew). The event lasted seven days. Leviticus records that Jews were to take branches and construct temporary shelters (booths, tabernacles) to live in for the duration of the feast. These booths were built anywhere outside the home: on roofs, within courtyards, on the streets, or in marketplaces. The feast commemorated when Israel lived in tents in the wilderness during their escape from Egypt. It also celebrated the completion of the harvest, similar to the modern holiday of Thanksgiving. Numerous animal and crop sacrifices were given to God and all work was forbidden, unless required for the feast itself. The Feast of Booths was a major national holiday, one of three events during the year where every male was to *"appear before the Lord your God in the place he chooses," (Deuteronomy 16:16)* which was typically in Jerusalem. Zechariah recorded that any families that didn't attend the feast would be plagued with no rain.

CHAPTER 20

The Feast of Booths

20.1 ARRIVAL IN JERUSALEM

John 7:11-36

The Jews were looking for him at the feast, saying, "Where is he?" There was a lot of complaining about him among the crowds. Some said, "He's good," while others said, "No, he misleads people." However, no one was speaking openly about him, out of fear of the Jews.

Halfway through the feast, Jesus went up to the Temple and taught. The Jews were amazed, saying, "How does this man know the writings[a] without an education?"

"My teaching isn't mine, it's his who sent me," Jesus replied. "If anyone is willing to do his will, he'll know about this teaching, whether it's from God or from me. Whoever speaks from himself is looking for his own glory. But whoever is looking for the glory of the one who sent him, he's true and there's no injustice in him. Didn't Moses give you the Law? Yet none of you obeys the Law. Why do you want to kill me?"

A. The Greek word *gramma* refers to any document or record and is where the English term "grammar" originates. It can be translated "**writings**," "letter," or "bill." It's used 13 times in the New Testament, most commonly in reference to a letter. *Graphe* is the more typical Greek word for the Jewish Scriptures, occurring 51 times.

Then the crowd answered him, "You have a demon! Who wants to kill you?"

"I did one deed and you're all amazed," Jesus answered. "Moses gave you circumcision (even though it's not from Moses, but from the fathers) and on the Sabbath you circumcise a man.[b] However, if a man gets circumcised on the Sabbath so Moses' Law won't be broken, why are you angry with me because I've healed a whole man on the Sabbath? Don't judge by appearances. Judge the righteous judgment."

So some of those in Jerusalem said, "Isn't this the man they want to kill? Look, he's speaking freely and they're not saying anything to him. Don't the leaders know whether this is actually the Christ? We know where this one's from, but no one will know where the Christ is from when he comes."[c]

Then Jesus taught in the Temple, crying out, "You know me and also know my origin. I haven't come of myself, but he who sent me is true, whom you don't know. I know him because I'm from him and he sent me."

So they wanted to arrest him, but no one laid a hand on him because his time hadn't come yet. But many in the crowd believed in him and said, "When the Christ comes, will he do more miracles than these?"

The Pharisees heard the crowd murmuring this about him, so the High Priests and the Pharisees sent officers to arrest him. Therefore Jesus said, "I'm with you for a short time and then I go to him who sent me. You'll look for me, but you won't find me, because you can't come where I am."

Then the Jews said to one another, "Where does this man plan to go that we won't find him? He isn't planning to go along with the dispersion[d] among the Greeks and teach the Greeks, is he? So what are these words he has said, 'You'll look for me but won't find me, because you can't come where I am'?"

B. *On the eighth day the body of his foreskin will be circumcised. – Leviticus 12:3*

C. It's unknown where the belief that the **Messiah's origins won't be known** comes from, but it may be an interpretation of the prophecy of Malachi 3:1, which states *"the master you desire will suddenly come into his Temple."* In keeping with this interpretation, the Mishnah states, "three come unawares: the Messiah, a found article, and a scorpion." However, Micah 5:2 predicted that the Messiah will come from Bethlehem.

D. After their exile to Babylon, Jews began dispersing throughout the world in a movement called the *diaspora*, which is the Greek word for "scatter." Much of the Jewish **dispersion** was forced, as captives were taken into exile by conquering nations or as refugees fleeing war or famine. Other times the relocation was voluntary, to pursue business or simply start

20.2 UNABLE TO ARREST JESUS

John 7:37-52

On the last and greatest day of the feast, Jesus stood up and shouted out, "If anyone's thirsty, let whoever believes in me come and drink, as the Scripture has said![e] And rivers of living water will flow out of his belly!"

He said this about the Spirit, which his believers were going to receive. The Spirit hadn't been given yet because Jesus hadn't been glorified.

When they heard these words, the people said, "This is definitely the prophet," while others said, "This is the Christ," and still others said, "The Christ isn't going to come from Galilee, is he? Hasn't the Scripture said that the Christ comes from David's family,[f] and from Bethlehem,[g] the village where David was from?"

So the crowd was divided because of him. Some of them wanted to arrest him, but no one laid a hand on him.

After the officers came back to the High Priests and the Pharisees, they asked them, "Why didn't you bring him in?"

"No one has ever spoken the way this man speaks," the officers answered.

"Have you been led astray too?" the Pharisees replied. "Have any of the leaders or the Pharisees believed in him? But this crowd that doesn't know the Law is cursed!"

Then Nicodemus – the one who came to him before, being one of

---

afresh elsewhere. Other nations similarly dispersed around the world, such as the Greeks around the time of Alexander the Great, settling along the Mediterranean coast. But more than others, the Jews retained their culture despite generations of living away from their homeland. Furthermore, they maintained ties by regularly travelling back to Jerusalem to worship in the Temple.

E. *Hey! Everyone who thirsts, come to the waters. And you who don't have money, come, buy and eat. Come, buy wine and milk without money and without cost. Why do you spend money for no bread and your work for no satisfaction? Listen to me carefully: eat well and pamper yourself with fatness. – Isaiah 55:1-2*

[Our fathers] all drank the same spiritual drink, because they drank from a spiritual rock that followed them. That rock was Christ. – 1 Corinthians 10:4

F. *The LORD swore a truth to David, which he won't return from: "I'll put the fruit of your belly on your throne. If your sons keep my covenant and my testimony, which I'll teach them, then their sons will also sit on your throne forever." – Psalm 132:11-12*

G. *As for you, Bethlehem Ephrathah, too small to be among the thousands from Judah, someone will go out from you to be Israel's ruler. His origins are ancient, from the days of eternity. – Micah 5:2*

them – tells them, "Does our Law judge a man before it hears from him first and knows what he's doing?"

"Are you from Galilee too?" they replied. "Look and see that no prophet comes from Galilee."

20.3 FORGIVENESS OF IMMORAL WOMAN

John 7:53-8:11

Everyone went home, but Jesus went to the Mount of Olives. At dawn, he came to the Temple again and all the people came to him, so he sat down and taught them.

Then the scribes and the Pharisees bring a woman who was caught having an affair.[h] After putting her in the middle, they say, "Teacher, this woman was caught having an affair and Moses commanded us in the Law to stone such women.[i] What do you say?"

H. Under Moses' Law, both the man and the woman **convicted of having an affair** were to be executed.

I. *If a man is found lying with a married woman, then the two of them will die – the man who lay with the woman and the woman. You'll burn the evil from Israel. If a virgin girl is engaged to a man and another finds her in the city and lies with her, then bring the two of them to the city gate and stone them to death – the girl because she didn't cry out in the city, and the man because he humiliated his neighbor's wife. So you'll burn the evil from among you. – Deuteronomy 22:22-24*

Sin

The term "**sin**" refers to the act of willfully violating moral law, as defined by God's commandments. The Hebrew word (*het*) that translates to "sin" literally means "go astray." Similar Hebrew terms, such as *pasha*, *aveira*, and *avone*, translate to "trespass," "transgression," and "iniquity," respectively. Genesis records that God made the human race without sin, but Adam and Eve, the first man and woman, disobeyed God's command not to eat fruit from a certain tree. For this, they were cursed and banished from Eden, the garden they were to live in. This is how Jews believed sin entered the world, bringing death, pain, and destruction with it. Although there was nothing to define sin before Moses' Law, Genesis records that, generations after Adam, the human race became so wicked that God regretted creating man in the first place. However, Moses' Law eventually came, which detailed what constituted sin and how it could be covered over (atoned for). This system became the basis of Jewish religion and culture.

The woman saw that the tree had good food, which her eyes wanted, and she desired the tree to make her wise, so she took its fruit and ate it. Then she gave it to her husband with her, and he ate it.... Then the LORD God asked, "What have you done?"

– Genesis 3:6,13

Sin's payment is death.

– Romans 6:23

They were saying this to test him, so they could accuse him. But Jesus crouched down and wrote on the ground with his finger. When they kept asking him, he straightened up and told them, "Whoever among you is without sin should throw the first stone at her."

Again he crouched down and wrote on the ground. When they heard it, they went out one by one, beginning with the oldest, until he was left alone with the woman in the middle. Straightening up, Jesus asked her, "Woman, where are they? Didn't anyone condemn you?"

"No one, Lord," she replied.

"I don't condemn you either," Jesus said. "Go, and from now on, don't sin anymore."

20.4 LIGHT OF THE WORLD

John 8:12-30

Then Jesus spoke to them again, "I am the light of the world. Whoever follows me won't walk in the dark but will have the light of life."

"You're witnessing about yourself," the Pharisees said, "so your testimony isn't true."

"Even if I witness about myself, my testimony is true," Jesus answered them, "because I know where I came from and where I'm going. But you don't know where I came from or where I'm going. You judge according to the body,[J] but I'm not judging anyone. But even if I do judge, my judgment is true, because I'm not alone. It's me and the Father who sent me. Even in your Law it's written that the testimony of two men is true. I am he who witnesses about myself, and the Father who sent me witnesses about me too."

So they asked him, "Where is your father?"

"You don't know me or my Father," Jesus answered. "If you knew me, you'd know my Father as well."

He spoke these words in the treasury, while he taught in the Temple. But no one arrested him, because his time hadn't come yet.

Again he told them, "I go away, but you'll look for me and die in your sin, because you can't come where I am going."

J. The Greek word *sarx* means "**body**" or "flesh," referring to the physical substance of the living body. It speaks to the worldly nature of man, particularly in terms of his imperfection and propensity for sin.

So the Jews said, "Certainly he won't kill himself, will he, since he says, 'You can't come where I am going'?"

"You're from below, but I'm from above," he told them. "You're of this world, but I'm not of this world. Therefore, I've told you that you'll die in your sins, because unless you believe that I am, you'll die in your sins."

So they asked him, "Who are you?"

"What have I been telling you from the start?" Jesus answered. "I have so much to say and to judge about you, but the one who sent me is true. And what I've heard from him I tell the world."

They didn't realize that he was talking to them about the Father. So Jesus said, "When you lift up the Son of Man, then you'll know who I am. But I do nothing on my own – I say this as the Father has taught me. And the one who sent me is with me. He hasn't left me alone, because I always do what pleases him."

As he said this, many believed in him.

20.5 JESUS AND ABRAHAM

John 8:31-59

Jesus was telling the Jews who had believed, "If you stay in my word, you're truly my disciples. Then you'll know the truth and the truth will set you free."[k]

"We're Abraham's seed, and we've never been slaves to anyone," they answered. "So how can you say, 'You'll be free'?"

"Truly truly, I tell you," Jesus replied, "everyone who sins is a slave to sin. The slave doesn't stay in the house forever, but the Son stays forever. So if the Son makes you free, you'll certainly be free. I know you're Abraham's seed, but you want to kill me because my word has no place in you. I say what I've seen with my Father, and you do what you've heard from your father too."

"Abraham is our father," they said.

"If you're Abraham's children, do Abraham's work,"[l] Jesus tells them. "But as it is, you're looking to kill me, a man who has told you

---

K. *The law of the Spirit of life in Christ Jesus has freed you from the law of sin and death. Because what the Law couldn't do – as it was weak through the body – God did by sending his own son in the image of a sinful body for the sin of the body. So the righteousness of the Law was completed in us, who don't walk by the body but by the Spirit. – Romans 8:2-4*

Israel Enslaved

The nation of **Israel has been enslaved** numerous times throughout its tumultuous history. In fact, Israel grew from a family of 70 into a nation under the Egyptians, who forced them into heavy labor. After their exodus from Egypt to Palestine, they were periodically oppressed by the Philistines and other Canaanite nations. Subsequent freedom ended when Assyria conquered Israel and Babylon conquered Judah, each enslaving all who survived the sieges. Persia assumed lordship thereafter, although it allowed the Jews to return home. Then the Greeks conquered and enslaved much of the Mediterranean world during Alexander the Great's campaigns. Periods of Jewish independence did occur, such as under David and Solomon, and during the Hasmonean dynasty, but never permanently. During the time of Jesus in the first century AD, the Roman Empire held power over the Jewish homeland, ruling through a series of client kings.

Look, we're slaves today. And as for the land you gave our fathers, to eat its fruit and goodness, look, we're slaves in it.

– Nehemiah 9:36

the truth, which I've heard from God. Abraham didn't do this. You're doing your father's work."

"We aren't bastard children!" they replied. "We have one Father – God!"

Then Jesus said, "If God were your Father, you'd love me,[m] because I came from God and now I'm here. I haven't come on my own – he sent me. Why don't you understand my words? It's because you can't hear my words. You're of your father the Devil[n] and you want to do your father's lusts. He was a murderer from the beginning and doesn't stand in the truth, because there's no truth in him. Whenever he tells a lie, he speaks from his own nature, because he's a liar and the father of doing so. But because I speak the truth, you don't believe me. Which one of you convicts me of sin? If I speak the truth, why don't you believe me? Whoever is of God hears God's words. This is why you don't hear: because you're not of God."[o]

"Don't we correctly say that you're a Samaritan and have a demon?" the Jews answered him.

"I don't have a demon," Jesus said, "but I honor my Father and you dishonor me. I don't look for my own glory, because there's someone

L. Abraham was the original patriarch of the Jews and the Jewish faith. So a command to "**do Abraham's work**" is analogous to a command to have faith and act accordingly.

M. *Whoever believes that Jesus is the Christ is born of God. And whoever loves the Father loves the one born of him. – 1 John 5:1*

N. *The sin-doer is of the Devil, because the Devil sinned from the beginning. – 1 John 3:8*

O. *We're from God. He who knows God listens to us. Whoever isn't from God doesn't listen to us. – 1 John 4:6*

else who looks and judges. I tell you, truly truly, if anyone keeps my word he'll never see death."[p]

"Now we know you have a demon," the Jews replied. "Abraham and the prophets died, but you say, 'If anyone keeps my word he'll never see death.' You're certainly not greater than our father Abraham who died, are you? The prophets died as well, so what do you make of yourself?"

"If I glorify myself, my glory is nothing," Jesus answered. "But it's my Father who glorifies me, about whom you say, 'He's our God.' You don't know him, but I know him. If I say I don't know him, I'd be a liar like you, but I do know him and keep his word. Your father Abraham was overjoyed that he might see my day. He saw it and was glad."

So the Jews said, "You're not even fifty years old and you've seen Abraham?"

"Truly truly, I tell you," said Jesus, "before Abraham existed, I am."[q]

So they picked up rocks to throw at him, but Jesus was hidden and went out of the Temple.

20.6 BLIND MAN HEALED, THEN TESTIFIES

John 9

Passing by, he saw a man blind since birth. His disciples asked him, "Rabbi, who sinned that he was born blind, he or his parents?"[r]

"Neither he nor his parents sinned," Jesus answered, "but so that God's work could be shown in him. We must do the work of the one who sent me as long as it's day. Night is coming, when no one can work.

P. *We see him – Jesus – who, for a little, was made lower than the angels, because suffering death crowned him with glory and honor, so that by God's grace he tasted death for everyone. – Hebrews 2:9*

Q. *God told Moses, "I Am who I Am... You'll say this to Israel's sons, 'I Am has sent you.'" – Exodus 3:14*

R. According to the Talmud, the Pharisees held that "there's no death without sin, and there's no suffering without iniquity." So the belief in ancient Judea was that someone was morally responsible for every physical defect or suffering. In this case, Jesus' disciples assumed that the man's **congenital blindness was caused by sin**, either by his parents or by himself in a pre-existential state. However, Ezekiel states the opposite is true, that each individual is responsible for his own sin.

The soul that sins will die. A son won't bear his father's punishment, nor will a father bear his son's punishment. The righteousness of the righteous will be on himself; the wickedness of the wicked will be on himself. – Ezekiel 18:20

The Pool of Siloam

In preparation for the impending Assyrian invasion and siege of Jerusalem in 701 BC, King Hezekiah blocked the stream flowing from the Gihon Spring near Jerusalem and diverted it into the city through an underground tunnel, which thereafter served as a freshwater source within the city walls. Buried and forgotten for centuries, the Siloam tunnel (also called Hezekiah's tunnel) was rediscovered in 1838 under Jerusalem. Excavations and an inscription in its wall have shown the tunnel to be a zigzagged passage over half a kilometer long that was carved through solid rock by two work crews digging from either end. It ended in a small reservoir, the **Siloam Pool**, which was discovered in 2005. Hezekiah's tunnel may or may not be related to a water tunnel that David had used generations earlier to conquer Jerusalem from the Jebusites. A tower was reportedly built nearby, which collapsed tragically sometime before Jesus' ministry. The Greek word *Siloam* comes from the Hebrew word *shiloah*, a derivative of *shalach* ("send" or "stretch out").

While I'm in the world, I'm the light of the world."

Saying this, he spat on the ground and made mud[s] from the spit, then he put the mud on his eyes and told him, "Go and wash in the Siloam Pool" (which translates to "Sent").

So he left and washed, and he returned seeing![t] Consequently, the neighbors and those who saw him before as a beggar asked, "Isn't this the one who used to sit and beg?" Others said, "That's him," while others, "No, but he's like him."

But he kept saying, "I'm the one!"

So they asked him, "How were your eyes opened?"

"The man called Jesus made mud and anointed my eyes," he answered. "Then he told me to go to Siloam and wash. So I went away and washed, and then I could see!"

"Where is he?" they asked him.

"I don't know," he replies.

Now the day when Jesus made the mud and opened his eyes was the Sabbath. So they bring him who was previously blind to the Pharisees. The Pharisees again asked him how he could see. So he told them, "He put mud on my eyes and I washed and then I could see."

Consequently, some of the Pharisees said, "This man isn't from God, because he doesn't observe the Sabbath." While others said, "How can a man who's a sinner do such signs?" So there was a division among them.

S. **Making mud** or clay was considered work and prohibited on the Sabbath by traditional Jewish law, but it wasn't explicitly prohibited in Moses' Law.

T. *Out of gloom and darkness, the blind's eyes will see. – Isaiah 29:18*

Then they ask the blind man again, "What do you say about him, since he opened your eyes?"

"He's a prophet," he replied.

The Jews didn't believe that he had been blind and then could see until they called his parents and asked them, "Is this your son, who you say was born blind? How can he see now?"

"We know this is our son and that he was born blind," his parents answered, "but we don't know how he sees now. Ask him, he's of age. He can speak for himself."

His parents said this because they were afraid of the Jews, because the Jews had agreed that if anyone confessed that he was the Christ, he would be excommunicated.[u] Therefore his parents said, "He's of age, ask him."

So a second time they called the man who had been blind, saying, "Give glory to God. We know this man is a sinner."

"I don't know whether he's a sinner," he answered, "but one thing I do know: I was blind, but now I see."

So they asked him, "What did he do to you? How did he open your eyes?"

"I've already told you and you didn't listen," he answered. "Why do you want to hear it again? You don't want to become his disciples too, do you?"

They scorned him and said, "You're his disciple, but we're Moses' disciples. We know God spoke to Moses, but as for him, we don't know where he's from."

"Well, this is amazing," the man answered. "You don't know where he's from and he opened my eyes. We know that God doesn't hear sinners, but if anyone fears God and does his will, he hears him. For eternity, it has never been heard that anyone has opened the eyes of someone born blind. If this man wasn't from God, he could do nothing."

"You were born completely in sin and yet you're lecturing us?" they answered.

So they threw him out.

U. *Aposynagogos* means "separate from the synagogue." This Greek term only occurs three times in the New Testament, all of them in John. Since the synagogue was the center of Jewish society and culture, to be banned from it was a bitter **excommunication** and meant expulsion from Jewish society.

Jesus heard that they had thrown him out. Finding him, he asked, "Do you believe in the Son of Man?"

"Lord, who is he so I can believe in him?" he answered.

"You've certainly seen him – he's the one talking with you," Jesus said.

"Lord, I believe!" he said, and he worshipped him.

"I came into this world for judgment," Jesus said, "so that those not seeing may see and that the seeing may become blind."

The Pharisees were with him and heard this. So they asked, "We aren't blind too, are we?"

"If you were blind, you'd have no sin," Jesus answered. "But because you say, 'We see,' your sin remains."

20.7 GOOD SHEPHERD

John 10:1-21

"Truly truly, I tell you that whoever doesn't come into the sheep's courtyard through the door, but climbs up another way, is a thief and a plunderer. But whoever comes in through the door is a shepherd to the sheep. The doorman opens to him and the sheep hear his voice. He calls his sheep by name and leads them out.[V] When he sends his own out, he goes ahead of them, and the sheep follow him because they know his voice. They won't follow a stranger but will run from him because they don't know the stranger's voice."

Jesus told them this illustration, but they didn't understand what he was telling them. So Jesus told them again, "Truly truly, I tell you, I am the door to the sheep. All who came before me were thieves and plunderers, but the sheep didn't hear them. I am the door. If anyone comes in through me, he'll be saved. He'll go in and out and find pasture. The thief just comes to steal, kill, and destroy, but I came that they might have life, and have an abundance!

"I am the good shepherd.[W] The good shepherd lays down his life for the sheep. The employee,[X] who's neither the shepherd nor the sheep's

V. *He'll feed his flock and gather the lambs with his arm and carry them in his chest. He'll lead those nursing. – Isaiah 40:11*

W. *The LORD is my shepherd. I lack nothing. – Psalm 23:1*

X. *"Woe, you shepherds destroying and scattering the sheep of my pasture!" declares the LORD. The LORD God of Israel says this about the shepherds who are shepherding my people,*

Sheep and Shepherds

Sheep were essential to life in the ancient Middle East and are mentioned more than any other animal in the Bible. They provided families with both food (lamb, mutton, milk) and clothing (wool, sheepskin). Furthermore, because their complex four-stomached digestive systems were able to process vegetation that other animals couldn't, sheep were ideal livestock for the arid terrain. However, unlike modern sheep that have been bred strictly for white wool, ancient sheep were likely white, brown, black, or a combination of colors. They also had long tails, unlike today's sheep that have their tails clipped as lambs for improved hygiene. In fact, fat sheep tails were prized as choice cuts of meat and often sacrificed as burnt offerings to God.

Shepherding, therefore, was a major industry. Because of their nomadic and solitary lifestyle, **shepherds** were often young sons of peasants or hired hands who had no children. Sheep are notoriously defenseless animals, prone to wander off into trouble if not carefully guarded. But because they're flock animals, with a strong natural instinct to follow a leader, sheep were easily domesticated as livestock. Early shepherds wouldn't drive their sheep from behind, but led them from out front – the sheep, familiar with their shepherd's voice, would follow them when he called.

A major task of ancient shepherds was to find regular fresh water for their flocks. However, because sheep bite off plants so close to the ground, flocks always had to be on the move and rotated through pastures to prevent destruction of flora by overgrazing. Thus shepherds were familiar with the location of wells and streams over a wide area.

At night, sheep would typically be housed in a sheepfold to protect against predators and thieves. Permanent sheepfolds were **courtyards** (*aule probaton*) enclosed by stone walls and open to the sky. A single entrance allowed the shepherd to guard access to his flock by sleeping in the doorway. If multiple flocks were penned overnight, each shepherd would call their own sheep in the morning to separate them out.

The Old Testament often used the analogy of a shepherd as the caretaker and leader of God's people. Furthermore, many of Israel's most prominent rulers (Abraham, Isaac, Jacob, Moses, David) worked as actual shepherds before assuming leadership of the nation. False shepherds, who led the people astray, were harshly denounced in the Bible.

The Lord God says this: "Look, I'll search for and seek my sheep myself. Like a shepherd cares for his herd in the day he's among his scattered sheep, so I'll care for my sheep and take them from all the places they were scattered on a cloudy and dark day. I'll bring them from the people and gather them from the countries, bringing them into their land. I'll feed them on Israel's mountains, by the streams and in all the settled land. I'll feed them in good pasture and their home will be on the high mountains of Israel. They'll lie there in a good home and eat from fat pastures on Israel's mountains. I'll feed my flock and lay them down," declares the Lord God. "I'll seek the lost, return the scattered, bandage the broken, and strengthen the sick...

"I'll set one shepherd over them, David, my servant, and he'll feed them. He'll feed them himself and shepherd them. And I, the LORD, will be their God, and David my servant will be a prince among them. I, the LORD, have spoken...

"As for you, my sheep, the sheep of my pasture, you are men and I am your God," declares the Lord God.

– Ezekiel 34:11-16, 23-24, 31

owner, sees the wolf coming and leaves the sheep and runs away, and then the wolf takes and scatters. He runs away because he's hired and doesn't care about the sheep. I am the good shepherd. I know my own and my own know me, just like the Father knows me and I know the Father. I lay my life down for the sheep. I have other sheep that aren't from this flock. I have to bring them too, and they'll hear my voice. They'll become one flock with one shepherd. The Father loves me because of this: I lay down my life so I can take it up again.[y] No one has taken it away from me, but I lay it down on my own. I have the authority to lay it down and I have the authority to take it up again. I've received this command from my Father."

The Jews were split because of these words. Many of them were saying, "He has a demon and he's insane. Why do you listen to him?"

While others were saying, "These aren't the words of someone demonized. A demon can't open blind eyes."

"You've scattered my flock and driven them away, and you haven't attended to them. Look, I'm going to attend to you for your evil actions," declares the LORD. – Jeremiah 23:1-2

Y. *The God of peace brought the sheep's great shepherd – Jesus our Lord – back from death through the blood of the everlasting covenant. – Hebrews 13:20*

CHAPTER 21

Love and Prayer

21.1 SEVENTY SENT OUT

Luke 10:1-12, 16

After this, the Lord appointed seventy others and sent them in pairs ahead of him to every city and place he was going to come. He told them: "The harvest is many, but the workers are few, so ask the Lord of the harvest to send workers out into his harvest. Go! Look, I send you out like lambs among wolves. Don't carry a money belt, bag, or shoes, and don't greet anyone on the way. Whatever house you enter, first say, 'Peace to this house.' If a son of peace is there, your peace will rest on him, but if not, it'll return to you. Stay in that house, eating and drinking whatever's from them, because the worker is worth his wages.[a] Don't keep moving from house to house. Whatever city that receives you when you enter it, go out into its streets and say, 'God's kingdom is near[b] to you.' But whatever city you enter that doesn't

A. *Does anyone ever soldier at his own expense? Who plants a vineyard and doesn't eat its fruit? Or who feeds a flock and doesn't consume the flock's milk? ... Moses' Law has written, 'You won't muzzle the ox while he's threshing'.... Don't those who do sacred work eat sacredly, and those at the altar divide what's from the altar? The Lord commanded this too, that those who announce the good news should live by the good news. – 1 Corinthians 9:7,9,13-14*

receive you, go out into its streets and say, 'Even the dust of your city that's sticking to our feet, we wipe it off against you. But know this: God's kingdom is near to you.' I tell you, it'll be better for Sodom in that day than for that city. Whoever listens to you, listens to me; whoever rejects you, rejects me; and whoever rejects me, rejects the one who sent me."

21.2 SEVENTY RETURN

Luke 10:17-24

The Seventy returned joyfully, saying, "Lord, even the demons submit to us in your name!"

"I watched Satan fall from heaven like lightning,"[c] he replied. "Look, I've given you authority to walk on snakes and scorpions,[d] and over all the power of the enemy. Nothing will injure you. But don't celebrate that spirits obey you – celebrate that your names are written in heaven."

At that moment, he was overjoyed[e] in the Holy Spirit and said, "I praise you, Father, the Lord of heaven and earth! You've hidden this from the wise and educated, but you've shown it to babies. Yes, Father, this was a good idea in your sight.

"Everything has been given to me by my Father. No one knows who the Son is except the Father, and who the Father is except the Son and anyone the Son wants to show."

But turning to the disciples, he told them by themselves, "Blessed are the eyes that see what you see, because I tell you that many prophets and kings wanted to see what you see, but didn't see, and to hear what you hear, but didn't hear."

B. Luke uses the Greek verb *eggizo* more than all the other New Testament writers combined. It means "bring **near**" or "approach." It speaks to the expectation of something coming soon, often in reference to God's kingdom.

C. *War happened in heaven: Michael and his angels warred with the dragon. The dragon and his angels warred, but they weren't powerful and there wasn't a place found for them in heaven anymore. So the great dragon was thrown down – the ancient snake, called the Devil and Satan, who deceives the whole world – he was thrown down to earth, and his angels were thrown down with him. – Revelation 12:7-9*

D. *You'll step on the lion and the cobra, and you'll stomp the lion cub and the snake. – Psalm 91:13*

E. The Greek verb *agalliao* is derived from *hallomai*, which can mean "jump" or "leap." It can refer to the action of water gushing or springing upwards. It was therefore a term of intense celebration and happiness that caused physical expression of such emotions, like leaping for joy. Here it's translated "**overjoyed**."

21.3 GOOD SAMARITAN

Luke 10:25-37

A lawyer stood up and tested him, saying, "Teacher, what should I do to inherit everlasting life?"

"What's written in the Law?" he answered. "How do you read it?"

"Love the Lord your God with all your heart, with all your soul, with all your strength, and with all your mind,"[f] he replied, "and your neighbor like yourself."[g]

"You've answered correctly," he said. "Do this and you'll live."[h]

But wanting to justify himself, he asked Jesus, "So who's my neighbor?"[i]

Jesus answered, "A man went down from Jerusalem to Jericho and fell among robbers. They stripped him, attacked him with blows, and left him half dead.[j] Now coincidently, a priest went down that road, but when he saw him, he passed by opposite him. Similarly, a Levite,[k] when he came to the place and saw him, passed by opposite him. But a Samaritan came along while on a journey, and when he saw him, he was moved. He came to him and bound up his wounds, pouring on oil and wine, then he put him on his beast, brought him to an inn, and took

F. *Hear, O Israel! The LORD is our God, the LORD is one! Love the LORD your God with all your mind, all your soul, and all your power. These words that I command you today will be on your mind. – Deuteronomy 6:4-6*

G. *Don't avenge or guard against the sons of your nation, but love your neighbor like yourself. I am the LORD. – Leviticus 19:18*

H. *Keep my rules and my judgments, through which a man can live if he does. I am the LORD. – Leviticus 18:5*

I. The Greek word *plesion* has traditionally been translated "**neighbor**," but can also mean "friend" or "fellow person," particularly referring to another Jew. The equivalent Hebrew word, *rea*, is derived from *ra'ah*, a verb meaning "pasture" or "feed," using the metaphor of sheep to suggest that one's *rea* is someone who grazes or feeds with you, that is, someone from your flock.

J. According to Moses' Law, all Jews become unclean for a week upon **touching a dead body** (*"Whoever touches the corpse of a man's soul will be unclean for seven days." Numbers 19:11*). So if either priests or Levites were on their way to Jerusalem to serve in their respective roles, becoming unclean would suspend their duties until they could be made clean again.

K. Priests were a special family of Levites descended from Aaron, Moses' brother. They were ultimately in charge of the Temple and associated religious duties. However, all other **Levites** also acted as priests of sort, but to a lesser extent, serving more supportive roles than Aaron's lineage. Levites were descendants of Jacob's son Levi and members of the Israelite tribe that bore his name. Instead of receiving a specific area of Canaan as Joshua divided it up, Levites were scattered in towns throughout the land so there would be priests among every tribe. Levites took care of the temple grounds, provided music, acted as doorkeepers, and prepared sacrifices to be offered by the priests.

Jericho

Northeast of Jerusalem, just west of the Jordan River, was the ancient city of **Jericho**, one of the oldest cities in the world. It sat low in the Jordan Valley, 258 meters (846 feet) below sea level, surrounded by mountainous terrain. The weather there was hot, with little rainfall each year, but plentiful freshwater springs made the area exceptionally fertile. It was renowned for its palm trees and was an attractive site for human settlement. A ford of the Jordan River nearby put Jericho at the intersection of major highways and trade routes.

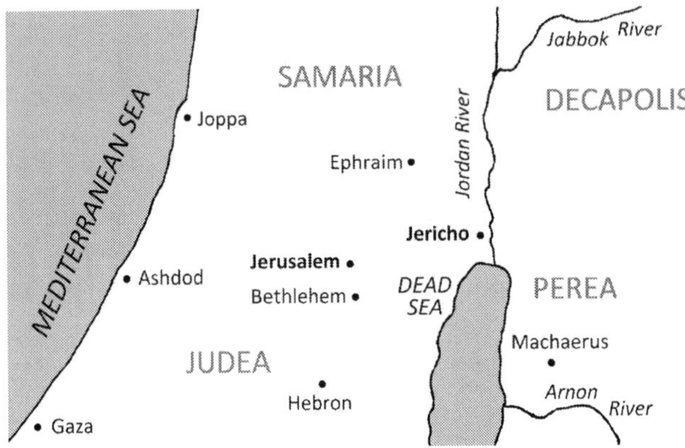

Like many ancient cities in the Middle East, Jericho has been built, destroyed, and rebuilt numerous times, and multiple settlements have been unearthed in its vicinity. Jericho's first and most notable reference in the Bible was during the beginning of Israel's campaign to conquer Canaan. The book of Joshua records that God told Joshua, Moses' successor, that the Israelite army should march around the well-fortified city for seven days, whereupon it would be miraculously delivered to them. Sure enough, Jericho's virtually impenetrable double walls collapsed on the seventh day and Israel destroyed the city. Unbeknownst to the Israelites at the time, Jericho was built in a seismically active area, experiencing earthquakes every few generations. Rahab, a Canaanite ancestor of Jesus, lived in the city at that time. Joshua then cursed the city, stating that whoever rebuilt its walls and gates would suffer the loss of his oldest and youngest sons. However, it wasn't until hundreds of years later that the curse was fulfilled, when *"Hiel the Bethelite built Jericho; he founded it at the loss of his firstborn Abiram and stood its gates at the loss of his youngest Segub, according to the LORD's word spoken through Joshua son of Nun." (1 Kings 16:34)* The city was allotted to Benjamin when the land was divided among Israel's tribes.

Further conquering and rebuilding of Jericho occurred under the Assyrians, Babylonians, and Persians. Following them, Alexander the Great (leading the Greek army) captured the area and lived there between 336 and 323 BC. It was later ruled by the Jews after the Maccabean Revolt. By New Testament times, Jericho had been acquired by the Romans and restored by Herod the Great, who eventually died in his palace there.

Starting high in the Judean mountains, the **road from Jerusalem to Jericho** was 27 kilometers (17 miles) long and included a huge descent of 1040 meters (3300 feet) to the bottom of the Jordan Valley, 258 meters below sea level. It was a notoriously dangerous highway, with rocky terrain providing innumerable hideouts for armed robbers waiting to ambush any travelers that passed by. However, despite the danger, the road from Jerusalem to Jericho was well-travelled for several reasons: Galilean Jews from the north journeyed on the east side of the Jordan River to avoid passing through loathsome Samaria, while travelling to and from Jerusalem; the residents of Jerusalem had limited options for bathing in large bodies of fresh water – the Jordan River at Jericho was one of the closest; and finally, the regular traffic of pilgrims, merchants, and soldiers going to and from Jerusalem kept this road well-trodden.

care of him. The next day, when he left, he took out two denarii[l] and gave them to the innkeeper, saying, 'Take care of him. Whatever else you spend, I'll repay you when I return.' Which of these three do you think proved to be a neighbor to the man who fell among the robbers?"

"The one who had mercy on him," he said.

Then Jesus told him, "Go and do the same."

21.4 VISIT TO MARTHA AND MARY

Luke 10:38-42

On their journey, he came into a village and a woman named Martha welcomed him into her home. She had a sister called Mary, who sat at the Lord's feet, listening to his words. But Martha was drawn away with all her service, so she came up and asked, "Lord, don't you care that my sister has left me to do all the serving by myself? Tell her to help me!"

"Martha, Martha," the Lord answered, "you're worried and troubled by so much, but only one thing is needed. Mary has chosen what's good, and it won't be taken from her."

21.5 PRAYER

Matthew 6:9-13a, 14-15; 7:7-12
Mark 11:25
Luke 11:1-13

After he had finished praying in some place, one of his disciples said, "Lord, teach us to pray, just like John taught his disciples."

So he told them, "When you pray, say, 'Our Father in the heavens, may your name be holy. May your kingdom come. May your desire be done on earth like it is in heaven. Give us enough bread every day. Forgive our debts as we forgive everyone in our debt. And don't lead us into temptation but rescue us from evil.'

"Whenever you stand praying, forgive, if you have something against someone, so your Father in heaven will forgive your failings[m]

L. **Two denarii** was two days' wages, which could potentially house and feed a healthy man in an inn for up to a month.

M. *Paraptoma* is a Greek noun meaning "fall beside," coming from *para* ("by") and *pipto* ("descend" or "fall"). It occurs rarely in the New Testament, but always in reference to moral violations and is typically translated as "transgression" or "trespass." Here it's rendered "**failing**."

The Heavens

The ancient Greeks believed in an afterlife called Elysium, which was where those chosen by the gods – the righteous and heroic – would spend eternity in happiness and enjoyment. This was distinct from Hades, where evil people were destined to suffer after death. Similarly, the Jews believed in **heaven**, a place where God dwelled and the righteous spent eternity with him after death. Hell was the opposite, where the evil were forever tortured apart from God. However, *ouranos*, the Greek word for "heaven" could also mean a number of other things within the context of the Greek-speaking Jewish society of Jesus' day.

The "first heaven" was understood to be simply the space that surrounded every creature on earth. It was synonymous with the atmosphere. After Jesus was baptized, God spoke as *"a voice out of the sky"* (page 46), but the word recorded in Greek is actually *ouranos*, heaven.

The "second heaven" was everything else in the universe beyond the earth – the space containing planets, stars, and galaxies far away. When Jesus talked about the end times, he said *"the stars will fall from heaven"* (page 243), that is, outer space.

The "third heaven" was the world beyond the physical realm. It was the spiritual realm of angels and demons, where non-physical beings like God himself were clearly seen and heard. This third heaven was what Paul had a vision of when he was *"caught up into paradise and heard inexpressible words"* (2 Corinthians 12:4). It wasn't necessarily related to a physical space, but another dimension of reality, a place "beyond the veil" so to speak.

Thus, heaven could mean a number of different things in the Bible, depending on the context. Indeed, sometimes all meanings were intended, as when Jesus instructed his disciples to address God as *"our Father in the heavens"* (page 175). The word he used was the plural form, encompassing all of the heavens from the atmosphere to rest of the universe to the heavenly realm where God is seen.

too. If you forgive others for their failings, your heavenly Father will forgive you too. But if you don't forgive others, your Father won't forgive your failings."

Then he said, "If one of you has a friend and goes to him at midnight and says, 'Friend, lend me three loaves, because another of my friends has shown up on a journey and I don't have anything to put before him.' From the inside he answers, 'Don't bother me. The door is already shut and my children are in bed with me. I can't get up and give you anything.' But I tell you, even though he won't get up and give it to him because he's his friend, he'll get up and give him as much as he needs because of his disrespect.[n]

"So I tell you, ask and it'll be given to you. Seek and you'll find. Knock and it'll be opened to you. Because everyone who asks receives, whoever seeks finds, and to whoever knocks, it'll be opened.

"What father among you will give his son a stone when he asks for bread? Or, if he asks for a fish, will he give him a snake instead? If he

N. Combining a negative prefix (*an-*) before the Greek word *aidos* ("modesty," "honor," "respect") produces *anaideia*, denoting immodesty, dishonor, or **disrespect**. *Anaideia* was also the name of the Greek goddess of shamelessness and ruthlessness.

asks for an egg, will he give him a scorpion? So if you, being evil, know how to give good gifts to your children, how much more will your Father in heaven give the Holy Spirit and what's good to those who ask him?

"So in everything, do to people like you want them to do to you, because this is the Law and the prophets."

CHAPTER 22

Further Teaching

22.1 GREED AND WEALTH

Matthew 5:25-26; 6:25-34
Luke 12:1a, 13-34, 54-59

Therefore, such countless[a] crowds gathered around that they were stepping on one another. Then someone out of the crowd said, “Teacher, tell my brother to divide the inheritance with me.”

“Man, who made me a judge or divider over you?” he replied. Then he told them, “Watch out and be on guard against every form of greed, because life doesn’t exist in possessions, even in an abundance of them.”

He told them a parable: “A rich man’s land was producing well and he thought to himself, ‘What will I do? I have nowhere to store my crops.’ Then he said, ‘This is what I’ll do: I’ll tear down my barns and build bigger ones, and I’ll store all my grain and my goods. Then I’ll tell my soul, “Soul, you have many goods stored up for many years. Relax! Eat, drink, and be happy!”’ But God said to him, ‘You fool! Tonight they’re demanding your soul from you, so who will own what you’ve prepared?’ Such is the man who stores up treasure for himself but isn’t

A. *Myrias* (Greek noun) translates to “ten thousand” or simply as a **countless**, innumerable amount. It’s where the English “myriad” comes from.

rich towards God."

Then he told his disciples, "This is why I tell you not to worry about life, what you'll eat or what you'll drink, nor your body and what you'll put on. Life is more than food and the body is more than clothes. Look at the ravens in the air – they don't sow, harvest, nor gather into barns or silos, but God, your heavenly Father, feeds them. How much more valuable are you than birds? And who of you can add a cubit[b] to his height by worrying? So if you can't even do something tiny, why do you worry about the rest? And why are you worried about clothing? Look how lilies[c] grow in a field – they don't work or spin,[d] but I tell you that not even Solomon in all his glory clothed himself like one of them. So if God clothes grass in the field like this, which is here today and thrown into the furnace tomorrow, how much more for you? You small-faiths! Don't worry, saying, 'What will we eat?' or 'What will we drink?' or 'What will we wear?' All the nations of the world look around for all

B. Ancient measurements of short distances were often based on body parts. For example, the **cubit** comes from the Latin *cubitum* ("elbow") and was the distance from the elbow to the tip of the middle finger, approximately 45 centimeters (18 inches). The equivalent Hebrew term was *ammah* and the Greek term was *pechys*, both of which are derived from the word for "elbow" in their respective languages. Other distances were based on the cubit and/or other body parts:

- Span: distance between extended thumb and little finger, equal to $^1/_2$ of a cubit
- Handbreadth: width of the hand at the knuckles, equal to $^1/_6$ of a cubit
- Finger: width of one finger, equal to $^1/_4$ of a handbreadth and $^1/_{24}$ of a cubit
- Fathom: width of the outstretched arms, equal to 4 cubits
- Rod, Reed: 6 cubits
- Mile: 1000 Roman paces

These measurements weren't universally standardized and varied somewhat between nations.

C. *Lilium* is the genus name of a type of flowering plant that grows from bulbs to produce prominent flowers. They're more commonly called true **lilies** worldwide, accounting for about 110 species. In ancient times, they grew wild across much of Europe, Asia, and North America, most often in woodlands. Lily bulbs house their resilient wintering organs when dormant, which grow annually to produce tall leafy herbs. The large fragrant flowers bloom in late spring or early summer with six petals (also called sepals) and come in various colors, often marked with spots or brush strokes.

In the Old Testament, 1 Kings 7 records that lily designs were used to decorate the Temple, while Song of Songs – a romantic poem between lovers – uses the lily as a metaphor of love. The Greek word *krinon* translates to lily in the New Testament, as does *shuwshan* (Hebrew) in the Old Testament, but these references may also refer to a flower in general.

D. **Spinning** was one of the many steps in converting freshly shorn wool into clothing. After cleaning, combing, and carding (disentangling), wool was spun into thread before being woven into cloth, dyed, and sewn into garments. The whole process was quite time consuming.

this, but your Father knows everything you need. Instead, look for his kingdom and his righteousness first and all this will be added to you. Don't be afraid, little flock, because your Father has happily chosen to give you the kingdom. So don't worry about tomorrow, tomorrow will worry about itself. Each day has enough trouble.

"Sell what you have and give to charity. Make money belts that won't wear out, an unfailing treasure in heaven, where no thief can come near nor moth can destroy. Because wherever your treasure is, your heart will be there too."

He was also telling the crowds, "When you see a cloud rising in the west, you immediately say, 'A storm is coming,' and so it happens. And when a south wind is blowing, you say, 'It'll be hot,' and it happens. You hypocrites! You examine the appearance of the earth and the sky, but why don't you examine the present?

"And why don't you judge what's right by yourself? Make friends quickly with your opposition and work to release yourself from him while you're on your way with him to the ruler, so that he doesn't drag you to the judge, and the judge give you to the officer, and then the officer throw you into prison. Truly I tell you that you won't come out of there until you've paid every last penny."[e]

22.2 REPENT OR DIE

Luke 13:1-9

At that time, someone there told him about the Galileans whose blood Pilate had mixed with their sacrifices. Jesus replied, "Do you think these Galileans[f] were sinners more than all the other Galileans because they suffered this way? No, I tell you, but unless you repent, you'll all be similarly destroyed. Or do you think the eighteen that the tower of Siloam[g] fell on and killed were in debt more than all the other men living in Jerusalem? No, I tell you, but unless you repent, you'll all be similarly destroyed."

Then he told this parable: "A man had a fig tree planted in his vine-

E. The *quadrans* was one of the smallest and least valuable Roman coins, worth one quarter of an assarion. It's often translated "**penny**."

F. The suffering of certain **Galileans** may have been a reference to Pilate's execution of people while offering sacrifices in the Temple. However, the incident not recorded outside the Bible.

G. The collapse of the **tower of Siloam**, which was built in southeast Jerusalem, is not mentioned outside the Bible either.

Figs

The plant genus *Ficus* – commonly known as the **fig** – refers to over 800 species of trees, shrubs, and vines. However, *Ficus carica* (common fig) and *Ficus sycomorus* (sycamore fig) are two of the most prevalent, native to much of the Mediterranean and the Middle East. The common fig is covered in smooth gray bark and grows up to 10 meters tall, shedding its multi-lobed leaves annually. Copious distasteful sap protects the plant from grazing animals and is a sticky irritant to human skin.

Syconium is the botanical term for the fig itself, derived from the Greek *sykon*, meaning "fig." It begins as a round fleshy bud enclosing thousands of tiny flowers. A highly specific symbiotic relationship occurs between tiny fig wasps and fig trees, where the syconium loosens slightly to allow a female wasp to crawl in. Once inside, the wasp pollinates the fig flowers and deposits her eggs inside some of them, forming galls. Wasp larvae develop in the galls and seeds develop in the pollinated flowers, all within the confines of the syconium. Over time, the wasp larvae mature and eat their way out, which triggers the syconium's development into a mature fruit with viable seeds. Edible fig crops occur twice per year.

Figs have been food to people and innumerable animal species since they first appeared, and fig trees were one of the first plant species to be bred for agriculture. The fruit can be eaten raw or pressed into cakes. They were also a key ingredient in ancient medicinal salves.

In the Bible, fig trees first appear in Eden, when Adam and Eve sewed clothes for themselves out of fig leaves after their fall. They are often mentioned in Israel's history in the context of wealth and prosperity.

yard. He came looking for fruit on it but didn't find any. So he told the vine worker, 'Look, I've been coming to look for fruit on this fig tree for three years, but I haven't found any.[h] Cut it down! Why does it even use up the ground?' But he answered, 'Sir, leave it for this year too, until I can dig around it and add some manure. If it bears fruit, then care for it; but if not, then cut it down.'"

H. *My beloved had a vineyard on a fat hill. He fenced it, de-stoned it, and planted vine shoots. He built a tower in the middle and dug a winepress. He expected it to produce grapes, but it produced a stench.... The vineyard of the* L*ORD of armies is Israel's house, and Judah's men are his delightful plant. He looked for justice, but look, slaughter. And for righteousness, but look, weeping. – Isaiah 5:1-2, 7*

22.3 CRIPPLED WOMAN HEALED

Luke 13:10-17

He was teaching in one of the synagogues on the Sabbath and a woman was there who had been frail from a spirit for eighteen years. She was hunched over[i] and couldn't straighten up completely. When Jesus saw her, he called her over and said, "Woman, you're freed from your frailty."

He laid his hands on her and immediately she straightened up and praised God. But the synagogue leader, upset that Jesus had healed on the Sabbath, responded to the crowd, "There are six days that work should be done, so come on them and get healed, not on the Sabbath day."

"You hypocrites!" the Lord replied. "Doesn't each of you release[j] his ox or his donkey on the Sabbath and lead him out from the manger to water him? So this woman, a daughter of Abraham, who has been bound[k] by Satan for eighteen years, look, shouldn't she have been released from this bond on the Sabbath day?"

Saying this, all of his opponents were embarrassed and the whole crowd celebrated over all the glorious things he was doing.

22.4 UNABLE TO STONE JESUS FOR BLASPHEMY

John 10:22-39

It was winter and the Dedication Feast was happening in Jerusalem. Jesus was walking in the Temple along Solomon's porch[l] when the Jews gathered around him and asked, "How long will you hold your breath? If you're the Christ, tell us openly."

I. *Syngkypto* is a Greek verb from *syn* ("with") and *kypto* ("stoop" or "bend forward"). It's translated here as "**hunched over**," but has also been rendered "bent over" or "bent double." This passage only occurs in Luke's account, who was reportedly a doctor from Antioch. His description of the frail hunched woman suggests some form of spinal arthritis, possibly involving fusion of her vertebrae. However, he also makes it clear that her problem was due to being "bound by Satan."

J. *Lyo* is Greek for "**release**" or "untie." It refers to the releasing of physical bonds, such as with prisoners, animals, or the straps of clothing. It can also refer to the divorce of a marriage, the annulment of a contract, breaking the law, or the dismissal of a gathering.

K. *Deo* is the opposite of *lyo*. It means "**bind**" or "tie." *Deo* is the root of *doulos*, the most common word for slavery in the New Testament.

L. The Jewish historian Josephus reported that along the east side of the Temple complex in Jerusalem was a covered walkway supported by pillars called **Solomon's porch**. He called it an "amazing" sight, built upon a massive retaining wall above the Kidron Valley. It was rebuilt on the site of the original porch Solomon built next to the first Temple in Jerusalem.

The Dedication Feast

While the Seleucid ruler Antiochus Epiphanes was away fighting in Egypt in 168 BC, rumors of his death prompted a deposed High Priest named Jason to overthrow Jerusalem in a Jewish revolt. However, upon his return in 167 BC, Antiochus furiously recaptured Jerusalem and massacred many of the Jews in Jerusalem. Furthermore, he outlawed Jewish religion and forced them to worship the Greek god Zeus. The Temple was desecrated with pagan offerings and anyone openly practicing Judaism was executed.

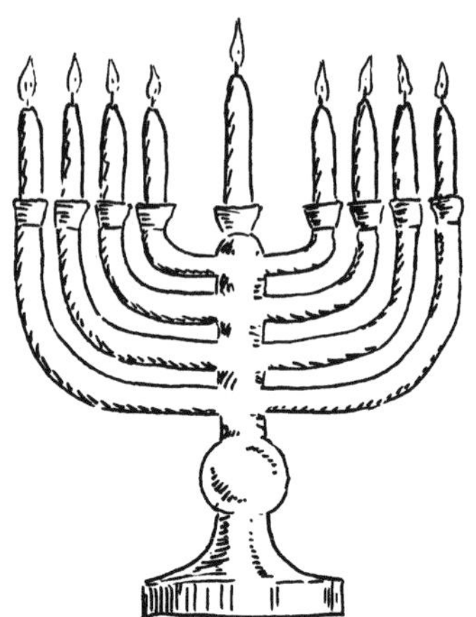

Because of this oppression, Orthodox Jews rebelled against their Greek rulers in the Maccabean Revolt, led by Judas Maccabee (Hebrew for "hammer") and his brothers. The civil war saw the Maccabean forces use guerilla tactics to defeat the Greek army, with victory coming after Antiochus died suddenly of disease while away on another campaign in 164 BC. The Maccabees then repossessed Jerusalem and reestablished Jewish religion. The Temple was rededicated after its desecration, which was thereafter commemorated by the **Dedication Feast** every winter. Tradition holds that the Maccabees could only find a small jug of oil, enough to sustain the Menorah (a seven-branched lampstand) for one day. However, the oil miraculously lasted eight days, leading to the feast's annual observance for the same time period. This feast was also known as the Feast of the Maccabees, while the traditional lighting of the menorah has led to it also being called the Feast of Lights. It's better known today as the Jewish holiday of Hanukkah.

"I've told you, but you don't believe me," Jesus answered. "The acts I do in my Father's name testify about me, but you don't believe because you're not my sheep. My sheep hear my voice – I know them and they follow me. I give them everlasting life and they'll never die. No one can take them out of my hand. My Father, who has given them to me, is greater than all, and no one can take them from the Father's hand. The Father and I are one."

The Jews picked up stones again to stone[m] him, but Jesus answered, "I've shown you many good acts from the Father. Which of them are you stoning me for?"

M. The usual method of capital punishment in Israel was by **stoning**. Moses' Law stated that people who broke certain commandments were to be stoned to death outside the city or camp. The two (or more) witnesses against the condemned criminal would throw the first stones and then the rest of the men of the community would join in. In such an execution, no individual could be identified as the one who ultimately killed the criminal – all bore the responsibility. Crimes that were punishable by stoning included breaking the Sabbath, child sacrifice, witchcraft, cursing God, idol worship, rebellion against one's parents, and having an affair.

"We aren't stoning you for a good act, but for blasphemy," the Jews answered, "and because, being a man, you make yourself God."

Then Jesus answered, "Hasn't it been written in your Law: 'I said you are gods'?[n] So if he called them gods, who the word of God came to – and the Scripture can't be broken – how do you tell the one whom the Father made holy and sent into the world, 'You're blaspheming' because I've said, 'I'm the Son of Man'? If I don't do my Father's actions, don't believe me. But if I do them, even though you don't believe me, believe the actions, so you can know and continue to know that the Father is in me and I am in the Father."

Therefore they were looking to arrest him again, but he escaped from their hands.

N. *I said, "You are gods, and all of you are sons of the Highest. But you'll certainly die as men and fall like one of the rulers." – Psalm 82:6*

CHAPTER 23

Discipleship

23.1 BELIEF IN PEREA

John 10:40-42

He went past the Jordan[a] again to the place where John was first baptizing, and he stayed there. Many came to him, saying, "John certainly didn't show us any signs, but everything John said about him is true!"

Many believed in him there.

23.2 ENTERING THE KINGDOM

Luke 13:22-33

He passed through one city and village into another, teaching and going on his way to Jerusalem. Then someone asked him, "Lord, will only a few be saved?"

A. The Roman province of Perea was the land **past the Jordan** River to the east. According to Josephus, Perea was bordered by the Jabbok River to the north, which drained into the Jordan, and the Arnon River to the south, which drained into the Dead Sea. Perea was originally a part of Herod the Great's domain, but Herod Antipas acquired it after his death.

"Try to enter through the narrow door," he answered, "because I tell you that many will search to enter but won't be able to. Once the housemaster[b] gets up and shuts the door – and you're standing outside, knocking on the door, saying, 'Lord, open up to us!' – he'll answer you, 'I don't know where you're from.' Then you'll say, 'We ate and drank with you, and you taught in our streets.' But he'll say, 'I tell you, I don't know where you're from. Leave me, all you evildoers!'[c] There will be weeping and teeth grinding when you see Abraham, Isaac, Jacob,[d] and all the prophets in God's kingdom, but you'll be thrown out. They'll come from east and west, and from north and south, and they'll recline in God's kingdom. And look, the last will be first and the first will be last."

Then some Pharisees came up to him, saying, "Go away and leave here, because Herod wants to kill you."

But he replied, "Go tell that fox, 'Look, I throw out demons and accomplish healings today and tomorrow, and on the third I'm finished. However, I have to travel today, tomorrow, and the next, because it can't be that a prophet would die outside Jerusalem."

23.3 SWOLLEN MAN HEALED | THREE PARABLES

Luke 14:1-24

When he went into the house of one of the Pharisee leaders on the Sabbath to eat bread, this happened: they were watching him closely, and look, in front of him was a man who appeared swollen.[e] Jesus asked the lawyers and the Pharisees, "Is it legal to heal on the Sabbath, or not?"

B. *Oikodespotes* is a combination of the Greek words for "house" (*oikos*) and "master" (*despotes*) and can be translated as "head of the house" or "landlord." A **housemaster** was just that: the owner and master of a household, which likely included his own family, his slaves' families, his land, and his livestock.

C. *Leave me, all of you troublemakers, because the LORD has heard the voice of my weeping. – Psalm 6:8*

D. **Abraham, Isaac, and Jacob** were the three most prominent patriarchs of Israel. Abraham was the man initially called by God to begin a holy nation; Isaac (Abraham's son) inherited this blessing; and Jacob (Abraham's grandson, who was renamed Israel) had twelve sons, which became the twelve tribes of Israel.

E. Luke uses the Greek word *hydropikos* in reference to a man's medical condition, which is a combination of *hydor* ("water") and a derivative of *optanomai* ("look at"). This description literally means he "looked watery," but perhaps a more appropriate translation is that the man "**appeared swollen**." This word has also been translated "suffering from dropsy." Dropsy is an old word for hydropsy, better known today as edema. This is the only occurrence of *hydropikos* in the Bible. Edema is excessive fluid in the tissues, caused by any

But they were silent. So he took hold of him, healed him, and sent him away. Then he said, "Who of you, if your son or ox falls into a well on the Sabbath, won't pull him out immediately?"

They couldn't respond to this. Then when he saw how the invited guests chose the first seats,[f] he told a parable: "When you're invited to a wedding party by someone, don't recline in the first seat, because someone more honored than you may have been invited too, and whoever invited both of you will come and say, 'Give your place to this man,' and then you'll go, humiliated, to sit in the last place. But when you're invited, go and recline in the last place, so that when the one who invited you comes, he can say, 'Friend, move up higher.'[g] Then you'll be honored in front of everyone reclining with you. Because everyone who lifts himself will be lowered, and whoever lowers himself will be lifted."[h]

He also said to the one who had invited him, "When you host a lunch or a dinner, don't invite your friends, your brothers, your relatives, or your rich neighbors, or they might invite you back, which will be your repayment. But when you host a party, invite the poor, the crippled, the lame, and the blind. You'll be blessed, because they can't repay you and you'll be paid back at the resurrection of the righteous."

When one of those reclining with him heard this, he said, "Everyone who will eat bread in God's kingdom is blessed!"

But he replied, "A man was hosting a great dinner and invited many. At dinnertime, he sent his slave to tell those invited, 'Come now, everything's ready!' but everyone made excuses. The first one said, 'I bought a field and I need to go see it, so please excuse me.' Another said, 'I bought five pairs[i] of oxen and I'm going to test them, so please

---

number of diseases, including failure of the heart, liver, or kidneys. It's unclear exactly what the man's diagnosis was, but it was significant enough to warrant the unusual description and consideration for healing.

F. Seats at a banquet were ranked by importance. Particularly at the head table, the centermost seat was considered highly prestigious in Jewish society. The Greek word for these spots was *protoklisia*, literally meaning "**first seats**," but it is also translated "chief seats" or "places of honor." An equivalent term, *protokathedria*, referred to the most prominent seats in the synagogue.

G. *Don't honor yourself before the king's face and don't stand with the great. Because it's better to be told, "Come up here," than to be lowered before the prince's face, whom your eyes have seen. – Proverbs 25:6-7*

H. *A man's pride will lower him, but a humble spirit will get honored. – Proverbs 29:23*

I. *Zeugos*, the Greek word for "**pair**," is essentially the same as the word for "yoke" (*zygos*), since two animals pulled together in one yoke.

excuse me.' Another said, 'I married a woman, so I can't come.' So the slave returned and reported this to his master. Then the housemaster got angry and told his slave, 'Quick, go out into the streets and alleys[j] of the city and bring the poor, the crippled, the blind, and the lame in here.' Then the slave said, 'Master, what you've commanded is done, but there's still room.' So the master told the slave, 'Go out to the highways and the hedges[j] and make them come, so my house will be filled. I tell you, none of those men who were invited will taste my dinner.'"

23.4 LOST AND FOUND

Matthew 18:12-14
Luke 15

All the tax collectors and sinners were coming near to listen to him, but the Pharisees and the scribes both grumbled, "This man accepts sinners and eats with them."

So he told them this parable: "What do you think? What man among you, if he has a hundred sheep and has lost one that has strayed, doesn't leave the ninety-nine in the wilderness and go after the lost and strayed one until he finds it? And if it happens that he finds it, I tell you truly, he puts it on his shoulders, overjoyed. Then when he comes home, he calls his friends and neighbors together, saying, 'Celebrate with me, because I've found my lost sheep!' So he celebrates over it more than the ninety-nine that haven't strayed. I tell you, there will be the same joy in heaven over one sinner who repents than over ninety-nine righteous who don't need repentance. So it's not the will of your Father in heaven that one of these little ones be lost.

"Or what woman, if she has ten coins and loses one, doesn't light a lamp, sweep the house, and look thoroughly until she finds it? And when she finds it, she calls her friends and neighbors together, saying, 'Celebrate with me, because I've found the coin I lost!' I tell you, there's the same joy in the presence of God's angels over one sinner who repents.

"A man had two sons," he said. "The younger told his father, 'Father, give me my part of the estate.'[k] So he divided his life between them. Not many days later, the younger son gathered everything and

J. **Streets and alleys** were located within city walls, while **highways and hedges** were outside. Hedges acted as barriers between property.

traveled to a land far away, and there he threw away his estate by living recklessly. When he had spent everything, a terrible famine occurred in that country and he became poor. So he joined himself to a resident of that country, who sent him into his fields to feed pigs. He would have happily filled his stomach with the pods[l] the pigs were eating, because no one gave him anything. But when he came to himself,[m] he said, 'How many of my father's workers have plenty of bread, but here I am dying of hunger?! I'll get up and go to my father and tell him, "Father, I've sinned against heaven and before you. I'm not worthy to be called your son anymore. Make me one of your workers."' So he got up and came to his father.

"But while he was still far away, his father saw him and was moved. He ran and fell on his neck and kissed him. Then the son said, 'Father, I've sinned against heaven and in your sight. I'm not worthy to be called your son anymore.' But the father told his slaves, 'Quick, bring out the best robe and put it on him, and put a ring on his hand and shoes on his feet. Bring the fattened calf[n] and kill it. Let's eat and celebrate! Because

---

K. Jewish **inheritance** laws stated that the firstborn son should receive *"a double portion of all he has, because he's the beginning of his strength." (Deuteronomy 21:17)* So in the case of having two sons, the older would have received two-thirds of his father's estate, and the younger one-third. It was disgraceful in Middle Eastern cultures for a son to ask for his inheritance before his father had died. It was analogous to the son wishing his father was dead.

L. Carob trees (*Ceratonia siliqua*) are flowering shrubs in the pea family that grow throughout the Mediterranean. Their fruit is a long **pod** that takes about a year to develop and ripen. Carob trees are also called St. John's trees, since the seeds in the pods resemble the shape of locusts, which was the unusual diet of John the Baptizer. Similarly, their Greek name, *keration*, translates to "little horn," due to their horned shape. As food, carob was usually dried or roasted and had a sweet taste, but was generally reserved for the poor, since it was so inexpensive. It was also a common means of feeding pigs.

M. The Greek expression that translates directly to "**came to himself**" is analogous to the English expression "came to his senses."

N. In ancient times, families would often keep at least one piece of livestock that was fed a robust diet to fatten it, making it a choice meal when butchered. It was also kept near the home in a pen, rather than running with the general herd, so its meat would be tender. Slaughtering and preparing the **fattened calf** (*siteutos moschos*) was done when celebrating a special event.

Three Words for Life

The Greek language has three words for "**life**:"

1. *Bios* refers to the quantity of time lived or the course of life itself, but could also refer to physical property possessed during one's life, such as wealth or land. *Bios* occurs few times in the Bible.
2. *Psyche* refers to the essence of a person's being, the vital force that animates each body, or one's personhood. It describes the quality or character of inner life – each person's source of feelings, desires, affection, and aversions. According to Christian theology, the *psyche* live on after physical death. *Psyche* occurs often in the Bible, but not always as "life" – it's also rendered "soul" or "breath." It's where the English word "psychology" (the study of mental function) originates.
3. *Zoe* refers to the true fullness of life. It's the highest state someone can exist in, as it incorporates vitality, vigor, and virtue. It typically describes God's life. *Zoe* occurs more frequently in the Bible than the other two words for "life."

In the passage of the Prodigal Son, the father "divided his life (*bios*)" between his two sons, while later the younger son is described as previously "dead and now he lives (*zoe*)!"

my son was dead and now he lives again! He was lost and has been found!' So they celebrated.

"Now his older son was in the field. When he came up to the house, he heard music and dancing, so he called one of the servants and asked what this could be. 'Your brother has arrived,' he answered, 'so your father has killed the fattened calf because he has received him back healthy.'[O] Then he got angry and wouldn't go in. His father came out and consoled him, but he answered his father, 'Look, I've been serving you for many years and have never come against your command, but you've never even given me a kid[P] to celebrate with my friends! Yet when your son came, who ate up your life with prostitutes, you killed the fattened calf for him!' Then he replied, 'Son, you're always with me and all I have is yours. But we had to celebrate and be happy, because your brother was dead and now he lives. He was lost and found.'"

23.5 SNEAKY MANAGER | WEALTH

Matthew 6:24
Luke 16:1-15, 19-31

He also told the disciples, "A rich man had a manager who was accused of throwing away his estate. He called him and said, 'What's

O. *Hygiaino* is a Greek verb that translates to "be sound," "be well," or "be whole." *Hygies*, the adjective form, is the root of the English word "hygiene," so it's rendered here as "**healthy**." However, its use in ancient times may also denote general well-being, similar to the modern expression of being "safe and sound."

P. A **kid** was a young goat from the herd, not a particularly special meal compared to the fattened calf.

this I hear about you? Give an explanation for your management, because you won't be manager anymore.' So the manager said to himself, 'What will I do, since my master is removing me from management? I'm not strong enough to dig and I'm ashamed to beg. I know what I'll do so that when I leave the management I'll be received into homes.'[q] He called each of his master's borrowers and asked the first, 'How much do you owe my master?' '100 baths[r] of oil,' he replied. So he said, 'Take your bill, sit down quickly, and write 50.' Then he said to another, 'How much do you owe?' '100 homers[s] of wheat,' he replied. So he tells him, 'Take your bill and write 80.' His master applauded the unrighteous manager because he acted so wisely, because the sons of this age are cleverer with themselves than the sons of light. So I tell you, make friends with the wealth of unrighteousness, so that when it fails, they'll welcome you into everlasting tents.

"Whoever's faithful with the small is faithful with the big as well, and whoever's unrighteous with the small is unrighteous with the big too. So if you haven't been faithful with unrighteous treasure, who will trust you with the true? And if you haven't been faithful with another's, who will give you your own? No servant can serve two masters, because either he'll hate one and love the other, or else be dedicated to one and scorn the other. You can't serve God and wealth."[t]

Now the Pharisees, who loved money, were listening to this and mocking him. So he told them, "You justify yourselves before men, but God knows your hearts, because the lofty among men is an abomination to God.

"There was a rich man that dressed in purple and sea silk,[u] happily

Q. *Whoever acquires souls is wise. – Proverbs 11:30*

R. One bath (*batos* in Greek) was a measurement of volume equal to about 40 liters (8-9 gallons), so **100 baths** was about 4000 liters. This large volume was about as much oil as 450 olive trees could produce in a year.

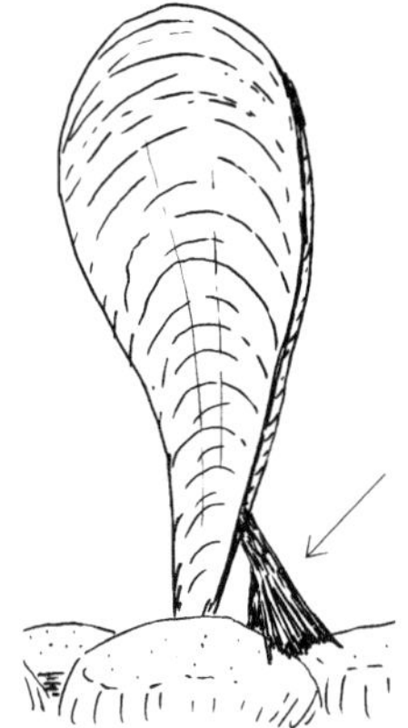

S. One homer was the largest Hebrew dry measure, equaling about 225 liters (60 gallons) of grain. It's the maximum amount of grain a donkey could carry, which is where the Hebrew term comes from (*hamor* means "donkey"). **100 homers**, therefore, is a huge amount of grain, the product of 100 acres of wheat.

T. *Mamon* is the Aramaic word for "treasure" or "riches," but was also understood to be the personification of **wealth** as a god or idol.

U. *Pinna nobilis* is a type of pen shell, a large saltwater clam, that lives in the Mediterranean Sea. These bivalve creatures produce shells up to a meter (3 feet) long and attach themselves to submerged rocks using strong filaments. These filaments, called byssus or

living every day in luxury. A poor, ulcerated man named Lazarus[v] was at his gate, longing to eat what fell from the rich man's table. Even the dogs came and licked his sores. Now the poor man died and was carried away by the angels to Abraham's chest, and the rich man died and was buried too. In hell,[w] he was in torment, but lifting his eyes he sees Abraham far away with Lazarus on his chest. So he cried out, 'Father Abraham, have mercy on me! Send Lazarus to dip his fingertip in water to cool my tongue, because I'm tormented by this flame!' But Abraham replied, 'Son, remember that during your life you had it good, while Lazarus had it bad. Now he's comforted here, while you're in agony. But besides all this, there's a huge divide established between us, so that those who want to cross over to you can't, and no one can cross over to us.' 'Then I beg you, father,' he said, 'send him to my father's house to warn them, because I have five brothers, so they won't come to this torturous place too!' But Abraham says, 'They have Moses and the prophets. Let them hear them.' 'No, father Abraham!' he replied. 'But if someone travels from death, they'll repent!' But he told him, 'If they don't listen to Moses and the prophets, they won't be convinced even if someone rises from death.'"

23.6 FAITH | SERVANTHOOD

Luke 17:5-10

Then the apostles told the Lord, "Increase our faith!"

"If you have faith like a mustard seed," the Lord replied, "you can tell this sycamine[x] tree, 'Uproot yourself and be planted in the sea!' and it'll obey you.

Egyptian flax, are exceptionally fine and can be woven into exquisite silk. This **sea silk** was light, warm, and strong, with a golden color that was said to never fade. It was very costly among ancient Mediterranean civilizations, including the Egyptians, Greeks, and Romans, and therefore was worn only by the wealthy. Byssus was woven into clothing up until the 20th century, when *Pinna nobilis* became threatened with extinction from over-harvesting.

V. The name **Lazarus** is a variant of the Hebrew name Eleazar, meaning "God has helped."

W. Hades (called Pluto by the Romans) was the Greek god of the underworld. According to mythology, he received his dominion in a division of worldwide sovereignty between his two brothers (Zeus received heaven to rule, while Poseidon received the sea). Hades' wife was Persephone, whom he abducted after falling in love with her. His dog, Cerberus, guarded the gates of the underworld and prevented those who crossed the river Styx from returning. In New Testament theology, Hades came to refer to the place of the dead as a location, rather than a diety personified, equivalent to the Hebrew word *sheol* ("grave"). In English, Hades is essentially **hell**, a place of constant suffering and separation from God.

"Who of you, who has a slave plowing or watching sheep, will tell him, 'Come now and recline,' when he comes in from the field? Won't you tell him, 'Make something for me to eat, then dress yourself and serve me while I eat and drink – you can eat and drink afterwards'? And do you thank the slave because he did what he was commanded? In the same way, when you do everything you're commanded, say, 'We're useless slaves. We've done what we ought to have done.'"

23.7 LAZARUS RESURRECTED

John 11:1-46

Now someone – Lazarus – was sick in Bethany,[y] the village of Mary and her sister Martha. Lazarus was the brother of Mary, who had anointed the Lord with perfume and wiped his feet with her hair. So the sisters sent to him, saying, "Lord, look, the one you love is sick."

But when Jesus heard about it, he replied, "This sickness won't end in death. It's for God's glory, so God's Son will be glorified."

Jesus loved Martha, her sister, and Lazarus. So when he heard he was sick, he stayed two days in the place he was. Then afterwards he tells his disciples, "Let's go to Judea again."

"Rabbi," the disciples reply, "the Jews wanted to stone you and now you're going back?"

But Jesus answered, "Aren't there twelve hours in a day? If anyone walks by day, he doesn't trip because he sees the light of the world. But if anyone walks by night, he trips because the light isn't in him."

He said this. Then afterwards he says, "Our friend Lazarus has gone to sleep, but I'm going to wake him up."

"Lord, if he has gone to sleep, he'll be saved," the disciples reply.

However, Jesus was talking about his death, whereas they thought he was talking about the resting sleep. So Jesus told them clearly,

X. Luke is the only Gospel writer who mentions a "**sycamine**" tree (*sycaminos* in Greek) in the Bible. Some say it's a reference to the black or white mulberry tree (*Morus nigra, Morus alba* respectively), which are native to Palestine. Others claim it's a reference to the sycamore tree, normally denoted by the Greek word *sykomorea*, which has leaves like a mulberry.

Y. Just east of Jerusalem, on the road up the Mount of Olives and down the mountains to Jericho, were the towns of Bethphage and **Bethany**. Bethphage comes from the Aramaic for "house of unripe figs," while Bethany's name means "house of misery" or "house of figs." Because Bethphage and Bethany were the last villages on the highway from Jericho to Jerusalem, they may have been where the poor and sick lived, away from the general

"Lazarus is dead, and I'm overjoyed that I wasn't there, so you can believe. Now let's go."

Then Thomas, called Didymus,[z] told the other disciples, "Let's go too, so we can die with him."

When Jesus came, he found he had already been in the tomb for four days. And since Bethany was close to Jerusalem – about 15 stadia[a] away – many of the Jews had come to Martha and Mary to comfort them regarding their brother. When Martha heard Jesus was coming, she went to meet him, while Mary sat in the house. Then Martha told Jesus, "Lord, if you had been here, my brother wouldn't have died. But even now, whatever you ask God for, God will give you."

population of Jerusalem and ideally located to receive donations from religious pilgrims travelling to the Temple.

Z. "Thomas" is derived from the Aramaic word for "twin," while *Didymus* is the Greek equivalent. Consequently, a man named Thomas in ancient Judea, where both Aramaic and Greek were spoken, would likely have been called **Didymus** as well.

Resurrection

The Greek *anastasis* is the act of rising up, typically translated "**resurrection**" in the Bible. It could refer to simply rising from a seat, or, more profoundly, coming back to life after death. Resurrection after death appears in various ancient religions and mythologies, but it's difficult to know exactly what early societies believed. For example, Greek mythology records the resurrection of various gods, such as Asclepius. However, despite the belief in Hades, an underworld where the spirit resides after death, widespread belief in universal resurrection – everyone coming back to life – doesn't seem to be commonly held among the ancient Greeks.

The Egyptians similarly believed in an afterlife, preparing extravagant tombs and treasures to provide for the dead in their next life. Yet resurrection from death wasn't part of their belief system either.

Judaism, however, held a different view. The Old Testament records three instances of overt bodily resurrection:

1. Elijah raised a young boy who had recently died of an illness (1 Kings 17:17-24).
2. Elisha raised a boy who died of an unknown head problem (2 Kings 4:18-37).
3. A man's corpse came to life after being thrown onto the long-dead bones of Elisha (2 Kings 13:21).

Additionally, some passages in the Hebrew Scriptures hint at universal resurrection. The writer of Psalm 49 had hope that God would *"redeem my soul from the hand of Sheol" (Psalm 49:15a)*. Job believed he would see God after death, saying *"Even after my skin's struck, I'll see God from my body" (Job 19:26)*. Likewise, Isaiah said, *"Your dead will live. Their corpses will rise. You, lying in the dirt, wake up and rejoice" (Isaiah 26:19)*. Finally, Daniel records, *"Many of those sleeping in the dust of the ground will wake up, these to everlasting life, but others to abuse and horror forever" (Daniel 12:2)*. Although these passages suggest some sort of resurrection, different sects of Judaism in the first century held different views on the subject, so it's unclear exactly what the general public believed.

[Abraham] figured that God could raise from death, and, in a way, he got [his son] back from there.

– Hebrews 11:19

"Your brother will be raised," Jesus says.

"He'll be raised in the resurrection on the last day," Martha replies.

"I am the resurrection and the life," Jesus told her. "Anyone who believes in me will live even if he dies, and everyone who lives and believes in me will never die. Do you believe this?"

"Yes, Lord," she replies. "I've believed that you're the Christ, God's Son, the one coming to the world."

After she said this, she went away and secretly called her sister Mary, saying, "The Teacher is here and he's asking for you."

Hearing this, she gets up. Then she came to him.

Jesus hadn't come into the village yet; he was still where Martha had met him. When the Jews who were in the house consoling Mary saw her get up quickly and leave, they followed her, thinking she was going to cry at the tomb. But when Mary got to Jesus, she saw him and fell at his feet, saying, "Lord, if you had been here, my brother wouldn't have died."

When Jesus saw her weeping, and also the Jews weeping with her, his spirit was stirred up[b] and troubled. He said, "Where have you laid him?"

Jesus wept.

A. One Greek stadium was about 600 feet long, so **15 stadia** was a distance of about 2.8 kilometers (1.7 miles).

Burial

Beginning with the patriarchs, Israel paid special attention to proper **burial**. Abraham purchased a cave for the final resting place of his wife, Sarah. Jacob commanded his body to be taken back to Canaan from Egypt for internment in a cave. And although Joseph was originally buried in Egypt when he died, his bones were unearthed and taken back to Israel's homeland during their exodus. Later, David commended the men who cared for the remains of Saul and his sons. Even executed criminals and enemies killed in battle were buried, since it was considered a great curse to remain unburied after death. Moses' Law states that unburied bodies polluted the land, while Ezekiel records that burying the dead cleansed the land.

Because of the hot climate of Palestine, the dead were buried promptly, often within a day or two of dying. However, customary burial called for careful preparation of the corpse. It was first washed to remove dirt, blood, or other bodily fluids. Then burial cloth was wrapped around it, with spices or perfumes within the folds. Internment occurred in a shallow grave dug by hand and covered with rocks (for the poor), or in a **tomb** carved into rock and sealed with stones (for the rich). Jews didn't regularly cremate their dead like the Babylonians, Greeks, or Romans. Nor did they embalm/preserve them or use coffins like the Egyptians.

Then the Jews said, "See how much he loved him!" But some said, "Couldn't this man, who opened blind eyes, have kept this man from dying?"

Then Jesus, stirred up again, comes to the tomb, which was a cave with a stone on it.

Jesus says, "Lift the stone off."

But Martha, the sister of the deceased, tells him, "Lord, he stinks by now! He has been in there for four days!"

"Didn't I tell you that if you believe, you'll see God's glory?" Jesus replies.

So they lifted the stone off. Then Jesus lifted his eyes and said, "Father, I thank you that you've heard me. I know you always hear me, but because of the crowd standing here I've said it, so they can believe you sent me."

After he said this, he shouted with a great voice, "Lazarus, come out!"

Then the deceased came out, tied hand and foot with linen, with a handkerchief[c] wrapped around his face.

"Untie him and let him go," Jesus tells them.

Therefore, many of the Jews who had come to Mary and saw what he had done believed in him. But some went to the Pharisees and told them what Jesus had done.

23.8 SANHEDRIN DECIDES TO KILL JESUS

John 11:47-54

The High Priests and the Pharisees held an assembly, saying, "What are we going to do? This man is doing many miracles. If we leave him like this, everyone will believe in him and the Romans will come and take away our land and our nation."

But one of them – Caiaphas,[d] the High Priest that year – said, "You know nothing, nor do you consider that it's worthwhile for one man to

B. The Greek word *embrimaomai* occurs five times in the New Testament, usually in the context of a stern rebuke or warning. It comes from the word *brimaomai,* which means "snort angrily." Thus *embrimaomai* is being **stirred up** or moved with anger.

C. The Greek *soudarion* is derived from the Latin word for "**handkerchief**," referring to a cloth used to wipe perspiration from the face or blow one's nose. The same word is used for the cloth used to wrap the head of a corpse. John uses this term twice, both in reference to burial clothes no longer needed by two resurrected men: Lazarus and Jesus.

die for the people so the whole nation isn't destroyed."

He didn't say this by himself, but being the High Priest that year, he prophesied that Jesus would die for the nation, and not only for the nation, but that he would gather God's scattered children into one. So they resolved to kill him from that day on.

Therefore, Jesus didn't walk publicly among the Jews anymore, but he went away to the land near the wilderness, to a city called Ephraim,[e] and stayed there with his disciples.

D. When Valerius Gratus, the Roman ruler of Judea, deposed Annas from the high priesthood in 15 AD, he appointed Eleazar, Annas' son, as his replacement for two years, and then **Caiaphas**, Annas' son-in-law, from 18 to 36 AD. Caiaphas was a Sadducee, a member of the Sanhedrin, and acted as High Priest during Jesus' three years of ministry.

E. **Ephraim** was the name of Joseph's second son, born in Egypt. He was the patriarch of the half-tribe of Ephraim, which became one of the most prominent tribes of the nation of Israel.

Ephraim was also the name of an ancient city, located just 15 kilometers north of Jerusalem. It was also called Ophrah and Ephron. The modern Palestinian town of Taybeh is built on its site, near the mountainous wilderness of Beth-Aven. The Bible records that Ophrah was originally within the territory of the tribe of Benjamin in central Israel (Joshua 18:23).

CHAPTER 24

To Jerusalem for the Last Time

24.1 TEN LEPERS HEALED

Luke 17:11-19

While he was travelling to Jerusalem, he passed through Samaria and Galilee, and as he entered a village, ten men with leprosy stood far off[a] and met him. They raised their voices, saying, "Jesus, Master! Have mercy on us!"

When he saw them, he said, "Go and show yourselves to the priests."[b]

As they were going, they were cleansed. One of them, when he saw that he was healed, returned praising God with a great voice, and he fell on his face at his feet, thanking him. He was a Samaritan.

"Weren't ten cleansed?" Jesus asked. "Where are the other nine? Was nobody found who returned to give God praise except this

A. *The leper with the lesions: his clothes will be torn, his hair disheveled, and he'll cover his mustache and shout, "Unclean, unclean!" He'll be unclean all the days he has the lesions. He's unclean. He'll live alone and his home will be outside the camp. – Leviticus 13:45-46*

B. *This is the law for the leper on the day he's cleansed: he'll go to the priest and the priest will go outside the camp. The priest will look and if the lesions of leprosy have been healed in the leper... the priest will cover him and he'll be clean. – Leviticus 14:2-3,20*

foreigner?"

Then he told him, "Stand up and go. Your faith has saved you."

24.2 PARABLES ON PRAYER

Luke 18:1-14

He told them a parable that they should pray all the time and not get discouraged: "There was a judge in a certain city who didn't fear God, nor did he respect man. And there was a widow in that city that kept coming to him, saying, 'Vindicate me from my opposition.'[c] He wouldn't for a while, but eventually he said to himself, 'I don't fear man nor do I respect God, but because this widow gives me so much trouble, I'll vindicate her, or else her coming to me endlessly will beat me down.'"

Then the Lord said, "Hear what the unrighteous judge says! Now won't God deliver his chosen, who cry out to him day and night? Will he be slow to help them? I tell you that he'll give them justice quickly. But when the Son of Man comes, will he find faith on the earth?"

Then he told this parable to those who trusted in their own righteousness and despised others:[d] "Two men went up to the Temple to pray, one a Pharisee and the other a tax collector. The Pharisee stood and prayed to himself, 'God, thank you that I'm not like others: cheaters, the unrighteous, adulterers, or like this tax collector. I fast twice a week and tithe on all I get.' But the tax collector, standing at a distance, wouldn't even lift up his eyes to heaven, but beat his chest,[e] saying, 'God, have mercy on me, a sinner!' I tell you, this man went down to his house justified rather than the other. Because everyone who honors himself will be humbled, but whoever humbles himself will be honored."[f]

C. *Antidikos* comes from *anti* ("against") and *dikos* ("justice" or "lawsuit"). It refers to one's opposing counsel or **opposition** in a court case. Similarly, the verb *ekdikeo*, also derived from *dikos*, translates "**vindicate**," "avenge," or "do justice."

D. *Why do you judge your brother? And why do you hate your brother? Because we'll all stand before God's platform. – Romans 14:10*

E. **Beating one's chest** was an outward sign of deep anguish or mourning.

F. *Humble yourself in the Lord's presence and he'll elevate you. – James 4:10*

24.3 DIVORCE

Matthew 19:1-12
Mark 10:1-12

After Jesus finished saying this, he gets up and goes from Galilee to Judea's border beyond the Jordan. Crowds gather around him again,

Marriage, Divorce, and the *Ketubah*

God created man in his image, and in the image of God he created them. He created them male and female. God blessed them and God told them, "Be fruitful and become many. Fill the earth and control it."

– Genesis 1:27-28

A helper wasn't found for Adam, so the LORD God made him fall into a trance and he slept. Then he took one of his ribs and closed his body under it. The LORD God built the rib he had taken from the man into a woman and brought her to the man. Then the man said, "Now this is bone from my bones and body from my body. She'll be called woman because she was taken from man."

This is why a man will leave his father and mother and join his wife. They'll be one body.

– Genesis 2:20-24

The Greek verb *apolyo* means "unbind" or "**release**," and is the term for the act of divorcing. The actual **divorce** itself is denoted by the Greek noun *apostasion.*

When a man takes and marries a wife, but she doesn't please his eyes because he finds something indecent with her, he can write a divorce certificate, hand it to her, and send her out of his house. But if she leaves his house and becomes another man's, and the subsequent husband hates her, writes a divorce certificate, hands it to her, and sends her out of his house, or if the subsequent husband who took her as his wife dies, then the initial husband who sent her away isn't able to take her as his wife again, because she has become unclean. That would be revolting to the LORD.

– Deuteronomy 24:1-4

"The LORD has witnessed regarding you and the wife of your youth, whom you've betrayed, even though she's your partner and your wife by covenant.... Beware in your spirit and let no one betray the wife of his youth. Because I hate divorce," says the LORD, the God of Israel.

– Malachi 2:16

In traditional Jewish marriages, the ***ketubah*** (Hebrew for "her writing") was a marriage contract that outlined the responsibilities of the husband. This one-sided agreement was signed by the groom, witnessed by two wedding guests, and read aloud during the wedding ceremony before being given to the new bride. The woman wasn't required to sign it, since she was the recipient of her husband's commitment. The *ketubah* was designed for the protection of women, in case their means of support (their husbands) should cease to provide for them, either due to death or divorce. It included three basic provisions for the wife: clothing, food, and conjugal rights. It could also include a specified amount of money if the marriage ended in divorce. Thus the *ketubah* was cherished by every Jewish wife, being her security. It was richly decorated and often displayed prominently in the home. It replaced the bride price (*mohar*), which was due to the woman's father at the time of marriage, and therefore enabled young prospective husbands to marry without fronting large sums of money. The Jewish *ketubah*, which awarded rights to married women, stood in stark contrast to many ancient civilizations' practice of possessing wives as mere property.

because many had followed him. As usual, he healed and taught them there. Pharisees came to him too, testing him by asking, "Is it legal for a man to release his wife for any reason?"

"What did Moses command you?" he answered.

"Moses allowed a man to write a certificate of divorce and release her," they reply.

"Moses wrote this command and let you release your wives because of your hard hearts," he answers, "but it wasn't this way from the beginning. Haven't you read that the Creator made them male and female from the beginning, and said, 'This is why a man will leave his father and mother and be joined[g] to his wife, and the two will become one body'? So they aren't two anymore, but one body. Therefore what God has joined, let no man separate."

In the house, the disciples asked him about this again. So he tells them, "I tell you that whoever releases his wife, except for fornication, and marries another, has an affair. And if she releases her husband and marries another man, she's having an affair."

Then the disciples say, "If the man's relationship with his wife is like that, it's better not to marry."

"Not all men accept these words, but only to whom it was given," he answered. "There are eunuchs[h] who were born like that from their

---

G. The Greek verb *kollao* is often translated "stuck" or simply "**join**," as it is here. However, it's derived from the noun *kolla*, meaning "glue." The equivalent Hebrew term – used in the original passage Jesus is quoting (Genesis 2:24) – uses a similar word (*dabaq*) that also refers to being stuck firmly together, as with glue. Thus a more literal translation may be "a man will leave his father and mother and be glued to his wife."

H. A castrated man in the ancient world was called a **eunuch**. His castration usually occurred early in life, typically without consent, before testosterone could virilize his body during puberty. Testosterone production increases dramatically in puberty and is required for the development of the masculine characteristics of the male body, such as voice deepening, body hair growth, muscle development, libido, and genital enlargement. Although some testosterone is still produced in the adrenal glands, the main source was gone for eunuchs entering puberty and therefore they would've lacked such characteristics. Even in adulthood, eunuchs would have looked more like large boys than men.

Lack of testosterone also reduces aggression and erectile function, making eunuchs ideal for managing harems, which is where the term eunuch originated (*eune* means "bed" or "harem;" *echo* means "hold" or "have"). Eunuchs also served as guards and servants within their master's bedrooms, with duties such as bathing and dressing royalty. Across Europe in the Middle Ages, *castrati* (Latin) were valuable in choirs for their high-pitched voices.

Eunuchs were usually slaves that lacked loyalties to the military, royalty, or a family of their own and were therefore viewed as trustworthy servants with little interest in their own dynasties. Many ancient empires employed them, often castrating boys taken as prisoners of war. Some eunuchs, however, were self-castrated for religious purposes. Furthermore, the term "eunuch" could also refer to a non-castrated but impotent or celibate man.

mother's womb; there are eunuchs who were castrated by men; and there are also eunuchs who castrated themselves for the kingdom of heaven. Whoever can accept this, accept it."

24.4 CHILDREN IN THE KINGDOM

Matthew 19:13-15
Mark 10:13-16
Luke 18:15-17

They were bringing babies and children to him, that he might put his hands on them, touch them, and pray. But his disciples scolded them. However, when Jesus saw this, he was angry and told them, "Leave the children alone and let them come to me. Don't stop them, because God's kingdom belongs to those like them. Truly I tell you, whoever doesn't receive God's kingdom like a child won't enter it."

He took them in his arms, put his hands on them, and blessed them. Then he left that place.

24.5 WEALTH IN THE KINGDOM

Matthew 19:16-30
Mark 10:17-31
Luke 18:18-30

As he was leaving on his way, a ruler ran up to him, knelt down, and asked, "Good Teacher, what good should I do to inherit everlasting life?"

"Why do you call me good and ask about what's good?" Jesus answered. "No one is good except God alone. But if you want to enter into life, keep the commandments."

"Which ones?" he asks.

"You know them," Jesus replied. "Don't murder, don't have an affair, don't steal, don't testify lies, don't cheat, honor your father and mother, and love your neighbor like yourself."[i]

"Teacher," he answers, "I've kept all of this since childhood. What am I still missing?"

Hearing this, Jesus loved him and said, "One thing you need if you want to be complete: go and sell everything you have and give it to the

I. *You won't avenge or guard against the sons of your nation, but you'll love your neighbor like yourself. I am the LORD. – Leviticus 19:18*

The Ten Commandments

On their journey from slavery in Egypt to dominion in Canaan, God gave Israel many laws, but among them were **Ten Commandments** that embodied the entire Law:

1. *I am the LORD your God, who brought you out of the land of Egypt, out of the house of slavery. Do not have other gods besides me.*
2. *Do not make an idol for yourself, nor any image of what is in heaven, nor beneath it on earth, nor in the water under the earth. Do not worship or serve them, because I, the LORD your God, am a jealous God. I punish the guilt of fathers on their children, for three and four generations of those who hate me, but I show goodness to thousands, to those who love me and keep my commandments.*
3. *Do not use the LORD your God's name hollowly, because the LORD will not leave the one who uses his name hollowly free.*
4. *Remember to keep the Sabbath day holy. You'll work and do all your business in six days, but the seventh day is a Sabbath to the LORD your God. Do not work on it, not you, your son or daughter, your man-servant or maid-servant, your animals, nor any foreigner living in your towns. Because the LORD made the skies, the earth, the sea, and everything in them in six days, but he rested on the seventh day. So the LORD blessed the Sabbath day and made it holy.*
5. *Honor your father and mother, so your days in the land the LORD your God gives you will be long.*
6. *Do not murder.*
7. *Do not have an affair.*
8. *Do not steal.*
9. *Do not testify lies against your neighbor.*
10. *Do not envy your neighbor's house. Do not envy your neighbor's wife, nor his man-servant or maid-servant, nor his ox or donkey, nor anything else your neighbor owns.*

– Exodus 20:2-17; Deuteronomy 5:6-21

These commandments were first delivered to Moses on two stone tablets while Israel was on the border of their promised land. However, after faithlessly failing to enter the land and spending 40 years in the desert as punishment, these Ten Commandments were again recorded just before Israel's second attempt at possessing Canaan. This second time they succeeded.

poor, and then you'll have treasure in heaven. Then come, follow me."

But when the young man heard these words, he became sad and went away depressed, because he was very wealthy and owned much property.[J] Looking around and seeing this, Jesus tells his disciples, "Truly I tell you, how hard it is for the wealthy to enter God's kingdom!"

The disciples were amazed at his words. But Jesus tells them again, "Children, how hard it is to enter God's kingdom! It's easier for a camel to pass through the eye of a needle than for the wealthy to enter God's kingdom."

Hearing this, they were even more blown away and asked him, "Then who can be saved?"

J. *One is rich, but it's all for nothing. Another is poor, but has much wealth. – Proverbs 13:7*

A Camel Through the Eye of a Needle

The largest animal in ancient Palestine was the **camel**, which could stand over 2 meters (7 feet) tall at the hump. They were domesticated primarily for their use as pack animals, but they also provided a source of milk, meat, and clothing.

Camels have a number of adaptations that help them withstand long periods without water, so they're ideally suited for the arid landscape of the Middle East and Northern Africa. Most notably, their humps are large deposits of fatty tissue that can be metabolized to produce water and energy when needed. Additionally, their red blood cells are oval shaped, ideal for functioning despite dehydration or over-hydration. Camels can tolerate extreme body temperatures that would normally kill other animals – their fur insulates them from heat during the day and cold at night. Their loping gait and wide feet allow them to walk easily on sand. Finally, their organs are so efficient at conserving water that their urine can come out thick like syrup and their feces so dry it can be burned as fuel for fires. Even exhaled water vapor is trapped and recycled in their nostrils. But however useful they were in ancient times, camels are notoriously stubborn and difficult to control. There is virtually no way to move a camel if it doesn't want to go.

In contrast to the largest animal, the oval (eye-shaped) opening at the end of a **needle** was one of the smallest openings in the ancient world.

Looking at them, Jesus said, "It's impossible with man, but not with God. Everything's possible with God."

Then Peter said, "Look, we've left everything we own and followed you. What will there be for us?"

"Truly I tell you," Jesus answered, "for you who've followed me, you'll sit on twelve thrones to judge the twelve tribes of Israel in the regeneration[k] when the Son of Man will sit on his glorious throne. Truly I tell you that there's no one who has left house or wife or brothers or sisters or mother or father or children or farms – because of my name, the good news, or God's kingdom – that won't receive a hundred times more houses and brothers and sisters and mothers and children and farms, as well as oppression, in this present time and everlasting life in

K. *Paliggenesia* is a combination of the Greek words *palin* ("new," "again") and *genesis* ("origin," "birth"). It translates here to "**regeneration**," referring to a rebirth within God's kingdom. In the apocalyptic book of Revelation, John records a vision of a regenerated *"new heaven and new earth, because the first heaven and the first earth passed away" (Revelation 21:1).*

the time to come.[l] But many of the first will be last and the last first."

24.6 PARABLE OF THE LANDLORD'S WAGES

Matthew 20:1-16

"The kingdom of heaven is like a landlord who went out early in the morning to hire workers for his vineyard. He agreed with the workers on a denarius for the day and sent them out into his vineyard. Then he went out at the third hour and saw others standing idly in the market, so he told them, 'Go to the vineyard too and I'll give you what's right.' So they went. He went out around the sixth and ninth hours and did the same. Then he went out around the eleventh hour[m] and found others standing there. 'Why have you been standing here idly all day?' he asks them. 'Because no one hired us,' they reply. So he tells them, 'Go to the vineyard too.'

"When evening came, the lord of the vineyard tells his manager, 'Call the workers and pay them their wages, starting with the last, up until the first.' So when those from the eleventh hour came, each one got a denarius. When the first came, they thought they'd get more, but each one got a denarius as well. When they got it, they complained to the landlord, saying, 'We bore the burden and the heat of the day, but you made the last, who only worked an hour, equal to us.' But he answered one of them, 'Friend, I'm not cheating you. Didn't we agree on a denarius? Take what's yours and go. I want to give the last the same as you. Isn't it legal to do what I want with what's mine? Or is your eye bad because I'm good?' So the last will be first and the first last."

24.7 JESUS PREDICTS HIS DEATH, THIRD TIME

Matthew 20:17-19
Mark 10:32-34
Luke 18:31-34

They were going along the road up to Jerusalem with Jesus leading

L. *But whatever was profit to me, I now count this as loss for Christ. And more so, I count everything as loss compared to the superiority of knowing Christ Jesus my Lord, for whom I've lost everything and count it all as garbage, that I might profit by Christ and be found in him as not having my own righteousness from the Law but that which is through faith in Christ, the righteousness that comes from God by faith. – Philippians 3:7-9*

M. The **third hour** of the day was mid-morning, about 9:00 am, three hours after sunrise. Similarly, the **sixth** and **ninth hours** were about 12:00 noon and 3:00 pm respectively, while the **eleventh hour** was near the end of the working day, around 5:00 pm.

them. They were amazed, but those following were afraid. Again he took the Twelve by themselves and told them on the way what was going to happen:

"Look, we're going to Jerusalem and everything the prophets wrote about the Son of Man will be completed. He'll be given to the High Priests[n] and the scribes, who'll condemn him to death and give him to the Gentiles. They'll mock him, slander him, and spit on him. And after they've whipped him, they'll crucify and kill him. Then on the third day he'll rise."

But the disciples understood none of this – it was hidden from them – so they didn't know what was said.

24.8 GREATEST MUST BE SERVANTS

Matthew 20:20-28
Mark 10:35-45

Then the mother of Zebedee's two sons – James and John – comes to Jesus with her sons, bowing down with a request. They ask him, "Teacher, we want you to do whatever we ask you."

"What do you want me to do for you?" he replied.

"Say that these two sons of mine will sit with you," she says, "one on your right and one on your left, in your kingdom and your glory."

"You don't know what you're asking for," Jesus said. "Can you drink from the cup I drink from or be baptized with the baptism I'm baptized with?"

"We can," they reply.

"You'll drink from the cup I drink from, and you'll be baptized with the baptism I am baptized with," Jesus says. "But to sit on my right my and left isn't mine to give – it's for whom it has been prepared for by my Father."

Upon hearing it, the ten were upset with the two brothers, James and John. But calling them together, Jesus says, "You know that those known as rulers of the Gentiles lord over them, and their great men have power over them. But it's not to be like this with you. Whoever

N. Even though there was only one acting High Priest at a time, all prior **High Priests** were still referred to by that title. The Sanhedrin therefore could have multiple High Priests in it at the same time, but only one would be in power. The same thing occurs today: a past president is still called "Mr. President" despite being out of office.

wants to become great among you must be your servant, and whoever wants to be first among you must be everyone's slave.[o] Even the Son of Man didn't come to be served, but to serve and give his life to ransom many."

24.9 ZACCHEUS | USING WHAT'S GIVEN TO YOU

Matthew 25:14-30
Mark 10:46a
Luke 19:1-28

They arrive at Jericho. He entered it and was passing through. A wealthy man was there named Zaccheus, a chief tax collector. Zaccheus was trying to see who Jesus was, but he couldn't see over the crowd because he was short. So he ran ahead and climbed a sycamore[p] tree to see him, because he was about to come that way. When Jesus arrived there, he looked up and said, "Zaccheus, come down quickly, because I need to stay at your house today."

He hurried down and happily received him. But when they saw it, they grumbled, saying, "He has become the guest of a sinner."

Zaccheus stopped and told the Lord, "Lord, look, I'll give half of my estate to the poor, and if I've cheated anyone of anything, I'll pay it back four times over."[q]

"Salvation has come to this house today, because he's a son of Abraham too," Jesus said. "The Son of Man came to look for and save the lost."

While they were listening to this, Jesus continued with a parable because he was close to Jerusalem and they thought God's kingdom was going to come immediately. He said, "A nobleman travelled to a country far away to take a kingdom and then return. So he called ten of his slaves and gave them ten minas, saying, 'Work with this until I

O. *Christ Jesus, being in the form of God, didn't consider being the same as God something to be seized, because he emptied himself, taking the form of a slave and being made in the image of men. – Philippians 2:5b-7*

P. The name sycamore has been applied to various trees and plants throughout history, but the **sycamore** fig (*Ficus sycomorus*), native to Palestine, was likely the tree referred to here. It can grow up to 15 meters (50 feet) tall, with a thick trunk and wide branches. Its figs were edible and therefore the tree was cultivated throughout the ancient Middle East, particularly in Egypt.

Q. *If a man steals an ox or a sheep, and butchers it or sells it, he'll pay five oxen for the ox and four sheep for the sheep. – Exodus 22:1*

come.' Then he left. However, his citizens hated him and sent messengers after him, saying, 'We don't want this one to rule us.'

"When he returned from taking the kingdom, he said to call those slaves whom he'd given money to so he could know the business they had done. So he comes and talks with them. The first came, saying, 'Master, your mina produced ten minas.' So he told him, 'Well done, good slave. Because you were faithful with little, you'll have power over ten cities.' The second came, saying, 'Master, your mina made five minas.' So he told him too, 'You'll be over five cities.' Another came, saying, 'Master, here's your mina. I kept it laid away in a handkerchief because I was afraid of you. You're a harsh man – you pick up what you didn't lay down and reap what you didn't sow.' 'You evil slave!' he replies. 'I'll judge you by your own words. Did you know that I'm a harsh man, picking up what I didn't lay down and reaping what I didn't sow? Then why didn't you put my money on a table,[r] so I could've used it with interest when I came?' Then he told those standing there, 'Take the mina from him and give it to the one with ten.' But they replied, 'Master, he already has ten minas.' 'I tell you, to everyone who has,

R. Moneychangers operated from **tables** (Greek *trapeza*) where they exchanged currencies for a small profit. The **interest** in these investments was denoted by the word for "birth" (*tokos*), since invested money figuratively breeds itself, producing more.

The Parable of the Minas/Talents

Both Matthew and Luke record a parable about a nobleman giving money to his slaves to invest during his absence. Here they're combined into one account, but there are some significant differences. In terms of the context, Matthew mentions the story amidst a large block of teaching on the coming of God's kingdom, delivered after Jesus' entry into Jerusalem. Luke, however, records the story as being told during a meal at a tax collector's house, quite apart from other teaching and prior to Jesus' entry into Jerusalem. Luke also includes extra narrative about the purpose of the nobleman's visit and the consequences for the citizens who opposed their king.

But the most striking difference between Matthew's and Luke's account is the currency: Luke states ten slaves received ten minas split amongst them; the first three turned a profit of ten, five, and zero minas, respectively. Conversely, Matthew states that three slaves received five, two, and one talent; the first two doubled their investment, while the third earned nothing. As a reward, Luke records that the slaves were appointed to govern cities, while Matthew's slaves were *"set over much."*

The **mina** was an ancient unit of weight equal to 100 shekels, about a kilogram by today's standards. It was also a unit of currency, worth 100 drachmas (one drachma was the usual wage of a day's labor). Thus one mina was the wage of working for about three months. The **talent**, however, was much larger, equaling about 60 minas. One silver talent would take a laborer over 15 years to earn. Matthew, who was previously a tax collector and presumably wealthy, quotes the larger amounts of money.

The details cited by Luke are used predominantly here.

more will be given. But from the one who doesn't have, even what he has will be taken away. Throw this useless slave out into the darkness outside where there's weeping and teeth grinding. And my enemies, who didn't want me as king, bring them here and kill them in front of me.'"

After saying this, he continued on ahead, going up to Jerusalem.

24.10 BLIND BARTIMAEUS HEALED

Matthew 20:29-34
Mark 10:46b-52
Luke 18:35-43

A large crowd followed as he was leaving Jericho[s] with his disciples. Two blind beggars – [one of them was] Bartimaeus, Timaeus' son – were sitting by the road. Hearing a crowd going by, they asked about it and were told that Jesus the Nazarene was passing by. When they heard it, they shouted, "Lord Jesus, son of David! Have mercy on me!"

Many of those leading the way scolded them to be quiet, but they shouted all the more, "Son of David! Have mercy on me!"

Jesus stopped and said, "Call them here."

So they call the blind men, saying, "Cheer up! He's calling for you. Get up!"

Throwing their coats aside,[t] they jumped up and went to Jesus, who asked, "What do you want me to do for you?"

"Lord, Rabboni,[u] to see again!" the blind men reply.

Jesus was moved, so he touched their eyes and said, "Receive your sight! Go, your faith has saved you."

Immediately they could see, and they followed him and glorified God on the road. When everyone saw it, they praised God.

S. Thousands of years of destruction and rebuilding of the ancient city of Jericho have left numerous settlements and ruins in the same general area. In particular, the Jericho mentioned in the Old Testament was largely ruined and abandoned, replaced with a new city to the south constructed by Herod the Great. Thus it's entirely possible that Jesus was **leaving Jericho** (as Matthew and Mark record) and entering a different Jericho (as Luke records) at the same time, all on the way from the Jordan River to Jerusalem.

T. A **blind man throwing** anything aside was highly unusual and unwise, since he didn't have the means to look for it afterwards. A coat, in particular, was likely a beggar's most valuable possession, being the only thing that kept him warm at night.

U. **Rabboni** is a variation of rabbi, possibly reflecting a difference in pronunciation or a higher designation.

CHAPTER 25

Entering the City

25.1 ARRIVAL AT BETHANY

John 2:13a; 11:55-12:1, 9-11

The Jewish Passover was near and many went up from the country to Jerusalem to purify themselves before the Passover. They were looking for Jesus and asking each other as they stood in the Temple, "What do you think? Won't he come to the feast?"

The High Priests and the Pharisees had given orders that if anyone knew where he was, he must report it so they could arrest him. Therefore, six days before the Passover, Jesus came to Bethany where Lazarus was, whom Jesus had raised from death. A large crowd of Jews learned he was there. They came not only because of Jesus but also to see Lazarus, whom he had raised from death. However, the High Priests planned to kill Lazarus too, because many Jews had left and believed in Jesus because of him.

25.2 ENTRY INTO JERUSALEM

Matthew 21:1-11, 14-17
Mark 11:1-11
Luke 19:29-44

John 2:13b; 12:12-19

The next day, they approach Jerusalem, near the Mount of Olives at Bethphage and Bethany. Jesus sends two disciples, saying, "Go into the village across from you and immediately as you enter it you'll find a donkey tied there with her colt, which no one has ever sat on. Untie them and bring them here to me. And if anyone asks you, 'What are you doing?' tell them, 'The Lord needs them,' and they'll send them here immediately."

So they went and did as Jesus had instructed them, finding it as he had told them. They found the colt tied at the door, outside in the street. They untie it. Its owners standing there asked them, "Why are you untying that colt?"

They responded, "The Lord needs it," just as Jesus had told them to. So they let them go.

They bring the donkey and the colt to Jesus, and throwing their coats on it, he sat on top of the coats. This happened to fulfill what was said through the prophet:

> "Tell Zion's daughter, 'Don't fear! Look, your king is coming to you, meek and mounted on a donkey, even on a colt, the son of an ass.'"[a]

His disciples didn't understand this at first, but when Jesus was glorified, they remembered that this was written about him and that they had done this to him.

The crowd, which was with him when he had called Lazarus out of the tomb and raised him from death, had witnessed about him. Therefore, the many crowds of people that had come to the feast went out to meet Jesus when they heard he was coming to Jerusalem, because they had heard he did this sign. Many in the crowd spread their coats on the road as he was going, and others spread palm branches they had cut from palm trees in the fields.

As they came close, near the descent from the Mount of Olives, the crowds of the disciples in front and behind happily praised God for all the miracles they had seen. They shouted,

---

A. The Greek *hypozygion* literally translates to "under the yoke," referring to a beast of burden. It appears twice in the New Testament, both in reference to a donkey. The actual Greek term for "donkey" is *onarion* or *onos*, so *hypozygion* is translated here as **ass**.

Celebrate fiercely, daughter of Zion! Shout, daughter of Jerusalem! Look, your king is coming to you. He's righteous and saving, poor and mounted on a donkey, even a colt, the son of an ass. –Zechariah 9:9

Palms

Three of the Gospel writers record that the crowds spread branches on the road before Jesus, in addition to their coats, but only John specifies that the branches were from **palm trees**. The only other time this tree is mentioned in the New Testament is in a vision John records in Revelation, where masses of people praise God with palm branches in their hands, celebrating God's salvation.

John's term for palm trees (*phoinix*) refers to the date palm (*Phoenix dactylifera*), a highly cultivated tree throughout the ancient world. It was grown for its dates (*dactylifera* means "date-bearing"), which are sweet, colorful, finger-like fruits with a hard pit in the center. Date palms have been grown for millennia in the Middle East and were plentiful in the first century Judean countryside.

Palm branches were used as symbols of Jewish nationalism since the Maccabean revolution, similar to how the maple leaf symbolizes Canada and the silver fern symbolizes New Zealand.

"Hosanna[b] to the son of David! Blessed is the one who comes in the name of the Lord,[c] the king of Israel! Blessed is the coming of the kingdom of our father David! Peace in heaven! Glory and hosanna in the highest!"

Some of the Pharisees in the crowd told Jesus, "Teacher, reprimand your disciples."

But he answered, "I tell you, if they keep quiet, the stones will shout out!"[d]

B. The old Hebrew word **hosanna** comes from the words for "save" (*yasha*), and "pray" or "now" (*na*). It's used as an entreaty or exhortation for salvation, similar to crying out, "Please save us!"

C. *Blessed is the one who comes in the name of the LORD. We've blessed you from the LORD's house. – Psalm 118:26*

D. *The stone will certainly shout out from the wall and the beam will answer from the wood. – Habakkuk 2:11*

So the Pharisees said to each other, "Look, the world has gone after him, and we can't help it at all!"

Approaching Jerusalem, he saw the city and wept over it, saying, "If only you'd known about the peace for you today! But it has been hidden from your eyes. The days will come when your enemies will throw up a barricade against you and surround you on all sides. They'll raze[e] you, and your children with you, and they won't leave one stone

E. Luke's use of the verb *edaphizo* means "flatten," "throw down," or "**raze**." In the case of Jerusalem, it refers to the city being destroyed and completely leveled.

The Destruction of Jerusalem

The Jews revolted from Roman rule in 66 AD due to excessive taxation and brutality, prompting the first Jewish-Roman War in 67 AD. Jewish independence was short-lived when the Roman army under Titus invaded Judea and conquered its fortified cities. The Jewish historian Josephus, who was employed by the Romans at the time, vividly recorded the events of the war that culminated in the **destruction of Jerusalem** in 70 AD.

The Roman army surrounded the city that spring, but the Jews continued to gather supplies from the countryside before safely returning behind Jerusalem's thick walls. To prevent this, a ditch and a barricade were built around the entire city and anyone caught trying to escape the city was crucified, with the corpse displayed as a warning to others. Thousands were executed this way. Other escapees were torn open while still alive by Roman soldiers looking for swallowed coins, although few produced any. The lengthy siege led to famine within Jerusalem, and hard-fought battles led to bitter frustration on both sides.

The Roman commander Titus, who would later become the Roman emperor, pitied the Jews as he fought against them. However, despite Titus' numerous attempts at negotiations, even to the point of barely escaping with his life from one of them, the Jews refused to yield. The Romans constructed ramps, battering rams, siege towers, and catapults to attack the city, stripping the countryside of trees to build their weapons of war. Jerusalem's walls were eventually broken in the early summer of 70 AD, but street fighting continued as the remaining rebels fortified themselves within the Temple. Towards the end, with Jerusalem's walls breached, the Romans ruthlessly slaughtered Jews indiscriminately: male and female, soldier and civilian, young and old. Similarly, the Jews' last stand in the Temple saw anyone able to hold a weapon fighting to the bitter end. Titus had planned to spare the Temple for Roman use later on, but a fire destroyed it and much of the city during the invasion. With the last Jewish stronghold burned, the Romans finally crushed the Jewish resistance, while refugees tried to escape the city through underground tunnels. The vast Temple treasury was melted down to mint coins commemorating Rome's success against the Jewish rebels.

After its fall, Jerusalem was leveled – walls, towers, Temple – by the embittered Roman soldiers who had endured such a hard-fought war. Small sections of the wall and towers were spared to house the Roman garrisons and demonstrate how great the city had previously been. The destruction was so extensive that afterwards the land was unrecognizable as the site of a great city. The fertile, beautiful landscape was replaced with desolate wasteland.

Over a million Jews died during the siege, from starvation, execution, or active combat. Piles of rotting corpses filled the streets, adding the stench of death to the smoke. As well, nearly 100,000 Jews were enslaved, while those few who managed to escape the Romans fled throughout the Mediterranean.

upon another, because you didn't recognize the time of your visitation."

When he entered Jerusalem, the whole city was stirred up, asking, "Who is this?"

"This is Jesus, the prophet from Nazareth in Galilee!" the crowds were saying.

Then Jesus entered the Temple. The blind and the crippled[f] came to him in the Temple and he healed them. But when the High Priests and scribes saw the wonderful things he had done, and the children shouting "Hosanna to the son of David!" in the Temple, they were upset. "Do you hear what they're saying?" they said.

"Of course!" Jesus replies. "Haven't you ever read, 'Out of the mouths of children and babies you've been praised'?"[g]

Then after seeing everything, he left the city for Bethany with the Twelve. And since it was late, they spent the night there.

25.3 FIG TREE CURSED | TEMPLE PURIFIED

Matthew 21:12-13, 18-19a
Mark 11:12-18
Luke 19:45-48
John 2:14-25

The next morning, after they had left Bethany to return to the city, he got hungry. In the distance he saw a lone fig tree full of leaves by the road, so he went to look for something on it. But when he got there, he found nothing but leaves, because it wasn't fig season. With his disciples listening, he tells it, "No one will ever eat your fruit again! You won't bear it anymore."

Then they come to Jerusalem. He entered the Temple, and inside he found those selling oxen, sheep, and doves,[h] and money changers[i] seated. So he made a whip from ropes and threw out all those who were

F. According to Moses' law, anyone with a physical defect was not allowed to enter the designated area to offer sacrifices to God, specifically the Tabernacle and the Temple. This included those who were **blind and crippled**. So for the blind and the crippled, and any others with physical ailments, to enter the Temple would likely have violated the Law.

G. *From the mouths of children and babies you've founded your strength, because of distress, to make hostility and revenge stop. – Psalm 8:2*

H. **Oxen, sheep, and doves** were all prescribed in Moses' Law as sacrifices to be made in the Temple for various purposes. It was presumably easier for those travelling from afar to purchase animals for sacrifice upon arrival than bring their own. Thus they were apparently bought and sold within the Temple complex.

buying and selling in the Temple, with the sheep and the oxen. He overturned the money changers' tables and poured out their coins. He overturned the dove sellers' seats, saying, "Take these away! Stop making my Father's house a market!"

He wouldn't let anyone carry merchandise through the Temple. Then he taught them, saying, "Isn't it written, 'My house will be called a house of prayer for all nations'?[j] But you've made it a cave of thieves!"[k]

His disciples later remembered that it was written, "Jealousy for your house will consume me."[l]

Then the Jews asked him, "What can you show us as a sign of your authority for doing this?"

"Destroy this Temple and in three days I'll raise it up!" Jesus answered.

"It took 46 years to build this Temple!" the Jews replied. "But you'll raise it up in three days?"

But he was speaking about his body as a temple. When he was raised from death, his disciples remembered that he had said this, and they believed the Scripture and the word Jesus had spoken.

He was teaching in the Temple daily, but when the High Priests, the scribes, and the peoples' leaders heard him, they looked for a way to destroy him, because they were afraid of him. However, they couldn't figure out what to do, since the whole crowd was blown away at his teaching and was hanging onto what they had heard.

So when he was at the Passover in Jerusalem, many believed in his

---

I. **Money changers** in the Temple turned a profit on exchanging currency. Because every Jewish male over 20 years old had to pay half a shekel into the Temple treasury annually, which could only be paid by Hebrew coins, money changers apparently abounded in the Temple area. The Greek term is *kollybistes*, derived from the small coin (*kollubos*) that money changers profited on each transaction. The term can also be translated "banker" or "broker."

J. *The foreigners' sons too, who are joined to the LORD... I'll bring them to my holy mountain and have them celebrate in my house of prayer. Their offerings and sacrifices will have favor on my altar, because my house will be called a house of prayer for all people. – Isaiah 56:6-7*

K. *"Has this house, called after my name, become a cave of thieves in your eyes? Look, I've seen it," says the LORD. – Jeremiah 7:11*

L. *Jealousy for your house has consumed me and the scorn of those you scorn has fallen on me. – Psalm 69:9*

M. Matthew records that the **fig tree withered** immediately after Jesus cursed it. However, Mark records it was withered when they found it the next day. The other Gospel writers don't record the event.

name during the feast, seeing the signs he was doing. But Jesus didn't trust them, because he knew them all; he didn't need anyone to testify about man, because he knew what was in man.

25.4 FIG TREE WITHERED

Matthew 21:19b-22
Mark 11:19-24
Luke 21:37-38

He taught in the Temple during the day, but when evening came, they would leave the city and stay on the mountain called Olive. But all the people would rise early to listen to him in the Temple.

As they were passing by the next morning, they saw the fig tree withered[m] to its roots. Reminded, the disciples were amazed. Then Peter says, "Rabbi, look, the fig tree you cursed has withered! How did it wither so soon?"

"Have faith in God," Jesus answers. "Truly I tell you, if you have faith and don't doubt in your heart, you won't only do this to the fig tree, but if you tell this mountain, 'Be lifted up and thrown into the sea,' and believe what you say, it'll happen. So I tell you, for everything you pray and ask for, believe that you've gotten it and it'll be so."

25.5 SON OF MAN MUST BE "LIFTED UP"

John 12:20-50

Some Greeks were going up to worship at the feast too. They came to Philip,[n] who was from Bethsaida in Galilee, saying, "Sir, we want to see Jesus."

So Philip comes and tells Andrew. Then Andrew and Philip come and tell Jesus. Jesus answers, "The time has come for the Son of Man to be glorified. I tell you, truly truly, unless a grain of wheat falls into the ground and dies, it stays alone. But if it dies, it produces much fruit. Whoever loves his life will lose it and whoever hates his life in this world

N. **Philip** is a Greek name meaning "friend." Three other disciples had Greek names in addition to their Hebrew names. Levi was called Matthew; Judas of James was apparently also called Thaddeus; and Simon was renamed Peter by Jesus. However, Philip is the only disciple with a Greek name alone, suggesting he may have been from a Greek family.

O. It's understandable that the Greeks in the crowd would think the voice of God from the sky was **thunder**. Zeus, the chief Greek deity, was the god of the sky and thunder.
The Lord thundered from heaven, and the Highest used his voice. – 2 Samuel 22:14

will keep it as everlasting life. If anyone serves me, he must follow me, because wherever I am, my servant must be there too. And if anyone serves me, the Father will honor him. My soul is upset, but what can I say, 'Father, save me from this time'? Rather, I came to this time for this reason. So Father, glorify your name."

Then a voice came from heaven: "I've glorified it and I'll glorify it again."

The crowd standing there heard it. Some said it was thunder,[o] while others said, "An angel spoke to him!"

But Jesus answered, "This voice hasn't come for me, but for you. Judgment is on this world, and now the ruler of this world will be thrown out. And if I'm lifted up above the earth, I'll pull everyone to myself."

He said this to show the kind of death he was going to die. Then the crowd answered him, "We've heard from the Law that the Christ will last forever,[p] so how can you say, 'The Son of Man must be lifted up'? Who is this Son of Man?"

"The light is with you for a little," Jesus answered. "So walk while you have the light, that the darkness won't catch you. Whoever walks in the dark doesn't know where he's going. While you have the light, believe in the light, so you can become sons of light."

Jesus said this, and then he left and hid. But even though he had done so many signs before them, they didn't believe, fulfilling the words spoken by Isaiah the prophet:

> "Lord, who has believed our words? And who has been shown the arm of the Lord?"[q]

This is why they couldn't believe. And Isaiah again said,

> "He has blinded their eyes and hardened their hearts, so they wouldn't see with their eyes and understand with their hearts, then turn and be healed."[r]

P. *My servant David will be king over them, and they'll all have one shepherd... My servant David will be their ruler forever. – Ezekiel 37:24-25*

Q. *Who has believed our message? And who has been shown the LORD's arm? – Isaiah 53:1*

R. *Go and tell this people, "Keep listening, but don't understand. Keep looking, but don't know. Make these people's hearts fat, their ears dense, and their eyes blind. Or else they might see with their eyes, hear with their ears, and understand with their hearts, and then return and be healed." – Isaiah 6:9-10*

Isaiah said this because he saw his glory and spoke of him. Nonetheless, many of the leaders believed in him, but they wouldn't say so for fear that the Pharisees would excommunicate them, because they loved glory from men more than glory from God.

Then Jesus shouted out, "Whoever believes in me doesn't just believe in me but in him who sent me. And whoever sees me sees the one who sent me. I've come as light in the world. Anyone who believes in me won't stay in the dark. If anyone hears my words but doesn't keep them, I don't judge him, because I didn't come to judge the world, but to save it. But whoever rejects me and doesn't accept my words does have someone who judges him: the words I've spoken will judge him on the last day. I haven't spoken on my own, but the Father who sent me commanded me with what to say and what to speak. I know his command is everlasting life, so what I speak, I speak just as the Father told me."

25.6 NICODEMUS' QUESTIONS

John 3:1-21

One night a man came to Jesus, a Pharisee named Nicodemus, a Jewish ruler. He said, "Rabbi, we know that you've come from God as a teacher, because no one can do these miracles that you do unless God is with him."

"Truly truly, I tell you," Jesus answered, "unless someone is born again,[s] he can't see God's kingdom."

"How can a man be born when he's old?" Nicodemus asks. "Can he go into his mother's womb again and be born?"

"Truly truly, I tell you that unless someone is born in water and in the Spirit,[t] he can't enter God's kingdom," Jesus answered. "Bodies birth bodies and spirit births spirit, so don't be surprised that I've told you, 'You must be born again.' The wind blows where it wants and you

S. The Greek phrase *gennao anothen* translates here as "**born again**," but it can also mean "born from above" or "born from a higher place."

So if anyone is in Christ, he's a new creation. The old is passed, and look, the new has come! – 2 Corinthians 5:17

T. The Greek word *pneuma* translates to "breath" or "wind." However, among ancient Greek physicians, it could also refer to the circulating air within a body, which was essential for consciousness and life. And since it could also signify a person's innermost being, *pneuma* is commonly translated as "**spirit**" in the Bible. This concept similarly occurred with the Hebrew word for "breath" (*ruwach*). "Spirit" is traditionally capitalized when referring to God's Holy Spirit (*hagios pneuma*), as it is here.

hear its sound, but you don't know where it comes from or where it's going. This is everyone born in the Spirit."

"How can this be?" Nicodemus asked him.

"You're Israel's teacher, but you don't understand this?" Jesus answered. "Truly truly, I tell you that we talk about what we know and witness about what we've seen, but you don't accept our testimony. So if I've told you about earthly things and you don't believe, how will you believe if I tell you about heavenly things? No one has gone up to heaven except the one who came down from heaven – the Son of Man. Just like Moses lifted up the snake[u] in the wilderness, the Son of Man must be lifted up too, so that whoever believes will have eternal life in him. Because God loved the world so much that he gave his only Son, so that whoever believes in him wouldn't die, but would have eternal life. God didn't send the Son into the world to judge it, but that it might be saved through him. Whoever believes in him is not judged, but whoever does not believe has already been judged, because he has not believed in the name of God's only Son. This is the judgment: the light came into the world, but men loved the darkness more than the light because their actions were evil. Everyone who does evil hates the light and doesn't come to the light for fear that his actions will be exposed. But whoever does the truth comes to the light[v] so his actions can be shown as having been worked out in God."

U. During Israel's journey through the desert, the book of Numbers records that they complained bitterly about their lack of food and water, despite divine provision up until then. Consequently, God sent "fiery snakes" that bit them, killing many. Israel quickly repented and begged for mercy, so God told Moses to make a similar **snake** out of bronze and raise it up on a pole, so that anyone who simply looked at it would live. The icon remained with Israel for hundreds of years until it was destroyed by King Hezekiah after Israel started worshiping it. This Jewish symbol of healing has been suggested as one of the origins of the modern medical symbol of snakes wrapped around a pole.

V. *We walk in the light like he is in the light. – 1 John 1:7a*

CHAPTER 26

Jesus' Authority Questioned

26.1 AUTHORITY QUESTIONED

Matthew 21:23-32
Mark 11:27-33
Luke 20:1-8

One day, they come to Jerusalem again to teach the people in the Temple and preach the good news. As he was walking into the Temple, the High Priests, the scribes, and the people's elders come up to him, saying, "What authority are you doing this by? Who gave you the authority to do all this?"

"I'll ask you a question too," Jesus replied. "If you answer me, I'll tell you about my authority. Answer me this: was John's baptism from heaven or from men?"

They discussed it among themselves, saying, "If we say it was from heaven, he'll say, 'Then why didn't you believe him?' But can we say it was from men?"

They were afraid of the people, that they would stone them to death, because everyone was convinced that John was a real prophet. So they answer Jesus, "We don't know."

"Neither will I tell you by what authority I act," Jesus replies. Then he also told them, "What do you think? A man had two sons, and he came to the first, saying, 'Boy, go work into the vineyard today.' 'No, I won't,' he answered, but later he regretted it and went. Then the man came to the second and said the same thing, and he answered, 'Yes, sir,' but he didn't go. Now which of the two did what his father wanted?"

"The first," they reply.

Then Jesus says, "Truly I tell you that the tax collectors and prostitutes are entering God's kingdom before you! John came to you in righteousness and you didn't believe him, but the tax collectors and prostitutes believed. And you, despite seeing, didn't even care afterwards, that you might believe."

26.2 VINEYARD AND EVIL GARDENERS

Matthew 21:33-46
Mark 12:1-12
Luke 20:9-19

Then he told the people, "Listen to another parable. A landlord planted a vineyard, fenced around it, dug a winepress, and built a tower. Then he rented it out to vine workers and traveled abroad for a

Vineyards and Vine Workers

The soil and climate of Canaan were well suited for growing grapes, so cultivating a **vineyard** was a common practice among landowning Jews. Vineyards were typically fenced or hedged to keep animals out, and a watchtower was built to protect against thieves. Grapes were harvested in September and their juice was fermented into wine or vinegar.

Landowners often hired others to tend the vines and harvest the grapes. The Greek word *ampelourgos* is derived from *ampelos* ("vine") and *ergon* ("work" or "business") and literally means "**vine worker**." It's translated as "vinedresser" in many Bible translations, but could also be rendered "gardener."

My beloved had a vineyard on a fat hill. He fenced it, de-stoned it, and planted vine shoots. He built a tower in the middle and dug a winepress. He expected it to produce grapes, but it produced a stench.

"So now, O residents of Jerusalem and men of Judah, judge between me and my vineyard. What more could I have done for my vineyard that I didn't do? When I expected it to produce grapes, didn't it produce a stench? So let me tell you what I'll do to my vineyard: I'll remove its hedge and it'll be burned. I'll break its wall and it'll be trampled. I'll make it desolate. It won't be pruned or cultivated, but briars and thorns will come. And I'll command the clouds not to rain on it too."

Because the vineyard of the LORD of armies is Israel's house, and Judah's men are his delightful plant. He looked for justice, but look, slaughter. And for righteousness, but look, weeping.

– Isaiah 5:1-7

long time. When the fruit season arrived, he sent a slave to the vine workers to collect the product of the vineyard from them. But they seized him, beat him, and sent him away empty.[a] Again, he sent another slave, but they beat him over the head, shamed him, and sent him away empty as well. He sent a third, whom they injured and threw out. He sent many others, more than the first few, but they did the same to them. They beat one, killed another, and stoned a third. Finally, the landlord said, 'What can I do?' He had one more, a son he loved. He sent him last, saying, 'Maybe they'll respect my son.' But when the vine workers saw the son, they said to each other, 'This is the heir! Come on, let's kill him and the inheritance will be ours!'[b] So they seized him, threw him out of the vineyard, and killed him. Now what will the lord of the vineyard do to the vine workers?"

"Let it never be!" they reply. "He'll come and destroy those awful wretches and give the vineyard to other vine workers who'll pay him its produce when it's due."

Then Jesus replies, "Haven't you read this Scripture: 'the stone the builders rejected has become the head corner; this was from the Lord and it's wonderful in our eyes'?[c] So I tell you that God's kingdom will be taken from you and given to a nation that will produce fruit. And whoever falls on this stone will be shattered, but whoever it falls on will be ground into dust."[d]

When the High Priests and the Pharisees heard his parables, they saw that he was speaking against them. So they were looking to arrest him, even right then. However, they were afraid of the crowds, because they considered him a prophet. So they went away.

A. The Greek word *kenos* means "**empty**" or "vain," used here to describe being empty-handed.

B. Jewish law stated in the Mishnah that unclaimed or **ownerless property could be claimed by anyone**. So land owned by an absent landowner with no legitimate heir could potentially be claimed by his slaves upon the landowner's death.

C. In ancient times, when a new structure was being constructed with a masonry foundation, the cornerstone was the first stone laid, and all subsequent stones were laid in reference to its position. Thus the cornerstone determined the layout of the entire building. It was often laid during a ceremony, with accompanying sacrifices. The Greek *kephale gonia* and Hebrew *ro'sh pinnah* translate directly to "**head corner**," as it appears here. Other translations commonly render this phrase "chief cornerstone" or "capstone."

The Lord God says this: "Look, I'm laying a stone in Zion, a tested stone, a precious corner established for the foundation. Whoever believes in him won't be rushed." – Isaiah 28:16

The stone the builders rejected has become the head corner. This is from the LORD and it's wonderful in our eyes. – Psalm 118:22-23

D. *[The LORD of armies] will become a sanctuary, but to both of Israel's houses, a stone to strike, a rock to trip, a trap and a snare for those living in Jerusalem. – Isaiah 8:14*

26.3 WEDDING FEAST

Matthew 22:1-14

Again, Jesus spoke to them in parables, saying, "The kingdom of heaven is like a king who had a wedding reception[e] for his son. He sent out slaves to call those he'd invited to the party, but they wouldn't come. Again he sent out more slaves saying, 'Tell those invited, "Look, the dinner's made, and the oxen and livestock are butchered. Everything's ready, so come to the feast!"' But they ignored him and went off, one to his farm, another to his business. The rest seized his slaves, then abused and killed them. The king was furious! He sent his armies to destroy those murderers and burn their city. Then he tells his slaves, 'The wedding's ready, but those invited aren't worthy. Go to the highways and invite everyone you find to the party.' The slaves went out into the streets and gathered everyone they found, both evil and good, and the hall was filled with diners. But when the king came in to see the guests, he saw a man not dressed in wedding clothes.[f] He asked him, 'Friend, how did you come in here without wedding clothes?' But the man was speechless. Then the king told his servants, 'Tie him up, hand and foot, and throw him outside into the dark, where there will be weeping and teeth grinding.' Because many are invited, but few are selected."

26.4 PAYING TAXES TO CAESAR

Matthew 22:15-22
Mark 12:13-17
Luke 20:20-26

The Pharisees watched him and discussed how they could trap him in his words so they could hand him over to the authority and power of the governor. So they send their disciples to him as spies pretending to be righteous, along with Herodians. "Teacher," they ask, "we know you're true and teach the way of God in truth. You aren't concerned about anyone, nor are you biased towards anyone. So tell us what you think: is it legal for us to pay the poll tax[g] to Caesar or not? Should we pay or not pay?"

But Jesus saw their trap. "You hypocrites," he answered. "Why are

E. *Gamos* is the Greek word for "wedding" or "wedding feast," similar to a modern **wedding reception**.

F. During Judean weddings, it may have been customary for the host to **provide wedding clothes** for his guests, especially if they were poor.

you testing me? Show me a denarius."

So they brought him a denarius. Then he says, "Whose image and engraving are these?"

"Caesar's," they reply.

"Then give to Caesar what is Caesar's," he tells them, "and to God what is God's."

So they couldn't catch him in his words before the people. Hearing his answer, they were speechless and completely amazed, so they left him.

26.5 MARRIAGE AFTER RESURRECTION | GREATEST COMMANDMENT

Matthew 22:23-33, 35-40
Mark 12:18-34a
Luke 20:27-39

That day, some Sadducees, who say there's no resurrection, come to Jesus, asking him, "Teacher, Moses wrote to us that if a man's brother dies and leaves a wife with no child, his brother should take the wife and raise children for his brother. Now, there were seven brothers with us. The first took a wife, but he died without children and left his wife to his brother. So the second one took her and died without children too. And the third as well, down to the seventh, each died without children. Finally, the woman died too. So, in the resurrection,

G. The Roman head tax or **poll tax** (*tributum capitis*) was a fixed amount that every man had to pay according the registry of the latest census. The poll tax generally fell on Roman subjects, not on Roman citizens. Consequently, it provoked bitterness towards Rome as the occupying power, promoting numerous revolts throughout the empire.

Sadducees

Unlike the Pharisees, with their countless additional rules and traditions, the **Sadducees** were a political and religious party of Jews that rejected anything not taught directly in Moses' Law. They also firmly believed there was no life, reward, or punishment after death. In fact, they denied the existence of angels, demons, or any spiritual world at all. Tradition held that they were descendants of Zadok the High Priest, who served under David and Solomon. Zadok was a descendant of Aaron, who was Moses' brother and the first High Priest of Israel. The term "Sadducee" is derived from Zadok's name. The Jewish historian Josephus records that Sadducees were among the most wealthy and prestigious of Judean society. They filled many roles in elite Jewish circles, primarily associated with Temple affairs. Sadducees acted as High Priests in Jerusalem's Temple and held seats in the Sanhedrin, the Jewish high court. Along with judging legal matters, their political roles also included mediation with the Romans and tax collection. However, despite their position and influence, the Sadducees had a reputation for being corrupt.

The Law of the Childless Widow

When brothers live together and one dies without a son, the wife of the deceased won't go outside to a man who's a stranger. Her husband's brother will go, take her as his wife, and do his duty. Then the firstborn she bears will be raised in the name of his dead brother, so his name won't be wiped out from Israel. But if the man doesn't want to take his brother's wife, then his brother's wife will go to the gate and tell the elders, "My husband's brother refuses to raise up a name for his brother in Israel. He won't do his duty."

Then the city elders will call him and speak with him. If he's adamant and says, "I don't want to take her," then his brother's wife will come into the elders' sight and remove the shoe from his foot and spit in his face. Then she'll say, "This is how it's done to the man who doesn't build his brother's house."

Then his name in Israel will be called, "The House of the Removed Shoe."

– Deuteronomy 25:5-10

In ancient Jewish culture, when a man died without a son, his property went to his closest male relative, often a brother, potentially leaving his widow and any daughters impoverished. Therefore, Moses' Law stated that the surviving brother should sleep with the widow so she could bear a son in the name of her deceased husband. This law preserved the dead man's inheritance, so *"his name won't be wiped out from Israel."* It also protected and provided for **widows without male children**, so they could retain the land of their deceased husband through their son.

This principle first appeared in the Bible in Genesis 38. The Bible records that Judah's firstborn son Er died, leaving his widow childless. Judah instructed his next son Onan to sleep with Er's widow to raise up a son for his dead brother. However, Onan *"spilled [his semen] on the ground so as to not give seed to his brother. But what he did was displeasing to the LORD, so he took his life too." (Genesis 38:9-10)* In refusing to impregnate his dead brother's wife, Onan was essentially attempting to steal his inheritance.

whose wife will she be, since all seven had married her?"

"You don't understand the Scriptures or the power of God," Jesus answered. "This is why you're mistaken. The sons of this age marry and are given in marriage, but those worthy to reach that age and the resurrection from death don't marry, nor are they given in marriage. They can't die anymore, because they're like angels in heaven. They're God's sons, being sons of the resurrection.

"But about the dead rising again: haven't you read what God spoke to you in Moses' book, regarding the bush, when God spoke to him, saying, 'I am the God of Abraham, the God of Isaac, and the God of Jacob'? He's not the God of corpses but of the living, because all live to him. You're very mistaken."

When the crowds heard this, they were blown away at his teaching, and the Sadducees didn't have the courage to question him about anything any longer. One of the scribes (a lawyer) came and heard them arguing, and, seeing that he had answered well, tested him by saying, "Well said, Teacher. Which commandment is the first and greatest of all the Law?"

Moses and the Burning Bush

The story of Moses encountering God in a **burning bush** is a pivotal moment in the history of the people of Israel. It marked the beginning of God's plan to deliver his people from slavery in Egypt and establish them as an independent nation in Palestine.

Moses was shepherding the flock of Jethro his father-in-law, the priest from Midian, and he led the flock to the western wilderness and came to Horeb, God's mountain. Then the LORD's angel appeared in a blazing fire in the middle of a bush. He saw it, and look, the bush was burning with fire, but the bush wasn't consumed.

"I have to turn and go see this great sight, why the bush isn't burned up," Moses said.

When the LORD saw that he had turned to see it, God called from the middle of the bush, saying, "Moses! Moses!"

"Here I am," he replied.

"Don't come near here," he said. "Slip the sandals off your feet, because the place you're standing is holy ground."

Then he also said, "I am the God of your father, the God of Abraham, the God of Isaac, and the God of Jacob."

So Moses hid his face, because he was afraid to look at God.

– Exodus 3:1-6

Jesus answered, "The first is, 'Hear, Israel! The Lord our God is one Lord. Love the Lord your God with all your heart, with all your mind, with all your soul, and with all your strength.'[h] This is the greatest and first commandment. And the second is like it: 'Love your neighbor like yourself.'[i] There's no other commandment greater than these; the entire Law and the prophets depend on them."

"Right, Teacher," the scribe replied. "You've spoken the truth, that he's one and there's no one else besides him. And to love him with all your heart, with all you understanding, and with all your strength, and to love your neighbor as yourself, is much more than all the offerings and sacrifices."

When Jesus saw that he had spoken wisely, he told him, "You aren't far from God's kingdom."

H. Based on the Hebrew word for "**hear**," the *Shema* (or *Sh'ma Yisrael*) is a Jewish proclamation of faith that comes from Deuteronomy 6:4. It was recited by pious Jews every morning and evening ("*when you lie down and when you rise*"), and at the beginning of synagogue services.

Hear, O Israel! The LORD is our God, the LORD is one! You will love the LORD your God with all your mind, all your soul, and all your power. The words, which I'm commanding you today, will be on your mind. You will teach them to your sons and talk about them when you sit in your house, when you walk on a road, when you lie down, and when you rise. – Deuteronomy 6:4-7

I. *You won't avenge or guard against the sons of your nation, but you'll love your neighbor like yourself. I am the LORD. – Leviticus 19:18*

The Temple in Jerusalem

The **Temple** in Jerusalem was the central place of corporate worship for all Jews and the focus of Jewish religion and culture. According to religious law, priests would ritually sacrifice animals here, and Jews from all over the world would visit it during national holidays. The Temple was intricately decorated with gold-plated walls, wood carvings, and tapestries. Facing east, the Temple complex was divided into various sections:

1. Temple Mount: The Temple and its courts were constructed on a massive rectangular plaza, elevated above the city. It had a thick wall surrounding it, with multiple gates and stairways leading up into it. Currently, the Temple Mount is the site of the Dome of the Rock, a Muslim holy site.
2. Court of Gentiles: The outermost courtyard of the Temple was where the whole nation periodically gathered to worship. However, a large market normally occupied much of this court. Gentiles were allowed into this outer court, but couldn't go beyond the Beautiful Gate to the inner courts.
3. Antonia Fortress: This was Herod's military barracks, built in the northwest corner of the Temple complex. Herod the Great built it in honor of his friend Mark Antony around 36 BC. Josephus described it as a central tower with four smaller towers on each corner. Its significant height offered a view of the entire Temple complex.
4. Solomon's Porch: The east wall of the Temple complex, within the Court of Gentiles, had a covered walkway supported by pillars.
5. Court of Women: Through the Beautiful Gate, the first of the inner courts, was as far as Jewish women could enter.
6. Court of Israel: Only Jewish men that were ceremonially clean could enter through the Nicanor Gate into this court, where the Temple could be viewed close up.
7. Court of Priests: A short wall separated this area from the Court of Israel. A huge sacrificial altar lay in this space, where animal sacrifices were made daily.
8. Porch: A short flight of stairs led up to the entrance of the Temple, which was flanked by two bronze pillars.
9. Storage rooms: Around the outside of the Temple building (within the Temple walls) were rooms to house the various utensils needed by the priests for their duties.
10. Holy Place: The first room inside Temple building itself was a large space with tall ceilings. Only priests were allowed to enter the Temple itself. An altar specifically for incense was located here.
11. Holy of Holies: Behind a large curtain, toward the rear of the Temple, was the most sacred and restricted space of the entire complex, where God's spirit was said to dwell. The room was gold-plated, and it housed the Ark of the Covenant (a gold chest that contained tablets inscribed with the Ten Commandments). According to Jewish Law, the Holy of Holies could only be entered once annually on the Day of Atonement by the High Priest after a series of purification rituals.

The original Jewish Temple was built by David's son Solomon, with construction starting around 966 BC and ending 7 years later. It represented the pinnacle of Israel's power and wealth under Solomon, attracting visitors from around the world. Israel's glorious Temple was plundered and destroyed during the Babylonian invasion of Jerusalem in 587 BC, with no trace of the original structure remaining to this day. However, under the Persian King Cyrus, Jewish exiles were allowed to return to Jerusalem and begin rebuilding the Temple in 538 BC, completing it 20 years later. This second Temple would remain until King Herod lavishly renovated it in 19 BC in an effort to please the Jews. It was Herod's Temple that Jesus visited during his time in Jerusalem. But this too was destroyed when Jerusalem was overthrown by the Romans in 70 AD.

In addition to serving as a place of worship, the Temple in ancient Jerusalem also served as a religious market, located in the Court of Gentiles, where pilgrims from all over the world could purchase animals for sacrifice.

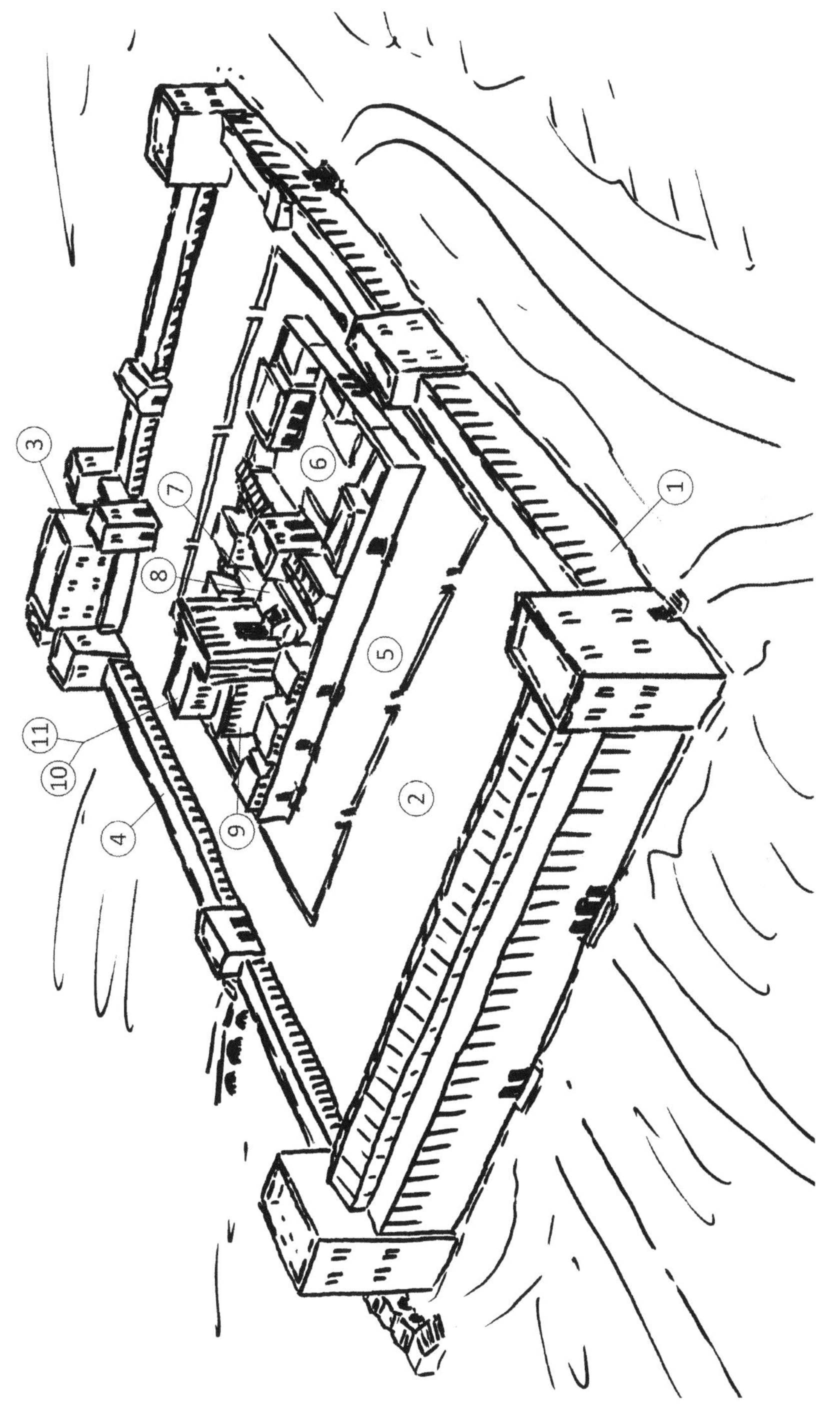
1
2
3
4
5
6
7
8
9
10
11

CHAPTER 27

Jesus Attacks His Critics

27.1 MESSIAH: THE SON OF DAVID AND LORD

Matthew 22:34, 41-46
Mark 12:34b-40
Luke 20:40-47

The Pharisees met together when they heard that Jesus had silenced the Sadducees. While they were gathered, Jesus asked them a question as he taught in the Temple: "Why do the scribes say that the Messiah is the son of David? What do you think about the Messiah? Whose son is he?"

"David's," they answer.

So he asks, "Then how does David call him 'Lord' by the Holy Spirit in the book of the Psalms, saying, 'The Lord said to my Lord, "Sit at my right hand, until I put your enemies under your feet"'?[a] If David himself calls him 'Lord,' how is he his son?"

But nobody could answer him a word. After that, nobody would dare question him anymore about anything, but the crowd happily listened to him.

A. *The LORD says to my Lord, "Sit at my right hand until I make your enemies a stool for your feet." – Psalm 110:1*

In his teaching, while all the people listened, he told his disciples, "Watch out for the scribes, who like to walk around in robes. They love the first seats at banquets and the head seats in the synagogues, and greetings in the market. But they devour widows' houses and make long prayers for show. This will get judged abundantly."

27.2 WOES TO PHARISEES

Matthew 23:1-13, 15-39
Luke 11:37-54; 13:34-35

After he had spoken, a Pharisee asks him to have breakfast with him. So he went in and reclined, but when the Pharisee saw that he hadn't first washed before the meal, he was amazed. But the Lord told him, "Woe, you scribes and Pharisees! You're hypocrites! You clean the outside of the cup and the plate, but inside you're full of theft, impulsivity, and evil! You fools, didn't the one who made the outside also make the inside? You blind Pharisee, clean the inside of the cup and the bowl first, then the outside will be clean too. But give what's inside you as charity, and look, everything will be clean for you."[b]

Then Jesus told the crowds and his disciples, "The scribes and the Pharisees have sat in Moses' seat,[c] so do everything they tell you, and do it carefully. But don't do what they do, because they say and don't do. They act to be noticed by men, because they make their phylacteries[d] wide and their tassels[e] long.

B. *To the pure, all is pure. But to the stained and faithless, nothing is pure, but both their mind and conscience are stained. – Titus 1:15*

C. Most synagogues had a stone chair at the front of the room where the teacher sat. Sitting on someone's seat represented becoming that person's successor, so sitting in **Moses' seat** was self-authorizing oneself as Moses' successor as a law teacher.

D. Based on a command from God recorded four times in the Torah – *"Put my words in your mind and your soul; tie them to your hand as a sign and they'll be bands between your eyes" (Deuteronomy 11:18)* – devout Jews wore **phylacteries** on their hands and heads. These small leather boxes contained a parchment inscribed with Scriptures and were worn by every Jewish male during morning prayer on all days except the Sabbath. They were commanded to wear them as a reminder of Israel's deliverance from Egypt. The Greek term *phylakterion* translates to "guard" or "protect," while the Hebrew term *towphaphah* means "band" or "frontlet."

E. **Tassels** were worn on the edges of Jewish clothing as a reminder to obey God's Law. These were also commanded in the Torah: *"Tell Israel's sons to make tassels on the corners of their clothes throughout the generations and put a blue cord on the tassel of each corner" (Numbers 15:38)*. A *mezuzah* (Hebrew for "doorpost") acted the same way, as a reminder of God's commands. They were inscribed on Jewish doorways, as it was written, *"You'll write [this] on the doorposts of your house and on your gates" (Deuteronomy 6:9)*.

"Woe, you scribes and Pharisees! You're hypocrites! You tithe mint, rue, anise, cumin, and every herb, but you've ignored the heavier laws – justice, mercy, faith, and God's love.[f] You should've done this without ignoring the others. You blind guides, who filter out a fly but swallow a camel![g]

F. *What will I come to the LORD with and bow before the high God with? Should I come with offerings, with year-old calves? Is the LORD happy with thousands of rams or with 10,000 rivers of oil? Should I give my firstborn for my rebellion, the fruit of my body for the sin of my soul? O man, he has already told you what's good. What does the LORD ask of you but to do justice, to love kindness, and to walk humbly with your God? – Micah 6:6-8*

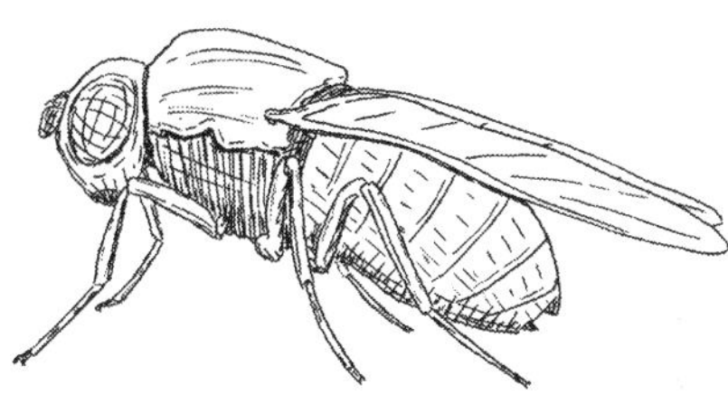

G. Strict Pharisees would routinely **filter** their drinks through a cloth to prevent the possibility of consuming an unclean insect (Moses' Law stated flies were forbidden as food). The **fly** in this passage may have been from the genus *Drosophila*, commonly known as the fruit fly. Fruit flies feed on over-ripe and rotting fruit, and they subsequently would have been a common contaminant in ancient wines. These tiny insects were among the smallest known animals in first century Judea. Conversely, the **camel** was arguably the largest animal in the Middle East at that time.

Tithing

Moses' Law dictated that a tenth of all income was holy and dedicated to God, to be given as an act of worship. This **tithe** applied to all grain, fruit, wine, oil, spices, and livestock accumulated each year. Every Jew was required to pay three tithes: one for the Levites and priests, who were responsible for religious duties throughout Israel; one for Temple use and upkeep, which included food for annual feasts; and one for the poor. It's not certain how and when these tithes occurred during each seven-year cycle. For those living far from Jerusalem, grain and fruit tithes could be purchased upon arrival for an additional 20%, presumably to facilitate lighter travelling. Livestock tithes, however, had to be transported as they were and consumed in Jerusalem.

The Hebrew (*ma'aser*) and Greek (*dekate*) words both mean "tenth." Similarly, the English "tithe" is from the Old English term meaning the same.

The practice of tithing began before Moses' Law was established and may have been a common custom in the ancient Middle East. Abraham, as the forefather of Israel, gave a tenth of all he owned to Melchizedek, the king of Salem (Jerusalem) and a priest of God. Similarly, Jacob promised God that *"of all you give me, I'll certainly give you a tenth" (Genesis 28:22)*. With its inclusion and regulation in Moses' Law, tithing became an integral part of Hebrew religion and economy. Both Malachi and Amos – prophets of the Old Testament – harshly denounced Israel for withholding and mismanaging tithes.

Among the spices mentioned as being tithed by the Pharisees, **mint** (Greek *hedyosmon*) is a fast-growing, sweet-smelling flowering plant that was used as a spice and medicine. It was best cultivated in cool, moist environments. **Rue** (*peganon*) was another garden herb, but unlike mint, it produced yellow flowers and a strong odor, and it was best grown in hot, dry soils. Rue was also used as a medicine, particularly to promote menstruation. **Anise** (*anethon*, often translated "dill") had a sweet flavor that was used to season food and liquor. Like many other spices, it was also used medicinally – anise was consumed in a tea to treat insomnia and promote lactation in nursing mothers. Finally, **cumin** (*kyminon*) was used for its strong aroma throughout the Middle East as a seasoning.

"Woe, you Pharisees! You love the first seats at banquets and the first seats in the synagogues, and greetings in the markets and being called 'Rabbi' by men. But don't be called 'Rabbi,' because one is your teacher and you're all brothers. And don't call someone on earth 'Father,' because one is your Father in heaven. Don't be called leaders, because one is your leader – the Christ. Instead, the greatest of you should be the servant. Whoever lifts himself will be lowered and whoever lowers himself will be lifted.

"Woe, you scribes and Pharisees! You're hypocrites! You travel by sea and land to make one convert,[h] and when he becomes one, you make him twice the son of hell as you are.

"Woe, you blind guides, who say, 'Swearing by the Temple is nothing, but swearing by the gold of the Temple is binding.' You fools! You blind men! Which is greater, the gold or the Temple that makes the gold holy?[i] And, 'Swearing by the altar is nothing, but swearing by the gift on the altar is binding.' You blind men! Which is greater, the gift or the altar that makes the gift holy?[j] So whoever swears by the altar swears by it and everything on it, and whoever swears by the Temple swears by it and him who lives in it. And whoever swears by heaven swears by the throne of God and him who sits on it.

"Woe, you scribes and Pharisees! You're hypocrites! You're like white tombs[k] that look beautiful on the outside, but on the inside are full of dead bones and everything filthy. You look righteous on the outside too, but on the inside you're full of hypocrisy and anarchy. You're like hidden tombs that people walk over unaware.

"Woe, you scribes and Pharisees! You're hypocrites! You build up the prophets' tombs and decorate the monuments of the righteous, saying, 'If we had been there in our fathers' days, we wouldn't have joined them in the blood of the prophets.' But your fathers killed them!

H. A Gentile who practiced Judaism was called a proselyte (Greek *proselytos*). It's the same word for "stranger" or "newcomer." Here it's translated "**convert**."

I. The Greek *hagiazo* means "**make holy**," "purify" or "dedicate to God." Commonly translated as "sanctify," it refers to setting something apart for divine purposes and cleansing it from impurity.

J. *You'll atone for the altar and sanctify it. Then the altar will be holy and whatever touches the altar will be holy. – Exodus 29:37*

K. Moses' Law dictated in Numbers that "*anyone in open land that touches a man's bone or a grave will be unclean for seven days.*" Therefore, Jews customarily **painted tombs white** to increase their visibility, especially at night. Although this improved their appearance, it didn't negate their uncleanness.

So you're witnesses against yourselves, that you're sons of those who murdered the prophets. You approve your fathers' actions, because they killed them and you build their tombs! So fill up the measure of your fathers. You snakes, you spawn of vipers! How will you escape the judgment of hell? This is why the wisdom of God[l] also said, 'Look, I'll send them prophets and apostles.' Some they'll kill, some they'll whip in their synagogues, and some they'll drive out from city to city, so that all the righteous blood of the prophets poured out on the earth since the foundation of the world will be charged against this generation, from the blood of Abel to the blood of Zechariah, Berechiah's son, who was murdered between the altar and the Temple. Yes, I tell you truly, all of this will come and be charged against this generation.

"O Jerusalem, Jerusalem, who kills the prophets and stones those sent to her! I've often wanted to gather your children like a hen gathers her chicks under her wings,[m] but you've refused it! Look, your house is

L. Jesus' quotation of the "**wisdom of God**" isn't found in the Old Testament.

M. *He'll cover you with his feathers and you can be sheltered under his wings. – Psalm 91:4*

Old Testament Martyrs

After being banished from Eden, the first man and woman – Adam and Eve – had two sons. Their older son, Cain, was a farmer, while their younger son, **Abel**, was a shepherd. Genesis records that Cain, whose offerings to God were inferior, murdered his brother Abel in a jealous rage. Then after God confronted him about the murder, he became cursed and ran away to the east.

Zechariah, on the other hand, was the name of dozens of men in the Old Testament. But most notably, **Zechariah, Berechiah's son**, was the author of the Old Testament book that bears his name. He was a priest and prophet to Judah during the Babylonian exile. He encouraged the returning Hebrew exiles to continue rebuilding the Temple. He also predicted the Messiah's coming, who would purify and deliver Israel.

However, **Zechariah, Jehoiada's son**, who lived much earlier (before Judah's fall to Babylon), seems to be the one referred to by Jesus as the man who "was murdered between the altar and the Temple." His brief story is recorded in 2 Chronicles 24:20-21. Zechariah's father Jehoiada helped save Prince Joash's life as a boy, and then established him as king over Judah. However, later in life, Jehoiada's son Zechariah condemned the people for their sin, so they approached King Joash to complain about Zechariah. Forgetting Jehoiada's kindness to him, the king ordered his son to be killed, and Zechariah was subsequently stoned within the Temple compound.

Thus the Old Testament account of the martyr Zechariah suggests his identity is Zechariah of Jehoiada. However, Matthew specifically records the martyr as Zechariah of Berechiah, who lived hundreds of years later and wrote the book of Zechariah. Whether Matthew (or someone after him) made a clerical error, or whether the later Zechariah was a descendant of the earlier, is unknown. However, despite the historical discrepancy, Jesus' citation of all the martyrs from Abel, the first to be killed for his righteousness, to Zechariah, the last recorded martyr in the Old Testament, incorporated the entirety of Hebrew history. Coincidentally, it's analogous to saying, "all the prophets from A to Z."

abandoned! I tell you, from now on you won't see me until it comes when you say, 'Blessed is he who comes in the name of the Lord!'"[n]

Then one of the lawyers replies, "Teacher, when you say this, you insult us too."

"Woe, you lawyers as well!" he said. "You tie up heavy burdens hard to bear and put them on men's shoulders, but you won't touch the burdens yourselves with even one of your fingers!

"Woe, you lawyers! And woe, you scribes and Pharisees! You're hypocrites! You've taken away the key of knowledge and shut the kingdom of heaven away from men. You haven't entered it yourselves, and you don't let those who are entering it come in!"

When he left there, the scribes and the Pharisees were very resentful and they interrogated him on much, plotting to catch him on something from out of his mouth.

N. *Blessed is the one who comes in the name of the LORD. We've blessed you from the house of the LORD. – Psalm 118:26*

CHAPTER 28

What will Come

28.1 GOD'S KINGDOM IS HERE | WIDOW'S GIFT

Mark 12:41-44
Luke 17:20-21; 21:1-4

After being asked by the Pharisees when God's kingdom was coming, he answered, "God's kingdom isn't coming with sights, nor will they say, 'Look here!' or 'There!' because look, God's kingdom is right here."

Then he sat across from the treasury and watched people putting coins into it. He looked up and saw many of the rich putting their many gifts into the treasury, but a poor widow came and put in two *lepta*, worth a penny.[a] He called his disciples and told them, "Truly I tell you, this poor widow put in more than all the others giving to the treasury. They all gave out of their excess, but she gave out of her poverty and put in all she owned, even her whole life."

A. The *lepton* was a thin brass coin, equal to half of a *quadrans* (translated here as "**penny**") and an eighth of an *assarion*. In the first century Judea, the average daily wage of an unskilled worker was one denarius, equal to 16 *asses* (*assarion* singular). The *lepton* was the smallest currency of the time, and therefore **two *lepta*** were worth almost nothing.

28.2 FUTURE PROPHECIES

Matthew 10:17-22; 24:1-31
Mark 13:1-27
Luke 12:11-12; 17:22-35, 37; 21:5-28

Jesus left the Temple, but as he was going, his disciples pointed out the Temple buildings with their beautiful stones and gifts. While they were talking about it, one of his disciples says, "Teacher, look! What great stones and what great buildings!"

"See all these great buildings?" Jesus replied. "Truly I tell you that the days will come when one stone won't be left upon another – they'll all be torn down."

As he was sitting on the Mount of Olives across from the Temple, his disciples Peter, James, John, and Andrew came on their own and asked him, "Tell us, when will this happen? And what will be the sign of your coming and the end of this age?"

"Make sure no one deceives you," Jesus answered them. "Many will come in my name, saying, 'I'm the Christ,' and, 'The time's close,' and they'll deceive many. But don't follow them. When you hear battles, commotion, and news of battles, don't be afraid. They must happen, but it's not the end. Nation will rise against nation and kingdom against kingdom. There will be huge earthquakes in places, and plagues and famines. There will be terrors and great signs from heaven.[b] All this is the start of the birth pains.

B. *When he broke the second seal... a red horse went out. The one sitting on it was allowed to take peace from the earth, so they'd kill each other, and a great sword was given to him.... When the lamb broke the fourth seal... look, I saw a pale horse. The one sitting on it was named Death, and Hades followed him. They were given authority over a quarter of the earth*

The Mount of Olives

East of Jerusalem, across the Kidron Valley, is a mountainous ridge that was populated by olive trees before Jerusalem's fall in 70 AD, aptly named the **Mount of Olives**. Its western slope faces Jerusalem, while its eastern slope is the edge of the arid Judean Desert that extends to the Dead Sea. The area has been used extensively as a burial ground, the graves of which are still present today. Low on its western slope was a garden called Gethsemane, meaning "oil press" in Aramaic, which was likely the processing site of the olives harvested from the mountainside above. The Mount of Olives is higher in elevation than nearby Jerusalem. Looking across the Kidron Valley, the view from the Mount of Olives was a panorama of the Temple complex and the rest of the city.

The Mount of Olives is mentioned occasionally in the Old Testament, most notably as the site where David escaped to the wilderness away from his son Absalom. Zechariah recorded a vision of the Mount of Olives being split in half, which people fled through to the east. It was also the likely site of pagan worship at various times in Israel's history, as a "high place" near Jerusalem.

"But before all this, watch out for men! They'll oppress and kill you, and every nation will hate you because of my name. They'll seize you and hand you over to courts and prisons, and you'll be whipped in their temples and synagogues. But you'll stand before synagogues, rulers, and kings because of me, as a witness to my name, to testify to them and to the nations. It'll be the basis[c] for your testimony, because the good news must be proclaimed to every nation and the whole world first, and then the end will come. When they take you and hand you over, don't worry about what to say in your defense, but say whatever's given to you then. It's not you speaking, but the Holy Spirit of your Father, who speaks through you. He'll teach you what to say at that time. So set your hearts beforehand not to defend yourselves, because I'll give you a mouth and a wisdom that your opposition won't be able to oppose or argue against.

"Many will trip, betray, and hate one another. Brother will betray brother to death, a father his child, and children will rise up against their parents and kill them.[d] You'll be betrayed by your parents, brothers, relatives, and friends, and they'll kill some of you. Many false prophets will rise up and mislead many, and most love will grow cold because of anarchy. You'll be hated by everyone because of my name, but not one hair of your head will die. The one who lasts until the end will be saved, and by your endurance you'll gain your souls.

"When you see Jerusalem surrounded by armies, know that the desolation is close. And when you see the abomination[e] of desolation

to kill with the sword, famine, death, and beasts of the earth.... I looked when he broke the sixth seal and there was a great earthquake. The sun became black like a sack of hair and the whole moon became like blood. The stars of the sky fell to the earth like a fig tree throws its unripe figs when a big wind shakes it. The sky was split like a rolled-up scroll, and every mountain and island was moved from its place. – Revelation 6:3-4,8-9,12-14

C. *Apobaino* literally means "walk out" in Greek. It's derived from the term *basis*, referring to something walked or stepped on. This is the origin of the English term "basis," which means "foundation" or "fundamental principle." Many Bibles translate *apobaino* as "get out" in reference to getting out of a boat. But when referring to a future moment for a particular action, it's often rendered "opportunity." Here it's simply "**basis.**"

D. *Don't trust a neighbor and don't trust a friend. Guard your lips from the one who lies in your arms. Because a son disrespects his father, a daughter rises against her mother, and a daughter-in-law against her mother-in-law. A man's enemies will be the men in his own house. But as for me, I'll watch for the LORD. I'll wait for the God of my salvation. My God will hear me. – Micah 7:5-7*

E. The **abomination of desolation** (*bdelygma eremosis* in Greek) mentioned by Matthew and Mark is a reference to a particular event prophesied by Daniel, recorded in the apocalyptical portion of his Old Testament book. Daniel uses this phrase three times (*shiqquwts shamen* in Aramaic). The first word of this phrase refers to an object of extreme hate and was used in the Old Testament as another term for "idol." It's typically translated "abomination," but

that the prophet Daniel spoke of standing in the holy place where he shouldn't be," – let the reader understand[F] – "then those in Judea must escape to the mountains, those in the city must leave, and those in the country must not enter the city. On that day, the one on the roof, whose belongings are in the house, must not come down and go inside to get them. And the one in the field must not go back for his coat. These are the days of revenge, so everything written will be fulfilled. But woe to the pregnant and those nursing babies in those days! Pray that it doesn't happen in winter or on a Sabbath. There will be great agony in the land and fury on this people. They'll fall by the edge of the sword and be taken captive to every nation. Jerusalem will be trampled underfoot by the Gentiles until the time of the Gentiles is finished. Those days will be a great oppression, beyond what has ever occurred since the beginning of God's creation until now, and it never will again. If the Lord hadn't shortened those days, nobody would've been saved. But because of his chosen, he shortened the days.

"The days will come," he told the disciples, "when you'll want to see one of the Son of Man's days, but you won't see it. And if anyone tells you, 'Look, here's the Christ!' or 'Look there!' don't believe it. False christs and false prophets will rise and show great signs and miracles to mislead the chosen, if possible. So watch out! Don't go away and don't follow. Look, I've told you beforehand. So if they tell you, 'Look, he's in the wilderness,' don't go. Or, 'Look, he's in the closet,' don't believe it. Just like lightning flashing in the east also shines in the west, so it'll be for the Son of Man in his day."

---

could also mean "bane" or "horror." The second word means "desolation," "barrenness," or "waste." Many views exist on what exactly the abomination of desolation is or was:

1. In 167 BC, the Seleucid ruler Antiochus Epiphanes returned to Jerusalem to find it had revolted against him. His furious recapture of the city and slaughter of the Jews culminated in his desecration of the Temple. Antiochus erected a statue of Zeus and sacrificed pigs (unclean animals) on the altar.
2. The fall of Jerusalem to the Romans in 70 AD saw the Gentile army conquer and destroy the Temple. Then they worshipped Roman standards on the temple mount.
3. Judah's king Manasseh built numerous altars to other gods in the 7th century BC. He also practiced sorcery and divination, even burning his own sons as sacrifices. He erected an idol in the Temple in Jerusalem.
4. The book of Revelation and other apocalyptical writings describe future events in which a beast or "anti-christ" will rule much of the world and oppose Israel.

F. Both Matthew and Mark use the unusual phrase *anaginosko noeo* in the middle of a lengthy quote by Jesus. It translates to "**let the reader understand**." This is a note from the narrator to the reader outside of the main text, and it's the only time in all the Gospels that this type of phrase occurs. Various ideas exist on why this phrase occurs here, but apparently the author deemed this information to be of particular importance to the audience he was addressing at the time.

"Where, Lord?" they ask.

"Vultures will gather wherever the corpse is," he replied. "First the Son of Man must suffer much and be rejected by this generation. Just like it happened in Noah's days, so it'll be in the Son of Man's days: they were eating and drinking, they were marrying and being given in marriage, until the day Noah entered the ark and the flood came and destroyed everyone. It'll be the same as Lot's days: they were eating and drinking, they were buying and selling, and they were planting and building. But on the day Lot left Sodom, fire and sulfur[g] rained down from heaven and destroyed them all. It'll be the same way on the day the Son of Man is revealed. Remember Lot's wife: whoever wants to keep his life will lose it, and whoever loses it will save it. I tell you, on that night there will be two in bed; one will be taken and the other left. There will be two women grinding together; one will be taken and the other left.

"In those days, right after the oppression, the sun will go dark, the moon won't give its light, the stars will fall from heaven, and the powers in the heavens will be shaken.[h] The nations will be distressed because of the mystery of the roaring sea and waves. Men will faint from fear and the expectation of things coming to the world. Then the sign of the Son of Man will appear in the sky. They'll see the Son of Man coming on the clouds of the sky with great power and glory,[i] and every tribe will weep and mourn. But when this starts to happen, cheer up and lift up your heads, because your deliverance is near. He'll send out his angels with a great trumpet and they'll gather together his chosen

G. *Theion* is a Greek noun derived from *theos*, meaning "god" or "divinity." *Theion* refers to a flammable solid material, which was thought to be elemental **sulfur**. It's also translated "brimstone," from the Middle English word for "burning stone." Sulfur is a yellow chemical element that oxidizes/burns to produce a thick smoke. Its solid yellow crystals melt into a thick red liquid, which burns with a faint blue flame. Elemental sulfur is most commonly found near hot springs and volcanoes. Sulfur was used for fumigation in ancient times – its smoke was thought to purify and/or heal people. In the Old Testament, sulfur (Hebrew *gophriyth*) represented God's judgment on immorality.

H. *Look, the day of the LORD is coming. It's cruel with rage and burning anger, to make the land a desolation and destroy its sinners. Heaven's stars and constellations won't flash their light. The sun will be dark when it rises and the moon won't shine its light.... So I'll make the heavens tremble and the earth will be shaken from its place at the rage of the LORD of armies in the day of his burning anger. – Isaiah 13:9-10,13*

I. *I kept seeing night visions. Look, someone like the Son of Man was coming with heaven's clouds. He came up to the Ancient of Days and was presented to him. Sovereignty, glory, and a kingdom were given to him, so that all people, nations, and languages would serve him. His sovereignty is an everlasting sovereignty that won't pass away, and his kingdom won't be destroyed. – Daniel 7:13-14*

from the four winds, from the ends of the earth to the ends of heaven."[j]

28.3 SIGNS OF THE END

Matthew 24:32-36, 42-51
Mark 13:28-37
Luke 12:35-48; 21:29-36

Then he told them a parable, "Look, learn from the fig tree and all the trees: when its branch gets soft and extends its leaves, you know that summer is close. So you too, when you see this happening, know that God's kingdom is close and that he's at the door. Truly I tell you, this generation won't pass away until all of this occurs. Heaven and earth will pass away, but my words will not. But no one except the Father knows the day or the time, not the angels nor the Son.

"Watch out and be ready, because you don't know when the time will come. Be dressed and keep your lamps lit like men waiting for their master to return from traveling to the wedding reception. He put his slaves in charge of his house upon leaving, giving each a job, and also telling the doorman to be ready. They'll immediately open to him when he returns and knocks. Blessed are the slaves whom the master finds alert when he comes. I tell you truly that he'll dress himself, have them recline, and come up and serve them. When he finds them so, they're blessed. So be ready in case he comes suddenly and finds you asleep, because you don't know when the lord of the house will come, whether in the evening, at midnight, when the rooster crows, or in the morning. What I tell you, I tell all: be ready!

"So watch out, because you don't know which day your Lord is coming. Know this: if the housemaster had known what time of night the thief was coming, he would have watched and not let his house be broken into. Because of this, you should be ready too, because the Son of Man is coming at a time you don't think."

"Lord," Peter said, "are you telling this parable to us or to everyone as well?"

"Who is the trustworthy and wise slave[k] that the master will put in

---

J. *If your outcasts are at the ends of the earth, the LORD your God will gather you and bring you from there. – Deuteronomy 30:4*

K. *Doulos* is the most common term for "**slave**" or "servant" in the New Testament. It has a male and female version – *doulos* for male and *doule* for female, translated as "slaves and maids" elsewhere in the text. *Doulos* is derived from *deo*, the Greek word for "bind."

charge of his house, to give out food rations at the right time?" the Lord answered. "Blessed is the slave whom the master finds doing so when he comes. Truly I tell you, he'll put him in charge of all he has. But if that slave is bad and says in his heart, 'My master will be a while,' and beats the others, both man-servants and maid-servants,[l] and eats and drinks with drunks, the slave's master will return on a day he doesn't realize and at a time he doesn't know. He'll cut him to pieces and put him in a place with the hypocrites, where there will be weeping and teeth grinding. The slave that knew his master's will, but didn't prepare and act according to his will, he'll be beaten much. But the one who didn't know and acted to deserve a beating will only get a little. Everyone who has been given much, much will be required of him, and if trusted with much, even more will be asked of him.

"Pay attention that your hearts don't get burdened with partying, drunkenness, and the worries of life, so that day won't come suddenly like a trap. Because it'll come for everyone living on the face of the earth. Be ready all the time, praying that you'll overpower and escape everything that's about to happen, and to stand before the Son of Man."

28.4 TEN VIRGINS

Matthew 25:1-13

"The kingdom of heaven is like ten virgins who took lamps[m] out to meet the groom. Five were fools and five were wise. When the fools took their lamps, they didn't take oil, but the wise took pots of oil with their lamps. Now the groom was late and they all got tired and fell asleep. Then at midnight there was a shout, 'Look, the groom! Come meet him!' Then all the virgins got up and lit their lamps, but the fools said to the wise, 'Give us some of your oil – our lamps are going out.' But the wise said, 'No, there won't be enough for both of us. Go to the sellers and buy some for yourselves.' But while they were away to buy more, the groom came and those prepared went in to the wedding

L. *Pais* is another term for "slave" or "servant," but it can also mean "boy." *Paidiske* is the female version, referring to a female servant or any young girl in general. Here they're translated "**man-servant**" and "**maid-servant**" respectively.

Oiketes is yet another term for "slave" or "servant." It's derived from *oikos* ("house") and is used specifically for those who served in the house.

M. Ancient **lamps** burned oil as fuel and were used as an alternative to candles, burning for hours on end. The fuel reservoirs were made of clay or metal, while a wick soaked up oil to feed the flame. Various oils could be used as fuel, depending on what was available in the area. In Judea, the most common fuel was olive oil.

Weddings

Jewish **weddings** were important affairs, but little is known about how exactly they occurred in ancient times. However, some events can be deduced from the Bible and Middle Eastern traditions. Apparently, the groomsmen would escort the bride and her wedding party to the groom's house at night. Her escorts (friends and family) would bring furniture and decorations for the new home. The groom, however, would be elsewhere, preparing his own wedding party. Later that night, the groom's party would light torches and proceed to the waiting bridal party, amidst cheers and shouts as he approached the house. An enormous feast would ensue, with various speeches and poems of congratulations. Jewish hospitality was a sacred duty and declining an invitation to a wedding reception was very insulting. The marriage was finally consummated by the entrance of the couple into the wedding chamber, which was the wife's canopied bed.

Draw me after you, let's run! The king has brought me into his bedrooms.

– Song of Songs 1:4

reception with him, and the door was shut. The other virgins came later, saying, 'Lord, Lord, open up for us!' But he answered, 'Truly I tell you, I don't know you.' So watch out, because you don't know the day or the time."

28.5 COMING JUDGMENT

Matthew 25:31-46

"When the Son of Man comes in his glory with all the angels, he'll sit on his glorious throne. All nations will be gathered in front of him and he'll sort them out, like a shepherd sorts sheep from goats. He'll put the sheep on his right and the goats on his left.

"Then the king will say to those on his right, 'You who are blessed by my Father, come inherit the kingdom made for you since the world's foundation. Because I was hungry and you fed me; I was thirsty and you gave me a drink; I was a stranger and you took me in; naked, and you clothed me; I was sick and you took care of me; I was in prison and you visited me.' The righteous will answer, 'Lord, when did we see you hungry and feed you, or thirsty and give you a drink? When did we see you as a stranger and take you in, or naked and clothe you? When did we see you sick or in prison and visit you?' The king will answer them, 'Truly I tell you, whatever you did for one of my brothers, even the smallest of them, you did for me.'

"Then he'll tell those on his left, 'Get away from me, you who are cursed, into the everlasting fire made for the Devil and his angels! Because I was hungry and you didn't feed me; I was thirsty and you gave

Goats

Like sheep, **goats** were exceptionally useful livestock in the ancient Middle East. Goat hair was woven into fabric, while the whole skins were used as clothing or wine/water containers. Goat's milk and meat was common food. According to Moses' Law, both sheep and goats were used in religious sacrifices. Goats were usually kept in herds with sheep, but unlike their gentle cousins, goats were independent, curious, and stubborn. The prophet Zechariah compared Israel's irresponsible leaders to male goats.

me nothing to drink; I was a stranger and you didn't take me in; naked, and you didn't clothe me; in prison, and you didn't visit me.' They'll answer, 'Lord, when did we see you hungry, thirsty, a stranger, naked, sick, or in prison and not care for you?' He'll reply, 'Truly I tell you, whatever you didn't do for someone else, you didn't do for me.' They'll go away to everlasting punishment, but the righteous to everlasting life."

CHAPTER 29

Betrayal Arranged

29.1 JESUS PREDICTS HIS DEATH, FOURTH TIME | THE SANHEDRIN PLOTS

Matthew 26:1-5
Mark 14:1-2
Luke 22:1-2

The Passover and the Feast of the Unleavened[a] were two days away. When Jesus had finished saying all this, he told his disciples, "You know that the Passover is coming in two days and that the Son of Man will be handed over to be crucified."

Then the High Priests, the scribes, and the leaders of the people got together in the courtyard of the High Priest, whose name was Caiaphas, to figure out how to secretly arrest Jesus and kill him. But they were afraid of the people, saying, "Not during the feast or the people might start a riot."

A. The first day of the Passover was called the **Feast of the Unleavened**, because only unleavened bread (flat, without yeast) could be eaten all week during the Passover. On that first evening, the Passover lamb was sacrificed and eaten.

29.2 MARY ANOINTS JESUS

Matthew 26:6-13
Mark 14:3-9
John 12:2-8

When Jesus was in Bethany at Simon the leper's house, they made him supper. Martha was serving and Lazarus was sitting with him. Then Mary came with a *litra*[b] of very expensive perfume – pure nard[c] – in an alabaster jar. As he was reclining, she broke the jar and poured it on Jesus' head, then she anointed his feet and wiped them with her hair. And the whole house was filled with the perfume's fragrance.

The disciples got angry when they saw it and scolded her, saying to one another, "What a waste!"

Then Judas Iscariot, one of his disciples, who was planning to betray him, says, "Why wasn't this perfume sold for over 300 denarii[d] and given to the poor?"

He didn't say this because he was concerned about the poor, but because he was a thief. He had the purse and would take from it.

Jesus knew they were scolding her and told them, "Why are you bothering this woman? Leave her alone! She has done something beautiful. You will always have the poor with you, and you can do good to them whenever you want, but you won't always have me. She has done what she could. When she poured this perfume on my body, she prepared me in advance for the day of my burial. I tell you truly, wherever the good news is preached in all the world, what this woman has done will be told in memory of her."

29.3 JUDAS AGREES TO BETRAY JESUS

Matthew 26:14-16
Mark 14:10-11
Luke 22:3-6

Then Satan entered Judas Iscariot of Simon, one of the Twelve, and put it in his heart to betray him. He went to the High Priests and

B. The ***litra*** was a unit of weight equal to 12.5 ounces (355 grams). A *litra* of nard in an alabaster jar would have been worth a small fortune in Judea during the first century.

C. High in the Himalayan mountain range of central Asia grows **nard** (*Nardostachys jatamansi*, also called spikenard), a fragrant plant that produces pink bell-shaped flowers. The aromatic oil extracted from these flowers was used as a perfume, incense, seasoning, and medicine. In the ancient Middle East, nard oil was an expensive commodity. It's mentioned twice in the romantic Song of Songs.

D. A common laborer would have to work a year to earn **300 denarii**.

commanders, saying, "What will you give me to hand him over to you?"

They were glad and promised to give him money. He agreed and they weighed out thirty silver coins for him. From then on, he looked for a chance to betray Jesus to them, away from the crowd.

Thirty Silver Coins

The Greek *argyrion* vaguely means "silver coin," possibly referring to any silver currency of the day. The *tetradrachm, stater,* and *shekel* were all possibilities, each worth approximately the same amount (about four days' wages). So **thirty silver coins** was the pay for about four months work.

This amount shows up twice in the Old Testament. Moses' Law valued a slave's life at thirty silver coins, to be paid to the slave's owner upon accidental death. Later, Zechariah received the same amount as wages, but he threw them to a potter working in the Temple after God sarcastically called the amount "glorious."

The LORD told me, "Throw it to the potter, the glorious price they valued me." So I took the thirty of silver and threw them to the potter in the LORD's house.

– Zechariah 11:13

CHAPTER 30

The Passover

30.1 PREPARATION FOR PASSOVER

Matthew 26:17-19
Mark 14:12-16
Luke 22:7-13

On the first day of the [Feast of the] Unleavened, when the Passover was sacrificed, his disciples ask him, "Where do you want us to prepare the Passover for you to eat?"

So he sends two of his disciples, Peter and John, and tells them, "Go into the city and a man will meet you carrying a water jug. Follow him and go into the house he enters. Tell the housemaster, 'The Teacher says, "My time is soon. Where's my room, where I can eat the Passover with my disciples?"' He'll show you a large room upstairs, spread out and ready. Prepare it for us there."

The disciples went to the city and found it just as he had said, so they did as Jesus had directed and prepared the Passover.

30.2 DISCIPLES' FEET WASHED

Matthew 26:20
Mark 14:17

Luke 22:14-16
John 13:1-20

Before the Passover Feast, Jesus knew that his time had come to leave this world and go to the Father. The Devil had already put it into the heart of Judas Iscariot of Simon to betray him. He loved his own, who were in the world, and he loved them to the end. He knew that the Father had put everything in his hands and that he had come from God and was going back to God.

That evening, he comes with the twelve apostles. When the time came, he reclined and told them, "I've really wanted to eat this Passover with you before I suffer, because I tell you that I won't eat it again until it's fulfilled in God's kingdom."

Then during supper he gets up from the meal and sets his coat aside. He took a towel and tied it around himself. He pours water into a wash-bowl. Then he began to wash the disciples' feet,[a] wiping them with the towel that was tied around himself. He comes to Simon Peter, who says, "Lord, are you washing my feet?"

"You don't realize what I'm doing now," Jesus answered, "but later you'll understand."

"You'll never wash my feet!" Peter says.

"If I don't wash you, you won't share with me," Jesus replied.

"Then not only my feet, Lord," Peter says, "but my hands and head too."

Then Jesus says, "Whoever has washed only needs to wash his feet. He's completely clean otherwise. And you are clean, but not all of you."

He said "not all of you are clean" because he knew who was betraying him.

When he had washed their feet, gotten his clothes, and reclined again, he told them, "Do you know what I've done to you? You call me Teacher and Lord, and you're right, I am. But if I, the Lord and Teacher, have washed your feet, you should wash each other's feet too.[b]

A. Sandals were the primary footwear in first century Judea, so walking any distance would cake travelers' feet with dirt. A host would therefore provide guests with water to wash their feet upon arrival. The host could also provide a servant to do the washing, or, as a sign of humility and deep respect, he could wash his guests' feet himself. Thus the task of **foot washing** was particularly humbling, if not degrading, since the foot – especially the dust of the foot – was considered unclean.

B. *Christ Jesus existed in the form of God, but didn't consider equality with God something to be seized. Instead, he emptied himself, taking the form of a slave. – Philippians 2:6-7*

I've given you an example to do just as I've done to you. I tell you, truly truly, a slave isn't greater than his master, nor is the sent greater than the sender. If you know this, you're blessed if you act on it.

"I'm not talking about all of you, because I know the ones I've chosen. But so the Scripture would be fulfilled, 'He who eats my bread has lifted his heel against me.'[c] From now on, I'm telling you before it happens, so when it does, you can believe that I am he. I tell you, truly truly, whoever receives who I send receives me, and whoever receives me receives him who sent me."

30.3 Greatness in the Kingdom, Again

Luke 22:24-30

Then an argument came up among them about which of them was considered the greatest. But he told them, "The kings of nations rule over them, and those with authority are called benefactors.[d] But this isn't your way. The one who's the greatest among you must be like the youngest, and the leader like the servant. Who is greater: the one who reclines or the one who serves? Isn't it the one who reclines? But among you, I am the one who serves. You've stood by me in my testing. Just like my Father gave me a kingdom, I give to you so you can eat and drink at my table in my kingdom. You'll sit on thrones to judge the twelve tribes of Israel."[e]

30.4 Betrayal Predicted

Matthew 26:21-25
Mark 14:18-21
Luke 22:21-23
John 13:21-30

After Jesus finished saying this, as they reclined and ate, he became upset in his spirit and testified, saying, "Truly truly, I tell you that one of you – someone eating with me – will betray me."

C. *Even my friend in peace, whom I trusted, who ate my bread, has lifted his heel against me. – Psalm 41:9*

D. The only time the Greek word *euergetes* occurs in the Bible is in Luke's Gospel. It's typically translated as "**benefactors.**" The word literally means "good work" and was applied those in power who showed favor to others. In particular, it was customary for Roman emperors (benefactors) to grant land on the frontier to retiring soldiers (beneficiaries). Thus it became a title of respect or flattery, particularly applied to emperors and kings, regardless of how evil or oppressive they might be.

E. *If we endure, we'll rule with him. – 2 Timothy 2:12*

The disciples looked at one another very sadly, not knowing who he was talking about. They asked each other which of them would do this, and one by one they each said, "Not me, Lord?"

Now the disciple Jesus loved was leaning against Jesus' chest. Simon Peter points to him and says, "Tell us who he's talking about."

So leaning back on Jesus' chest, he asks him, "Lord, who is it?"

"One of the Twelve," Jesus replies. "Someone who dips his hand in the bowl with me will betray me. I'll dip this piece[f] and give it to the one who it is. Look, the betrayer's hand is with mine on the table. The Son of Man will certainly go just as it's written about him, as it was determined. But woe to the man who betrays the Son of Man! It'd be better for that man to have never been born."

Then he dipped the piece. He takes it and gives it to Judas of Simon Iscariot. And Judas, who was betraying him, said, "Not me, Rabbi?"

"You've said it yourself," Jesus answers.

After the piece, Satan entered him and Jesus told him, "Whatever you do, do it quickly."

None of those reclining knew why he had told him this. Some guessed that Jesus was telling him, "Buy the things we need for the feast," because he had the purse, or that he should give something to the poor.

Then, immediately after getting the piece, he left.

It was night.

30.5 BREAD AND WINE

Matthew 26:26-29
Mark 14:22-25
Luke 22:17-20
John 13:31a
1 Corinthians 11:23b-25

After he left, while they were still eating, Jesus took bread, blessed[g] it, and gave thanks.[h] Then he broke it and gave it to them, saying, "Take

F. John is the only Gospel writer that records Jesus handing Judas a **piece** of food. The Greek word for such a piece is *psomion*, which can also mean "fragment," "crumb," or "morsel." What Jesus gave was presumably a piece of unleavened bread dipped in the communal meat dish.

G. All four Gospel writers use the word *eulogeo* to mean "**bless**," "praise," or "consecrate." It translates literally to "give a good word" and is where the English "eulogy" comes from.

this and eat it. This is my body, given for you. Do this to remember me."

After they ate, he took a cup,[i] gave thanks, and gave it to them, saying, "Drink this, all of you, and share it among yourselves. This cup is the new covenant in my blood, poured out for you and for the forgiveness of the sins of many. Do this to remember me as often as you drink. Truly I tell you that I won't drink the fruit of the vine again from now until the day I drink it fresh with you in God's kingdom – my Father's kingdom – when it comes."

They all drank from it.

30.6 PETER'S DENIAL PREDICTED

Matthew 26:31-35
Mark 14:27-31
Luke 22:31-38
John 13:31b, 32b-38

"The Son of Man is glorified and God is glorified in him," Jesus says. "God will also glorify him in himself, and he'll glorify him right away. Little children, I'm with you a for little longer. You'll look for me, but like I told the Jews I tell you too: you can't come where I'm going. I give you a new command: love each other.[j] Love each other just like I've loved you. This is how all men will know you're my disciples, if you have love for each other."

Then Simon Peter asks, "Where are you going, Lord?"

"Where I'm going, you can't follow me now, but you'll follow me

---

H. *Eucharisteo* also begins with the Greek prefix *eu-*, meaning "good," and the whole word translates to **"give thanks.**" The English "eucharist" originates from *eucharisteo*, which is the Christian practice of ritually eating bread and drinking wine (or an equivalent drink) in remembrance of Jesus. It's also called "Communion," "The Lord's Supper" or "The Blessed Sacrament."

I. According to the Mishnah, Jewish tradition held that all Jews were to drink **four cups of wine** during the Passover Feast, representing the four promises that God made to Israel before the original Passover, as Israel was being delivered from slavery in Egypt. Based on the words that Moses recorded, the four promises began with "I'll bring you," "I'll deliver you," "I'll redeem you," and "I'll take you" – a cup of wine for each of them.

Tell Israel's sons, "I am the LORD, and I'll bring you out from the Egyptian's burdens and I'll deliver you from their service. I'll redeem you too, with an extended arm and great judgments. Then I'll take you as my people and I'll be your God. Then you'll know that I am the LORD your God, who brought you out from the Egyptian's burdens. I'll bring you to the land that I lifted my hand to give to Abraham, Isaac, and Jacob, and I'll give it as your possession. I am the LORD." – Exodus 6:6-8

J. *This is the message you've heard from the start: love each other. – 1 John 3:11*

Covenants

Jeremiah is the only Old Testament writer that mentions a **new covenant**, in contrast to the "old" Abrahamic covenant. This new covenant is where the term "New Testament" comes from, through its Latin translation. The writer of Hebrews quotes Jeremiah's words regarding this new covenant in the largest single citation of Old Testament text within the New Testament. Covenants were customarily sealed with blood in ancient Middle Eastern societies. Moses sealed the Abrahamic covenant with bulls' blood.

"Look, the days are coming," the LORD announces, "when I'll make a new covenant with Israel's house and Judah's house, unlike the covenant I made with their fathers in the day I took their hand to bring them from the land of Egypt – my covenant that they broke, even though I was their husband," the LORD announces. "However, this is the covenant I'll make with Israel's house after those days," the LORD announces. "I'll put my law inside them and I'll write it on their hearts. I'll be their God and they'll be my people. They won't teach anymore, a man to his neighbor and a man to his brother, saying, 'Know the LORD,' because they'll all know me, from the smallest to the greatest," the LORD announces, "because I'll forgive their guilt and not remember their sin anymore."

– Jeremiah 31:31-34

If the first [covenant] had been faultless, there wouldn't have been any place to look for a second. But fault was found.... And when he said, "new," he made the first old, and the old and aging have nearly disappeared.

– Hebrews 8:7-8,13

Moses wrote down all of the LORD's words. Then he got up early in the morning and built an altar under the mountain with twelve pillars for Israel's twelve tribes. He sent boys from Israel's sons and they brought up offerings and sacrificed bulls for peace to the LORD. Moses took half of the blood and put it in bowls, and scattered the other half of the blood on the altar. Then he took the book of the covenant and read it in the people's ears, and they said, "We'll do and hear everything the LORD has said!"

So Moses took the blood and scattered it on the people, saying, "Look, the blood of the covenant, which the Lord has made with you upon all these words."

– Exodus 24:4-8

later," Jesus answered. "You'll all trip up tonight, because it's written, 'I'll strike the shepherd and the flock of sheep will be scattered.'[k] But after I've been raised, I'll go to Galilee ahead of you."

"Why can't I follow you now, Lord?" Peter asks. "Even if everyone trips, I never will. I'll lay my life down for you!"

"Will you lay down your life for me?" Jesus replies. "Simon, Simon. Look, Satan has demanded to sift you like wheat. But I've prayed for you, that your faith won't fail. So when you've returned, strengthen your brothers."

"Lord, I'm ready to go to both prison and death with you!" he answered.

K. *"Wake up, sword, against my shepherd and against the man, my neighbor," declares the Lord of armies. "Strike the shepherd so the sheep will be scattered, and I'll turn my hand against the small." – Zechariah 13:7*

"I tell you, truly truly Peter," he said, "tonight, before the rooster crows twice, you'll deny that you know me three times."

But Peter insists, "Even if I have to die with you, I'll never deny you!"

And they all said the same too. Then he told them, "When I sent you out without a purse, a bag, or sandals, did you lack anything?"

"Nothing," they said.

"But now, whoever has a purse should take it, and a bag too," he said. "And whoever doesn't have a sword should sell his coat to buy one. I tell you, what's written must be fulfilled in me: 'He was counted with the lawless,'[l] because whatever refers to me is fulfilled."

"Lord look, here are two swords," they said.

"That's enough," he replied.

L. *I'll give him a part with the great, and he'll divide the plunder with the strong, because of this: he poured himself out to death and was counted with the lawless, but he carried the sin of many and interceded for the lawless. – Isaiah 53:12*

CHAPTER 31

In the Room Upstairs

31.1 WHERE JESUS IS GOING

John 14

"Don't let your heart become upset. Believe in God and believe in me too. There are many rooms in my Father's house. If there weren't, I wouldn't tell you so, because I go to make a room for you. And if I go and make a room for you, I'll come back and bring you with me, so you can be where I am. You know the way to where I'm going."

"Lord," Thomas says, "we don't know where you're going, so how do we know the way?"

"I'm the way, the truth, and the life," Jesus answers. "Nobody comes to the Father except through me. If you knew me, you'd know my Father too.[a] So from now on, you know him and you've seen him."

Then Philip says, "Lord, show us the Father. That'll be enough for us."

A. *We know that God's Son has come and has given us understanding so we can know the one who's true. And we're in the one who's true, his son Jesus Christ. This is the true God and everlasting life. – 1 John 5:20*

"Have I been with you this long and you still don't know me, Philip?" Jesus replies. "Whoever has seen me has seen the Father,[b] so how can you say, 'Show us the Father'? Don't you believe that I am in the Father and the Father is in me? The words I tell you I don't say on my own, but the Father living in me is doing his work. Believe me, I am in the Father and the Father is in me. Or believe because of the work itself. I tell you, truly truly, whoever believes in me will do the things I do, and even greater things, because I go to the Father. I'll do whatever you ask in my name, so the Father will be glorified through the Son. If you ask me for anything in my name, I'll do it.

"If you love me, you'll keep my commands.[c] I'll ask the Father and he'll give you another Helper[d] – the Spirit of truth – to be with you forever. The world can't have him because it doesn't see him or know him, but you know him because he lives with you and will be in you.

"I won't leave you like orphans, because I'll come back to you. Soon the world won't see me anymore, but you'll see me. And because I live, you'll live too. On that day, you'll know that I am in my Father, you are in me, and I am in you. Whoever has my commands and keeps them is the one who loves me. My Father will love whoever loves me, and I'll love him and show myself to him."

Then Judas (not Iscariot) says, "Lord, what has happened that you'll show yourself to us and not to the world?"

"If anyone loves me, he'll do what I say," Jesus answered. "My Father will love him, and we'll come to him and make our home with him. Whoever doesn't love me doesn't do what I say. The words you hear aren't mine, they're the Father's who sent me.

"I've told you this while living with you, but the Helper – the Holy Spirit, who the Father will send in my name – he'll teach you everything and make you remember everything I've told you. Peace I leave with you; my peace I give you. However, I don't give like the world gives. Don't let your heart become upset or let it be afraid. You've heard me

B. *[God's Son] is the image of the invisible God, the firstborn of all creation. – Colossians 1:15*

C. *This is love for God: keeping his commandments. – 1 John 5:3a*

D. *Parakletos* occurs five times in the Bible, all mentioned by John. The word literally means "called to one's side" and translates to "advocate," "**helper**," or "comforter." Non-biblical Greek writings use the word in reference to court cases and legal action, as a lawyer representing a client would literally "stand by his side" and advocate for him before a judge.

If anyone sins, we have a Helper with the Father: Jesus Christ the righteous. He's the appeasement for our sins, and not only for ours, but for the whole world's too. – 1 John 2:1-2

tell you, 'I go away, but I'll come back to you.' If you love me, you'll be happy that I go to the Father, because the Father is greater than I am. I've told you before it happens so you'll believe when it does happen. I won't talk with you much longer, because the ruler of the world is coming and he has nothing in me. But I do what the Father tells me so the world will know that I love the Father.

"Now get up. Let's get out of here."

31.2 VINE AND BRANCHES | LOVE EACH OTHER | OPPOSITION

John 15, 16:1-4

"I'm the true vine and my Father is the gardener. He removes every branch that doesn't produce fruit,[e] and he prunes[f] everyone that does produce fruit so that he'll produce more fruit. You're already pruned because of the words I've told you. Stay in me and I in you. Just like a branch can't produce fruit by itself unless it stays in the vine, neither can you unless you stay in me. I'm the vine, you're the branches. Whoever stays in me, and I in him, will produce much fruit, but apart from me you can't do anything. If anyone doesn't stay in me, he's thrown away and dries up like a branch. They'll be gathered up and tossed into the fire to be burned. But if you stay in me, my words live in you, and whatever you want will be done for you. My Father is glorified by this: when you produce lots of fruit, proving you're my disciples. Just like the Father has loved me, I've loved you too. Stay in my love. If you do what I command, you'll live in my love, just as I've done what my Father commands and stayed in his love. I've told you this so my joy will be in you, that you'll be full of joy.

"This is my command: love each other,[g] just like I've loved you. No

E. *The fruit of the Spirit is love, joy, peace, patience, kindness, goodness, faith, meekness, and self-control. Against these there is no law. – Galatians 5:22-23*

F. The Greek word *kathairo* means "clean" or "purge." It can also mean "**prune**" in reference to vines and trees.

G. *Whoever confesses that Jesus is God's Son, God stays in him and he in God. We've known and believed the love God has for us. God is love and the one who stays in love stays in God, and God stays in him. Love is complete in us in this way so we can speak openly on judgment day, because we're in this world too, like he is. There's no fear in love because mature love throws out fear. Fear holds punishment and the one who fears isn't mature in love. We love because he loved us first. If someone says, "I love God," but hates his brother, he's a liar. The one who doesn't love the brother he has seen can't love the God he hasn't seen. And we have this commandment from him: the one who loves God should love his brother too. – 1 John 4:15-21*

one has greater love than when someone lays down his life for his friends. And you're my friends if you do what I command. I don't call you slaves anymore, because a slave doesn't know what his master is doing. I've called you friends, because I've let you know everything I've heard from my Father. You didn't choose me, I chose you. I established you that you'd go and produce fruit that would last, so the Father will give you whatever you ask in my name. This is what I command you: love each other.

"If the world hates you, understand that it hated me first. If you were of the world, the world would love its own. But you aren't of the world, because I chose you out of the world, which is why the world hates you. Remember what I told you: a slave isn't greater than his master. If they've mistreated me, they'll mistreat you too.[h] And if they've kept my word, they'll keep yours too. But they'll do all this to you because of my name, because they don't know who sent me. If I hadn't come and told them, they wouldn't have sin, but now they have no excuse for their sin. Whoever hates me hates my Father too. If I hadn't done things with them that nobody else has done, they wouldn't have sin. But now they've seen and still hated me and my Father. This fulfills the words written in their Law, 'They hated me freely.'[i]

"I'll send you a Helper from the Father. He's the Spirit of truth that goes out from the Father, and he'll witness for me when he comes. So you will witness too, because you've been with me from the start.

"I've told you this so you won't trip up. They'll excommunicate you. And a time is coming when everyone who kills you will think he's offering God a service. They'll do this because they don't know the Father or me. But I've told you this so that when the time comes, you'll remember I've told it to you. I didn't tell you this at the start, because I was with you."

31.3 WHY JESUS IS GOING

John 16:5-33

"Now I'm going back to the one who sent me, but none of you asks

H. *Certainly, all who want to live godly in Christ Jesus will be mistreated. – 2 Timothy 3:12*

I. The Greek word *dorean* and its equivalent Hebrew term *chinnam* both mean "**freely**" or "without cost." However, in the context of being hated, they more loosely mean "without cause" or "undeservedly," similar to the English phrase "for no good reason."

Those who freely hate me are more than the hairs on my head. Those who would destroy me are powerful, wrongfully my enemies. What I didn't steal, I have to repay. – Psalm 69:4

me, 'Where are you going?' Sadness has filled your hearts because I've told you this. But I tell you the truth, it's better that I leave, because if I don't go, the Helper won't come to you. But if I go, I'll send him to you. When he comes, he'll convict the world about sin, righteousness, and judgment: about sin, because they don't believe in me; about righteousness, because I go to the Father, and you won't see me anymore; and about judgment, because this ruler of the world has been judged.

"I have much more to tell you, but you can't handle it now. When the Spirit of truth comes, he'll guide you into every truth. He won't speak on his own, but he'll speak whatever he hears and he'll report on what will come. He'll glorify me because he'll take what's mine and announce it. Everything the Father has is mine – that's why I said that he'll take what's mine and announce it.

"In a little while you won't see me anymore, but a little while again and you'll see me."

Then his disciples asked each other, "What's this he's saying? 'In a little while you won't see me anymore, but a little while again and you'll see me,' and 'because I go to the Father'? What's this 'little while' he says? What's he talking about?"

Jesus knew what they wanted to ask him, so he said, "Are you looking into this together, that I said, 'In a little while you won't see me anymore, but a little while again and you'll see me'? I tell you, truly truly, you'll grieve and cry, but the world will celebrate. You'll grieve, but your sadness will turn into joy. Whenever a woman is in labor, she has pain because her time has come.[J] But after she gives birth to her baby, she doesn't remember her agony anymore because of the joy that a person was born into the world. So you have sadness too, but I'll see you again. Your heart will celebrate and nobody will take your joy away. On that day you won't have to ask me about anything. Truly truly, I tell you that if you ask the Father for anything in my name, he'll give it to you. Up until now you haven't asked for anything in my name, but ask and you'll get it, so your joy will be fulfilled.

"I've said all this in metaphors, but a time is coming when I won't speak figuratively – I'll tell you about the Father clearly. On that day, you'll ask in my name, but I'm not saying that I'll ask the Father for

J. *Like the pregnant coming to her delivery, she writhes and cries in her pain. We were this way before you, LORD. We were pregnant and we writhed. We delivered only the wind.... But look, the LORD is coming. – Isaiah 26:17-18,21*

you. The Father loves you himself because you've loved me and have believed that I came from the Father. I came from the Father into the world. But I'm leaving the world again and going to the Father."

Then his disciples say, "Look, now you're talking clearly and not speaking figuratively. Now we know that you know everything and don't need anyone to question you. Because of this, we believe you came from God."

"Do you believe me now?" Jesus answered. "Look, a time is coming – which has already come – for you to scatter, everyone on his own, leaving me alone. However, I'm not alone, because of my Father. I've told you this so you can have peace in me. In the world you will have trouble, but cheer up, I've conquered the world!"[k]

31.4 PRAYER FOR BELIEVERS

John 17

Jesus said this. Then lifting his eyes to heaven, he continued, "Father, the time has come. Glorify your Son so the Son can glorify you. You've given him power over everybody[l] so he can give everlasting life to everyone you've given him. This is everlasting life: to know you, the one true God, and Jesus, the Christ you've sent. I've glorified you on earth, finishing the work you gave me to do. Now Father, glorify me together with yourself, with the glory I had with you before the world.

"I've shown your name to the men you gave me from the world. They were yours, you gave them to me, and they've kept your word. Now they understand that everything you've given me is from you. The words you gave me, I gave to them, and they've received them and understood that I came from you. They've believed you sent me, so I ask this for them. I don't ask it for the world, but for those you gave me. They're yours. Everything of mine is yours, and yours is mine. They've glorified me. I'm not in the world anymore – I come to you – but they're in the world. Holy Father, keep them in your name, which you gave me, so they can be one just like us. I've kept them in the name[m] you gave me – your name – while I was with them. I've watched them

K. *However, in all this, we over-conquer through the one who loved us. – Romans 8:37*

L. The Greek *pas* means "all" or "every," while *sarx* refers to the physical substance of the body, that is, the flesh of both man and animal. Here the phrase *pas sarx* is translated "**everybody**," but it has traditionally been translated "all flesh."

M. *He has a name written on him that no one knows except himself. Dressed in a robe immersed in blood, his name is called "The Word of God." – Revelation 19:12-13*

so that none of them would be destroyed, except the son of destruction, so the Scripture would be complete. But now I come to you. I say this in the world so my joy can be complete in them. I gave your word to them and the world hated them because they aren't of the world, like I'm not of the world. I don't ask that you'd take them from the world, but that you'd keep them from evil. They aren't of the world, just like I'm not of the world. Make them holy in the truth. Your word is truth. I sent them into the world like you sent me into the world. I made myself holy for them, so they can be made holy in the truth too.

"I don't ask this only for them, but also for those who believe in me through their word, that they can all be one. Father, just like you're in me and I'm in you, they can be in us as well, so the world can believe you sent me. I gave them the glory you gave me so they can be one, like we're one. I in them and you in me, so they can be completely one, so the world can know that you've sent me and that you've loved them, just like you've loved me. Father, I want them – those you've given me – to be with me where I am too, so they can see my glory. You gave it to me because you loved me before the foundation of the world.

"Righteous Father, even though the world didn't know you, I knew you, and they knew you sent me. I've shown them your name. I show it so the love you've loved me with can be in them, and I in them."

CHAPTER 32

Betrayal

32.1 PRAYER IN GETHSEMANE

Matthew 26:30, 36-46
Mark 14:26, 32-42
Luke 22:39-46
John 18:1

After Jesus said this, they sang a hymn[a] and he left. He went across the Kidron Ravine to the Mount of Olives, into the garden there with his disciples following him, as was his routine. So Jesus comes to the place called Gethsemane and tells his disciples, "Sit here until I've gone and prayed."

But he takes Peter and James and John, Zebedee's two sons, with him. Then he became upset and distressed. "My soul is grieved enough to die," he tells them. "Stay here and watch out with me. Pray that you won't give in to temptation."

He went on a little further, about a stone's throw, and fell to the ground on his face and prayed, "Dad![b] My Father! If it's possible, let this

A. *Hymneo* is a Greek verb that means "**sing a hymn**," derived from the noun *hymnos*, which is a sacred song that praises God, a nation, or a hero. It's different from *psalmos*, meaning "chords," derived from *psallos*, meaning "pluck" or "vibrate," in reference to playing the stings of a musical instrument. *Psalmos* is the Greek term for the Old Testament book of Psalms.

The Kidron Valley and Gethsemane

On the east side of Jerusalem was the **Kidron** Valley, running north to south. Only John mentions Jesus crossing it en route to Gethsemane. The word he uses for "valley" is *cheimarros*, from the words *cheimon* ("winter," "storm") and *rheo* ("flow," "torrent"). It's traditionally translated "valley," but the word literally means "winter-torrent." It could also be translated "**ravine**" or "gorge." A stream ran through the Kidron after heavy rains, typically in the winter months, but the ravine was otherwise dry. Either way, the valley separated Jerusalem on the west from the Mount of Olives on the east as it carved southward through the Judean Desert towards the Dead Sea. The Kidron Valley appears occasionally in the Old Testament: David escaped eastward across it as he fled from a coup led by his son Absalom; idols and pagan symbols were burned there by King Asa, King Josiah, and King Hezekiah during various purifications of Judah; and it was a popular cemetery for Jerusalem's inhabitants.

The Gihon Spring was located on the Kidron's western slope, which was diverted underground into Jerusalem by King Hezekiah. On the other side, **Gethsemane** was a garden on the ascent to the Mount of Olives.

hour pass by me. You can do anything. Take this cup away! But not what I want, what you want."

He comes back to the disciples and finds them sleeping. "Simon, are you asleep?" he asks Peter. "Couldn't you watch out with me for one hour? Watch and pray so you won't give in to temptation. The spirit's willing, but the body is weak."

He went away again a second time and prayed the same words, saying, "My Father, if this can't pass unless I drink it, do your will."

Then he came back and found them sleeping again, because their eyes were heavy. And they didn't know how to answer him.

He left them a third time and prayed, saying the same thing again. Then an angel from heaven appeared to him, strengthening him, because he was in such anguish and was praying so hard that his sweat became like drops of blood[C] falling on the ground. Then he got up from praying.

He comes back to the disciples, who were sleeping from sadness, and says, "Are you still sleeping and resting? Enough, the time has come. Look, the Son of Man is being betrayed into the hands of sinners. Get

B. *Abba* is an informal, intimate title for one's father, similar to "**Dad**" in English.

All who are led by God's spirit, these are God's sons. You haven't received a spirit of slavery that leads to fear again, but you've received a spirit of adoption, by which we cry "Dad! Father!" The Spirit himself witnesses with our spirit that we're God's children, and if children, heirs too – God's heirs and co-heirs with Christ. Indeed, if we suffer with him, we'll be glorified too. – Romans 8:14-17

C. Under extreme distress, the capillaries around sweat glands can rupture, leading to blood-tinged sweat upon perspiration. This rare condition is called **hematidrosis**, which literally means "bloody water disorder."

up, let's go. Look, the one betraying me is here!"

32.2 ARREST

Matthew 26:47-56
Mark 14:43-52
Luke 22:47-53
John 18:2-11

Look, while he was he was still speaking, Judas, one of the Twelve, immediately comes leading a crowd from the High Priests, the Pharisees, the scribes, and the people's elders. Now Judas, the one betraying him, knew the place, because Jesus met there with his disciples often. So after getting the cohort[d] and the officers from the High Priests, Judas comes with torches, lanterns, swords, and clubs. He had given them a sign, saying, "The one I kiss is him. Arrest him and take him away securely."

Knowing everything that was coming, Jesus went forward. "Who are you looking for?" he asks.

"Jesus the Nazarene," they answered.

"I am,"[e] he says.

But when he said, "I am," they pulled back and fell to the ground. Judas, who was betraying him, was standing with them too.

"Who are you looking for?" he asked them again.

"Jesus the Nazarene," they answered.

"I told you, I am," Jesus said. "So if you're looking for me, let them leave." This fulfilled the words he had spoken: "I didn't lose one of those you gave me."[f]

After arriving, Judas immediately went up to him, saying, "Hail, Rabbi!"

Then he kissed him.

"Judas, my friend," Jesus told him, "you betray the Son of Man with a kiss? Do what you came for."

D. A Roman **cohort** was 500-600 soldiers, which comprised one tenth of a legion. There was likely a cohort in Jerusalem stationed at Antonia Fortress next to the Temple.

E. "**I Am**" is one the names God uses for himself in the Old Testament. His Hebrew name יהוה, abbreviated as YHWH in English, is derived from this phrase.

F. *I've kept them in the name you gave me – your name – while I was with them. I've watched them so none of them was destroyed, except the son of destruction, so the Scripture would be complete. – John 17:12*

Then they grabbed Jesus and arrested him. But look, when those around him saw it happening, they asked, "Lord, should we attack with the swords?"

Then Simon Peter, who was one of those standing there with Jesus, reached and pulled out the sword he had. He hit the High Priest's slave, cutting off his right ear. The slave's name was Malchus. But Jesus tells Peter, "Stop! None of this. Put your sword back in its place in the sheath. Everyone who picks up the sword will die by the sword.[g] Don't you realize that I can call my Father to immediately provide over twelve legions[h] of angels? But then how will the Scriptures be fulfilled, which say it has to happen like this? Won't I drink from the cup the Father has given me?"

So he touched his ear and healed him. Then Jesus told the crowds of High Priests, Temple guards, and elders who had come against him, "Have you come out with swords and clubs to arrest me, like you would against a thief? I was with you, sitting and teaching in the Temple every day, but you didn't arrest me then. But this hour and the power of darkness are yours. This has all happened to fulfill the Scriptures of the prophets."

Then all the disciples left him and fled. A young man was following him, wearing only a sheet.[i] They grab him. But he left the sheet behind and escaped naked.

G. *If anyone is for captivity, he'll go to captivity. And if anyone kills with the sword, he must be killed with the sword. – Revelation 13:10*

H. One Roman legion was an army of about 5000 soldiers, so **twelve legions** would've been 60,000, a massive force in ancient Judea.

I. **Sheets** of fine linen (*sindon* in Greek) were reserved for the wealthy and as burial clothes for the dead.

CHAPTER 33

Trials

33.1 FIRST JEWISH TRIAL

John 18:12-14, 19-24

The cohort, the commander, and the Jewish officers arrested Jesus and tied him up. They took him to Annas[a] first, who was the father-in-law of Caiaphas, the High Priest that year. Caiaphas had advised the Jews that it was beneficial for one man to die for the people.

The High Priest questioned Jesus about his disciples and his teaching, but Jesus answered, "I spoke to the world openly. I always taught in a synagogue and in the Temple, where all Jews gather. I said nothing secretly. So why do you question me? Ask those who heard what I told them. They know what I said."

After he said this, an officer[b] standing there gave Jesus a punch,

A. When Quirinius was governor of Syria, he appointed **Annas**, son of Seth, as High Priest in 6 or 7 AD. Annas served in that position until 15 AD, when he was deposed by Valerius Gratus for illegally executing criminals, which was forbidden under Roman rule. Gratus was the Roman ruler of Judea from 15 to 26 AD; he was replaced by Pontius Pilate. However, despite losing his official title, Annas remained a highly influential figure in Jewish society, especially since his five sons, grandson, and son-in-law acted as High Priests for decades after him.

B. The Greek *hyperetes* literally means "under rower," a term from Greek mariners, referring to someone who serves beneath another. In the New Testament, this position denotes an **officer** or attendant, serving rulers by enacting their judgments and penalties.

saying, "Is this how you answer the High Priest?"

"If I said something wrong, say what's wrong," Jesus replied. "But if right, why did you hit me?"

So Annas sent him tied up to Caiaphas the High Priest.

33.2 PETER'S DENIALS | SECOND JEWISH TRIAL

Matthew 26:57-75
Mark 14:53-72
Luke 22:54-65
John 18:15-18, 25-27

Having arrested Jesus, his captors led him to Caiaphas' house, the High Priest. Then all the High Priests, the elders, and the scribes gather together.

Simon Peter followed him at a distance with another disciple, until the courtyard[c] of the High Priest. The High Priest knew that disciple, so he went into the High Priest's courtyard with Jesus, but Peter stood outside at the door. So the other disciple, whom the High Priest knew, went out and talked to the doorkeeper and brought Peter inside. The slaves and officers were sitting and warming themselves at the charcoal fire they had made in the middle of the courtyard, since it was cold. Peter sat with them to watch the outcome, warming himself at the fire.

As Peter was outside, one of the High Priest's maid-servants, who was the doorkeeper, saw him in the light as he sat warming himself. Gazing at Peter, she comes and says, "You were with Jesus the Nazarene[d] too. Aren't you this man's disciple?"

But he denies it in front of them all: "I'm not. Woman, I don't know what you're talking about."

Then he went out into the gateway.[e]

Meanwhile, the High Priests and the entire council kept looking for a witness against Jesus to have him killed, but they couldn't find any. Many were testifying lies[f] about him, but their testimonies weren't the same. Later, two stood up and came forward. They testified lies about

C. In first century Judean houses, the **courtyard** (*aule*) was an uncovered area within the outer walls. The buildings of the house typically surrounded the courtyard.

D. Mark records that the maid-servant called Jesus a **Nazarene**, while Matthew records that she called him a Galilean. Nazareth was a town in the province of Galilee, so one could be both a Nazarene and a Galilean.

E. Near the main entryway, the **gateway** (*proaulion*) was literally the "fore-courtyard," referring to the space directly behind the door.

him, saying, "We heard him say, 'I'll destroy this handmade temple of God and build another one non-handmade[g] in three days.'"

But even in this their testimonies weren't the same. Then the High Priest stood forward and asked Jesus, "Won't you answer? What are they testifying about you?"

But Jesus kept quiet and didn't answer. So the High Priest asks him again, "I command you by the living God to tell us: are you the Christ, the Son of the blessed God?"

"You've said it," Jesus answers. "I am. And I tell you that after this, you'll see the Son of Man sitting at the right hand of power, coming in the clouds of heaven."[h]

Tearing his robes,[i] the High Priest says, "He has blasphemed![j] What more do we need witnesses for? Look, you've heard the blasphemy. What do you think?"

They all judged him guilty of death. Then some of the men holding Jesus spat in his face, and they covered his head and punched him, while others slapped him. They mocked him, saying, "Prophesy to us, Christ! Who hit you?" And they said much else, blaspheming against him. Then the officers took him for a beating.

Back down in the courtyard, another maid-servant saw Simon Peter and told those standing there, "This one was with Jesus of Nazareth.

F. The Greek verb *pseudomartyreo* comes from *martyria* ("witness," "testimony") and *pseudes* ("false," "lying"). It refers to giving false testimony, translated here as "**testify lies**." *Pseudomartyreo* is the Greek word for the action forbidden in Moses' ninth commandment: *"Do not testify lies against your neighbor"* (Exodus 20:16).

G. Something **handmade**, that is, something physically made by people, was denoted by the Greek adjective *cheiropoietos*. It's opposite, *acheiropoietos*, refers to something not made by human hands, that is, something **non-handmade**.

We know that if this earthly tent, which is our home, is destroyed, we have another building from God, a non-handmade home, everlasting in heaven. – 2 Corinthians 5:1

H. *I kept seeing night visions. Look, someone like the Son of Man was coming with heaven's clouds. He came up to the Ancient of Days and was presented to him. – Daniel 7:13*

I. Tearing one's clothes was a sign of anguish in the Bible. Jacob tore this clothes when he was told his son Joseph had been killed (Genesis 37:34). David tore his clothes upon hearing of the death of King Saul and his son Jonathan, David's best friend (2 Samuel 1:11). Judah's king Josiah did the same as he listened to the Law and realized the people were living in sin (2 Kings 22:11). However, the High Priest wore special robes to identify his position while he was serving. These garments were considered holy. Deliberately **tearing priestly robes** violated Moses' Law.

The priest that is highest among his brothers ... will not tear his clothes. – Leviticus 21:10

J. According to Moses' Law, **blasphemy** was punishable by the execution of the blasphemer.

The one who blasphemes the name of the LORD will certainly be killed. The whole congregation will certainly stone him. The foreigner as well as the native will be killed if he

He's one of them!"

But he denied it again. "Woman, I'm not!" he said with an oath. "I don't know the man!"

A little later, one of the High Priest's slaves was standing there. He was related to the one whose ear Peter had cut off. He insisted and again said to Peter, "You were certainly with them, because you're a Galilean too. It's clear by your accent! And didn't I see you in the garden?"

But he cursed and swore, "Man, I don't know this man you're talking about!"

Immediately, while he was still speaking, a rooster crowed a second time. Then the Lord turned and looked at Peter, and Peter remembered the words Jesus had told him, "Before a rooster crows today twice, you'll deny me three times."

Then he left and wept bitterly.

33.3 THIRD JEWISH TRIAL | JUDAS' REGRET

Matthew 27:1,3-10
Mark 15:1a
Luke 22:66-71
Acts 1:18-19

When morning came, all the elders – both the High Priests and the scribes – gathered in a council to have Jesus killed. They brought him into their assembly, saying, "If you're the Christ, tell us."

"If I tell you, you won't believe," he replied. "And if I ask a question, you won't answer. But from now on the Son of Man will sit at God's right hand of power."[k]

Then they asked, "So are you God's Son?"

"Yes," he told them, "I am."

"What do we need witnesses for?" they said. "We've heard it ourselves from his own mouth!"

When Judas, who had betrayed him, saw that he had been condemned, he regretted it and returned the thirty silver coins to the High Priests and the elders, saying, "I've sinned by betraying innocent blood!"

blasphemes that name. – Leviticus 24:16

K. *The LORD says to my Lord, "Sit at my right hand until I make your enemies a stool for your feet." – Psalm 110:1*

The Death of Judas

There are two different accounts of **Judas Iscariot's death** in the Bible. Matthew records that he hung himself after betraying Jesus, while Luke (in Acts) records that he fell in his field and burst open. There are various theories that explain the two accounts:

1. Judas indeed hung himself, but his body fell to the ground and broke apart, being in an advanced state of decay. Perhaps it occurred when he was cut down from the rope or as his corpse was being carried across his field for burial (his land was converted into a graveyard after his death).
2. The Greek word *apagcho* (typically translated "strangle" or "hang") didn't refer to Judas' death at all, but to his intense emotional state, similar to the English expression "all choked up."
3. One of the Gospel writers may have transcribed it incorrectly.

Biblical scholars are divided on the issue.

"What's that to us?" they replied. "See to yourself."

So he threw the silver coins into the Temple, then went away and hung himself.

The High Priests took the silver coins and said, "It isn't legal to put them into the treasury, since it's the price of blood."

They counselled together and bought the potter's field with it for strangers to be buried. So this man got a field for the price of his wickedness. And falling head first, he burst in the middle and all his organs poured out. Everyone living in Jerusalem found out about it, so the field was called *Hakeldama*,[l] which is Blood Field in their own language, and so it's called to this day. Then the prophet Jeremiah's words[m] were fulfilled: "They took the thirty silver coins, the price that I had been valued by Israel's sons, and they gave them for the potter's field, as the Lord instructed."[n]

33.4 FIRST ROMAN TRIAL

Matthew 27:2, 11-14
Mark 15:1b-5

L. ***Hakeldama*** comes from the Aramaic words *cheleq* ("portion" or "territory") and *dam* ("blood").

M. Matthew records that the prophecy about the thirty silver coins is from the Old Testament book of **Jeremiah**, but the book of Zechariah actually contains the passage that matches it best. Jeremiah, however, contains text regarding interaction with a potter (19:1-2) and purchasing a field for a different amount of silver (32:6-12).

N. *The Lord told me, "Throw it to the potter, the glorious price they valued me at." So I took the thirty of silver and threw them to the potter in the Lord's house. – Zechariah 11:13*

Luke 23:1-12
John 18:28-38

Then the whole crowd of them got up and took Jesus away, tied up. They lead him from Caiaphas into the palace. They gave him to Pilate the governor while it was early, but they didn't go into the palace themselves so they wouldn't become unclean and could therefore still eat the Passover. Instead, Pilate went out to them.

"What are your charges against this man?" he asks.

"If he weren't wicked, we wouldn't have given him to you," they answered.

"Then take him and judge him yourselves with your own Law,"

Pontius Pilate

Succeeding Valerius Gratus in 26 AD, **Pontius Pilate** was the fifth ruler of Judea under Rome, holding power until 36 AD. Despite the scant historical record of his early life, Pilate was likely from a middle-class Italian family and had army experience before his appointment as prefect or procurator in Judea, since his primary function there was military. He was also responsible for tax collection and judging legal cases beyond the authority of the local councils – the Jews were allowed to self-govern, but any executions required Roman approval. Pilate resided in Caesarea on the Mediterranean coast with his wife Claudia Procula, but he travelled extensively throughout the province. Especially during the Passover, Pilate would've been expected to be present in Jerusalem to keep the peace.

According to the historians Philo and Josephus, Pilate was insensitive towards Jewish religion and customs, which led to various conflicts with the Jews. For example, Josephus records that the Jews became outraged at Roman images secretly brought into Jerusalem by Pilate's soldiers at night. After days of protests, Pilate threatened to put the Jewish protesters to death, to which the Jews showed their necks and declared that that would be better than their Law being violated. Pilate eventually conceded and removed the images. A similar event occurred when Pilate displayed golden shields from Herod's palace in Jerusalem. This time, it took a reproach from the Roman Emperor Tiberius to prompt their transfer to Caesarea to restore the peace. Pilate also used Temple money to build an aqueduct, then attacked and killed Jewish protesters who objected to his actions. Philo stated that Pilate was stubborn, relentless, and had a furious temper. He ruled Judea amidst allegations of bribery, theft, insults, illegal executions, and cruelty. Finally, after a bloody conflict with Samaritan pilgrims, Pilate was deposed by Vitellius, Syria's governor, and stood trial in Rome for his conduct. From there, Eusebius records that he was exiled to Gaul (modern-day France), where he committed suicide. He was replaced in Judea by Marcellus, who reigned briefly before Marullus took his place.

When in Jerusalem, Pilate would most certainly have stayed in Herod's **palace**. As the second most prominent building in the city (after the Temple), it served as the residence of the ruling Roman authority whenever he was there. Josephus records that the palace was luxurious and richly decorated, built from massive white marble stones. It had tall towers and contained many bedrooms. However, most of it was demolished along with the rest of the city in 70 AD during Jerusalem's destruction. In the New Testament, this palace was called the *praitorion*, a Latin word referring to the tent of the highest ranking officer in a Roman military camp. When the Romans occupied a city, they typically resided in the largest building there, which was Herod's palace in Jerusalem. Many Bibles translate it as "Praetorium," but here it's simply "palace." The word *praitorion* could also refer to the elite guard for the Roman ruler, as Paul mentions in the biblical book of Philippians.

Pilate said.

"We can't kill anyone," the Jews replied. This fulfilled the word Jesus had spoken, as a sign for the type of death he would die.[O]

So Pilate returned to the palace and called Jesus. As Jesus stood before the governor, he asked him, "Are you the king of the Jews?"

"Are you saying this on your own or did others tell you about me?" Jesus replied.

"Am I a Jew?" Pilate asked. "Your own people and the High Priests gave you to me. What have you done?"

"My kingdom isn't of this world," Jesus answered. "If my kingdom were of this world, my servants would fight for me to not be given to the Jews. But my kingdom isn't of this place."

"Then you're a king?" Pilate asked.

"I am a king, just as you say," Jesus answers. "I was born for this and I came to the world for this: to witness to the truth. Everyone in the truth hears my voice."

"What is truth?" Pilate replies.

After saying this, he went back to the Jews. The High Priests and the elders accused him of much, saying, "We found him corrupting our nation and preventing taxes from being paid to Caesar. He said that he's the Christ and a king."

So Pilate asks him again, "Won't you answer? Don't you see and hear how many accusations they've testified against you?"

But Jesus didn't answer him regarding any of the charges, so Pilate the governor was quite amazed.

Then Pilate tells the High Priests and the crowds, "I find this man not guilty."

However, they became even stronger,[P] saying, "He stirs up the people! He has taught all over Judea, beginning in Galilee, and now here!"

When Pilate heard this, he asked if the man was a Galilean, and when he learned that he was under Herod's jurisdiction, who was also

O. *Just like Moses lifted up the snake in the wilderness, the Son of Man must be lifted up too. – John 3:14*

P. Luke is the only Gospel writer to use the word *epischyo*, a combination of *epi* ("on" or "over") and *ischyo* ("be strong"). Here it's translated "**become stronger**," but in other translations it's "insist."

in Jerusalem that day, he sent him to Herod.[q]

Herod was very happy to see Jesus. He had heard about him and had wanted to see him for a long time, because he had hoped to see him do some miracle. He questioned him with much talking, but he answered nothing. Meanwhile, the High Priests and the scribes stood there accusing him fiercely. Then after Herod and his soldiers scorned[r] and mocked him, they dressed him in a magnificent robe and returned him to Pilate. So Herod and Pilate became friends that day; they had been enemies before then.

33.5 SECOND ROMAN TRIAL | JESUS BEATEN | BARABBAS RELEASED

Matthew 27:15-30
Mark 15:6-19
Luke 23:13-16, 18-25
John 18:39-40, 19:1-16

Pilate called the High Priests, the leaders, and the people, telling them, "You brought me this man as if he turned people astray. But look, I've investigated this before you and found this man not guilty of the accusations you've made against him. No, neither did Herod, who returned him back to us. Look, he has done nothing to deserve death, so I'll punish him and release him."

Now at the Passover Feast, the Jews had a tradition that the governor would release one prisoner for them, whoever they asked for. A notorious prisoner named Barabbas[s] had been arrested and thrown into prison with rebels[t] who had murdered during a rebellion in the city. He was also a thief. So when the crowd gathered and approached, and asked him to do as he had done before, Pilate answered, "Which of these two do you want me to release for you: Barabbas or Jesus, called the Christ, the king of the Jews?"

He knew that the High Priests had handed him over out of envy.

Q. The **Herod** ruling at the time of Jesus' trials was Herod Antipas, the son of Herod the Great.

R. Only Luke uses *exoutheneo*, although Mark uses a variant of it (*exoudeneo*). It literally translates to "of nothing," meaning "be worthless" or "considered of no account." It's usually rendered "despise," "**scorn**," or "treat with contempt."

S. **Barabbas** is a Hebrew name meaning "father's son."

T. Barabbas is nonspecifically called a *stasiastes* ("insurrectionist," "**rebel**," "rioter"), which may have referred to his being a Zealot. Zealots were a political party that had a reputation for riots and murders in opposition of Roman rule. One of Jesus' disciples, Simon, was a former Zealot.

But the High Priests and the elders convinced the crowds and stirred them up to have Barabbas released for them instead, and to kill Jesus. They all shouted together, "Take him away! Release Barabbas for us!"

Pilate asked them again, "Then what should I do with the one you call the king of the Jews?"

"Crucify him!" they shouted.

Pilate, wanting to release Jesus, took him and had him whipped.[u] So the governor's soldiers took Jesus away into the courtyard of the palace. They gather the whole cohort. After stripping him, they dressed him in a purple robe. Then the soldiers braided a crown from thorns and put it on his head, and they put a stick in his right hand. They mocked him and saluted him, saying, "Hail, King of the Jews!"[v] while they knelt and bowed before him. Then they slapped him in the face and spat on him, and they took the stick and hit him over the head with it.[w]

Then Pilate came out again. He tells them, "Look, I'm bringing him

U. Roman floggings had a reputation for being terribly brutal. *Mastigoo* is the Greek term for such an act, which can be translated "**whip**," "scourge," or "flog." Numerous lashings were applied to the victim's back, sides, and buttocks. Braided leather thongs with interwoven metal, stone, and bone sliced through soft tissue so the victim's shredded flesh would expose underlying muscle, fascia, and bones. The Jews limited the number of lashings to a maximum of 39, but the Romans had no such limit. The victims of Roman floggings often didn't survive.

V. The standard word used to greet Caesar was *chairo*, often translated "Hail, Caesar!" It's used here for Jesus ("**Hail, King of the Jews!**"). As well as a salutation, *chairo* also means "rejoice" or "be well." Angels greeted Jesus' mother Mary the same way with news of her pregnancy ("Rejoice, favored one!"). Judas Iscariot used the same ("Hail, Rabbi!") during Jesus' betrayal in Gethsemane.

The Color Purple

Purple was the most precious of ancient dyes, made from the desiccated (dried) mucous glands of *Murex* sea snails. The process of extracting the pigmented glands from the spiny shells was notoriously stinky and laborious. Hundreds of thousands of mollusks were needed to produce even a small amount, making it very costly. Purple fabric was part of Israel's Tabernacle and Jerusalem's Temple. It was also the color of royal robes, like the one Mark and John record that Jesus wore.

Matthew, however, recorded that Jesus wore a red robe. Unlike purple from shellfish, red dye in first century Judea was produced from the dried bodies of female *Kermes* insects. These small bugs feed on the sap of oak trees indigenous to the Mediterranean region. Their dried bodes were crushed to produce a rich red dye that was used throughout Europe until the Middle Ages. The English words "crimson" and "carmine" – both referring to deep red – are derived from the Greek word *kermes*.

Whatever the color of Jesus' robe, both purple and red dyes were considered luxurious and typically reserved for the rich and royalty. It may have been an old military cloak from the soldiers' barracks.

out so you'll know that I find him not guilty."

Then Jesus came out wearing the crown of thorns and the purple robe. "Look, the man!" Pilate tells them.

Seeing him, the High Priests and the officers all shouted, "Crucify, crucify!"

"Take him and crucify him yourselves," Pilate tells them. "I find him not guilty."

But the Jews answered, "We have a law, and by that law he must die because he made himself to be God's Son."

When Pilate heard these words, he became even more afraid and returned to the palace. "Where are you from?" he asks Jesus.

But Jesus gave no reply. So Pilate says, "Won't you speak to me? Don't you know I have the power to release you and the power to crucify you?"

"You wouldn't have any power over me if it hadn't been given to

W.*His appearance was wrecked beyond that of any man, and his form beyond any of the sons of men. – Isaiah 52:14*

Thorns

In addition to their obvious physical discomfort, **thorns** represented the curse of sin to Jews. Genesis records that the first two people, Adam and his wife Eve, committed the first sin by deliberately disobeying God. Consequently, God banished them from their home and cursed them. Part of this curse was against the earth itself, which became less fruitful and required strenuous labor to produce food. Additionally, thorns began growing along the ground to further afflict them.

The ground is cursed because of you. You'll eat from it in pain all the days of your life. Thorns and weeds will grow for you and you'll eat plants from the field. You'll eat bread by the sweat of your face until you return to the ground, because you were taken from it. You are dust and you'll return to the dust.

– Genesis 3:17-19

you from above," Jesus answered. "This is why the one who gave me to you has the bigger sin."

Because of this, Pilate tried to release Jesus, but the Jews shouted out, "If you release him, you're no friend of Caesar![x] Everyone who makes himself a king speaks against Caesar!"

When Pilate heard these words, he brought Jesus out and sat on the throne at a place called the Pavement, which is *Gabbatha*[y] in Hebrew. It was about the sixth hour[z] on the preparation day for the Passover. He tells the Jews, "Look, your king!"

But they shouted out, "Away, away! Crucify him!"

While he was sitting on his throne, his wife sent to him, saying, "Do nothing with that righteous one. Last night I suffered much in a dream because of him."

So Pilate asks them, "Should I crucify your king? Why? What evil has he done? I've found nothing in him deserving death. So I'll punish him and release him."

But the High Priests answered, "We have no king but Caesar![a] Crucify him!"

They persisted, shouting out with great voices for him to be crucified, and their voices were overpowering. When Pilate saw that he wasn't accomplishing anything, but that a riot was starting instead, he took water and washed his hands before the crowd, saying, "I'm innocent of this man's blood. See to yourselves."

X. "***Friend of Caesar***" was a phrase within the Roman government referring to the ruling elite that were loyal to the Emperor. Losing the status of *amici Caesaris* meant political ruin. Because Pilate had recently been rebuked by the Roman Emperor Tiberius for being too harsh with the Jews, another report from the Jewish leaders of further unfavorable behavior toward them was a loaded threat. Pilate could not afford more bad news about him in Rome, so the pressure was on to do everything possible to maintain his status as a "friend of Caesar".

Y. Although John records that ***Gabbatha*** is a Hebrew word, it's actually Aramaic, which was the common language of the Jews at the time. It literally means "elevation" or "ridge," referring to its height above the surrounding area. The Greek term is *lithostrotos*, which means "spread with stones" and is translated "pavement." These two characteristics – that it's elevated and paved – have traditionally identified *Gabbatha* with the site where the Sanhedrin gathered to judge court cases on a large paved surface in the northeast section of the Temple. This platform may have been part of the Antonia Fortress adjacent to the Temple. The paved surface was reportedly made of huge square slabs of stone, possibly arranged in a mosaic.

Z. The **sixth hour** was at noon.

A. *The LORD said to Samuel, "Listen to the people's voice regarding all they say, because they haven't rejected you. They've rejected me from being king over them." – 1 Samuel 8:7*

Then everyone said, "His blood will be on us and our children!"

So wanting to make the crowd content, Pilate announced that their request would happen. He released Barabbas for them, the man they had asked for, who had been thrown into prison for rebellion and murder. And, after having Jesus whipped, he handed him over to them to be crucified, as they wanted.

Crucifixion

The Latin word *crux* ("cross") is where the English term "**crucifixion**" comes from, but the original Greek accounts of Jesus' death use the word *stauros* ("stake"), which evolved to mean "crucify" over time. Crucifixion was a form of capital punishment performed by affixing a criminal to a wooden cross for a long, drawn-out death. This method of execution was used throughout ancient history, particularly during the Assyrian, Median, Persian and Greek empires. Similarly, the Romans used it as their most severe form of execution, reserved for slaves and criminals. No Roman citizen could be crucified, as it was considered too agonizing and disgraceful. In fact, the pain of crucifixion was so terrible that a new word – excruciating ("out of the cross") – was used to describe it.

Exactly what the cross looked like or how the criminal was nailed to it isn't clear, but most scholars agree a variety of forms were employed. Crucifixion evolved from the practice of impaling dead bodies on stakes to discourage civil disobedience. Over time, victims wouldn't be killed beforehand and horizontal beams were attached to better accommodate a hanging body. The arms of the victim were first attached to a cross-beam with ropes, leather straps, and/or large iron nails. This was then raised onto a vertical stake that had been permanently planted in the ground. Finally, the feet or legs were fastened to the stake in a similar fashion. The victim was then be left to hang naked from the cross. The strain of hanging by one's arms for extended periods would likely have dislocated both shoulders. With the body supported by outstretched arms, hyperinflation of the chest cavity would prevent adequate exhalation, so the victim of crucifixion had to painfully push himself up on his nailed legs to exhale each breath. Eventually, death came by exhaustion and subsequent asphyxiation (inability to breathe). This process could take days in otherwise healthy people, but if a beating or whipping had occurred prior to crucifixion, death would come sooner due to the prior trauma and hypovolemia (excessive blood loss).

The Roman guards charged with performing crucifixion could only leave the site after the victim had died. So to speed the process, legs could be broken to prevent breathing, thereby causing death in a matter of minutes. There were no survivors of Roman crucifixions – soldiers would have ensured their victims were definitely dead, since their own lives would've been forfeited if anyone lived. Once expired, crucified corpses were often left on display to deter future crime. Barring customary burial, they would've decayed on the cross, exposed to the weather and scavenging animals.

Crucifixion was abolished by the Roman emperor Constantine in 337 AD upon his conversion to Christianity. Although the cross originally represented guilt, punishment, and shame, it became a sacred symbol of Christianity and was therefore no longer used for execution.

Despite the thousands of crucifixions that were recorded to have occurred, only one crucified body has been discovered to date. In 1968, the remains of a crucified man were found in Jerusalem. Large spikes had been driven laterally through the heel bones. However, his wrist bones were intact, suggesting spikes had been driven through the bones of his forearms rather than the hands, if at all.

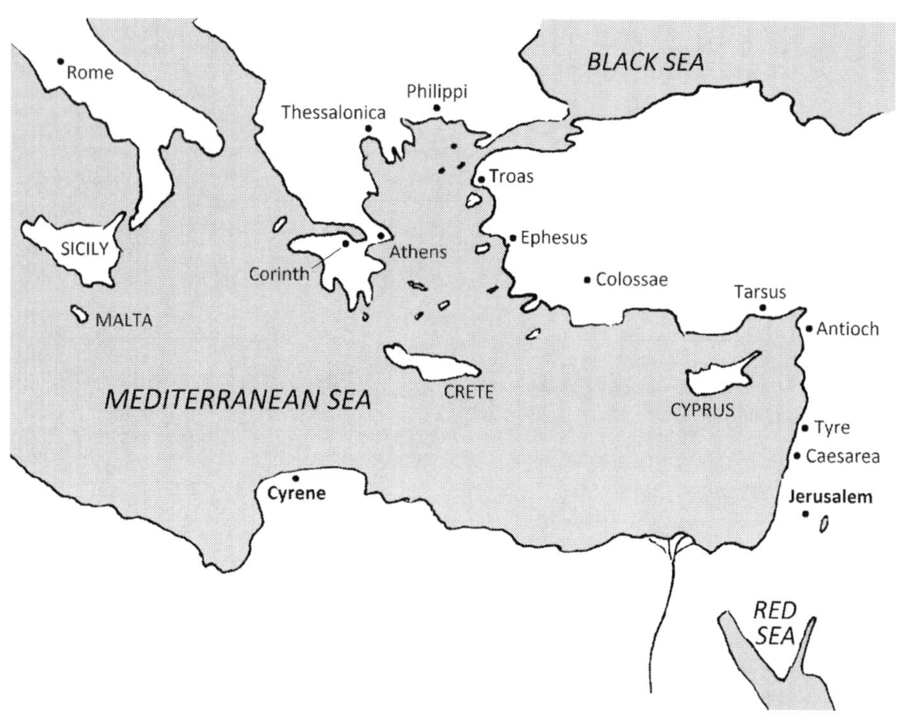

The City of Cyrene

On the north coast of Africa, directly south of Greece, was the ancient Greek colony of **Cyrene**, now in modern-day Libya. Founded in 630 BC, Cyrene quickly rose to prominence among other Greek settlements on the African coast and was known for its temple to the Greek god Apollo. The city had a prominent Greek population and a Jewish minority. It became a Roman province in 74 BC.

Cyrene was known for its export of silphium, a plant that was pictured on many of its coins. Silphium's valuable resin, worth its weight in silver, was traded throughout the Mediterranean. Unfortunately, it was so popular in ancient times that it was harvested to extinction in the first century AD. Overgrazing by livestock, the inability to cultivate it, and desertification of the land may have also contributed to its disappearance. Silphium's identity is controversial, but most experts agree it was from the genus *Ferula*, a family of tough flowering plants related to carrot and parsley. Like other spices of the time, silphium was used as a seasoning and as a medicine. Fever, cough, indigestion, pain, and warts were all reportedly relieved by its healing properties. Silphium may also have been used as an early contraceptive or abortifacient (pregnancy-terminating drug), and it may be the origin of the traditional heart shape in connection with sexuality and love (its seeds were heart-shaped). The last known silphium from Cyrene was recorded to have been eaten by the Roman emperor Nero in the first century.

With Cyrene's primary local export gone and multiple earthquakes wreaking havoc, the city was deserted by the seventh century AD, despite efforts at restoration. All that remains today are ruins near the Libyan city of Shahhat.

CHAPTER 34

Crucifixion

34.1 To Golgotha

Matthew 27:31-34
Mark 15:20-23
Luke 23:26-33a
John 19:17

After they had mocked him, they took off the purple robe and put his clothes back on him. Then they lead him out carrying his own cross to crucify him. Two criminals were also led to be killed with him.

As they were coming out, they took someone passing by on his way in from the country (Simon from Cyrene, the father of Alexander and Rufus) and put the cross on him. Then they force him to carry it behind Jesus.

Many crowds of people were following him, with women wailing and lamenting for him. But Jesus turned to them and said, "Daughters of Jerusalem, don't cry for me. Instead, cry for yourselves and your children. Look, the days are coming when they'll say, 'Blessed are the barren, the wombs that never birthed, and the breasts that never nursed.' They'll tell the mountains, 'Fall on us,' and the hills, 'Cover us.'[a] Because if they do this when the tree is green, what'll happen when it's dry?"

Golgotha

Golgotha is derived from the Hebrew or Aramaic term for "skull place." The Latin equivalent is *Calvaria*, where the term "Calvary" comes from. Presumably, *Golgotha* was where the vertical stakes of crosses for crucifixion were permanently located, while horizontal crossbeams were temporarily affixed (with the victim nailed to it) for executions as they arose. Its exact location is unknown, but tradition holds that it was on a hill just west of Jerusalem, beside major highways. Archeologists have discovered evidence of an abandoned rock quarry from the first century in the same area, with tombs cut into the bottom of the cliff faces. The name *Golgotha* may also originate from an outcropping of rock shaped like a skull, or simply from the numerous executions that occurred there and abandoned skulls that could potentially be found. It may also refer to the buried bones of a cemetery nearby. Rome had a similar location reserved for executions just outside its Porta Esquilina.

So they bring him to a place called *Golgotha*, which means "Skull Place" in Hebrew. And they tried to give him wine mixed with myrrh,[b] but after tasting it, he wouldn't drink any.

34.2 CRUCIFIXION

Matthew 27:35-44
Mark 15:24-27, 29-32
Luke 23:33b-43
John 19:18-25a

They crucify him at the third hour.[c] But Jesus said, "Father, forgive them. They don't know what they're doing."

Two thieves[d] are also crucified with him, one on his right and one on his left, with Jesus in between.

After they had crucified Jesus, the soldiers took his coat and made four parts – one part for each soldier. However, the shirt was seamless, woven from one piece, so they said to each other, "Let's not tear it, but cast lots for whose it'll be."

A. *The high places of vanity – the sin of Israel – will be destroyed. Thorns and thistles will grow on their altars. Then they'll tell the mountains, "Cover us!" And the hills, "Fall on us!" – Hosea 10:8*

B. **Wine mixed with myrrh** may have been a primitive anesthetic. Some traditions hold that the women of Jerusalem gave this drink to victims of crucifixion to ease their pain. Mark records that the additive to wine was myrrh, while Matthew records that the additive was *chole*, meaning "bile" or "gall," possibly in reference to myrrh.

C. The **third hour** of the day was around nine o'clock in the morning.

D. Theft wasn't normally punishable by death under Roman law. It's possible that the **two thieves** crucified with Jesus were rebels or zealots. Barabbas was also a rebel that was labelled a thief.

Casting Lots

Casting lots was a popular form of gambling in the ancient Middle East. The Hebrew phrase for it, *yadad gowral*, directly translates to "throwing pebbles," but there is some discrepancy as to what the practice actually looked like. It may have been an early form of dice. Another theory is that various small objects (pebbles, pieces of wood, pottery shards) with their owners' names scratched onto them were placed into a container, and then upon shaking them together, a single object was drawn at random. However it occurred, casting lots was used throughout Israel's history to determine God's will. As Joshua was dividing up Canaan among Israel's twelve tribes, portions of land were assigned by lot. Years later, Israel's first king, Saul, was identified the same way. And the Old Testament prophet Jonah was chosen by lot to be thrown overboard to appease God and calm a fierce storm.

Lots are thrown into the lap, but every decision is from the LORD.

– Proverbs 16:33

So casting lots for who should take what, they divide his clothes among them. The soldiers did this to fulfill the Scripture, "They divided my coat among them and cast lots for my clothes."[e]

Pilate had written the charge against him, which read, "This is Jesus the Nazarene, King of the Jews." They put it above his head on the cross, then they sat down and guarded him as people stood there watching. Many Jews read the inscription, since the place Jesus was crucified was close to the city, and it was written in Hebrew, Latin, and Greek.

The High Priests had told Pilate, "Don't write, 'King of the Jews,' but that he said, 'I am the king of the Jews.'" But Pilate had answered, "I've written what I've written."

Passers-by blasphemed him, shaking their heads and saying, "Destroy the Temple and rebuild it in three days? Ha! If you're God's Son, come down from the cross and save yourself!"

The rulers – the High Priests, the elders, and the scribes – mocked him and scoffed at him among themselves the same way, saying, "He saved others, but he can't save himself. Is he the Christ, chosen by God, the king of Israel? Let him come down now so we can see and believe! He trusts God – he even said, 'I'm God's Son' – so now let God rescue him if he pleases."[f]

The soldiers mocked him too, coming up and offering him vinegar,[g] saying, "Save yourself, if you're the king of the Jews!"

E. *I can count all my bones. They look and stare at me. They divide my coat among them and cast lots for my clothes. – Psalm 22:17-18*

F. *Roll with the LORD. Let him rescue if he's pleased with him. – Psalm 22:8*

Even the thieves crucified with him insulted him the same way. One of the criminals hanging there was blaspheming him, saying, "Aren't you the Christ? Save yourself and us!"

But the other scolded him, saying, "Don't you fear God, since you're under the same judgment? It's the right thing for us – we're getting what we deserve for our actions. But this one has done nothing wrong."

Then he said, "Jesus, remember me when you come into your kingdom!"

"Truly I tell you," he replied, "you'll be with me in paradise today."

34.3 DEATH

Matthew 27:45-56
Mark 15:33-41
Luke 23:44-49
John 19:25b-30

At the sixth hour,[h] the whole land became dark until the ninth hour,

G. *Posca* was a common drink among the Roman army and lower civilian classes of the first century. It was a concoction of **vinegar**, water, and herbs. When batches of wine were improperly stored, bacteria fermented the ethanol (alcohol) into acetic acid (vinegar), thereby spoiling it. The term *posca* is Latin, but the Greek equivalent *oxos* comes from word for "sharp," referring to its pungent flavor. It's often translated as "vinegar" in the Bible.

H. The **sixth hour** of the day was at noon, while the **ninth hour** was around three o'clock in the afternoon.

Paradise

The Greek word *paradeisos* originates from the Persian word for "a wall around," referring to an enclosed park or orchard that was maintained for hunting parties. Tradition holds that when a Persian king wanted to honor someone, he invited him to join him in **paradise**, that is, in his private garden. The Hebrew *pardec* similarly means "park" or "garden" in the Old Testament, appearing in Scripture after Israel's exile, which suggests its adoption from the Persians. Paradise was later associated with Eden, the original garden for Adam and Eve. The word only appears three times in the New Testament:

1. Spoken by Jesus while on the cross, referring to the afterlife.
2. Recorded by Paul in a vision he had of being taken up into paradise, where he *"heard unspeakable words that were illegal for a man to say." (2 Corinthians 12:4)*
3. Recorded by John in his apocryphal book of Revelation, quoting Jesus telling the church of Ephesus, *"For whoever conquers, I'll let him eat from the tree of life, which is in God's paradise." (Revelation 2:7b)*

There's certainly discrepancy as to what paradise is in the spiritual sense. Some believe it's a utopia where virtuous souls wait before resurrection and entry into heaven, in contrast to *Sheol*, where the wicked go. Others believe it's simply another term for heaven. The theories about its definition abound.

because the sun failed.[i] Then around the ninth hour Jesus shouted with a loud voice, "*Eli, Eli, lama sabachthani?*" which translates to, "My God, my God, why have you abandoned me?"

When the bystanders heard it, some said, "Look, he's calling Elijah."

Standing by Jesus' cross were his mother, his mother's sister, Mary of Clopas,[j] and Mary Magdalene. When Jesus saw his mother and the disciple he loved standing there, he tells his mother, "Woman, look, your son!" Then he tells the disciple, "Look, your mother!" From then on the disciple took her as his own.

After this, knowing everything had been done, Jesus says, "I'm thirsty," to fulfill the Scripture.

A jar full of vinegar was there, so someone immediately ran and filled a sponge with the vinegar. Putting it on a hyssop[k] stick, they raised it to his mouth and gave him a drink.[l] But the rest said, "Let's see if

I. *Ekleipo* (Greek verb) means "**fail**" or "stop," and is where the English "eclipse" comes from. Astronomically, an eclipse is when an object in space temporarily obscures the view of another, either directly or by casting a shadow. A total solar eclipse is when the moon's complete shadow falls on the earth, blocking direct sunlight from reaching the earth's surface. Up to five partial solar eclipses occur annually, but because the moon's orbit is elliptical and tilted at five degrees to the earth's orbit around the sun, total solar eclipses are rare. They occur at the same place on earth about every 400 years, lasting up to seven minutes each time.

Both Matthew and Luke record darkness occurring at midday during Jesus' crucifixion. Whether this was due to a solar eclipse or some miraculous sign is uncertain.

J. In Greek, when speaking about a person as "of" another, it usually referred to a man being the "son of" another. For example, "Judas of James" meant "Judas, son of James." However, referring to a woman this way was different – "of" typically meant "wife of" rather than "daughter of." So "**Mary of Clopas**" was likely "Mary, wife of Clopas," rather than Clopas' daughter.

K. The minty shrub **hyssop** thrived throughout the warm, dry climates of Europe and the Middle East. It grew well in rocky terrain, even sprouting straight out of walls. Woody stems supported numerous straight branches, which bore thin leaves and purple flowers.

Israel used hyssop branches in various purification ceremonies in the Temple and to apply blood from the Passover lamb to their doorways. King David alluded to its cleansing properties in his repentant Psalm 51.

The Hebrew and Greek words for hyssop (*ezowb* and *hyssopos* respectively) may also have referred to a number of aromatic herbs in Palestine.

L. *Scorn has broken my heart so that I'm sick. I looked for sympathy, but none was there, and for comforters, but found none. They gave me poison as my food and they gave me vinegar to drink for my thirst. – Psalm 68:21-22*

Elijah will come and take him down and save him."

After Jesus drank the vinegar, he gave up a loud cry[m] again, saying, "Father, I set my spirit in your hands.[n] It's finished!"

After saying this, he bowed his head, exhaled, and gave up his spirit. Then look, the veil[o] of the Temple tore in two, from top to bottom. The earth shook and rocks split apart. Tombs opened up and many bodies of the holy were raised from their sleep. They came out of their tombs after his resurrection, went into the holy city, and were seen by many.

Now the centurion standing in front of him, and those guarding Jesus with him, saw the earthquake and how he had exhaled. When they saw what was happening, they were frightened and praised God, saying, "This man was certainly innocent. He truly was God's Son!"

All the crowds that had gathered for the event returned beating their chests when they saw what had happened. All his friends and the women, who had followed Jesus and ministered to him from when he was in Galilee, had also been watching this from far off. Among them were Mary Magdalene; Mary, the mother of Little James[p] and Joseph; the mother of Zebedee's sons; Salome; and many other women who came up to Jerusalem with him.

34.4 DEATH ENSURED

John 19:31-37

It was the preparation day for the Sabbath, a big preparation.[q] The Jews asked Pilate that their legs be broken so they could take the bodies

M. Crucifixion led to a slow death. Terrible pain led to difficulty breathing, which caused a gradual loss of consciousness that faded into death. Thus Jesus' **loud cry** and abrupt death would have been quite unusual.

N. *I set my spirit in your hands. You've ransomed me, LORD, God of truth. – Psalm 31:5*

O. Separating the Holy Place and the Holy of Holies in the Temple was a massive curtain, also referred to as a **veil**. Exodus records that Israel's Tabernacle, a large tent that functioned as the Temple on their journey from Egypt to Canaan, also had such a curtain. It was made of fine purple and red linen, with heavenly images woven into it. It hung across the inside of the Temple from golden hooks and poles. The curtain of Herod's Temple was presumably similar to the original curtain of the Tabernacle. The only person who could pass behind it into the Holy of Holies, where the presence of God was said to live, was the High Priest once a year after a week of purification rituals. There he would burn incense, offer sacrifices for himself and the rest of the nation, and receive whatever messages God had for his people.

P. *Iakobos micros* translates to "James the Less" or "**Little James.**" This is not likely the same James as either of Jesus' disciples or Jesus' brother.

away, that they wouldn't stay on the cross for the Sabbath. So the soldiers came and broke the first man's legs, and those of the other who was crucified with him. But coming to Jesus, they didn't break his legs when they saw that he was already dead. Then one of the soldiers stabbed his side with a spear, and blood and water[r] immediately came out.

The one who has seen this has witnessed it, and his witness is true. He knows he's telling the truth, so you can believe too. This happened to fulfill the Scripture, that "not one of his bones will be broken."[s] And another Scripture says again, "They'll look on the one they stabbed."[t]

Q. Preparation was made every sixth day of the week so no work would be done on the Sabbath. On the day before the Passover Sabbath, it was an exceptionally **big preparation**, due to the nature of the weeklong feast when all work was banned.

R. Pericardial and pleural effusions (fluid around the heart and lungs) caused by the strain of crucifixion or another disease process could be liberated with a puncture to the thorax, causing "**blood and water**" to flow out of the wound.

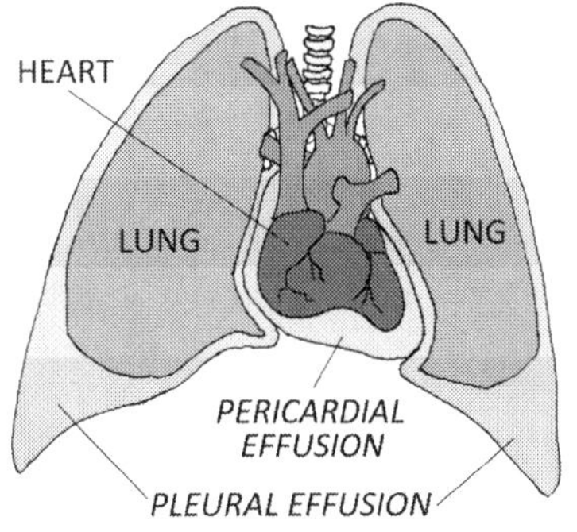

S. *They'll leave none [of the Passover lamb] until morning, nor break its bones, to act according to all the rules of the Passover. – Numbers 9:12*

The troubles of the righteous are many, but the LORD saves him from all of them. He keeps all his bones and not one is broken. – Psalm 34:20

T. *I'll pour out the spirit of grace and appealing on David's house and on those living in Jerusalem, so they'll look at me whom they've stabbed. They'll mourn for him, like mourning for a son, and they'll cry bitterly over him, like the bitter weeping over a firstborn. – Zechariah 12:10*

Psalm 22

No other Psalm is quoted more often in the New Testament than David's anguished **Psalm 22**. Jesus quoted the first verse of the original Hebrew as he hung from the cross. Since the Psalms were not numbered in the first century, it's possible that quoting the first line was a reference to the whole song.

My God, my God, why have you left me? The words I cry are far from my salvation. O my God, I call out by day, but you don't answer, and by night, but I don't have rest. Yet you are holy, you who are seated on Israel's praise. Our fathers trusted you – they trusted you and you saved them. They called out to you and were saved. They trusted you and weren't disappointed.

But I'm a worm not a man, the scorn of men and despised by people. All who see me mock me. They purse their lips and shake their head. "Roll[1] *with the* LORD*. Let him rescue if he's pleased with him."*

But you're the one who burst me from the womb, and you made me trust while on my mother's breasts. I've been thrown on you since birth; you've been my God since my mother's womb.

Don't be far from me, because trouble is near and there's no one to help. Many bulls have turned around me, strong ones from Bashan[2] *have surrounded me. They open their mouths wide like a ravenous roaring lion. I'm poured out like water and all my bones are separated. My heart is like wax, melted inside me. My strength is dried up like a clay pot and my tongue sticks to my jaw. You put me in the dirt of death. Dogs have turned around me, an assembly of evil has encircled me. They've pierced my hands and feet and I can count all my bones. They look and stare at me. They divide my coat among them and cast lots for my clothes.*

But you, LORD*, don't be far. O my strength, hurry to help me. Rescue my soul from the sword and my only [life] from the hand*[3] *of the dog. Save me from the lion's mouth. You answer me from the horns of aurochs.*[4]

I'll tell my brothers about your name and I'll praise you in the midst of the congregation. Praise the LORD*, you who fear him. Honor him, all Jacob's seed. Stay with him, all Israel's seed. Because he hasn't despised or detested the oppression of the poor. Nor has he hidden his face, but he heard when he called out.*

My praise in the great congregation comes from you and I'll fulfill my promises in front of those who fear him. The poor will eat and be satisfied and those who ask for him will praise the LORD*. May your heart live forever! All the ends of the earth will remember and return to the* LORD *and all the families of the nations will worship in front of you. Because the kingdom is the* LORD*'s and he rules nations. All the fat*[5] *on earth will eat and worship, and all who descend into the dirt will bow in front of him, even without a living soul. His seed will serve him and the Lord will be spoken of to the generations. They'll come and announce his righteousness to a people yet to be born, that he has done it.*

[1] The Hebrew word *galal* literally means "**roll**," often used in the Old Testament as the word to denote moving a large stone aside. However, it has also been translated as "commit" when entrusting plans or a person to God. This coincidentally aligns with the modern slang usage of roll: to "roll with the LORD" essentially means to be faithful to him.

[2] The Old Testament records that when Israel was entering Canaan, Og the king of **Bashan** marched his army out against them. Israel, however, annihilated him and his people and conquered his land. Bashan and all the territory east of the Jordan River was then renamed Gilead.

[3] *Yad* is the Hebrew word for "**hand**." As a symbol of strength, it also means "power."

[4] The **auroch** was a type of wild cattle that once lived across Europe and Asia. They are now extinct; the last one died in the 1600s. They looked similar to modern bulls, with a large muscular body and massive horns pointing forward. Many Bibles translate the Hebrew term *re'em* as "wild ox."

[5] In Hebrew, *dashen* means "**fat**." When referring to people, it can also mean "prosperous."

CHAPTER 35

Buried

35.1 BURIAL

Matthew 27:57-66
Mark 15:42-47
Luke 23:50-56
John 19:38-42

Joseph was a good and righteous man from the Jewish city of Arimathea[a] who was waiting for God's kingdom. He had become Jesus' disciple too, but secretly, out of fear of the Jews. He was also a rich man and a prominent councilor, but he hadn't voted for their plan and action. So after this, when evening came, he bravely went to Pilate and asked for Jesus' body, because it was the preparation before the Sabbath. Pilate wondered if he was dead by then, so he called the centurion and asked him if he had died. Learning of it from the centurion, he ordered the body given to Joseph.

The place of the crucifixion had a garden and the garden had his own new tomb, which he had cut into the rock. No one had ever been laid in it. Nicodemus, who had first come to [Jesus] at night, came too,

A. There is no record of a city named **Arimathea** outside the Bible. It may have been the town of Ramathaim-Zophim (also called Ramah or Ramatha) northwest of Jerusalem, which was known as the birthplace of the prophet Samuel.

bringing about 100 *litra*[b] mixture of myrrh and aloe.[c] So Joseph bought clean cloth, and they took him down and wrapped him in it with perfume, according to Jewish burial traditions. Then they took his body away. Because the tomb was so close and it was the Jewish preparation day and the Sabbath was dawning, they laid Jesus there and rolled a big stone over the opening of the tomb.[d] Then they left.

The women who had come with him from Galilee – Mary Magdalene and the other Mary (of Joses) – followed them and saw the tomb where his body was laid, and they sat across from the grave. Then the women went back and got ointments and perfumes ready, but they rested on the Sabbath, according to the commandment.

The next day, after the preparation, the High Priests and the Pharisees gathered with Pilate, saying, "Sir, we remember that while he was still alive, that deceiver said, 'After three days, I'll rise.' So order the grave secured until the third day or else his disciples might come, steal him, and tell the people he has risen from death. Then the last deception will be worse than the first!"

"You have guards," Pilate replied. "Go and secure it however you can."

So they went and secured the grave by sealing the stone and setting a guard.

B. **100 *litra*** was equal to about 35 kilograms (78 pounds). This was an enormous amount of balm, far beyond all normal proportions.

C. The ancient Greeks and Romans used a pulp from the succulent ***Aloe** vera* plant to treat wounds, while the Egyptians used it for embalming corpses.

D. *If a man has committed a sin deserving death and is killed and hung on a tree, his corpse won't stay on the tree. Certainly bury him the same day – because whoever is hung is cursed by God – so that you won't make your land unclean, which the LORD your God gave you as an inheritance. – Deuteronomy 21:22-23*

CHAPTER 36

The Tomb is Empty

36.1 WOMEN AT THE EMPTY TOMB

Matthew 28:1-8a
Mark 16:1-8a
Luke 24:1-8, 10a
John 20:1

After the Sabbath, Mary Magdalene, Joanna, Mary of James,[a] Salome,[b] and the other women brought the spices they had prepared to anoint him with. Very early in the morning on the first day of the week, as the sun is dawning, they come to look at the tomb. But they asked each other, "Who will roll the stone away from the entrance of the tomb for us?"

But look, a huge earthquake had occurred and an angel from the Lord had come down from heaven, rolled away the stone, and sat down on it. He looked like lightning and his clothes were white like snow. The guards were so scared that they shook and became like the dead.

Looking up, [the women] see the stone rolled away, even though it

A. **Mary of James** was likely the mother of "Little" James and Joses (Joseph).

B. **Salome** is traditionally identified as the mother of James and John, two of Jesus' disciples, but this relation is not mentioned in the Bible.

was very large. Then going into the tomb, they were baffled to not find the Lord Jesus' body. Look, instead they saw two young men (angels)[c] sitting to the right, wearing brilliant white clothing. The women were shocked and terrified, and they bowed with their faces on the ground. But they tell them, "Don't be so surprised and don't be scared! I know you're looking for Jesus the Nazarene who was crucified. But why are you looking for the living among the dead? He's not here. He has risen! Look, come see the place they laid him. Remember what he told you in Galilee, that the Son of Man had to be given into the power of wicked men and be crucified, but that he would rise on the third day. Now go quickly and tell Peter and his disciples that he has risen from death! Look, he's going to Galilee ahead of you and you'll see him there, just like he said. Look, I've told you!"

Then they remembered his words.

They quickly left the tomb and ran away, shaking from the joyful excitement and fear that had gripped them.

36.2 PETER AND JOHN AT EMPTY TOMB

Matthew 28:8b
Mark 16:8b
Luke 24:9, 10b-12
John 20:2-10

They run back from the tomb to tell his disciples and they come to Simon Peter and the other disciple Jesus loved. They were so afraid that they said nothing. But [Mary Magdalene] says, "They've taken the Lord out of the tomb and we don't know where they've put him!"

They were telling this to the apostles – the Eleven and all the rest – but their words sounded like nonsense[d] and they didn't believe them. But Peter and the other disciple got up, went out, and ran to the tomb. The two were running together, but the other disciple ran faster, ahead of Peter, and got to the tomb first. Looking in, he sees only the cloth lying there, but he didn't go inside. Then Simon Peter arrives after him, and, after entering the tomb, he sees the cloth lying there too. But the handkerchief that had been over his head was rolled up and lying alone

C. Mark, a youth (Greek *neaniskos*); Luke, two men; and John doesn't record what they initially saw in the open tomb, but later states that two angels were there. The different accounts are reconciled here as "...they saw **two young men (angels)** sitting...." In the Bible, angels often appeared in the form of men.

D. The only time the Greek word *leros* occurs in the Bible is in the context of confusing speech, translated here as "**nonsense**." *Leros* is the root of the English word "delirious."

in another place, not with the other cloth. Then the other disciple, who had arrived first, went in too and believed when he saw it. But they didn't understand the Scripture yet, that he had to rise from death. So the disciples went back to their homes wondering what had happened.

CHAPTER 37

Alive!

37.1 MARY AND MARTHA SEE JESUS

Matthew 28:9-10
John 20:11-18

Mary was standing outside the tomb weeping. Then looking inside, she sees two angels in white sitting where Jesus' body had been laid, one at the head and one at the feet. They ask her, "Woman, why are you crying?"

"Because they took my lord away," she replies, "and I don't know where they've put him."

Then look, Jesus met them:[a] after she had said this she turned around and saw Jesus standing there, but she didn't know it was him.

"Woman, why are you crying?" Jesus asks her. "Who are you looking for?"

Thinking he was a gardener,[b] she says, "Sir, if you've taken him, tell me where you've put him, so I can take him away."

A. Matthew records that **Jesus met "them,"** referring to the women who had visited the tomb early in the morning. John, however, records that Jesus only appeared to Mary.

B. Someone who tended or guarded gardens was a *kepouros* in Greek, derived from the words for "garden" (*kepos*) and "watcher" (*ouros*). It only occurs once in the Bible, used by John, and is translated here as "**gardener**."

Then Jesus says, "Mary!"

Upon turning, she says, "Rabboni!" (which in Hebrew means "Teacher") and they came and held onto his feet as they worshipped him.

"Don't hold on to me, because I haven't gone up to the Father yet," Jesus tells them. "Don't be afraid! Go, report to my brothers so they'll leave for Galilee. They'll see me there. Tell them, 'I go up to my Father and your Father, my God and your God.'"

So Mary Magdalene comes, announcing to the disciples, "I saw the Lord!" and that he had told her this.

37.2 SOLDIERS TOLD TO LIE

Matthew 28:11-15

While they were going, some of the guards went into the city and reported everything that had happened to the High Priests. When they gathered and consulted with the elders, they gave the soldiers enough money, telling them, "Say, 'His disciples came at night and took him away while we were asleep.' And to keep you from worrying, if this comes to the governor's ears, we'll persuade him otherwise."

So they took the money and did as they were told, and this story spread among the Jews, even up to today.[c]

37.3 TWO DISCIPLES TRAVEL WITH JESUS

Luke 24:13-35
1 Corinthians 15:5a

Look, that same day two of them were going to Emmaus, a village about 60 stadia from Jerusalem, talking with each other about everything that had happened. As they were talking and debating, Jesus came up and travelled with them, but their eyes didn't recognize him. He asked them, "What's this talk you're discussing with each other as you go?"

Then they stood still, looking sad. One of them, named Cleopas, answered him, "Are you the only one visiting Jerusalem who doesn't know what has happened these last few days?"

C. Matthew's Gospel was written sometime between 80 and 90 AD, so "**today**" refers to that time period, during the early years of the church.

The Town of Emmaus

The modern location of **Emmaus** isn't known, but the traditional site is the city of Emmaus-Nicopolis, 160 stadia (18 miles, 29 kilometers) west of Jerusalem and the site of a church founded by Cleopas. Although the city rose to prominence during the Hasmonean dynasty, it was burned by the Romans in 4 BC, around the time of Jesus' birth. Emmaus was later renamed Nicopolis under the Romans and Imwas under the Muslims, which is its current name. However, the distance of 160 stadia would have been nearly impossible to walk twice in one day, contrary to Luke's account.

Another possibility is the town of Colonia Amosa, 35 stadia (4 miles, 6.5 kilometers) west of Jerusalem, along the road to Imwas. Its name is derived from the Latin word for "colony," where 800 Roman soldiers settled to live after the First Jewish Revolt (66-73 AD). The town was close to the ruins of Bet Mizza, prompting it to be called Mozah, but its modern name of Qalunya is derived from its Roman name.

Yet another possible Emmaus is the town of El-Kubeibeh ("little dome"), **60 stadia** (7 miles, 11 kilometers) northwest of Jerusalem, where Crusaders built a church centuries later.

"What?" he asked.

"Everything about Jesus the Nazarene," they replied. "He was a powerful prophet in action and speech before God and all the people. The High Priests and our leaders gave him over to be sentenced to death and crucified. We had hoped it was he who would free Israel. But apart from all this, it's the third day since this has happened. However, some of our women amazed us earlier when they didn't find his body at the tomb. They came and said they'd also seen a vision of angels, who said he was alive! Some of those with us went to the tomb and found it just like the women said, but they didn't see them."

"O you foolish men," he told them, "slow to believe in your heart everything that the prophets have said! Didn't the Messiah need to suffer this way and then go into his glory?"

So starting with Moses and all the prophets, he explained the things in the Scriptures regarding himself. Then, approaching the village they were going to, he seemed like he was going farther, but they begged him, saying, "Stay with us! It's almost evening and the day is ending."

So he went in to stay with them. After he had laid back with them, he took bread, blessed it, broke it, and gave it to them. Then their eyes opened and they recognized him. But he disappeared from them! They said to each other, "Weren't our hearts burning inside us while he spoke to us on the road, as he explained the Scriptures to us?"

Then they got up at that hour and went back to Jerusalem. They found the Eleven gathered, and those with them, who said, "The Lord really has risen! He appeared to Simon (Cephas)!"

Then they described what had happened on the road and how they had recognized him while breaking bread.

37.4 DISCIPLES VISITED

Luke 24:36-43
John 20:19-23

It was the evening of that day, the first of the week, and the doors were shut for fear of the Jews. While they were saying this, Jesus came and stood there among the disciples. "Peace to you," he tells them.

But they were startled and became afraid, thinking they were seeing a ghost. "Why are you upset?" he said. "Why are doubts coming up in your hearts? Look at my hands and feet. It's me! Touch me and see. A ghost doesn't have flesh and bones like you see that I have."

So after he said this, he showed them his hands, his feet, and his side. But because of their joy and surprise, they still couldn't believe. So he said, "Do you have anything here to eat?"

They gave him some cooked fish, and he took it and ate in front of them. Then the disciples celebrated when they saw the Lord. Jesus told them again, "Peace to you. Just like the Father sent me, I send you too."

After he said this, he blew on them. "Receive the Holy Spirit," he says. "If you forgive anyone's sins, they've been forgiven. If you hold on to them, they've been held."

37.5 DISCIPLES VISITED, WITH THOMAS

John 20:24-31
1 Corinthians 15:5b

One of the Twelve, Thomas, called Didymus, wasn't with the other disciples when Jesus came. But when they told him, "We've seen the Lord!" he said, "I won't believe unless I see and put my finger on the nail marks on his hands and put my hand on his side."

Eight days later, his disciples were inside again and Thomas was with them. Then, with the doors shut, Jesus comes. He stood there among them and said, "Peace to you."

Then he tells Thomas, "Reach your finger here and look at my hands. Reach your hand here and put it on my side. Don't be faithless but faithful!"

"My Lord and my God!" Thomas answered.

"Have you believed because you've seen me?" Jesus replies. "Blessed are those who have believed without seeing me."

There are many other miracles that Jesus did before the disciples which aren't written in this book. However, this has been written so you can believe that Jesus is the Christ, God's Son, and that you can have life in his name by believing.[d]

37.6 APPEARANCE WHILE FISHING | PETER'S SECOND CONFESSION

John 21:1-24

After this, Jesus showed himself to the disciples again at the Tiberias Sea. This is how: Simon Peter; Thomas, called Didymus; Nathaniel, from Cana in Galilee; those of Zebedee;[e] and another two of his disciples were together. Simon Peter tells them, "I'm going fishing."

"We'll go with you too," they reply.

So they went and got in the boat, but they caught nothing that night. As it was becoming morning, Jesus was standing on the beach, but the disciples didn't know it was him. So Jesus asks them, "Children, don't you have anything to eat?"

"No," they answered.

Then he said, "Throw your net on the right[f] side of the boat and you'll find some."

So they threw it out, but then they couldn't pull it in because of the multitude of fish. Then the disciple Jesus loved tells Peter, "It's the Lord!"

When Simon Peter heard that it was the Lord, he put on his coat (he was bare) and threw himself into the sea. However, the other disciples came in the boat, dragging the net of fish, because they weren't far from land, about 200 cubits.[g]

D. *If you confess with your mouth that Jesus is Lord and believe in your heart that God raised him from death, you'll be saved; because the heart believes, for righteousness, and the mouth confesses, for salvation. – Romans 10:9-10*

E. James and John were the sons of Zebedee, that is, **those of Zebedee**.

F. *Dexios* is the Greek word for "**right**," in the directional sense, as the opposite of left. It doesn't have the same double meaning as the English "right," which can also mean morally correct. A more accurate translation of *dexios* in the context of a boat may be "starboard."

G. Since 1 cubit was about 18 inches long, **200 cubits** was a distance of about 100 yards.

When they got to land, they see a charcoal fire[h] laid out with fish and bread over them. Then Jesus tells them, "Bring some of the fish you've just caught."

Simon Peter went out and pulled the net to land, full of 153 big fish. But even with so many, the net didn't rip.

"Come, have breakfast," Jesus tells them.

None of the disciples dared to ask him, "Who are you?" knowing it was the Lord. Then Jesus comes, takes bread, and gives it to them, with fish likewise. This was already the third time that Jesus was shown to the disciples after being raised from death.

After they had breakfast, Jesus asks Simon Peter, "Simon of John, do you love me more than this?"

"Yes, Lord," he replies, "you know I love you."

So he says, "Feed my lambs."

Then he asks him again, for the second time, "Simon of John, do you love me?"

H. *Anthrakia* (Greek noun) refers to a pile of burning coals, translated here as "**charcoal fire**." Of all the Gospel writers, only John uses this word, and only twice in the whole Bible. The first occurrence is when Peter denied knowing Jesus in the High Priest's courtyard (page 274); the second is here, when Peter confessed his love and devotion for Jesus. In both scenes, Peter is standing around a charcoal fire.

Four Words for Love

The Greeks had four words that translate to "**love**" in English, each with a different meaning:

1. *Agape* refers to deep, genuine love or charity. It's active, unconditional, selfless, and sacrificial. *Agape* is used to describe feelings towards one's children and spouse, as well as God's love for mankind. It's by far the most commonly used word for "love" in the Bible. In fact, the Gospel writer John states in one of his letters that *"God is love (agape)." (1 John 4:8)*
2. *Eros* refers to passionate, sensual desire and intimacy. It's not necessarily sexual, but it's most often used in the context of romance and typically denotes attraction of some sort. *Eros* is the root of the English "erotic." It occurs often in ancient Greek literature and is the name of the Greek god for sexual love (also known as Cupid to the Romans). However, *eros* isn't mentioned in the Bible.
3. *Phileo* refers to deep friendship. It describes the warmth, loyalty, and affection towards friends, family, and community. It occurs often in Greek literature and the Bible.
4. *Storge* refers to natural affection, particularly describing a parent's feelings towards children. It's the least common of the four, predominantly used within the context of family relationships. *Storge* isn't mentioned in the Bible, but its opposite, *astorgos* ("without natural affection"), occurs twice. Additionally, *storge* occurs in Paul's letter to the Romans in combination with *phileo* as *philostorgos* ("tender love", Romans 12:10).

In the passage about Peter's confession of Christ on the beach, Jesus' first two questions to Peter use the word *agape*, while Jesus' final question and all of Peter's responses use *phileo*.

"Yes, Lord," he replies, "you know I love you."

So he says, "Take care of my sheep."

He asks him a third time, "Simon of John, do you love me?"

Peter became sad because he asked, "Do you love me?" a third time. "Lord," he said, "you know everything. You know I love you."

So Jesus says, "Feed my sheep. Truly truly, I tell you that when you were younger, you dressed yourself and walked wherever you wanted. But when you get old, you'll reach out your hands for someone else to dress you and bring you where you don't want to go."

He said this to show the kind of death he would glorify God with.[i] Then after saying this, he told him, "Follow me!"

Turning around, Peter sees the disciple Jesus loved following, the one who had also leaned back on his chest at dinner and asked, "Lord, who's your betrayer?" Seeing him, Peter says, "Lord, what about him?"

"If I want him to wait until I come, what's it to you?" Jesus answers. "You, follow me!"

So this word went around throughout the brothers that this disciple wouldn't die. But Jesus didn't tell him he wouldn't die, but that, "If I want him to wait until I come, what's it to you?"

This is the disciple witnessing to this, who wrote this down, and we know his witness is true.

37.7 APPEARANCE IN GALILEE

Matthew 28:16-20
1 Corinthians 15:6-7

The eleven disciples went to Galilee, to the mountain Jesus had set, and worshipped him when they saw him there. But some doubted. Then Jesus came and spoke to them, saying, "I've been given all power in heaven and on earth. So go and make disciples from every nation, baptizing them in the name of the Father, the Son, and the Holy Spirit, and teaching them to keep everything I've commanded you. And look,

I. Church tradition holds that **Peter was executed** in 64 AD, during a time of great persecution against Christians. The story goes that Peter was in the process of escaping Rome when he saw Jesus walking back into the city. Peter asked him where he was going, to which Jesus replied, "I've come to be crucified again." Peter understood this to mean his suffering, so he returned to the city and was subsequently crucified. But because he considered himself unworthy to be killed the same way that Jesus was, he insisted on being crucified upside down on the cross.

I'm with you every day, even to the end of time."

After that, he appeared to over five hundred brothers at once, many of whom remain until now,[j] but some are asleep. Then he appeared to James, and then all the apostles.

37.8 ASCENSION

Luke 24:44-53
Acts 1:3-12

After his suffering, he showed himself alive, appearing to them with much proof over forty days and speaking about God's kingdom. Then gathering them together, he said, "These words that I spoke while I was still with you are mine, that everything written about me in Moses' Law, the prophets, and the Psalms must be completed."

Then he opened their minds to understand the Scriptures and told them, "It's written that the Christ would suffer and rise from death on the third day,[k] and that repenting for the forgiveness of sins would be announced in his name to every nation,[l] starting in Jerusalem. You're witnesses of this. Look, I'm sending out my Father's promise on you. But stay in the city until you're dressed with power from on high."

So he commanded them not to leave Jerusalem. "Wait for the Father's promise, which you heard from me. John baptized in water, but you'll be baptized in the Holy Spirit before many days."

Then he led them out until Bethany. When they had come together, they asked him, "Lord, are you restoring the kingdom of Israel at this time?"

"It's not for you to know the times or the seasons the Father has set by his own control," he replied. "But you'll receive power when the Holy Spirit comes upon you. You'll be my witnesses both in Jerusalem and all of Judea and Samaria, and even to the end of the earth."

After he said this, he raised his hands and blessed them. As he was

J. Paul the Apostle wrote a letter to the church of Corinth in Greece around 55 AD during his time in Ephesus, which became the New Testament book of 1 Corinthians. Thus "**now**" in Paul's letter is about 25 years after Jesus' death.

K. The Old Testament doesn't explicitly state that "**the Christ would suffer and rise from death on the third day**." However, it does state that the Messiah would suffer and that he would live forever (Isaiah 53).

L. Similarly, there is no explicit claim in the Old Testament that "**repenting for the forgiveness of sins would be announced in his name to every nation**," but there are multiple passages describing God's plan of salvation for the nations (Psalm 67:2-3; Isaiah 49:6).

blessing them, he left for heaven, being lifted up as they watched, until a cloud took him out of sight. While they were staring at the sky as he was leaving, two men in white clothes stood there beside them, saying, "Men of Galilee, why are you standing here staring at the sky? This Jesus, taken from you to heaven, will come the same way that you saw him go to heaven."

So after worshiping him, they returned from the mountain called Olive, which is near Jerusalem, a Sabbath's journey away.[m] They returned to Jerusalem with great joy, praising God in the Temple all the time.

M. Based on Old Testament passages about the restriction of work on the Sabbath, a **Sabbath's journey** was no more than 2000 cubits (1000 yards, ½ mile, 0.9 kilometers).

Omitted Passages

Many ancient manuscripts of the New Testament have been found, but all are copies of the original documents that make up the complete New Testament canon. The very oldest manuscripts are considered the most accurate, and logically so – the more times a text has been copied, the greater its chance of containing errors. In fact, few manuscripts found to date are exactly the same. The bulk of differences are clerical errors in grammar or spelling that are easily reconciled. However, some major differences are the addition of certain words or passages. Since some newer manuscripts contain text that the oldest ones do not, it suggests that that text wasn't a part of the original document, but was added later. These portions of Scripture are typically denoted by large square brackets in most Bibles – [ ] – but tend to be **omitted** in *THE STORY OF JESUS*.

One of the largest and most popular of these "extra" passages is the ending of Mark's Gospel, which describes Jesus' post-resurrection appearances, similar to the other Gospels. It also includes Jesus' famous Great Commission, unique to Mark, which is not a part of the earliest New Testament manuscripts.

Go into all the world and preach the good news to all creation. Whoever has believed and has been baptized will be saved, but whoever has not believed will be condemned. These signs will follow the believers: they'll throw out demons in my name; speak with new tongues; pick up snakes; and if they drink death, it won't hurt them. They'll lay hands upon the unwell and they'll get better.

– Mark 16:15-18

CHAPTER 38

The Birth of the Church

38.1 DISCIPLES GATHER | JUDAS REPLACED

John 21:25
Acts 1:1-2, 13-17, 20-26

Theophilus,[a] the first account I wrote was about everything Jesus did and taught until the day he was taken up, after he had commanded his chosen apostles by the Holy Spirit. There's also much more that Jesus did, but if it's written as one, I think the whole world wouldn't be able to contain the books written.

When they returned, they went up to the room upstairs where they were living. They were: Peter, John, James, and Andrew; Philip and Thomas; Bartholomew and Mathew; James of Alphaeus, Simon the Zealot, and Judas of James. They all had the same passion,[b] devoted to prayer, along with the women, Jesus' mother Mary, and his brothers.

In those days, Peter stood up among the brothers – a crowd of 120 people was there with them – saying, "Brothers, the Scriptures had to

A. Similar to his first book, Luke begins Acts with an introduction addressed to someone named **Theophilus**.

B. *Homothymadon* is the combination of the Greek words *homo* ("same," "together") and *thymos* ("passion," "anger"), translated here as "having the **same passion**." It's used almost exclusively in the book of Acts to convey a sense of unified fervent action.

be fulfilled, which the Holy Spirit predicted by David's mouth about Judas, who became a guide to Jesus' captors. He was counted as one of us and had his part in this ministry. It's written in the book of Psalms, 'Let his home become deserted and let nobody live in it,'[c] and, 'Let another take his position.'[d] So one of the men who has been with us for all the time the Lord Jesus went in and out among us – starting with John's baptism until the day he was lifted up from us – one of them must become a witness of his resurrection with us."

So they put two forward: Joseph (called Barsabbas[e] and also called Justus) and Matthias. Then they prayed, "Lord, you know everyone's heart. Show us which of these two you've chosen to take Judas' place in this ministry and apostleship, which he passed up to go to his own place."

They drew lots for them and the lot fell to Matthias, so he was voted to the eleven apostles.

38.2 HOLY SPIRIT COMES | PETER PREACHES

Acts 2:1-36

When the day of Pentecost[f] came, they were all together by themselves. Suddenly, a sound came from heaven like a fierce wind blowing that filled the whole house where they were seated. Then fiery tongues appeared and divided to sit on every one of them. They were filled with the Holy Spirit and spoke with other tongues, as the Spirit gave them speech.

Other Jews were living in Jerusalem then, devoted men from every nation under heaven. When this sound occurred, a crowd gathered, confused, because everyone was hearing them speak in their own language.[g] They were surprised and amazed, saying, "Look, aren't they

---

C. *May their camp be deserted and may no one live in their tents. – Psalm 69:25*

D. *Let his days be few. Let another take his position. – Psalm 109:8*

E. **Barsabbas** is a Hebrew name meaning "son of the Sabbath."

F. Fifty days after the Passover, on the first day of the eighth week, the Jews celebrated the harvest during the Feast of Weeks, also called *Shavuot* (Hebrew for "weeks"). The Greek name for this day was **Pentecost**, meaning "fiftieth." This festival celebrated the anniversary of God's gift of the Torah (Moses' Law) to Israel while on their journey through the desert to Canaan.

You'll count from the day after the Sabbath, from the day you brought in the wave [offering], there will be seven whole Sabbaths. You'll count fifty days after the seventh Sabbath, then you'll offer a new grain [offering] to the LORD. – Leviticus 23:15-16

G. *He'll certainly speak to this people through stuttering lips and another tongue. – Isaiah 28:11*

all Galileans who are speaking? How does each of us hear them in the language we were born into? Parthians, Medes and Elamites; residents of Mesopotamia, Judea and Cappadocia, Pontus and Asia, Phrygia and Pamphylia, Egypt and the regions of Libya around Cyrene; visitors from Rome, both Jews and converts; Cretans and Arabs. We hear them talking about God's magnificence in our own tongues!"

They were all amazed and dumbfounded. They kept asking each other, "What does this mean?" But others were mocking them, saying, "They're full of juice."[h]

But Peter stood with the Eleven and raised his voice, announcing to them, "Men of Judea and all of you living in Jerusalem, give ear[i] to my words and know this: these men aren't drunk, like you assume. It's the third hour[j] of the day! But this was said through Joel the prophet:

> 'It'll be in the last days,' God says, 'that I'll pour out my Spirit on everybody. Your sons and daughters will prophesy, your youths will see visions, and your elders will dream dreams. I'll even pour out my Spirit on my slaves in those days – both slaves and maids – and they'll prophesy. I'll give wonders in the heavens above and signs on the earth below – blood, fire, and the haze of smoke. The sun will be changed into darkness, and the moon into blood, before the great and glorious day that the Lord comes. And it'll happen that all who call on the name of the Lord will be saved.'[k]

"Men of Israel, listen to these words: Jesus the Nazarene – a man God proved to you with miracles, wonders, and signs, which God did through him among you, as you know – he was given according to God's purpose and knowledge beforehand. You nailed him by the hands of the lawless and killed him. But God raised him, ending the agony[l] of death, because it wasn't strong enough to hold him under it. David

H. Freshly trodden grapes produced **juice**, which could be fermented to produce wine. This unfermented (non-alcoholic) juice was denoted by the Greek *gleukos*, derived from *glykys*, meaning "sweet." This passage contains the only occurrence of *gleukos* in the Bible.

I. *Enotizomai* only occurs once in the Bible. It's a verb formed by combining the Greek preposition *en* ("in," "with") and *ous* ("ear"). It could be translated "**give ear to**," "lend your ears," or simply "hear."

J. The **third hour** was mid-morning, around nine o'clock.

K. *It'll come after this that I'll pour my Spirit on everybody. Your sons and daughters will prophesy, your elders will dream dreams, and your youths will see visions. I'll even pour out my Spirit on the slaves and maids in those days. I'll show wonders in the heavens and on the earth – blood, fire, and columns of smoke. The sun will change into darkness and the moon into blood before the great and fearful day the LORD comes. And it'll be that all who call on the name of the LORD will be saved. – Joel 2:28-32*

Nations Surrounding Jerusalem

In the book of Acts, Luke lists religious pilgrims from many nations, having travelled to Jerusalem ("J" on the map) from virtually every direction around it.

1. **Parthian Empire**: a rival empire to Rome northeast of Judea, beyond the Tigris and Euphrates Rivers; now modern-day Iran.
2. **Media**: northern Persia, south of the Caspian Sea.
3. **Elam**: southern Persia, north of the Persian Gulf; centered on its capital city, Susa.
4. **Mesopotamia**: "land between the rivers," the fertile flood plains of the Tigris and Euphrates.
5. **Judea**: a Roman province whose capital was Jerusalem, but much of the territory lay south of the city.
6. **Cappadocia**: the arid, mountainous land occupying much of modern-day central Turkey.
7. **Pontus**: southern coast of the Black Sea.
8. **Asia Minor**: the Anatolian peninsula, particularly the western portion, which was the land between the Black Sea (north), Aegean Sea (west), and Mediterranean Sea (south).
9. **Phrygia**: central Anatolia, around the Sakarya River.
10. **Pamphylia**: southern Anatolia, along the northern Mediterranean coast.
11. **Egypt**: northeast African nation, centered on the Nile River.
12. **Cyrene**: Greek colony in northern Africa, on the Mediterranean coast of modern-day Libya.
13. **Rome**: central Italian city, capital of the Roman Empire.
14. **Crete**: an island in the Mediterranean, south of Greece; once the center of the Minoan civilization.
15. **Arabian Peninsula**: the desert southeast of Jerusalem, bordered by the Red Sea (west), Indian Ocean (south), Persian Gulf (east).

Jews from all these nations, and possibly more, were living in or visiting Jerusalem at the time. In addition to Aramaic (from their Jewish homeland) and Greek (common to much of the world), they would have also spoken languages native to their respective nations.

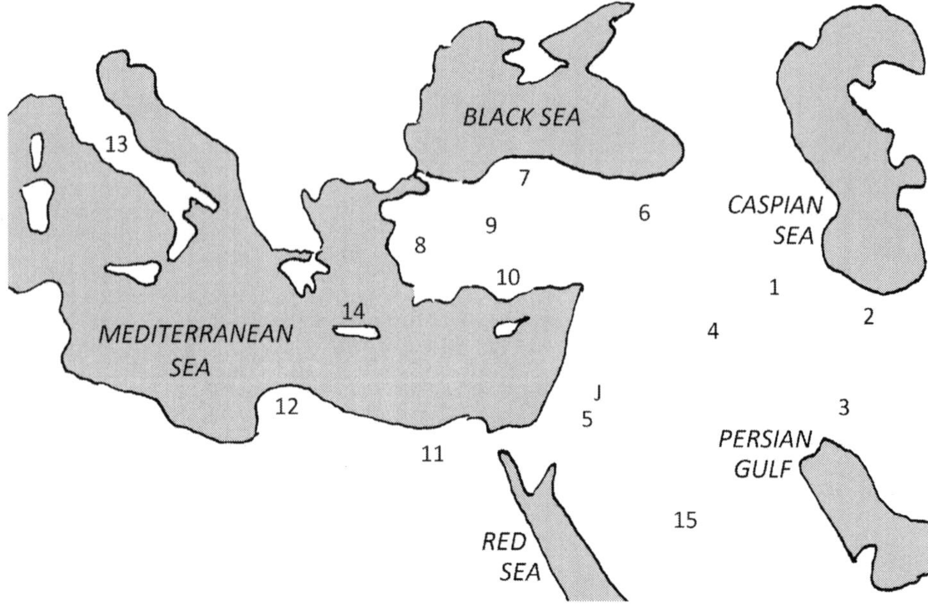

spoke about him:

> 'I saw the Lord with me through it all, because he's at my right hand, so I won't be shaken. So my heart was happy and my tongue overjoyed! And even more, my body will live in hope as well, because you won't abandon my soul to hell, nor let your holy one see decay. You've shown me the ways of life and you'll fill me with happiness with your face.'[m]

"Brothers, I can tell you freely about David the patriarch: he died and was buried, and his tomb is with us to this day. But because he was a prophet and knew that God had sworn a promise to him, to seat the fruit of his loins on his throne,[n] he saw beforehand and spoke of the Christ's resurrection, that he wasn't abandoned to hell, nor did his body see decay. God has risen up this Jesus, which we're all witnesses to! So being raised up to the right side of God, and receiving the promised Holy Spirit from the Father, he poured this out, which you see and hear. Because it wasn't David who rose up to heaven, but he says,

> 'The Lord said to my Lord, "Sit at my right until I make your enemies a footrest for your feet."'[o]

So, all of Israel's house, know for sure that God made him both Lord and Christ, this Jesus, whom you crucified."

38.3 CHURCH EXPANDS

Acts 2:37-47

They were cut to the heart as they listened. They asked Peter and the rest of the apostles, "Brothers, what should we do?"

"Repent and be baptized, each of you, in the name of Jesus Christ for the forgiveness of sins," Peter replied. "Then you'll receive the gift

---

L. *Odyne* is Greek for "overwhelming grief" or "**agony**." The related word used here, *odin*, refers specifically to the pain experienced during childbirth.

M. *I've set the LORD continually before me. I won't be shaken because he's at my right hand. So my heart is happy and my glory celebrates. My body will live safely too, because you won't abandon my soul to the grave, nor will you put your holy one in a pit. You've made me know the path of life. The fullness of joy is in your face and your right hand has pleasure forever. – Psalm 16:8-11*

N. *The LORD swore a truth to David, which he won't return from: "I'll put the fruit of your belly on your throne. If your sons keep my covenant and my testimony, which I'll teach them, then their sons will sit also on your throne forever." – Psalm 132:11-12*

O. *The LORD says to my Lord, "Sit at my right hand until I make your enemies a stool for your feet." – Psalm 110:1*

of the Holy Spirit. The promise is for you, your children, and all who are far away, however many the Lord our God will call."

With many other words he testified and called to them, saying, "Be saved from this crooked generation!"

Then those who received his words were baptized and about three thousand souls were added that day. They were devoting themselves to the apostles' teaching and the community, and to breaking bread and prayer.

Fear was in everyone, and many wonders and signs happened through the apostles. All who believed were together and held everything commonly; they sold their land and possessions to share among them all, as anyone might have need. They devoted themselves with the same passion daily in the Temple. And they had meals together, happily breaking bread throughout the houses with simple hearts, while praising God and finding favor with all people. And the Lord was daily adding to those who were saved.

[The Son] is the image of the invisible God and the firstborn of all creation. Everything was created by him, in heaven and on earth, visible and invisible. Whether thrones, lordships, leaders, or powers, everything was created through him and for him. He's before everything and everything is held together in him. He's also the head of the body, the church. And he's the beginning, the firstborn from death, so he'll come to have the first place in everything. Because it was his good idea for all fullness to live in him and to transfer everything back to himself, having made peace through the blood of his cross and through [God], whether this on earth or that in heaven.

– Colossians 1:15-20

APPENDIX A

Chronology of the Gospels

CH.	PG.	PASSAGE	MATT	MARK	LUKE	JOHN
1.1	15	Luke's purpose	-	1:1	1:1-4	-
1.2	16	John's prologue: the "word"	-	-	-	1:1-18
1.3	17	Jesus' genealogy	1:1-17	-	3:23b-38	-
2.1	23	John's birth foretold to Zacharias	-	-	1:5-25	-
2.2	25	Jesus' birth foretold to Mary	-	-	1:26-38	-
2.3	26	Mary visits Elizabeth	-	-	1:39-56	-
2.4	27	John's birth	-	-	1:57-80	-
3.1	31	Joseph's dream	1:18-25	-	-	-
3.2	32	Jesus' birth	-	-	2:1-20	-
3.3	34	Jesus presented at the Temple	-	-	2:21-39	-
3.4	36	Magi visit	2:1-23	-	2:40	-
3.5	39	Passover in Jerusalem	-	-	2:41-52	-
4.1	41	John's ministry	3:1-12	1:2-8	3:1-18	-
5.1	45	Jesus' baptism	3:13-17	1:9-11	3:21-23a	-
5.2	46	Temptation in the wilderness	4:1-11	1:12-13	4:1-13	-
5.3	47	John's testimony	-	-	-	1:19-34
5.4	48	First disciples	-	-	-	1:35-51
5.5	50	First miracle: water to wine	-	-	-	2:1-12
5.6	51	Jesus greater than John	-	-	-	3:22-36
5.7	52	Samaritan woman	4:12	1:14a	3:19-20	4:1-42
6.1	57	Return to Galilee	4:17	1:14b-15	4:14-15	4:43-45
6.2	58	Capernaum child healed from Cana	-	-	-	4:46-54
6.3	59	Rejection in Nazareth	-	-	4:16-30	-
6.4	60	Travel to Capernaum	4:13-16	-	4:31a	-
7.1	63	Four disciples called	4:18-22	1:16-20	5:1-11	-
7.2	65	Demonized man healed	-	1:21-28	4:31b-37	-
7.3	65	Peter's mother-in-law healed	8:14-17	1:29-34	4:38-41	-

CH.	PG.	PASSAGE	MATT	MARK	LUKE	JOHN
7.4	66	Travel and healing through Galilee	4:23-25	1:35-39	4:42-44	-
7.5	67	Leper healed	8:2-4	1:40-45	5:12-16	-
7.6	68	Paralytic healed	9:1-8	2:1-12	5:17-26	-
7.7	69	Matthew called	9:9-13	2:13-17	5:27-32	-
7.8	71	Feasting vs. fasting	9:14-17	2:18-22	5:33-39	-
8.1	73	Cripple healed on the Sabbath	-	-	-	5:1-3a, 5-47
8.2	77	Picking grain on the Sabbath	12:1-8	2:23-28	6:1-5	-
8.3	78	Hand healed on the Sabbath	12:9-21	3:1-12	6:6-11	-
9.1	81	Twelve apostles chosen; blessings and woes	5:1-12 10:2-4	3:13-19	6:12-26	-
9.2	83	Interpretations of the Law	5:13-24, 27-48 6:22-23	9:49-50 14:34-35	6:27-36 11:33-36 16:16-18	-
9.3	87	Religious hypocrisy	6:1-8, 16-18	-	-	-
9.4	88	True treasure; judgment	6:19-21 7:1-6	-	6:37-42	-
9.5	89	Narrow road; false prophets; obedience	7:13-29 8:1	-	6:43-44, 46-49	-
10.1	91	Centurion's servant healed	8:5-13	-	7:1-10	-
10.2	93	Widow's son resurrected		-	7:11-17	-
10.3	93	John's questions	11:2-19	-	7:18-35	-
10.4	95	Woe to Chorazin and Bethsaida	11:20-30	-	10:13-15	-
10.5	97	Sinful woman anoints Jesus' feet	-	-	7:36-50	-
11.1	99	Women followers	-	-	8:1-3	-
11.2	99	Accusations and blasphemy	12:22-37, 43-45	3:20-30	6:45 11:14-15, 17-28 12:10	-
11.3	102	Sign requested	12:38-42	-	11:16, 29-32	-
11.4	103	Spiritual family	12:46-50	3:31-35	8:19-21	-
12.1	105	Parable of soils	13:1-23	4:1-20	8:4-18	-
12.2	107	Parables of seeds and yeast	13:24-35	4:26-34	13:18-21	-
12.3	109	Parable of seeds explained; more parables of the kingdom	13:36-53	-	-	-
13.1	111	Storm calmed	8:18, 23-27	4:35-41	8:22-25	-
13.2	112	Legion thrown out	8:28-34	5:1-20	8:26-39	-
13.3	115	Jairus' daughter and bleeding woman healed	9:18-26	5:21-43	8:40-56	-
13.4	117	Blind and others healed	9:27-34	-	-	-
13.5	118	Hometown disbelief	13:54-58	6:1-6a	-	-
14.1	119	Worker shortage	9:35-38	6:6b	-	-
14.2	119	Twelve sent out	10:1, 5-16, 23-42; 11:1	6:7-13	9:1-6 12:2-9, 49-53 14:25-33	-
14.3	122	John executed by	14:1-12	6:14-29	9:7-9	-
15.1	125	Five thousand fed	14:13-23	6:30-46	9:10-17	6:1-15
15.2	127	Walking on water	14:24-33	6:47-52	-	6:16-21
15.3	128	Bread of life	14:34-36	6:53-56	-	6:22-58
15.4	131	Some disciples leave	-	-	-	6:59-71
16.1	133	Outer vs. inner cleanliness	15:1-20	7:1-15, 17-23	-	7:1

CH.	PG.	PASSAGE	MATT	MARK	LUKE	JOHN
16.2	135	Phoenician girl healed	15:21-28	7:24-3	-	-
16.3	137	Healing in Decapolis	15:29-31	7:31-37	-	-
16.4	137	Four thousand fed	15:32-39a	8:1-9	-	-
16.5	138	Warning against hypocrisy	15:39b-16:12	8:10-21	12:1b	-
16.6	139	Blind man in Bethsaida healed	-	8:22-26	-	-
17.1	141	Peter's confession of Christ	16:13-20	8:27-30	9:18-21	-
17.2	143	Jesus predicts his death, first time	16:21-28	8:31-9:1	9:22-27	-
17.3	144	Meeting with Moses and Elijah	17:1-13	9:2-13	9:28-36	-
18.1	147	Moonstruck boy healed	17:14-20	9:14-29	9:37-43a	-
18.2	148	Jesus predicts his death, second time	17:22-23	9:30-32	9:43b-45	-
18.3	149	Paying the two drachmas	17:24-27	-	-	-
18.4	149	Greatness in the kingdom	18:1-10	9:33-43, 45, 47-48	9:46-50; 17:1-3a	-
18.5	151	Forgiveness	18:15-35	-	17:3b-4	-
19.1	155	Following Jesus	8:19-22	-	9:57-62	-
19.2	156	Discussion with Jesus' brothers	-	-	9:51-56	7:2-10
20.1	157	Arrival in Jerusalem	-	-	-	7:11-36
20.2	159	Unable to arrest Jesus	-	-	-	7:37-52
20.3	160	Forgiveness of immoral woman	-	-	-	7:53-8:11
20.4	161	Light of the world	-	-	-	8:12-30
20.5	162	Jesus and Abraham	-	-	-	8:31-59
20.6	164	Blind man healed, then testifies	-	-	-	9
20.7	167	Good shepherd	-	-	-	10:1-21
21.1	171	Seventy sent out	-	-	10:1-12, 16	-
21.2	172	Seventy return	-	-	10:17-24	-
21.3	173	Good Samaritan	-	-	10:25-37	-
21.4	175	Visit to Martha and Mary	-	-	10:38-42	-
21.5	175	Prayer	6:9-13a, 14-15 7:7-12	11:25	11:1-13	-
22.1	179	Greed and wealth	5:25-26 6:25-34	-	12:1a, 13-34, 54-59	-
22.2	181	Repent or die	-	-	13:1-9	-
22.3	183	Crippled woman healed	-	-	13:10-17	-
22.4	183	Unable to stone Jesus for blasphemy	-	-	-	10:22-39
23.1	187	Belief in Perea	-	-	-	10:40-42
23.2	187	Entering the kingdom	-	-	13:22-33	-
23.3	188	Swollen man healed; three parables	-	-	14:1-24	-
23.4	190	Lost and found	18:12-14	-	15	-
23.5	192	Sneaky manager; wealth	6:24	-	16:1-15, 19-31	-
23.6	194	Faith; servanthood	-	-	17:5-10	-
23.7	195	Lazarus resurrected	-	-	-	11:1-46
23.8	198	Sanhedrin decides to kill Jesus	-	-	-	11:47-54
24.1	201	Ten lepers healed	-	-	17:11-19	-
24.2	202	Parables on prayer	-	-	18:1-14	-
24.3	203	Divorce	19:1-12	10:1-12	-	-
24.4	205	Children in the kingdom	19:13-15	10:13-16	18:15-17	-
24.5	205	Wealth in the kingdom	19:16-30	10:17-31	18:18-30	-
24.6	208	Parable of the landlord's wages	20:1-16	-	-	-

CH.	PG.	PASSAGE	MATT	MARK	LUKE	JOHN
24.7	208	Jesus predicts his death, third time	20:17-19	10:32-34	18:31-34	-
24.8	209	Greatest must be servants	20:20-28	10:35-45	-	-
24.9	210	Zaccheus; using what's given to you	25:14-30	10:46a	19:1-28	-
24.10	212	Blind Bartimaeus healed	20:29-34	10:46b-52	18:35-43	-
25.1	213	Arrival at Bethany	-	-	-	2:13a 11:55-12:1 12:9-11
25.2	214	Entry into Jerusalem	21:1-11, 14-17	11:1-11	19:29-44	2:13b 12:12-19
25.3	217	Fig tree cursed; Temple purified	21:12-13, 18-19a	11:12-18	19:45-48	2:14-25
25.4	219	Fig tree withered	21:19b-22	11:19-24	21:37-38	-
25.5	219	Son of man must be "lifted up"	-	-	-	12:20-50
25.6	221	Nicodemus' questions	-	-	-	3:1-21
26.1	223	Authority questioned	21:23-32	11:27-33	20:1-8	-
26.2	224	Vineyard and evil gardeners	21:33-46	12:1-12	20:9-19	-
26.3	226	Wedding feast	22:1-14	-	-	-
26.4	226	Paying taxes to Caesar	22:15-22	12:13-17	20:20-26	-
26.5	227	Marriage after resurrection; greatest commandment	22:23-33, 35-40	12:18-34a	20:27-39	-
27.1	233	Messiah: the son of David and Lord	22:34, 41-46	12:34b-40	20:40-47	-
27.2	234	Woes to Pharisees	23:1-13, 15-39	-	11:37-54 13:34-35	-
28.1	239	God's kingdom is here; widow's gift	-	12:41-44	17:20-21 21:1-4	-
28.2	240	Future prophecies	10:17-22 24:1-31	13:1-27	12:11-12 17:22-35, 37 21:5-28	-
28.3	244	Signs of the end	24:32-36, 42-51	13:28-37	12:35-48 21:29-36	-
28.4	245	Ten virgins	25:1-13	-	-	-
28.5	246	Coming judgment	25:31-46	-	-	-
29.1	249	Jesus predicts his death, fourth time; the Sanhedrin plots	26:1-5	14:1-2	22:1-2	-
29.2	250	Mary anoints Jesus	26:6-13	14:3-9	-	12:2-8
29.3	250	Judas agrees to betray Jesus	26:14-16	14:10-11	22:3-6	-
30.1	253	Preparation for Passover	26:17-19	14:12-16	22:7-13	-
30.2	254	Disciples' feet washed	26:20	14:17	22:14-16	13:1-20
30.3	255	Greatness in the kingdom, again	-	-	22:24-30	-
30.4	255	Betrayal predicted	26:21-25	14:18-21	22:21-23	13:21-30
30.5	256	Bread and wine (*1 Corinthians 11:23b-25*)	26:26-29	14:22-25	22:17-20	13:31a
30.6	257	Peter's denial predicted	26:31-35	14:27-31	22:31-38	13:31b, 32b-38
31.1	261	Where Jesus is going	-	-	-	14
31.2	263	Vine and branches; love each other; opposition	-	-	-	15 16:1-4
31.3	264	Why Jesus is going	-	-	-	16:5-33
31.4	266	Prayer for believers	-	-	-	17
32.1	269	Prayer in Gethsemane	26:30, 36-46	14:26, 32-42	22:39-46	18:1
32.2	271	Arrest	26:47-56	14:43-52	22:47-53	18:2-11

Ch.	Pg.	Passage	Matt	Mark	Luke	John
33.1	273	First Jewish trial	-	-	-	18:12-14, 19-24
33.2	274	Peter's denials; second Jewish trial	26:57-75	14:53-72	22:54-65	18:15-18, 25-27
33.4	278	First Roman trial	27:2, 11-14	15:1b-5	23:1-12	18:28-38
33.5	280	Second Roman trial; Jesus beaten; Barabbas released	27:15-30	15:6-19	23:13-16, 18-25	18:39-40 19:1-16
34.1	287	To Golgotha	27:31-34	15:20-23	23:26-33a	19:17
34.2	288	Crucifixion	27:35-44	15:24-27, 29-32	23:33b-43	19:18-25a
34.3	290	Death	27:45-56	15:33-41	23:44-49	19:25b-30
34.4	292	Death ensured	-	-	-	19:31-37
35.1	295	Burial	27:57-66	15:42-47	23:50-56	19:38-42
36.1	297	Women at the empty tomb	28:1-8a	16:1-8a	24:1-8, 10a	20:1
36.2	298	Peter and John at empty tomb	28:8b	16:8b	24:9, 10b-12	20:2-10
37.1	301	Mary and Martha see Jesus	28:9-10	-	-	20:11-18
37.2	302	Soldiers told to lie	28:11-15	-	-	-
37.3	302	Two disciples travel with Jesus (*1 Corinthians 15:5a*)	-	-	24:13-35	-
37.4	304	Disciples visited	-	-	24:36-43	20:19-23
37.5	304	Disciples visited, with Thomas (*1 Corinthians 15:5b*)	-	-	-	20:24-31
37.6	305	Appearance while fishing; Peter's confession, again	-	-	-	21:1-24
37.7	307	Appearance in Galilee (*1 Corinthians 15:6-7*)	28:16-20	-	-	-
37.8	308	Ascension (*Acts 1:3-12*)	-	-	24:44-53	-
38.1	311	Disciples gather; Judas replaced (*Acts 1:1-2, 13-17, 20-26*)	-	-	-	21:25
38.2	312	Holy Spirit comes; Peter preaches (*Acts 2:1-36*)	-	-	-	-
38.3	315	Church expands (*Acts 2:37-47*)	-	-	-	-

Omitted passages (see sidebar on *Omission of Scripture*, page 309)

Matthew 6:13b
Matthew 18:11
Matthew 23:14
Mark 7:16
Mark 9:44, 46
Mark 11:26
Mark 15:28
Mark 16:9-20
Luke 9:55b-56a
Luke 17:36
Luke 23:17
John 5:3b-4
John 13:32a

APPENDIX B

Index of Topics

APPENDIX C

Index of Scripture References

APPENDIX D

Index of Illustrations

APPENDIX E

Jesus' Miracles

MIRACLE	TYPE	PAGE	MATT	MARK	LUKE	JOHN
Water changed to wine	Provisional	50	-	-	-	2:1-11
Official's son healed	Healing	58	-	-	-	4:46-54
Escape from Capernaum cliff	Transport	60	-	-	4:28-30	-
First big catch of fish	Nature	63	-	-	5:1-11	-
Unclean spirit thrown out	Spiritual	65	-	1:21-27	4:33-37	-
Peter's mother-in-law healed	Healing	65	8:14-15	1:29-31	4:38-39	-
Many healed in evening	Healing	65	8:16-17	1:32-34	4:40-41	-
Leper healed	Healing	67	8:2-4	1:40-45	5:12-14	-
Paralytic healed	Healing	67	9:1-8	2:1-12	5:17-26	-
Sick man healed at Bethesda	Healing	73	-	-	-	5:1-15
Withered hand healed	Healing	78	12:9-14	3:1-6	6:6-11	-
Centurion's servant healed	Healing	91	8:5-13	-	7:1-10	-
Widow's son resurrected	Healing	93	-	-	7:11-17	-
Blind, deaf, demonized man healed	Spiritual, Healing	99	12:22-23	-	11:14	-
Storm calmed	Nature	111	8:23-27	4:35-41	8:22-25	-
Demons thrown into pigs	Spiritual	112	8:28-33	5:1-20	8:26-39	-
Bleeding woman healed	Healing	115	9:20-22	5:25-34	8:42-48	-
Jairus' daughter resurrected	Healing	116	9:18-26	5:21-43	8:40-56	-
Two blind men healed	Healing	117	9:27-31	-	-	-
Deaf, demonized man healed	Spiritual, Nature	117	9:32-34	-	-	-
5000 fed	Provisional	126	14:13-21	6:30-44	9:10-17	6:1-15
Walking on water	Nature	127	14:22-33	6:45-52	-	6:16-21
Many healed at Gennesaret	Healing	128	14:34-36	6:53-56	-	-
Demon thrown out of Syrophoenician girl	Spiritual	136	15:21-28	7:24-30	-	-

Deaf man, others healed at Sea of Galilee	Healing	137	15:29-31	7:31-37	-	-
4000 fed	Provisional	138	15:32-39	8:1-9	-	-
Blind man healed at Bethsaida	Healing	139	-	8:22-26	-	-
Moonstruck boy healed	Spiritual, Healing	148	17:14-20	9:14-29	9:37-43	-
Coin found in fish's mouth	Nature	149	17:24-27	-	-	-
Disappearance from treasury	Transport	164	-	-	-	8:59
Man born blind healed	Healing	165	-	-	-	9
Hunched woman healed	Healing	183	-	-	13:10-17	-
Man with edema healed	Healing	189	-	-	14:1-6	-
Lazarus resurrected	Healing	198	-	-	-	11:1-45
Ten lepers healed	Healing	201	-	-	17:11-19	-
Blind Bartimaeus healed	Healing	212	20:29-34	10:46-52	18:35-43	-
Fig tree withered	Nature	219	21:18-22	11:12-14, 20-25	-	-
Malchus' ear healed	Healing	272	-	-	22:49-51	-
Disappearance in Emmaus	Transport	303	-	-	24:30-31	-
Appearance without Thomas	Transport	304	-	-	24:36	20:19
Appearance with Thomas	Transport	304	-	-	-	20:26
Second big catch of fish	Nature	305	-	-	-	21:4-11
Ascension to heaven	Transport	309	-	-	24:51	-

APPENDIX F

Jesus' Parables

PARABLE	TOPIC/MORAL	PAGE	MATT	MARK	LUKE
Lamp Under a Basket	Righteous living as a witness to God	83	5:14–15	4:21–25	8:16–18
Wise and Foolish Builders	Heeding God's call, wisdom	90	7:24-27	-	6:47-49
Two Borrowers	Forgiveness	97	-	-	7:41-43
Sower	Receiving God's word with a receptive heart	105	13:3-23	4:3-20	8:4-15
Growing Seed	Growth of God's kingdom	107	-	4:26-29	-
Weeds	Judgment	107	13:24-30, 36-43	-	-
Hidden Treasure	Value of God's kingdom	109	13:44	-	-
Pearl	Value of God's kingdom	109	13:45-46	-	-
Mustard Seed	Growth of God's kingdom	108	13:31-32	4:30-32	13:18-19
Yeast	Growth of God's kingdom	108	13:33	-	13:20-21
Fishing Net	Judgment	110	13:47-50	-	-
Unforgiving Slave	Forgiveness	152	18:23-35	-	-
Good Samaritan	Loving your neighbor	173	-	-	10:30-37
Midnight Friend	Persistence	176	-	-	11:5-8
Rich Fool	Folly of wealth	179	-	-	12:16-21
Barren Fig Tree	Producing spiritual fruit	182	-	-	13:6-9
Lost Sheep	God's heart for the lost	190	18:12-14	-	15:4-7
Lost Coin	God's heart for the lost	190	-	-	15:8-10
Prodigal Son	God's heart for the lost	190	-	-	15:11-32
Shrewd Manager	Using wealth to one's eternal advantage	192	-	-	16:1-9

Rich Man and Lazarus	Luxury and suffering	194	-	-	16:19-31
Unrighteous Judge	Persistence	202	-	-	18:1-8
Pharisee and Tax Collector	Self-righteousness and humility	202	-	-	18:9-14
Hiring Vineyard Workers	Salvation based on grace rather than actions	208	20:1-16	-	-
Talents, Minas	Using one's abilities	210	25:14-30	-	19:11-27
Two Sons	Obedience	224	21:28-32	-	-
Wicked Vine Workers	Not heeding God's messengers	224	21:33-45	12:1-12	20:9-19
Wedding Reception	Responding to God's offer	226	22:1-13	-	14:16-24
Waiting Servant	Preparation for God's arrival	244	24:42-51	13:33-37	12:35-48
Budding Fig Tree	Recognizing signs of God's arrival	244	24:32-35	13:28-32	21:29-33
Ten Virgins	Preparation for God's arrival	245	25:1-13	-	-

Note: Only Matthew, Mark, and Luke record Jesus' parables, which are stories that illustrate a spiritual or moral principle. John's Gospel contains allegories and metaphors that relate spiritual principles to worldly subjects, but these typically aren't in the form of a story.

APPENDIX G

Acknowledgments

THE STORY OF JESUS team would like to acknowledge the following individuals:

Trista-Lee Russell
Rose Kovacs
Darian Kovacs
Scott Rude
Joseph Kraftchick
Blair Nielsen
Graf-Martin Communications Inc

Their contributions, feedback, and encouragement were invaluable in turning the idea of *THE STORY OF JESUS* into a reality.

Major literary and electronic references used in creating *THE STORY OF JESUS* include, but aren't limited to:

Barker, Kenneth (Editor). *The Zondervan NASB Study Bible*. Zondervan, 1999.

Dictionary.com, LLC. *Dictionary.com* (online). Web. Multiple times from 2008 to 2017.

HarperCollins Christian Publishing. *Bible Gateway* (online). Web. Multiple times from 2008 to 2017.

Patterson, Dorothy (Editor). *The Woman's Study Bible, NKJV*. Thomas Nelson Inc, 1995.

Sowing Circle. *Blue Letter Bible* (online). Web. Multiple times from 2008 to 2017.

Strong, James. *Strong's Exhaustive Concordance: New American Standard Bible*. Lockman Foundation, 1998.

Walker, G. Allen (Editor). *Holy Bible Modern Literal Version*. Createspace, 2017.

Wikimedia Foundation, Inc. *Wikipedia* (online). Web. Multiple times from 2008 to 2017.

Youngblood, Ronald F. (Editor). *Nelson's New Illustrated Bible Dictionary*. Thomas Nelson Inc, 1995.

NOTES

Books by DB Ryen

Bibles:

The Story of Jesus: All Four Gospels In One (Study Bible), 2nd Edition

The Story of Jesus: All Four Gospels In One (Just The Word), 2nd Edition

Historical (Biblical) Fiction:

Never The Same: Twelve Lives Changed By Jesus

Non-Fiction ('Let's Be Real' Series):

Birth Control for Christians

Faith: Mountains, Mustard, and Everything in Between

Children's Stories:

Rory the Knight and the Giant Squid

Rory the Knight and the Anaconda

Rory the Knight and the Grumpy Old Alligator

Rory the Knight and the Grizzlies

Spaceman Bren and the Slime Monster

Spaceman Bren and the Planet of Apes

Spaceman Bren on Spider Planet

Daisy Mermaid and the Shipwreck

Princess Telsa and the Ogre

"Look, I'm coming [back] quickly. My payment is with me, to repay everyone as he has done. I'm the alpha and the omega, the first and the last, the beginning and the end... Yes, I'm coming quickly."

Amen! Come, Lord Jesus!

– Revelation 22:12-13,20b